# Praise for *Hands-On Generative AI with Transformers and Diffusion Models*

An essential technical guide that delivers clear, hands-on instructions
for implementing stable diffusion and fine-tuning language models.
A must-have for any AI developer's bookshelf.

—*Vicki Reyzelman, chief AI solutions architect, Mave Sparks*

As a comprehensive and practical guide for anyone eager to master generative AI, this
book blends theory with real-world applications. From the fundamentals of language
models and diffusion techniques to advanced topics like fine-tuning and creating text-
to-image applications, the authors provide actionable Python code and clear insights
that empower readers to build, innovate, and stay ahead in this rapidly evolving
field. Their expertise and hands-on approach make this book an invaluable resource
for both beginners and experienced practitioners alike.

—*Anil Sood, senior manager, Ernst & Young US*

An invaluable guide that demystifies generative AI, blending practical
insights with hands-on techniques and examples covering various domains.
A must-read for those interested in the future in AI.

—*Vishwesh Ravi Shrimali,*
*an engineer in the automobile industry*

The book is an incredibly well-crafted guide that makes complex AI concepts accessible
to a wide spectrum of readers. The authors bring clarity to transformers and diffusion
models, making this a fantastic read for anyone looking to truly understand the
fundamental building blocks driving today's generative AI.

—*Sai M Vuppalapati,*
*data and AI/ML platforms product manager, Tubi TV*

This book is a treasure trove for anyone curious about the potential of AI-generated content. With a focus on solving relevant real life problems and hands-on guidance, it skillfully bridges complex concepts and makes generative AI approachable for enthusiasts and professionals alike. A must-read for anyone ready to dive into this dynamic field and explore the power of generative AI.

—*Lipi Deepaakshi Patnaik, senior software developer, Zeta*

This book is exactly what you need to get started with generative AI: from comprehensive explanations to thoughtful tips and do-it-yourself exercises, it has it all. An excellent guide for anyone looking to learn how to use, adapt and evaluate generative AI models.

—*Luba Elliott, AI art curator,* elluba.com

Omar, Pedro, Apolinário, and Jonathan present an impressive blend of technical depth and intuitive guidance, empowering readers to bring innovative generative AI solutions to life with clarity and purpose. Through clear explanations of transformers and diffusion models, their in-depth development and applications across text, images, and audio, they make the complex world of AI both accessible and actionable. This work equips the next generation of innovators to confidently navigate GenAI's technical, ethical, and practical challenges.

—*Aditya Goel, AI consultant*

This book is excellent for anyone starting their journey with generative AI. The authors guide us through this complex topic in a simple and intuitive way.

—*Zygmunt Lenyk, research engineer, Odyssey*

*Hands-On Generative AI with Transformers and Diffusion Models* offers a comprehensive, accessible guide to the core concepts and applications of generative AI. The authors skilfully cover essential topics, from transformers and diffusion models to creative applications, making it a must-read for those looking to master GenAI technologies.

—*Gourav Singh Bais, senior data scientist*
*and senior technical content writer, Allianz Services*

The essential guide for developers to master the tools and concepts behind the biggest AI revolution in the last decade. This is such a serious competitor to my own book that I fear for our royalties!

—*Lewis Tunstall, machine learning engineer at Hugging Face*
*and coauthor of* Natural Language Processing with Transformers

# Hands-On Generative AI with Transformers and Diffusion Models

*Omar Sanseviero, Pedro Cuenca,*
*Apolinário Passos, and Jonathan Whitaker*

**Hands-On Generative AI with Transformers and Diffusion Models**

by Omar Sanseviero, Pedro Cuenca, Apolinário Passos, and Jonathan Whitaker

Published by O'Reilly Media, Inc., 1005 Gravenstein Highway North, Sebastopol, CA 95472.

O'Reilly books may be purchased for educational, business, or sales promotional use. Online editions are also available for most titles (*https://oreilly.com*). For more information, contact our corporate/institutional sales department: 800-998-9938 or *corporate@oreilly.com*.

| | |
|---|---|
| **Acquisitions Editor:** Nicole Butterfield | **Indexer:** BIM Creatives, LLC |
| **Development Editor:** Jill Leonard | **Interior Designer:** David Futato |
| **Production Editor:** Gregory Hyman | **Cover Designer:** Karen Montgomery |
| **Copyeditor:** Krsta Technology Solutions | **Illustrator:** Kate Dullea |
| **Proofreader:** Sharon Wilkey | |

December 2024:     First Edition

**Revision History for the First Edition**

2024-11-22:     First Release

See *http://oreilly.com/catalog/errata.csp?isbn=9781098149246* for release details.

978-1-098-14924-6

[LSI]

# Table of Contents

# Part II. Transfer Learning for Generative Models

## Part III.   Going Further

# Preface

Generative AI is a revolutionary technology that has rapidly transitioned from lab demos to real-world applications, impacting billions. It can create new content—images, text, audio, videos, and more—by learning patterns from existing data, thereby enhancing creativity, augmenting data, or assisting in many tasks. For instance, a generative AI model trained on music can compose new melodies, while one trained on text can generate stories or even programming code.

This book isn't just for experts—it's for anyone who wants to learn about this fascinating new field. We won't focus on building models from scratch or diving straight into complicated mathematics. Instead, we'll leverage existing models to solve real-world problems, helping you to build a solid intuition around how these techniques work and providing the foundation for you to keep exploring.

This hands-on approach, we hope, will help you get up and running quickly and efficiently with generative AI. You'll learn how to use pretrained models, adapt them for your needs, and generate new data with them. You'll also learn how to evaluate the quality of generated data and explore ethical and social issues that may arise from using generative AI. This exposure will allow you to stay up-to-date with new models and help you identify areas that you may want to explore more deeply.

## Who Should Read This Book

Given the impressive products and news you might have seen about generative AI, it's normal to be excited, or worried, about it! Whether you're curious about how programs can generate images, want to train a model to tweet in your style, or are looking to gain a deeper understanding of products like ChatGPT, this book is for you. With generative AI, we can do all of that and many other things, including these:

- Write summaries of news articles
- Generate images based on a description

- Enhance the quality of an image
- Transcribe meetings
- Generate synthetic speech in your voice style
- Incorporate new subjects or styles into image-generation models, like creating images of "your cat dressed as an astronaut"

No matter your reason, you've decided to learn about generative AI, and this book will guide you through it.

# Prerequisites

This book assumes that you are comfortable programming in Python and have a foundational understanding of what machine learning is, including basic usage of frameworks like PyTorch or TensorFlow. Having practical experience with training models is not required, but it will be helpful to understand the content with more depth. The following resources provide a good foundation for the topics covered in this book:

- *Hands-On Machine Learning with Scikit-Learn, Keras, and TensorFlow*, 2nd ed., by Aurélien Géron (O'Reilly)
- *Deep Learning for Coders with fastai and PyTorch* by Jeremy Howard and Sylvain Gugger (O'Reilly)

If you feel intimidated by the prerequisites, don't worry! The book is designed to enhance your intuition and provide a hands-on approach to help you get started.

# What You Will Learn

This book is divided into three parts:

- In Part I, "Leveraging Open Models", we'll introduce the fundamental building blocks of generative AI. You'll learn how to use pretrained models to generate text and images. This part will help you understand the basics of the field and understand the big picture.
- Part II, "Transfer Learning for Generative Models", is all about fine-tuning, showcasing ways to take existing models and adapt them to your needs. We'll walk you through how to *teach* a diffusion model a new concept, customize a transformer model to classify text and reply in conversations, and explore advanced techniques for working with large models on limited hardware. Don't worry if this is the first time you read about transformer or diffusion models; you'll learn about them soon.

- In Part III, "Going Further", we'll extend the ideas from the previous parts, generating new modalities such as audio and getting creative with new applications. After you've read this book, you'll have a solid understanding of the methods and techniques on which generative applications are built.

# How to Read This Book

We designed the book to be read in order, but we have kept the chapters as self-contained as possible so that you can jump around to the parts that interest you most. Many of the ideas covered in this book apply to multiple modalities, so even if you are interested in only one particular domain (such as image generation), you may still find it valuable to skim through the other chapters.

We've included exercises and code examples throughout the book, designed to help you get hands-on with the material. Try to complete these exercises as you go along, and where possible, see if you can adapt the examples to your use cases. Trying things out for yourself will help you build a much deeper understanding of the material.

Finally, most chapter summaries list additional resources for further reading. We encourage you to explore these resources to deepen your understanding of the topics covered in the book. You don't need to read these resources before you progress to a new chapter; you can come back later, whenever you are ready to go deeper into the subjects that interest you.

# Software and Hardware Requirements

To get the most out of this book, we highly recommend running the code examples as you read along. Experimenting with the code by making changes and exploring different scenarios will enhance your understanding. Working with transformers and diffusion models can be computationally intensive, so having access to a computer with an NVIDIA GPU is beneficial. While a GPU is not mandatory, it will significantly speed up training times.

You can use any of multiple online options, such as Google Colaboratory (*https://oreil.ly/y1MHw*) and Kaggle Notebooks (*https://oreil.ly/Pkqq7*). Follow these instructions to set up your environment and follow along:

*Using Google Colab*
> Most code should work on any Google Colab instance. We recommend you use GPU runtimes for chapters with training loops.

*Running code locally*
> To run the code on your computer, create a Python 3.10 virtual environment using your preferred method. As an example, you can do it with conda like this:

```
conda create -n genaibook python=3.10
conda activate genaibook
```

For optimal performance, we recommend using a CUDA-compatible GPU.[1] If you don't know what CUDA is, don't worry, we'll explain it in the book.

Many support utilities and helper functions are used throughout the book. To access them, please install the *genaibook* package:

```
pip install genaibook
```

This will, in turn, install the libraries required to run transformers and diffusion models, along with *PyTorch*, *matplotlib*, *numpy*, and other essentials.

All code examples and supplementary material can be found in the book's GitHub repository (*https://oreil.ly/handsonGenAIcode*). You can run all the examples interactively in Jupyter Notebooks, and the repository will be regularly updated with the latest resources.

# Conventions Used in This Book

The following typographical conventions are used in this book:

*Italic*
　　Indicates new terms, URLs, email addresses, filenames, and file extensions.

`Constant width`
　　Used for program listings, as well as within paragraphs to refer to program elements such as variable or function names, databases, data types, environment variables, statements, and keywords.

This element signifies a tip or suggestion.

This element signifies a general note.

---

1　Rather than GPU, you can also use the MPS device, which might work on Macs with Apple Silicon, but we have not tested this configuration extensively.

This element indicates a warning or caution.

# Using Code Examples

Supplemental material (code examples, exercises, etc.) is available for download at *https://oreil.ly/handsonGenAIcode*.

If you have a technical question or a problem using the code examples, please send email to *support@oreilly.com*.

This book is here to help you get your job done. In general, if example code is offered with this book, you may use it in your programs and documentation. You do not need to contact us for permission unless you're reproducing a significant portion of the code. For example, writing a program that uses several chunks of code from this book does not require permission. Selling or distributing examples from O'Reilly books does require permission. Answering a question by citing this book and quoting example code does not require permission. Incorporating a significant amount of example code from this book into your product's documentation does require permission.

We appreciate, but generally do not require, attribution. An attribution usually includes the title, author, publisher, and ISBN. For example: *"Hands-On Generative AI with Transformers and Diffusion Models* by Omar Sanseviero, Pedro Cuenca, Apolinário Passos, and Jonathan Whitaker (O'Reilly). Copyright 2025 Omar Sanseviero, Pedro Cuenca, Apolinário Passos, and Jonathan Whitaker, 978-1-098-14924-6."

If you feel your use of code examples falls outside fair use or the permission given above, feel free to contact us at *permissions@oreilly.com*.

# How to Contact Us

Please address comments and questions concerning this book to the publisher:

O'Reilly Media, Inc.
1005 Gravenstein Highway North
Sebastopol, CA 95472
800-889-8969 (in the United States or Canada)
707-827-7019 (international or local)
707-829-0104 (fax)
*support@oreilly.com*
*https://oreilly.com/about/contact.html*

We have a web page for this book, where we list errata, examples, and any additional information. You can access this page at *https://oreil.ly/handsonGenAI*.

For news and information about our books and courses, visit *https://oreilly.com*.

Find us on LinkedIn: *https://linkedin.com/company/oreilly-media*.

Watch us on YouTube: *https://youtube.com/oreillymedia*.

# State of the Art: A Moving Target

*State of the art* (SOTA) is used to describe the highest level of performance currently achieved in a particular task or domain. In the field of generative AI, the SOTA is constantly changing as new models are developed and new techniques are discovered. This book will provide you with a solid grounding in the fundamentals of generative AI, but by the time you read it, new models will have been released that outperform the ones we discuss here.

Rather than trying to chase the ever-shifting *best*, we've tried to focus on general principles that will help you understand how the models work in a way that will be useful even as the field continues to evolve. New models rarely come out of nowhere and often build on the ideas of previous models. By understanding the fundamentals, you'll be better equipped to understand the latest developments as they happen.

# Acknowledgments

We would like to express our deepest gratitude to the incredible O'Reilly team, particularly Jill Leonard, for her amazing guidance and support throughout this entire process. Special thanks to Nicole Butterfield, Karen Montgomery, Kate Dullea, Gregory Hyman, and Kristen Brown for their invaluable advice and contributions, from initial scoping to the creation of the beautiful cover and illustrations.

We are deeply grateful to our technical reviewers: Vishwesh Ravi Shrimali, David Mertz, Lipi Deepaakshi Patnaik, Luba Elliott, Anil Sood, Sai Vuppalapati, Ranjeeta Bhattacharya, Rajat Dubey, Bryan Bischof, Vladislav Bilay, Gourav Singh Bais, Aditya Goel, Lakshmanan Sethu Sankaranarayanan, Zygmunt Lenyk, Youssef Hosn, Vicki Reyzelman, Lewis Tunstall, Sayak Paul, and Vaibhav Srivastav. Their insightful feedback was instrumental in shaping this book.

We would also like to extend our gratitude to the Hugging Face team for their inspiration and collaboration, particularly Clémentine Fourrier for her insights on model evaluation, Sanchit Gandhi for his guidance on audio-related topics, and Leandro von Werra and Lewis Tunstall for helping us navigate the book-writing process. The Hugging Face team continues to inspire us with its brilliance and kindness, helping bring this project to life.

A heartfelt thank you to the countless friends, collaborators, and contributors who have shaped the open-source ecosystem that we are proud to be part of. We are grateful to the entire ML community for advancing the research, tools, and resources that form the heart of this book. This work was crafted in Jupyter Notebooks, and we owe special thanks to Jeremy Howard, Hamel Husain, and all the contributors to Quarto and nbdev for making this possible.

## Jonathan

I am very grateful to the community of researchers and hackers sharing their ideas and pushing forward what is possible. To Jeremy Howard, Tanishq Abraham, and the rest of the fastdiffusion crew who came together to learn all we could about these ideas. And to my amazing coauthors, without whom this book could not have happened!

## Apolinário

I am grateful to my coauthors Omar, Pedro and Jonathan for the co-creation of this book. Combining technology education and creativity has been a fun challenge to tackle. I thank my friends who understand and support me even when I come along to hang out carrying my laptop around and my Hugging Face colleagues for always being supportive.

## Pedro

Writing a book is a lot of fun, but it unfairly exacts sacrifices from the people you love. I'm super lucky to have had the support of María José, my partner in life. She made it easy for me to work on it, and when I was stuck she helped with common sense reasoning that, frankly, is anything but common. I apologize to my Mom and Dad for always bringing my laptop when I visit, to my son Pablo for not exploring Hyrule or Eorzea as much as we'd have liked, and to my son Javier for sometimes talking too much about work and too little about life. They are the best.

I'm truly inspired by my amazing coauthors. I admire and look up to them and can't believe how lucky I am to learn from them, every day. This extends to the Hugging Face folks, whose enthusiasm and humility provide a primordial soup where things happen, and to the open ML community at large, whose work is always advancing the field but not always getting the credit it deserves.

Thank you.

## Omar

Thank you, Michelle, for your constant encouragement throughout this process, for all the brainstorming sessions, and for your support over the past two years. I couldn't have completed this project without you. Hikes are back on the table!

To my parents, Ana and Walter, thank you for nurturing my love for books from the very beginning and for supporting me to become the person I am today.

Lastly, I want to thank my amazing coauthors—Pedro, Poli, and Jonathan. This journey has been truly fun, and I'm so grateful that we accomplished this together.

# Leveraging Open Models

PART I

Leveraging Open Models

# CHAPTER 1

# An Introduction to Generative Media

Generative models have become widely popular in recent years. If you're reading this book, you've probably interacted with a generative model at some point. Maybe you've used ChatGPT to generate text, used style transfer in apps like Instagram, or seen the deepfake videos that have been making headlines. These are all examples of generative models in action!

In this book, we'll explore the world of generative models, starting with the basics of two families of generative models, transformers and diffusion, and working our way up to more advanced topics. We'll cover the types of generative models, how they work, and how to use them. In this chapter, we'll cover some of the history of how we got here and take a look at the capabilities offered by some of the models, which we'll explore in more depth throughout the book.

So, what exactly is generative modeling? At its core, it's about teaching a *model* to *generate* new data that resembles its training data. For example, if I train a model on a dataset of images of cats, I can then use that model to generate new images of cats that look like they could have come from the original dataset. This is a powerful idea, and it has a wide range of applications, from creating novel images and videos to generating text with a specific style.

Throughout this book, you'll discover popular tools that make using existing generative models straightforward. The world of machine learning (ML) offers numerous *open-access* models, trained on large datasets, available for anyone to use. Training these models from scratch can be costly and time-consuming, but open-access models provide a practical and efficient alternative. These *pretrained* models can generate new data, classify existing data, and be adapted for new applications. One of the most popular places to find open-access models is Hugging Face (*https://oreil.ly/ evFEx*), a platform with over two million models for many ML tasks, including image generation.

# Generating Images

As an example of an *open source* library, we'll kick off with *diffusers*. This popular library provides access to state-of-the-art (SOTA) diffusion models. It's a powerful, simple toolbox that allows us to quickly load and train diffusion models.

By going to the Hugging Face Hub and filtering for models that generate images based on a text prompt (`text-to-image`) (*https://oreil.ly/oVajm*), we can find some of the most popular models, such as Stable Diffusion and SDXL. We'll use Stable Diffusion 1.5, a diffusion model capable of generating high-quality images. If you browse the model website, you can read the *model card*, an essential document for discoverability and reproducibility. There, you can read about the model, how it was trained, intended use cases, and more.

Given we have a model (Stable Diffusion) and a tool to use the model (*diffusers*), we can now generate our first image! When we load models, we'll need to send them to a specific hardware device, such as CPU (`cpu`), GPU (`cuda` or `cuda:0`), or Mac hardware called Metal (`mps`). The *genaibook* library we mentioned in the Preface has a utility function to select an appropriate device depending on where you run the example code. For example, the following code will assign `cuda` to the `device` variable if you have a GPU:

```
from genaibook.core import get_device

device = get_device()
print(f"Using device: {device}")

Using device: cuda
```

Next, we'll load Stable Diffusion 1.5. The *diffusers* library offers a convenient, high-level wrapper called `StableDiffusionPipeline`, which is ideal for this use case. Don't worry about all the parameters for now—the highlights include the following:

- There are many models with the Stable Diffusion architecture, so we need to specify the one we want to use. We are going to use `stable-diffusion-v1-5/stable-diffusion-v1-5`, a mirror of the original Stable Diffusion 1.5 model released by RunwayML.

- We need to specify the *precision* we'll load the model with. Precision is something you'll learn more about later. At a high level, models are composed of many *parameters* (millions or billions of them). Each parameter is a number learned during training, and we can store these parameters with different levels of precision (in other words, we can use more bits to store the model). A larger precision allows the model to store more information, but it also requires more memory and computation. On the other hand, we can use a lower precision by setting `torch_dtype=float16` and use less memory than the default `float32`. When doing inference (a fancy way of saying "executing" the models), using `float16` is usually fine.[1]

The first time you run this code, it can take a bit: the pipeline downloads a model of multiple gigabytes, after all! If you load the pipeline a second time, it will redownload the model only if there has been a change in the remote repository that hosts the model on Hugging Face.[2] Hugging Face libraries store the model locally in a cache, making things much faster for subsequent loads:

```python
import torch
from diffusers import StableDiffusionPipeline

pipe = StableDiffusionPipeline.from_pretrained(
    "stable-diffusion-v1-5/stable-diffusion-v1-5",
    torch_dtype=torch.float16,
    variant="fp16",
).to(device)
```

Now that the model is loaded, we can define a *prompt*—the text input the model will receive. We can then pass the prompt through the model and generate our first image based on that text! Try inputting the following prompt:

```python
prompt = "a photograph of an astronaut riding a horse"
pipe(prompt).images[0]
```

---

1 You might wonder about the `variant` parameter. For some models, you might find multiple checkpoints with different precision. When specifying `torch_dtype=float16`, we download the default model (`float32`) and convert it to `float16`. By also specifying the `fp16` variant, we're downloading a smaller checkpoint already stored in `float16` precision, which requires half the bandwidth and storage to download it. Check the model you want to use to find out if there are multiple precision variants.

2 Hugging Face repositories are Git-based repositories under the hood.

Exciting! With a couple of lines of code, we generated a new image. Play with the prompt and generate new images. You might notice two things. First, running the same code will generate different images each time. This is because the diffusion process is *stochastic* in nature, meaning it uses randomness to generate images. We can control this randomness by setting a *seed*:

```
import torch
torch.manual_seed(0)
```

Second, the generated images are not perfect. They might have artifacts, be blurry, or not match the prompt at all. We'll explore these limitations and how to improve the quality of the generated images in later chapters. For instance:

- Chapters 4 and 5 dive into all the components behind diffusion models and how to get from text to new images. They rely on foundational methods like AutoEncoders—introduced in Chapter 3—that can learn efficient representations from input data and reduce the compute requirements to build diffusion and other generative models.

- In Chapter 7, you'll learn how to teach new concepts to Stable Diffusion. For example, we can teach Stable Diffusion the concept of "my dog" to generate images of the author's dog in novel scenarios, such as "my dog visiting the moon".

- Chapter 8 shows how diffusion models can be used for more than just image generation, such as editing images with a prompt or filling empty parts of an image.

# Generating Text

Just as *diffusers* is a very convenient library for diffusion models, the popular *transformers* library is extremely useful for running transformer-based models and adapting to new use cases. It provides a standardized interface for a wide range of tasks, such as generating text, detecting objects in images, and transcribing an audio file into text.

The *transformers* library provides different layers of abstractions. For example, if you don't care about all the internals, the easiest is to use `pipeline`, which abstracts all the processing required to get a prediction. We can instantiate a pipeline by calling the `pipeline()` function and specifying which task we want to solve, such as `text-classification`:

```
from transformers import pipeline

classifier = pipeline("text-classification", device=device)
classifier("This movie is disgustingly good!")

[{'label': 'POSITIVE', 'score': 0.9998536109924316}]
```

The model correctly predicted that the sentiment in the input text was positive. By default, the text-classification pipeline uses a sentiment analysis model under the hood, but we can also specify other transformer-based text-classification models.

Similarly, we can switch the task to text generation (`text-generation`), with which we can generate new text based on an input prompt. By default, the pipeline uses the GPT-2 model. The transformer pipeline uses a default maximum number of words to generate, so don't be surprised if the output is truncated. You'll learn later how to change this:

```
from transformers import set_seed

# Setting the seed ensures we get the same results every time we run this code
set_seed(10)

generator = pipeline("text-generation", device=device)
prompt = "It was a dark and stormy"
generator(prompt)[0]["generated_text"]

It was a dark and stormy year, and my mind went blank," says the 27-year-old,
who has become obsessed with art, poetry and music since moving to France.
"I don't really know why, but there are things
```

Although GPT-2 is not a great model by today's standards, it gives us an initial example of transformers' generation capabilities while using a small model. The same concepts you learn about with GPT-2 can be applied to models such as Llama or Mistral, some of the most powerful open-access models (at the time of writing). Throughout the book, we'll strike a balance between the quality and size of the models. Usually, larger models have higher-quality generations. At the same time, we want people with consumer computers or access to free services, such as Google Colab, to be able to create new generations by running code:

- Chapter 2 will teach you how transformer models work under the hood. We'll dive into different types of transformer models and how to use them for generating text.

- Chapter 6 will teach you how to continue training transformer models with our data for different use cases. This will allow us to make conversational models like those you might have used with ChatGPT or Gemini. We'll also discuss efficient training approaches so that you can train transformer models on your computer.

## Generating Sound Clips

Generative models are not limited to images and text. Models can generate videos, short songs, synthetic spoken speech, protein proposals, and more!

Chapter 9 dives deep into audio-related tasks that can be solved with ML, such as transcribing meetings and generating sound effects. For now, we can limit ourselves to the now-familiar *transformers* pipeline and use the small version of MusicGen, a model released by Meta to generate music conditioned on text:

```
pipe = pipeline("text-to-audio", model="facebook/musicgen-small", device=device)
data = pipe("electric rock solo, very intense")

print(data)

{'audio': array([[[0.12342193, 0.11794732, 0.14775363, ..., 0.0265964 ,
        0.02168683, 0.03067675]]], dtype=float32), 'sampling_rate': 32000}
```

Later, you'll learn how audio data is represented and what these numbers are. Of course, there's no way for us to print the audio file directly in the book! The best alternative is to show a viewer in our notebook or save the audio to a file we can play with our favorite audio application. For example, we can use IPython.display() for this:

```
import IPython.display as ipd

display(ipd.Audio(data["audio"][0], rate=data["sampling_rate"]))
```

## Ethical and Societal Implications

While generative models offer remarkable capabilities, their widespread adoption raises important considerations around ethics and societal impact. It's important to keep them in mind as we explore the capabilities of generative models. Here are a few key areas to consider:

*Privacy and consent*

The ability of generative models to generate realistic images and videos based on very little data poses significant challenges to privacy. For example, creating synthetic images from a small set of real images from an individual raises questions about using personal data without consent. It also increases the risk of creating deepfakes, which can be used to spread misinformation or harm individuals.

*Bias and fairness*

Generative models are trained on large datasets that contain biases. These biases can be inherited and amplified by the generative models, as we'll explore in Chapter 2. For example, biased datasets used to train image-generation models may generate stereotypical or discriminatory images. It's important to consider mitigating these biases and to ensure that generative models are used fairly and ethically.

*Regulation*

Given the potential risks associated with generative models, there is a growing call for regulatory oversight and accountability mechanisms to ensure responsible development. This includes transparency requirements, ethical guidelines, and legal frameworks to address the misuse of generative models.

It's important to approach generative models with a thoughtful and ethical mindset. As we explore the capabilities of these models, we'll also consider the ethical implications and how to use them responsibly.

# Where We've Been and Where Things Stand

The research into and development of generative models began decades ago with efforts focused on rule-based systems. As computing power and data availability increased, generative models evolved to use statistical methods and ML. With the emergence of deep learning as a powerful paradigm in ML and breakthroughs in the fields of image and speech recognition, generative models have advanced significantly. Although invented decades ago, Convolutional Neural Networks (CNNs) and Recurrent Neural Networks (RNNs) have become widely popular in the last decade. CNNs revolutionized image-processing tasks, and RNNs brought sequential data-modeling capabilities, enabling tasks like translating text and text generation.

The introduction of Generative Adversarial Networks (GANs) by Ian Goodfellow in 2014, and variants such as Deep Convolutional GANs (DCGANs) and conditional GANs, brought a new era of generative models. GANs have been used to generate high-quality images and applied to tasks like style transfer, enabling users to apply artistic styles to their images with astonishing realism. Although quite powerful, the quality of GANs has been surpassed by diffusion models in recent years.

Similarly, although RNNs were the to-go tool for language modeling, transformer models, including architectures like GPT, achieved SOTA performance in Natural Language Processing (NLP). These models have demonstrated remarkable capabilities in tasks such as language understanding, text generation, and machine translation. GPT, in particular, became extremely popular because of its ability to generate coherent and contextually relevant text. Not long afterward, a huge wave of generative language models emerged.

The field of generative AI is more accessible than ever because of the rapid expansion of research, resources, and development in recent years. A growing community interested in the area, a rich open source ecosystem, and research facilitating deployment have led to a wide range of applications and use cases. Since 2023, a new generation of models that can generate high-quality images, text, code, videos, and more has emerged; examples include ChatGPT, DALL·E, Imagen, Stable Diffusion, Llama, Mistral, and many others.

## How Are Generative AI Models Created?

Typically, the creation of AI models comes down to big budgets or open source.

Several of the most impressive generative models in the past couple of years were created by influential research labs in big, private companies. OpenAI developed ChatGPT, DALL·E, and Sora; Google built Imagen, Bard, and Gemini; and Meta created Llama and Code Llama.

There's a varying degree of openness in the way these models are released. Some can be used via specific UIs, some have access through developer APIs, and some are just announced as research reports with no public access at all. In some cases, code and model weights are released as well: these are usually called *open source* releases because those are the essential artifacts necessary to run the model on your hardware. Frequently, however, they are kept hidden for strategic reasons.

At the same time, an ever-increasing, energetic, and enthusiastic community uses open source models as the clay for their creativity. All types of practitioners, including researchers, engineers, tinkerers, and amateurs, build on top of one another's work and come up with novel solutions and clever ideas that push the field forward, one commit at a time. Some of these ideas make their way into the theoretical corpus of knowledge where researchers draw from, and new impressive models that use them come out after a while.

Big models, even when hidden, serve as inspiration for the community, whose work yields fruits that serve the field as a whole.

This cycle can work only because some of the models are open source and can be used by the community. Companies that release open source models don't do it for altruistic reasons but because they discover economic value in this strategy. By providing code and models that are adopted by the community, they receive public scrutiny with bug fixes, new ideas, derived model architectures, or even new datasets that work well with the models released. Because all these contributions are based on the assets they published, these companies can quickly adopt them and thus move faster than they would on their own. When Meta released Llama, one of the most popular language models (LMs), a thriving ecosystem organically grew around it.

Both established and new companies alike, including Meta, Stability AI (Stable Diffusion), or Mistral AI, have embraced varying degrees of open source as part of their business strategy. This is as legitimate as the strategy of competing companies that prefer to keep their trade secrets behind closed doors (even if those companies can also draw from the open source community).

At this point, we'd like to clarify that model releases are rarely truly open source. Unlike in the software world, source code is not enough to fully understand an ML system. Model weights are not enough either: they are just the final output of the model training process. Being able to exactly replicate an existing model would require the source code used to train the model (not just the modeling code or the inference code), the training regime and parameters, and, crucially, all the data used for training. None of these, and particularly the data, are usually released.

If there were access to these details, it would be possible for the community and the public to understand how the model works, explore the biases that may afflict it, and better assess its strengths and limitations. Access to the weights and model code provides an imperfect estimation of all this knowledge, but the actual hard data would be much better. On top of that, even when the models are publicly released, they often come out with a special license that does not adhere to the Open Source Initiative's definition of open source. This is not to say that the models are not useful or that the companies are not doing a good thing by releasing them, but it's an important context to keep in mind and one of the reasons we'll often say *open access* instead of *open source*.

Be that as it may, there has never been a better time to build generative models or *with* generative models. You don't need to be an engineer in a top-notch research lab to come up with ideas to solve the problems that interest you or to contribute to the field. We hope you find these pages helpful in your journey!

# Summary

Hopefully, after generating your first images, text, and audios, you'll be excited to learn how diffusion and transformers work under the hood, how to adapt them for new use cases, and how to use them for different creative applications. Although this chapter focused on high-level tools, we'll build solid foundations and intuition on how these models work as we embark on our generative journey. Let's go ahead and learn about the principles of generative models!

# CHAPTER 2

# Transformers

Many trace the most recent wave of advances in generative AI to the introduction of a class of models called *transformers* in 2017. Their most well-known applications are the powerful large language models (LLMs), such as Llama and GPT-4, used by hundreds of millions daily. Transformers have become a backbone for modern AI applications, powering everything from chatbots and search systems to machine translation and content summarization. They've even branched out beyond text, making waves in fields like Computer Vision, music generation, and protein folding. In this chapter, we'll explore the core ideas behind transformers and how they work, with a focus on one of the most common applications: language modeling.

Before we dive into the details of transformers, let's take a step back and understand what language modeling is. At its core, a language model (LM) is a probabilistic model that learns to predict the next word (or *token*) in a sequence based on the preceding or surrounding words. Doing so captures the language's underlying structure and patterns, allowing the model to generate realistic and coherent text. For example, given the sentence "I began my day eating", an LM might predict the next word as "breakfast" with a high probability.

So, how do transformers fit into this picture? Transformers are designed to handle long-range dependencies and complex relationships between words efficiently and expressively. For example, imagine that you want to use an LM to summarize a news article, which might contain hundreds or even thousands of words. Traditional LMs, such as RNNs, struggle with long contexts, so the summary might skip critical details from the beginning of the article. Transformer-based LMs, however, show strong results in this task. Besides high-quality generations, transformers have other properties, such as efficient parallelization of training, scalability, and knowledge transfer, making them popular and well suited for multiple tasks. At the heart of this innovation lies a mechanism called *self-attention*, which allows the model to weigh the importance of each word in the context of the entire sequence.

To help us build intuition about how LMs work, we'll use code examples that interact with existing models, and we'll describe the relevant pieces as we find them. Let's get to it.

# A Language Model in Action

In this section, we will load and interact with an existing small (pretrained) transformer model to get a high-level understanding of how they work. In recent years, companies, research labs, and open communities have released thousands of open models that you can use.

We'll pick a small model you can run directly in your hardware, but consider that the same principles apply to the larger (over 100 times larger!) and more powerful models that have since been released. Some good examples of small models are as follows:

*GPT-2 (137M)*
> This model made headlines in 2019 for its (then) impressive text-generation capabilities. Although small and almost quaint by today's standards, GPT-2 illustrates how these LMs work.

*Qwen2 (494M)*
> This is an Alibaba model and part of the Qwen family. The Qwen family has models with 500 million to over 100 billion parameters.

*SmolLM (135M)*
> This is a model by Hugging Face trained with very high-quality data. The authors released models with 135 million, 360 million, and 1.7 billion parameters.

Chapter 6 will provide more insights into picking the suitable model for your use case. For now, we suggest exploring one of the models in the preceding list (or all of them!).

# Tokenizing Text

Let's begin our journey to generate text based on an initial input. For example, given the phrase "it was a dark and stormy", we want the model to generate words to continue it. Models can't receive text directly as input; their input must be data represented as numbers. To feed text into a model, we must first find a way to turn sequences into numbers. This process is called *tokenization*, a crucial step in any NLP pipeline.

An easy option would be to split the text into individual characters and assign each a unique numerical ID (Figure 2-1). This scheme could be helpful for languages such as Chinese, where each character carries much information. In languages like English, this creates a small token *vocabulary*, and there will be few unknown tokens (characters not found during training) when running inference. However, this method requires many tokens to represent a string, which is bad for performance and erases some of the structure and meaning of the text—a downside for accuracy. Each character carries little information, making it hard for the model to learn the underlying structure of the text.

*Figure 2-1. In character-level tokenization, each letter has its own ID, with all instances of the same letter having the same ID. In this example, the IDs correspond to their position in the alphabet.*

Another approach could be to split the text into individual words (Figure 2-2). While this lets us capture more meaning per token, it has the downsides that we need to deal with more unknown words (e.g., typos or slang), we need to deal with different forms of the same word (e.g., "run", "runs", and "running"), and we might end up with a very large vocabulary, which could easily be over half a million words for languages such as English.

*Figure 2-2. In word-level tokenization, the same word always has the same ID*

Modern tokenization strategies strike a balance between these two extremes, splitting the text into subwords that capture both the structure and meaning of the text while still being able to handle unknown words and different forms of the same word (Figure 2-3). Characters that are usually found together (like most frequent words) can be assigned a single token that represents the whole word or group. Long or complicated words, or words with many inflections, may be split into multiple tokens, where each one usually represents a meaningful section of the word.

There is no single best tokenizer; each LM comes with its own. The differences between tokenizers reside in the number of tokens supported and the tokenization strategy. For example, the GPT-2 tokenizer averages 1.3 tokens per word.[1]

---

1 You can explore various tokenizers interactively in the Tokenizer Playground (*https://oreil.ly/fDJCc*).

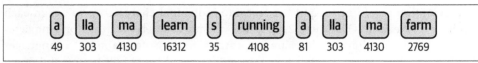

| a | lla | ma | learn | s | running | a | lla | ma | farm |
|---|-----|-----|-------|---|---------|---|-----|-----|------|
| 49 | 303 | 4130 | 16312 | 35 | 4108 | 81 | 303 | 4130 | 2769 |

*Figure 2-3. In this example of subword tokenization, llama is split into two tokens because it was likely not a common word in the data used to create the tokenizer*

Let's find out how the Qwen tokenizer handles a sentence. We'll first use the *transformers* library to load the tokenizer corresponding to Qwen. Then we'll run the input text (also called *prompt*) through the tokenizer to encode the string into numbers representing the tokens. We'll use the `decode()` method to convert each ID back into its corresponding token for demonstration purposes:

```
from transformers import AutoTokenizer

# Use the id of the model you want to use
# GPT-2 "openai-community/gpt2"
# Qwen "Qwen/Qwen2-0.5B"
# SmolLM "HuggingFaceTB/SmolLM-135M"

prompt = "It was a dark and stormy"
tokenizer = AutoTokenizer.from_pretrained("Qwen/Qwen2-0.5B")
input_ids = tokenizer(prompt).input_ids
input_ids
```

```
[2132, 572, 264, 6319, 323, 13458, 88]
```

```
for t in input_ids:
    print(t, "\t:", tokenizer.decode(t))
```

```
2132    :  It
572     :  was
264     :  a
6319    :  dark
323     :  and
13458   :  storm
88      :  y
```

As shown, the tokenizer splits the input string into a series of tokens and assigns a unique ID to each. Most words are represented by a single token, but when using the Qwen and GPT-2 tokenizers, "stormy" is represented by two tokens: one for " storm" (including the space before the word) and one for the suffix "y". This allows the model to learn that "stormy" is related to "storm" and that the suffix "y" is often used to turn nouns into adjectives. On the other hand, the SmolLM tokenizer does not split any of the words in this particular sentence. Each model is usually paired with its own tokenizer, so always use the proper tokenizer when using a model. The three models of this section have vocabularies that go from 50,000 to 150,000 tokens, which allows them to represent almost any input text.

Even though we usually talk about *training* tokenizers, this has nothing to do with training a model. Model training is stochastic (nondeterministic) by nature, whereas we train a tokenizer using a statistical process that identifies which subwords are the best to pick for a given dataset. How to choose the subwords is a design decision of the tokenization algorithm. Therefore, tokenization training is deterministic. We won't dive into different tokenization strategies, but some of the most popular subword approaches are Byte-level Byte-Pair Encoding (BPE), used in GPT-2, WordPiece, and SentencePiece.

## Predicting Probabilities

GPT-2, Qwen, and SmolLM were trained as *causal language models* (also known as *autoregressive*), which means they were trained to predict the next token in a sequence, given the preceding tokens. The *transformers* library has high-level tools that enable us to use such a model to generate text or perform other tasks quickly. It is helpful to understand how the model makes its predictions by directly inspecting them on this language-modeling task. We begin by loading the model:

```
from transformers import AutoModelForCausalLM

model = AutoModelForCausalLM.from_pretrained("Qwen/Qwen2-0.5B")
```

Note the use of `AutoTokenizer` and `AutoModelForCausalLM`. The *transformers* library supports hundreds of models and their corresponding tokenizers. Rather than having to learn the name of each tokenizer and model class, we will use `Auto Tokenizer` and `AutoModelFor*`. For the automatic model class, we need to specify for which task we're using the model, such as classification (`AutoModelForSequence Classification`) or object detection (`AutoModelForObjectDetection`). In the case of Qwen2, we'll use the class corresponding to the causal language-modeling task. When using the automatic classes, *transformers* will pick an adequate default class based on the configuration of a model. For example, under the hood, *transformers* will use `Qwen2Tokenizer` and `Qwen2ForCausalLM`.

If we feed the tokenized sentence from the previous section through the model, we get a result with 151,936 values for each token in the input string:

```
# We tokenize again but specifying the tokenizer that we want it to
# return a PyTorch tensor, which is what the model expects,
# rather than a list of integers
input_ids = tokenizer(prompt, return_tensors="pt").input_ids

outputs = model(input_ids)
outputs.logits.shape  # An output for each input token

torch.Size([1, 7, 151936])
```

The first dimension of the output is the number of batches (1 because we just ran a single sequence through the model). The second dimension is the sequence length, or the number of tokens in the input sequence (7 in this case). The third dimension is the vocabulary size. We get a list of ~150,000 numbers for each token in the original sequence. These are the raw model outputs, or *logits*, that correspond to the tokens in the vocabulary. For every input token, the model predicts how likely each token in the vocabulary is to continue the sequence up to that point. With our example sentence, the model will predict logits for "It", "It was", "It was a", and so on. Higher logit values mean the model considers the corresponding token a more likely continuation of the sequence. Table 2-1 shows the input sequences, the most likely token ID, and its corresponding token.

Logits are the raw output of the model (a list of numbers such as [0.1, 0.2, 0.01, ...]). We can use the logits to select the most likely token to continue the sequence. However, we can also convert the logits into probabilities, as we'll do soon.

*Table 2-1. The most likely token to continue input sequences according to the Qwen2 model*

| Input sequence | ID of most likely next token | Corresponding token |
| --- | --- | --- |
| It | 374 | is |
| It was | 264 | a |
| It was a | 2244 | great |
| It was a dark | 323 | and |
| It was a dark and | 13458 | storm |
| It was a dark and | 88 | y |
| It was a dark and stormy | 3729 | (let's figure this one) |

Let's focus on the logits for the entire prompt and learn how to predict the next word of the sequence. We can find the index of the token with the highest value by using the argmax() method:

```
final_logits = model(input_ids).logits[0, -1]  # The last set of logits
final_logits.argmax()  # The position of the maximum

tensor(3729)
```

3729 corresponds to the ID of the token the model considers most likely to follow the input string "It was a dark and stormy". Decoding this token, we can find out that this model knows a few story tropes:

```
tokenizer.decode(final_logits.argmax())

' night'
```

So "night" is the most likely token. This makes sense considering the beginning of the sentence we provided as input. The model learns how to *pay attention* to other tokens by using a mechanism called *self-attention*, which is the fundamental building block of transformers. Intuitively, self-attention allows the model to identify how much each token contributes to the meaning of the sequence.

 Transformer models contain many of these attention layers, each one specializing in some aspect of the input. Contrary to heuristics systems, these aspects or features are learned during training, instead of being specified beforehand.

Let's now find out which other tokens were potential candidates by selecting the top 10 values with `topk()`:

```python
import torch

top10_logits = torch.topk(final_logits, 10)
for index in top10_logits.indices:
    print(tokenizer.decode(index))
```

```
 night
 evening
 day
 morning
 winter
 afternoon
 Saturday
 Sunday
 Friday
 October
```

We need to convert logits into probabilities to better understand how confident the model is about each prediction. We can do that by comparing each value with all the other predicted values and normalizing so that all the numbers sum up to 1. That's precisely what the `softmax()` operation does. The following code uses `softmax()` to print out the top 10 most likely tokens and their associated probabilities according to the model:[2]

```python
top10 = torch.topk(final_logits.softmax(dim=0), 10)
for value, index in zip(top10.values, top10.indices):
    print(f"{tokenizer.decode(index):<10} {value.item():.2%}")
```

```
 night     88.71%
 evening   4.30%
 day       2.19%
```

---

2 We use < to align the token to the left, 10 to specify the width of the field, and .2% to format the probability as a percentage with two decimal places.

```
morning    0.49%
winter     0.45%
afternoon  0.27%
Saturday   0.25%
Sunday     0.19%
Friday     0.17%
October    0.16%
```

Before going further, we suggest you experiment with the preceding code. Here are some ideas for you to try:

*Change a few words*

Try changing the adjectives (e.g., "dark" and "stormy") in the input string and find out how the model's predictions change. Is the predicted word still "night"? How do the probabilities change?

*Change the input string*

Try different input strings and analyze how the model's predictions change. Do you agree with the model's predictions?

*Grammar*

What happens if you provide a string that is not a grammatically correct sequence? How does the model handle it? Look at the probabilities of the top predictions.

## Generating Text

Once we know how to get the model's predictions for the next token in a sequence, it is easy to generate text by repeatedly feeding the model's predictions back into itself. We can call `model(ids)`, generate a new token ID, add it to the list, and call the function again. To make it more convenient to generate multiple words, *transformers* autoregressive models have a `generate()` method ideal for this case. Let's explore an example:

```
output_ids = model.generate(input_ids, max_new_tokens=20)
decoded_text = tokenizer.decode(output_ids[0])

print("Input IDs", input_ids[0])
print("Output IDs", output_ids)
print(f"Generated text: {decoded_text}")
```

```
Input IDs tensor([ 2132,   572,   264,  6319,   323, 13458,    88])
Output IDs tensor([ 2132,   572,   264,  6319,   323, 13458,    88,  3729,
          13,   576, 12884,   572,  6319,   323,   279,  9956,   572,  1246,
        2718,    13,   576, 11174,   572, 50413,  1495,   323,   279])
Generated text: It was a dark and stormy night. The sky was dark and the
wind was howling. The rain was pouring down and the
```

When we ran the `model()` forward method in the previous section, it returned a list of logits for each token in the vocabulary (151,936). Then, we had to calculate the probabilities and pick the most likely token. The `generate()` method abstracts this logic away. It makes multiple forward passes, predicts the next token repeatedly, and appends it to the input sequence. The method provides us with the token IDs of the final sequence, including both the input and new tokens. Then, with the tokenizer `decode()` method, we can convert the token IDs back to text.

We can use many possible strategies to perform generation. The one we just did, picking the most likely token, is called *greedy decoding* (Figure 2-4). Although this approach is straightforward, it can sometimes lead to suboptimal outcomes, especially in generating longer text sequences. Greedy decoding can be problematic because it doesn't consider the overall probability of a sentence, focusing only on the immediate next word. For instance, given the starting word "Sky" and the choices "blue" and "rockets" for the next word, greedy decoding might favor "Sky blue" since "blue" initially appears more likely following "Sky". However, this approach might overlook a more coherent and probable overall sequence like "Sky rockets soar". Therefore, greedy decoding can sometimes miss out on the most likely overall sequence, leading to less-optimal text generation.

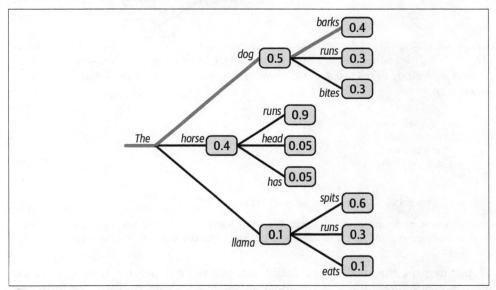

*Figure 2-4. This greedy decoding example generates "The dog barks" because "dog" is the most likely second token with a probability of 0.5, and "barks" is the most likely token following "The dog"*

Rather than selecting one token at a time, techniques such as *beam search* (see Figure 2-5) explore multiple possible continuations of the sequence and return the most likely *sequence* of continuations. Shown in the following code example, this approach keeps the most likely `num_beams` of hypotheses during generation and chooses the most likely one.

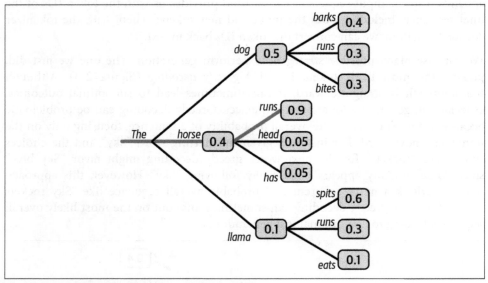

*Figure 2-5. This beam search example finds a more likely sequence: "The dog barks" has a total probability of 0.5 × 0.4 = 0.2, while "The horse runs" has a probability of 0.4 × 0.9 = 0.36*

```
beam_output = model.generate(
    input_ids,
    num_beams=5,
    max_new_tokens=30,
)
```

```
print(tokenizer.decode(beam_output[0]))
```

```
It was a dark and stormy night. The wind was howling, and the rain was
pouring down. The sky was dark and gloomy, and the air was filled with
the
```

Depending on the model, you might get somewhat repetitive results. Although not frequently used, there are multiple parameters we can control to perform less-repetitive generations. Let's consider two examples:

`repetition_penalty`

How much to penalize already generated tokens, avoiding repetition. A good default value is 1.2.

```
bad_words_ids
```
A list of tokens that should not be generated (e.g., to avoid generating offensive words).

Let's explore what we can achieve by penalizing repetition:

```
beam_output = model.generate(
    input_ids,
    num_beams=5,
    repetition_penalty=2.0,
    max_new_tokens=38,
)

print(tokenizer.decode(beam_output[0]))

It was a dark and stormy night. The sky was filled with thunder and
lightning, and the wind howled in the distance. It was raining cats
and dogs, and the streets were covered in puddles of water.
```

Which generation strategy to use? As often is true in ML, it depends. Beam search works well when the desired length of the text is somewhat predictable. This is the case for tasks such as summarization or translation but not for open-ended generation, where the output length can vary greatly, leading to repetition. Although we can inhibit the model to avoid repeating itself, doing so can also lead to it performing worse. Also note that beam search will be slower than greedy search as it needs to run inference for multiple beams simultaneously, which can be an issue for large models.

When we generate with greedy search and beam search, we push the model to generate text with a distribution of high-probability next words, as can be seen in Figure 2-6.[3] Interestingly, high-quality human language does not follow a similar distribution. Human text tends to be more unpredictable. The authors of an excellent paper (*https://arxiv.org/abs/1904.09751*) about this counterintuitive observation conjecture that human language disfavors predictable words—people optimize against stating the obvious. The paper proposes a method called *nucleus sampling*.

Before discussing nucleus sampling, let's discuss sampling. With sampling, we pick the next token by sampling from the probability distribution of the next tokens. This means that sampling is not a deterministic generation process. If the next possible tokens are "night" (60%), "day" (35%), and "apple" (5%), rather than choosing "night" (with greedy search), we will sample from the distribution. In other words, there will be a 5% chance of picking "apple" even if it's a low-probability token and leads to a nonsensical generation. Sampling avoids creating repetitive text, hence leading to more diverse generations.

---

3 In statistics, a distribution is a way of describing how the values of a variable are spread out. It tells us how often different values of the variable occur.

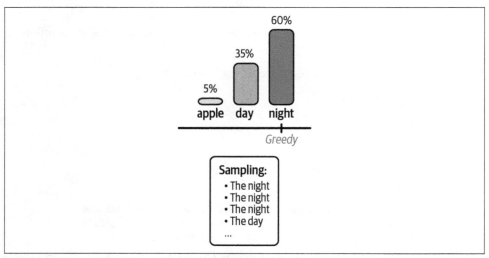

*Figure 2-6. Greedy generation will always pick the most likely next token, while sampling will pick the next token by sampling from the probability distribution*

Sampling is done in *transformers* by using the do_sample parameter:

```
from transformers import set_seed

# Setting the seed ensures we get the same results every time we run this code
set_seed(70)

sampling_output = model.generate(
    input_ids,
    do_sample=True,
    max_new_tokens=34,
    top_k=0,  # We'll come back to this parameter
)

print(tokenizer.decode(sampling_output[0]))
```

```
It was a dark and stormy night. Kevin said he was going to stay up all
night, staring at the cloudless stars, wondering, what if I lost my
dream.He'd been teasing her about
```

We can manipulate the probability distribution before we sample from it, making it sharper or flatter using a temperature parameter. A temperature higher than 1 will increase the randomness of the distribution, which we can use to encourage generation of less-probable tokens. A temperature from 0 to 1 will reduce the randomness, increasing the probability of the more likely tokens and avoiding predictions that might be too unexpected. A temperature of 0 will move all the probability to the most likely next token, which is equivalent to greedy decoding, as can be seen in Figure 2-7.

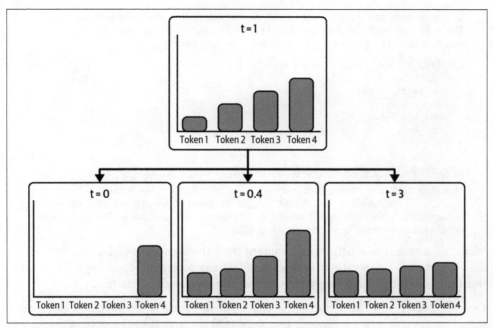

*Figure 2-7. Effect of temperature on the token probability distribution*

Compare the effect of this temperature parameter on the generated text in the following example:

```
sampling_output = model.generate(
    input_ids,
    do_sample=True,
    temperature=0.4,
    max_new_tokens=40,
    top_k=0,
)

print(tokenizer.decode(sampling_output[0]))
```

It was a dark and stormy night in 1878. The only light was the moon, and the only sound was the distant roar of the thunder. The only thing that could be heard was the sound of the storm

```
sampling_output = model.generate(
    input_ids,
    do_sample=True,
    temperature=0.001,
    max_new_tokens=40,
    top_k=0,
)

print(tokenizer.decode(sampling_output[0]))
```

```
It was a dark and stormy night. The sky was dark and the wind was howling.
The rain was pouring down and the lightning was flashing. The sky was dark
and the wind was howling. The rain was pouring down

sampling_output = model.generate(
    input_ids,
    do_sample=True,
    temperature=3.0,
    max_new_tokens=40,
    top_k=0,
)

print(tokenizer.decode(sampling_output[0]))

It was a dark and stormy 清晨一步
            女人们都 BL 咻任何时候 بن تص attendees*sinruitmentโลกnuresindi
ambassadors eventData 原来是 exaлENCE hemisphere worldsɯ.Anyar 久◆ Sous dapat
HVιşísdía.inventory emptiedfuncpping {\Sex
```

Well, the first test is much more coherent than the second one. The second, which uses a very low temperature, is repetitive (similar to greedy decoding). Finally, the third sample, with an extremely high temperature, gives gibberish text.

One parameter you likely noticed is top_k. What is it? *Top-K sampling* is a simple sampling approach in which only the *K* most likely next tokens are considered. For example, using top_k=5, the generation method will first filter the most likely five tokens and redistribute the probabilities so that they add to 1:

```
sampling_output = model.generate(
    input_ids,
    do_sample=True,
    max_new_tokens=40,
    top_k=5,
)

print(tokenizer.decode(sampling_output[0]))

It was a dark and stormy night in New York. The city was on the brink
of a violent storm. The sky above was painted with a mix of bright red
and orange. It was a sign, but the storm had arrived
```

Hmm…this could be better. An issue with Top-K sampling is that the number of relevant candidates in practice could vary greatly. If we define top_k=5, some distributions will still include tokens with very low probability, while others will consist of only high-probability tokens.

The final generation strategy we'll visit is *Top-p sampling* (also known as nucleus sampling). Rather than sampling the *K* words with the highest probability, we will use all the most likely words whose cumulative probability exceeds a given value. If we use top_p=0.94, we'll first filter only to keep the most likely words that cumulatively have a probability of 0.94 or higher, as can be observed in Figure 2-8. We then redistribute the probability and do regular sampling. Let's check this out in action.

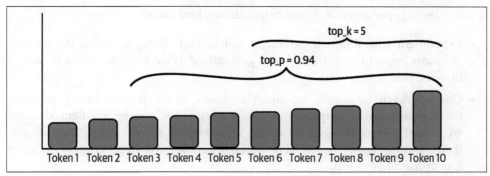

*Figure 2-8. Effect of* `top_k` *and* `top_p` *on the token probability distribution. With* `top_k=5`, *only the five most likely tokens are considered. With* `top_p=0.94`, *we include all tokens until they cumulatively have a probability of 0.94.*

In *transformers*, we can use Top-p sampling and modify the probability with the `top_p` parameter:

```
sampling_output = model.generate(
    input_ids,
    do_sample=True,
    max_new_tokens=40,
    top_p=0.94,
    top_k=0,
)

print(tokenizer.decode(sampling_output[0]))
```

```
It was a dark and stormy night in the skies of Morrowind, and a particularly
ruthless fighter had decided that these careless tourists at Carrabine
should be dealt with with maximum cruelty. The chief of this important
operation was appointed by
```

Both Top-K and Top-p are commonly used in practice. They can even be combined to filter out low-probability words but have more generation control. The issue with the stochastic generation methods is that the generated text doesn't necessarily contain coherence.

We've explored three generation methods: greedy search, beam-search decoding, and sampling (with temperature, Top-K, and Top-p providing further control). Those are lots of approaches! If you feel underwhelmed by the model generations, consider that it's a model with a few hundred million parameters; the fact that it can generate coherent text is already impressive! New models spawn billions or even hundreds of billions of parameters and are trained with higher-quality data, so switching to a more modern or larger model will lead to better results. You can find an online interactive demo (*https://oreil.ly/bH8AJ*) to visualize how `temperature`, `top_p`, and `top_k` impact a generation distribution.

If you want to experiment with generation further, here are some suggestions:

- Experiment with different parameter values. How does increasing the number of beams impact the quality of your generation? What happens if you reduce or increase your `top_p` value?

- One approach to reduce repetition in beam search is introducing penalties for n-grams (word sequences of *n* words). This can be configured using `no_repeat_ngram_size`, which avoids repeating the same n-gram. For example, if you use `no_repeat_ngram_size=4`, the generation will never contain the exact four consecutive words.

- Top-K can lead to discarding high-quality tokens, and Top-p can lead to including some low-probability tokens. For a more dynamic approach, you can use Min-P (`min_p`), which multiplies `min_p` by the top token's probability, and then include only tokens above that percentage. In other words, Min-P defines a dynamic threshold based on the top token's probability.

- A newer method, contrastive search, can generate long, coherent output while avoiding repetition. This is achieved by considering both the probabilities predicted by the model and the similarity with the context. This can be controlled via `penalty_alpha` and `top_k`.[4]

If all this sounds too empirical, it's because it is. Generation is an active area of research, with new papers coming up with different proposals, such as more sophisticated filtering. We'll briefly discuss these in the final chapter. No single rule works for all models, so it's always important to experiment with different techniques.

## Zero-Shot Generalization

Generating language is a fun and exciting application of transformers, but writing fake articles about unicorns is not the reason they are so popular.[5] To predict the next token well, these models must *learn* a fair amount about the world. We can take advantage of this to perform various tasks. For example, instead of training a model dedicated to translation, we can prompt a sufficiently powerful LM with an input like this:

---

4 An excellent deep dive into contrastive search is Tian Lan's "Generating Human-Level Text with Contrastive Search" blog post (*https://oreil.ly/VFc42*).

5 The first example in the GPT-2 release blog post (*https://oreil.ly/Nz0C7*) was famously a news story about unicorns.

```
Translate the following sentence from English to French:
Input: The cat sat on the mat.
Translation:
```

I typed this example with GitHub Copilot active, and it helpfully suggested "Le chat était assis sur le tapis" as a continuation of the prompt—a perfect illustration of how an LM can perform tasks not explicitly trained for. The more powerful the model, the more tasks it can perform without additional training. This flexibility makes transformers quite powerful and has made them so popular in recent years.

To check this in action for ourselves, let's use Qwen as a classification model. Specifically, we'll classify movie reviews as positive or negative—a classic benchmark task in the NLP field. We'll use a *zero-shot* approach to make things interesting, which means we won't provide the model with any labeled data. Instead, we'll prompt the model with the text of a review and ask it to predict the sentiment.

We can use a generative model as a classifier in multiple ways. Usually, we begin by inserting the movie review into a prompt template that provides context for the model. This prompt template could instruct the model to simply return the sentiment of the review (and ask to limit it as `positive` or `negative`). An alternative trick, especially needed with a small model like GPT-2 or the small Qwen, is to look at its prediction for the next token and find out which possible token is assigned a higher probability: `positive` or `negative`? Let's go with this approach and find the IDs corresponding to those tokens:

```
# Check the token IDs for the words ' positive' and ' negative'
# (note the space before the words)
tokenizer.encode(" positive"), tokenizer.encode(" negative")

([6785], [8225])
```

Once we have the IDs, we can run inference with the model and generate a label based on the probabilities:

```
def score(review):
    """Predict whether it is positive or negative

    This function predicts whether a review is positive or negative
    using a bit of clever prompting. It looks at the logits for the
    tokens ' positive' and ' negative', and returns the label
    with the highest score.
    """
    prompt = f"""Question: Is the following review positive or
negative about the movie?
Review: {review} Answer:"""

    input_ids = tokenizer(prompt, return_tensors="pt").input_ids ❶
    final_logits = model(input_ids).logits[0, -1] ❷
```

```
        if final_logits[6785] > final_logits[8225]: ❸
            print("Positive")
        else:
            print("Negative")
```

❶ Tokenize the prompt.

❷ Get the logits for each token in the vocabulary. Note that we're using `model()`
rather than `model.generate()`, as `model()` returns the logits for each token in
the vocabulary, while `model.generate()` returns only the chosen token.

❸ Check if the logit for the `positive` token is higher than the logit for the `negative`
token.

We can try out this zero-shot classifier on a few fake reviews to evaluate how it does:

```
score("This movie was terrible!")

Negative

score("That movie was great!")

Positive

score("A complex yet wonderful film about the depravity of man")   # A mistake

Negative
```

In the GitHub repo for this book (*https://oreil.ly/handsonGenAIcode*), you'll find a
dataset of labeled reviews and code to assess the accuracy of this zero-shot approach.
Can you tweak the prompt template to improve the model's performance? Can you
think of other tasks that could be performed using a similar approach?

The zero-shot capabilities of recent models have been a game-changer. As the models
improve, they can perform more tasks out-of-the-box, making them more accessible
and easier to use and reducing the need for specialized models for each task.

## Few-Shot Generalization

Despite the release of ChatGPT and the quest for the perfect prompts, zero-shot
generalization (or prompt tuning) is not the only way to bend powerful LMs to
perform arbitrary tasks.

Zero-shot is the extreme application of a technique called *few-shot generalization*, in
which we provide the LM with a few examples about the task we want it to perform
and then ask it to provide similar answers for us. Instead of training the model, we
show some examples to influence generation by increasing the probability that the
continuation text follows the same structure and pattern as our prompt. Let's try an

example. Apart from providing examples, providing a short description of what the model should do, e.g., "Translate English to Spanish", will help with higher-quality generations:

```
prompt = """\
Translate English to Spanish:

English: I do not speak Spanish.
Spanish: No hablo español.

English: See you later!
Spanish: ¡Hasta luego!

English: Where is a good restaurant?
Spanish: ¿Dónde hay un buen restaurante?

English: What rooms do you have available?
Spanish: ¿Qué habitaciones tiene disponibles?

English: I like soccer
Spanish:"""
inputs = tokenizer(prompt, return_tensors="pt").input_ids
output = model.generate(
    inputs,
    max_new_tokens=10,
)

print(tokenizer.decode(output[0]))
```

```
Translate English to Spanish:

English: I do not speak Spanish.
Spanish: No hablo español.

English: See you later!
Spanish: ¡Hasta luego!

English: Where is a good restaurant?
Spanish: ¿Dónde hay un buen restaurante?

English: What rooms do you have available?
Spanish: ¿Qué habitaciones tiene disponibles?

English: I like soccer
Spanish: Me gusta el fútbol

English:
```

We state the task we want to achieve and provide four examples to set the context for the model. Hence, this is a four-shot generalization task. Then we ask the model to generate more text to follow the pattern and provide the requested translation. Here are some ideas to explore:

- Would this work with fewer examples?
- Would it work without the task description?
- How about other tasks?
- How do GPT-2 and SmolLM score in this setting?

 GPT-2, given its size and training process, is not very good at few-shot tasks, and it's even worse at zero-shot generalization. How is it possible you could have used it for sentiment classification as in the previous section? We cheated a bit: we didn't look at the text generated by the model, but just checked whether the probability for " positive" was larger than the " negative" probability. Understanding how models work under the hood can unlock powerful applications even with small models. Remember to think about your problem; don't be afraid to explore.

GPT-2 and Qwen 0.5B are examples of *base models*. Some base models in the style of Qwen have zero-shot and few-shot capabilities that we can use at *inference* time. Another approach is to *fine-tune* a model: we take the base model and keep training it a bit longer on domain- or task-specific data. We don't always need the extreme generalization capabilities showcased by the most powerful models in the world; if you only want to solve a particular task, it will usually be cheaper and better to fine-tune and deploy a smaller model specialized on a single task.

It's also important to note that *base models are not conversational*; although you can write a nice prompt that will help make a chatbot with a base model, it's often more convenient to fine-tune the base model with conversational data, hence improving the conversational capabilities of the model. That's precisely what we'll do in Chapter 6. Recent LLM releases tend to include both a base model and an official model with conversational capabilities. In the case of the small Qwen model, this would be Qwen2-0.5B-Instruct (*https://oreil.ly/WO2QB*).

# A Transformer Block

After our brief experiments using LMs, we are ready to introduce an architecture diagram for transformer-based language-generation models shown in Figure 2-9.

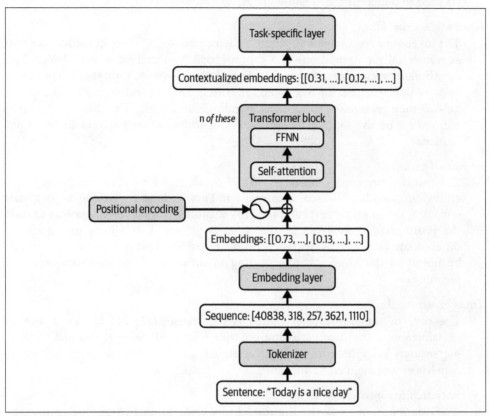

*Figure 2-9. Architecture of a transformer-based language model*

The high-level pieces involved include the following:

*Tokenization*

The input text is broken into individual tokens. Each token has a corresponding ID used to index the token embeddings.

*Input token embedding*

The tokens are represented as vectors called *embeddings*. These embeddings serve as numerical representations that capture basic information of each token. You can think of vectors as a (long) list of numbers, where each number corresponds to a particular aspect of the token's meaning. During training, a model learns how to map each token to its corresponding embedding. The token embedding will always be the same for each token, regardless of its position in the input sequence.

*Positional encoding*

The transformer model has no notion of order, so we need to enrich the token embeddings with positional information. This is done by adding a positional encoding to the token embeddings. This encoding is a set of vectors that encode the position of each token in the input sequence. This allows the model to differentiate between tokens based on their position in the sequence, which can be useful as the same token appearing in different places can have different meanings.

*Transformer blocks*

The core of the transformer model is the transformer block. The power of transformers comes from stacking multiple blocks, allowing the model to learn increasingly complex and abstract relationships between the input tokens. It consists of two main components:

*Self-attention mechanism*

This mechanism allows the model to weigh the importance of each token in the context of the entire sequence. It helps the model understand the relationships between tokens in the input. The self-attention mechanism is the key to the transformer's ability to handle long-range dependencies and complex relationships between words, and it helps generate coherent and contextually appropriate text.

*Feed-forward neural network*

The self-attention output is passed through a feed-forward neural network, which further refines the representation of the input sequence.

*Contextual embeddings*

The output of the transformer block is a set of contextual embeddings that capture the relationships between tokens in the input sequence. Unlike the input embeddings, which are fixed for each token, the contextual embeddings are updated at each layer of the transformer model based on the relationships between tokens. The embeddings capture rich and complex semantic information about the token in the context in which it appears.

*Prediction*

An additional layer processes the final representation into a task-dependent final output. In the case of text generation, this involves having a linear layer that maps the contextual embeddings to the vocabulary space, followed by a softmax operation to predict the next token in the sequence.

Of course, this is a simplification of the transformer architecture. Diving into the internals of how self-attention works or the internals of the transformer block is beyond the scope of this book. However, understanding the high-level architecture of a transformer model can be helpful to grasp how these models work and how they can be applied to various tasks. This architecture has enabled transformers to achieve unprecedented performance in various tasks and domains, and you'll find them cropping up again and again—not only in the rest of this book, but also in the discipline as a whole.

# Transformer Model Genealogy

At the beginning of the chapter, we experimented with Qwen to autoregressively generate text. Qwen, an example of a decoder-based transformer, has a single stack of transformer blocks that process an input sequence. This is a popular approach today, but other architectures have been developed over the years. This section provides a brief overview of the genealogy of transformer models.

## Sequence-to-Sequence Tasks

The original transformer paper (*https://arxiv.org/abs/1706.03762*) used a seemingly more complicated architecture called the encoder-decoder architecture (Figure 2-10). Although the encoder-decoder architecture was popular until 2023, it has been superseded by decoders in most research labs.

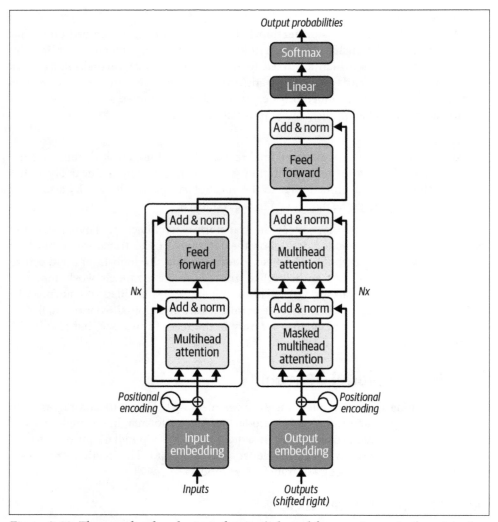

*Figure 2-10. The encoder-decoder transformer (adapted from an image in the original transformer paper (https://arxiv.org/abs/1706.03762))*

The transformer paper focused on machine translation as the example sequence-to-sequence task. The best results in machine translation at the time were achieved by RNNs, such as long short-term memory (LSTM) and gated recurrent units (GRUs)—don't worry if you're unfamiliar with them. The paper demonstrated better results by focusing solely on the *attention* method and showed that scalability and training were much easier. Important factors like excellent performance, stable training, and easy scalability are why transformers took off and were adapted to multiple tasks, as the next section explores in more depth.

In encoder-decoder models, like the original transformer model described in the paper, one stack of transformer blocks, called the *encoder*, processes an input sequence into a set of rich representations, which are then fed into another stack of transformer blocks, called the *decoder*, that decodes them into an output sequence. This approach to convert one sequence into a different one is called *sequence-to-sequence*, or *seq2seq*, and is naturally well suited for tasks such as translation, summarization, or question answering.

For example, you feed an English sentence through the encoder of a translation model, which generates a rich embedding that captures the meaning of the input. Then the decoder generates the corresponding French sentence by using this embedding. The generation happens in the decoder one token at a time, as we saw when generating sequences earlier in the chapter. However, the predictions for each successive token are informed not just by the previous tokens in the sequence being generated but also by the output from the encoder.

The mechanism by which the output from the encoder side is incorporated into the decoder stack is called *cross-attention*. It resembles self-attention, except that each token in the input (the sequence being processed by the decoder) attends to the context from the encoder rather than other tokens in its sequence. The cross-attention layers are interleaved with self-attention, allowing the decoder to use both contexts within its sequence and the information from the encoder.

After the transformer paper, existing sequence-to-sequence models, such as Marian NMT, incorporated these techniques as a central part of their architecture. New models were developed using these ideas. A notable one is BART (*http://arxiv.org/abs/1910.13461*) (short for Bidirectional and Auto-Regressive Transformers). During pretraining, BART corrupts input sequences and attempts to reconstruct them in the decoder output. Afterward, BART is fine-tuned for other generation tasks, such as translation or summarization, leveraging the rich sequence representations achieved during pretraining. Input corruption, by the way, is one of the key ideas behind diffusion models, as we'll discuss in Chapter 4.

## Encoder-Only Models

As we've discussed, the original transformer model was based on an encoder-decoder architecture that has been further explored in models such as BART or T5. In addition, the encoder or the decoder can be trained and used independently, giving rise to distinct transformer families. The first sections of this chapter explored decoder-only, or autoregressive models. These models are specialized in text generation using the techniques we described and have shown impressive performance, as demonstrated by ChatGPT, Claude, Llama, and Gemma.

Encoder models, on the other hand, are specialized in obtaining rich representations from text sequences and can be used for tasks such as classification or to prepare semantic *embeddings* for a multitude of documents that can be used in retrieval systems. The best-known transformer encoder model is probably BERT (*http://arxiv.org/abs/1810.04805*), which introduced the masked LM objective that was later picked up and further explored by BART.

Causal language modeling predicts the next token given the previous ones—it's what we did with Qwen. The model can attend to only the context on the left of a given token. A different approach used in encoder models is called *masked language modeling* (MLM). MLM, proposed in the famous BERT paper, pretrains a model to learn to "fill in the blanks." Given an input text, we randomly mask some tokens, and the model must predict the hidden tokens, as shown in Figure 2-11. Unlike causal language modeling, MLM uses both the sequence at the masked token's left and right, hence the *B* of *Bidirectional* in BERT's name. This helps create strong representations of the given text. Under the hood, these models use the encoder part of the transformer's architecture.

We just discussed encoder-decoder and decoder-only architectures. A common question is why one might need an encoder-decoder model for tasks like translation if decoder-only models like Qwen and Llama can show good results. Encoder-decoder models are designed to translate an entire input sequence to an output sequence, making them well-suited for translation. In contrast, decoder-only models focus on predicting the next token in a sequence. Initially, decoder-only models like GPT-2 were less capable in zero-shot learning scenarios than more recent models like GPT-4, but this was due to more than just the absence of an encoder. The improvement in zero-shot capabilities in advanced models like GPT-4 is also due to larger training data, better training techniques, and increased model sizes. While encoders in seq2seq models play a crucial role in understanding the full context of input sequences, advancements in decoder-only models have made them more effective and versatile, even for tasks traditionally relying on seq2seq models.

Let's look at some code. Rather than using the `AutoModel` and `AutoTokenizer` classes we used before, let's introduce a higher-level *transformers* API called `pipeline`. This API allows you to easily load a model for a given task. The `pipeline` API takes care of all the pre- and post-processing, and hence, it's a great way to quickly try out models:

```
from transformers import pipeline

fill_masker = pipeline("fill-mask", model="bert-base-uncased")
fill_masker("The [MASK] is made of milk.")
[{'score': 0.19546695053577423,
  'token': 9841,
  'token_str': 'dish',
  'sequence': 'the dish is made of milk.'},
 {'score': 0.1290755718946457,
  'token': 8808,
  'token_str': 'cheese',
```

```
  'sequence': 'the cheese is made of milk.'},
 {'score': 0.10590697824954987,
  'token': 6501,
  'token_str': 'milk',
  'sequence': 'the milk is made of milk.'},
 {'score': 0.04112089052796364,
  'token': 4392,
  'token_str': 'drink',
  'sequence': 'the drink is made of milk.'},
 {'score': 0.03712352365255356,
  'token': 7852,
  'token_str': 'bread',
  'sequence': 'the bread is made of milk.'}]
```

It's good to know that the milk is made of milk! What happens under the hood? The encoder receives the input sequence and generates a contextualized representation for each token. This representation is a vector of numbers that captures the meaning of the token in the context of the entire sequence. The encoder is usually followed by a task-specific layer that uses the representations to perform tasks such as classification, question answering, or masked language modeling, as shown in Figure 2-11. The encoder is trained to generate representations that are useful for tasks that require a good understanding of the input.

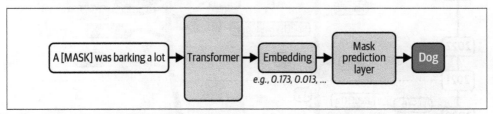

*Figure 2-11. Encoder models output semantic embeddings that can be used to solve tasks such as predicting a token in the middle of a sequence*

Between encoder-only, decoder-only, and encoder-decoder models, companies and research labs have released a large number of new open and closed language models, such as GPT-4, Mistral, Falcon, Llama, Qwen, Yi, Claude, Bloom, Gemma, and hundreds more. Figure 2-12 presents a nonexhaustive genealogy of transformer models, showing their fruitful impact on the NLP landscape as of 2024.

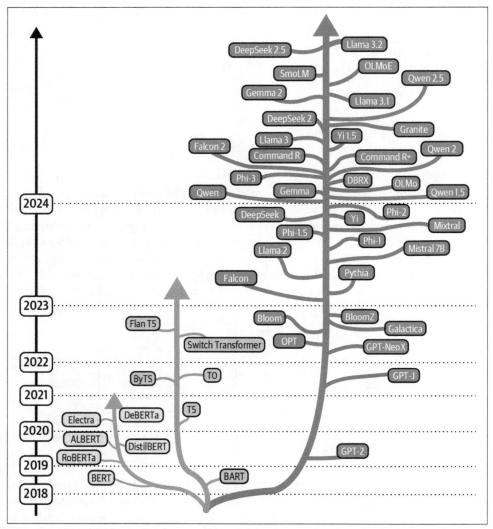

*Figure 2-12. A timeline of open encoder-only (red), encoder-decoder (green), and decoder-only (blue) model releases*

# The Power of Pretraining

Having access to existing models is quite powerful. Transformer models have shown SOTA performance across many other language tasks, such as text classification, machine translation, and answering questions based on an input text. Why do transformers work so well?

The first insight is the usage of the attention mechanism, as hinted at across the chapter. Attention mechanisms allow the transformer model to attend to long sequences and learn long-range relationships. In other words, transformers can estimate the relevance of some tokens to other tokens.

The second key aspect is their ability to scale. The transformer architecture has an implementation optimized for parallelization, and research has shown that these models can scale to handle high-complexity and high-scale datasets. Although initially designed for text data, the transformer architecture can be flexible enough to support different data types and handle irregular inputs.

The third key insight is the ability to do *pretraining* and *fine-tuning*. Traditional approaches to a task, such as movie-review classification, were limited by the availability of labeled data. A model would be trained from scratch on a large corpus of labeled examples, attempting to predict the label from the input text directly. This approach is often referred to as *supervised learning*. However, it has a significant drawback: it requires a large amount of labeled data to train effectively. This is a problem because labeling data is expensive and time-consuming. There might not even be any available data in many domains.

To address this need for a large amount of labeled data, researchers began looking for a way to pretrain models on existing data that could then be fine-tuned (or adjusted) for a specific task. This approach is known as *transfer learning* and is the foundation of modern ML in many fields, such as NLP and Computer Vision. Initial works in NLP focused on finding domain-specific corpora for the LM pretraining phase, but papers such as ULMFiT (*http://arxiv.org/abs/1801.06146*) showed that even pretraining on generic text such as Wikipedia could yield impressive results when the models were fine-tuned on downstream tasks, such as sentiment analysis or question answering. This set the stage for the rise of transformers, which turned out to be highly well suited for learning rich representations of language.

The idea of pretraining is to train a model on a large unlabeled dataset and then fine-tune it to a new target task, for which one would require much less labeled data (Figure 2-13). Before graduating to NLP, transfer learning had already been very successful with the CNNs that form the backbone of modern Computer Vision. In this scenario, one first trains a large model with a massive amount of labeled images in a classification task. Through this process, the model learns common features that can be leveraged on a different but related problem. For example, we can pretrain a model on thousands of classes and then fine-tune it to classify whether a picture is that of a hot dog.

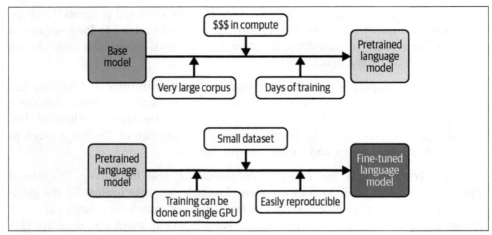

*Figure 2-13. While pretraining a base model can require a significant amount of resources, fine-tuning an existing model on a new task or domain is significantly cheaper*

With transformers, things are taken further with self-supervised pretraining (training with unlabeled data). We can pretrain a model on large, unlabeled text data. How? Let's think about causal models such as GPT. The model predicts which is the next token. Well, we don't need any labels to obtain training data! Given a corpus of text, we can mask the tokens after a sequence and train the model to learn to predict them. As in the Computer Vision case, pretraining gives the model a meaningful representation of the underlying text. We can then fine-tune the model to perform another task, such as generating text in the style of our tweets or a specific domain (e.g., your company chat). Given the model has already learned a representation of language, fine-tuning will require much less data than if we trained from scratch.

For many tasks, a rich representation of the input is more important than being able to predict the next token. For example, if you want to fine-tune a model to predict the sentiment of a movie review, MLMs would be more powerful. Models such as GPT-2 are designed to optimize for text generation rather than for building powerful representations of the text. On the other hand, models such as BERT are ideal for this task. As briefly mentioned before, the last layer of an encoder model outputs a dense representation of the input sequence, called *embedding*. This embedding can then be leveraged by adding a small, simple network on top of the encoder and fine-tuning the model for the specific task. As a concrete example, we can add a simple linear layer on top of the BERT encoder output to predict the sentiment of a document. We can take this approach to tackle a wide range of tasks:

*Token classification*
    Identify each entity in a sentence, such as a person, location, or organization.

*Extractive question answering*

Given a paragraph, answer a specific question and extract the answer from the input.

*Semantic search*

The features generated by the encoder can be handy to build a search system. Given a database of a hundred documents, we can compute the embeddings for each. Then, we can compare the input embeddings with the documents' embeddings at inference time, hence identifying the most similar document in the database.[6]

The preceding list is not exhaustive and also includes text similarity, anomaly detection, named entity linking, recommendation systems, and document classification.

Let's use a BERT-based model that was fine-tuned to perform sequence classification to determine whether the sentiment of a text is positive or negative. Once again, we'll use the `pipeline` API to load the model and perform the classification:

```
from transformers import pipeline

classifier = pipeline(
    "text-classification",
    model="distilbert/distilbert-base-uncased-finetuned-sst-2-english",
)
classifier("This movie is disgustingly good!")

[{'label': 'POSITIVE', 'score': 0.9998536109924316}]
```

This classification model can analyze reviews and predict their sentiment, as we did in "Zero-Shot Generalization" on page 28 and "Few-Shot Generalization" on page 30. "Challenges" on page 52 shows how to evaluate classification models and compare a zero-shot setup and this fine-tuned model.

# Transformers Recap

We've discussed three types of architectures:

*Encoder-based architectures*

Encoder-based architectures such as BERT, DistilBERT, and RoBERTa are ideal for tasks that require understanding the entire input.[7] These models output contextualized embeddings that capture the meaning of the input sequence. We

---

6 This oversimplifies how semantic search works, but we'll get a chance to build a simple search system using semantic embeddings in "Challenges" on page 52. This is the core of retrieval-augmented generation.

7 DistilBERT is a smaller model that preserves 95% of the original BERT performance while having 40% fewer parameters. RoBERTa is a powerful BERT-based model trained for longer with different hyperparameters.

can then add a small network on top of these embeddings and train it for a new specific task that relies on the semantic information.

*Decoder-based architectures*
Decoder-based architectures such as GPT-2, Qwen, Gemma, and Llama are ideal for new text generation.

*Encoder-decoder architectures*
Encoder-decoder architectures, or seq2seq, such as BART and T5, are great for tasks that require generating new sentences based on a given input, such as summarization or translation.

"Wait," you might say, "I can handle all these tasks with ChatGPT or Llama." That's true. Given the vast and growing amount of training data, computing power, and training optimizations, the quality of generative models has significantly improved. Their zero-shot capabilities have come a long way compared to those of a few years ago.

There are two main schools of thought here. One perspective is that, given the resources, fine-tuning a model for your specific task and domain will yield better results than using a generalist pretrained model. For example, if you want to use a GPT-like model to generate character dialogues in real time within a game, fine-tuning it with similar data beforehand might improve performance. Similarly, if you need a model to extract entities from a dataset of chemistry papers, it might make sense to fine-tune an encoder-based model with relevant chemistry texts.

On the other hand, with the rise of high-quality, low-cost generalist models that perform well across a variety of tasks, some argue that fine-tuning might be unnecessary for most use cases. Instead, prompt engineering could be a more effective and cheaper approach.

Seq2seq models were initially successful because they can encode variable-length input sequences into embeddings that summarize the input information. The decoder then uses this context to generate output. Recently, decoder-only models have gained popularity because of their simplicity, scalability, efficiency, and parallelization. In practice, different types of models are employed depending on the task; there's no single "golden" model that works for everything.

With over a million open models, you might wonder which one to use. Chapter 6 will help you navigate this landscape, providing guidelines on how to choose the right model for your task and requirements as well as how to fine-tune a model for your specific needs.

# Limitations

At this point, you might wonder about potential issues with transformers. Let's briefly go over some of the limitations:

*Transformers are very large*

Research has consistently shown that larger models perform better. Although that's quite exciting, it also brings concerns. First, some of the most powerful models require tens of millions of US dollars to train—just in computing power. That means that only a small set of institutions can train very large base models, limiting the kind of research that institutions without those resources can do. Second, using such amounts of computing power can also have ecological implications—those millions of GPU hours are, of course, powered by lots of electricity. Third, even if some of these models are open source, running them might require many GPUs. Chapter 6 will explore some techniques to use these LLMs even if you don't have multiple GPUs at home. Even then, deploying them in resource-constrained environments is a frequent challenge.

*Sequential processing*

If you recall the decoder section, we had to process all the previous tokens for each new token. That means that generating the 10,000th token in a sequence will take considerably longer than generating the initial one.[8] In computer science terms, transformers have quadratic time complexity with respect to the input length. This means that as the length of the input increases, the time taken for processing grows quadratically, making it challenging to scale them to very long documents or use these models in some real-time scenarios. While transformers excel in many tasks, their computational demands require careful consideration and optimization when being used in production. That said, there has been a lot of research on making transformers more efficient for extremely long sequences, such as clever caching techniques, ring attention, and Infini-attention.

*Fixed input size*

Transformer models can handle a maximum number of tokens, which depends on the base model. The number of tokens the model can attend to is called the *context window*, and it is essential to look into when picking a pretrained model. You cannot simply pass entire encyclopedias to transformers, expecting they will be able to summarize them, but this is changing quickly. While some pretrained models can handle up to only 512 tokens, having models that can handle up to 32,000 tokens is more common nowadays. New techniques allow scaling to

---

8 We can cache things to avoid processing tokens from scratch. Even then, for each new token, the model must attend to all the previous tokens.

hundreds of thousands or even millions of tokens! For example, Llama 3.1 can handle 131,000 tokens, which is close to the length of this book!

*Limited interpretability*
   Transformers are often criticized for their lack of interpretability.[9]

All of these limitations are active research areas. People have been exploring how to train and run models with less computing power (e.g., QLoRA, which we'll explore in Chapter 6), make generation faster (e.g., Flash Attention and assisted generation), enable unconstrained input sizes (e.g., RoPE and attention sinks), and interpret the attention mechanisms.

One big concern is the presence of biases in models. If the training data used to pretrain transformers contains biases, the model can learn and perpetuate them. This is a broader issue in ML but is especially relevant to transformers. Let's revisit the fill-mask pipeline. Let's say we want to predict the most likely profession. As you can check out in the following example, the results differ if we use the word "man" versus "woman":

```
unmasker = pipeline("fill-mask", model="bert-base-uncased")
result = unmasker("This man works as a [MASK] during summer.")
print([r["token_str"] for r in result])

result = unmasker("This woman works as a [MASK] during summer.")
print([r["token_str"] for r in result])

['farmer', 'carpenter', 'gardener', 'fisherman', 'miner']
['maid', 'nurse', 'servant', 'waitress', 'cook']
```

Why does this happen? To enable pretraining, researchers usually require large amounts of data, leading to scraping all the content they can find. This content might be of all kinds of quality, including toxic content (which can be, to some extent, filtered out). The base model might end up engraining and perpetuating these biases when being fine-tuned. Similar concerns exist for conversational models, where the final model might generate toxic content learned from the pretraining dataset.

# Beyond Text

Transformers have been used for many tasks representing data as text. A clear example is code generation: rather than training an LM with English data, we can use lots of code, and, by the same principles we just learned, it will learn how to autocomplete code. Another example is using transformers to answer questions from a table, such as a spreadsheet.

---

9 Among the lines of research on this, using sparse AutoEncoders (*https://arxiv.org/abs/2406.04093*) to extract interpretable features from transformers is becoming increasingly popular.

As transformer models have been so successful in the text domain, considerable interest has sparked in other communities to adapt these techniques to other modalities. This has led to transformer models being used for tasks such as image recognition, segmentation, object detection, video understanding, and more, as shown in Figure 2-14.

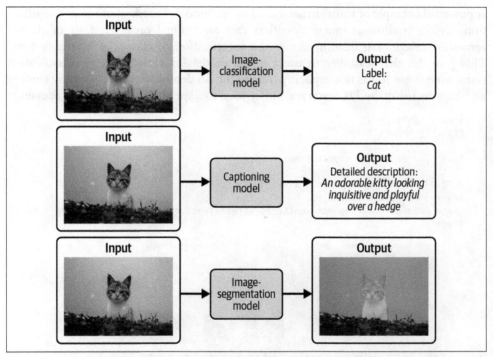

*Figure 2-14. Transformer models can be used for tasks such as classifying images, detecting objects, and segmenting images*

CNN have been widely used as the go-to SOTA models for most Computer Vision techniques. With the introduction of Vision Transformers (ViTs) (*http://arxiv.org/abs/2010.11929*), there has been a switch in recent years to explore how to tackle vision tasks with attention and transformer-based techniques. ViTs don't discard CNNs entirely: in the image-processing pipeline, CNNs extract feature maps of the image to detect high-level edges, textures, and other patterns. The feature maps obtained from the CNNs are then divided into fixed-size, nonoverlapping patches. These patches can be treated similarly to a sequence of tokens, so the attention mechanism can learn the relationships between patches in different places.

Unfortunately, ViTs required more data (300 million images!) and compute than CNNs to get good results. Further work has happened in recent years; for example, the DeiT model was able to leverage a transformer-based architecture with midsized datasets (1.2 million images) thanks to using augmentation and regularization techniques common in CNNs. Other models such as DETR, SegFormer, and Swin Transformer have pushed the field further, supporting many tasks such as image classification, object detection, image segmentation, video classification, document understanding, image restoration, super-resolution, and others.

A powerful example of transformer-based image models is zero-shot image classification. Unlike traditional image classifiers that are trained on a fixed set of classes, zero-shot image classification allows the specification of classes at inference time. This provides the flexibility to use a single model for various image-classification tasks, even those it was not explicitly trained for. To demonstrate, let's start by loading an image by using the *PIL* library, a widely used tool for vision-related preprocessing:

```
import requests
from PIL import Image

from genaibook.core import import SampleURL

# Download an image and load it with the PIL library
url = SampleURL.CatExample
image = Image.open(requests.get(url, stream=True).raw)
image
```

Now, let's use the high-level `pipeline` to use a model for the given task:

```
pipe = pipeline(
    "zero-shot-image-classification", model="openai/clip-vit-base-patch32"
) ❶
```

```
labels = ["cat", "dog", "zebra"]  ❷
pipe(image, candidate_labels=labels)  ❸
image

[{'score': 0.9936687350273132, 'label': 'cat'},
 {'score': 0.006043245084583759, 'label': 'dog'},
 {'score': 0.0002880473621189594, 'label': 'zebra'}]
```

❶ Load the openai/clip-vit-base-patch32 model (*https://oreil.ly/Q2tPc*).

❷ Define the classes we want to use at inference time.

❸ Pass the image and labels through the pipeline to get the model predictions.

As we'll explore in Chapter 9, transformer models can also be used for audio tasks, such as transcribing audio or generating synthetic speech or music. Under the hood, the same fundamental principles of pretraining and attention mechanisms persist, but each modality has different data types, requiring different approaches and modifications.

Other modalities where transformers are being explored are as follows:

*Graphs*
An excellent introductory read is "Introduction to Graph Machine Learning" (*https://oreil.ly/TK9vt*) by Clémentine Fourrier. Using transformers for graphs is still very exploratory, but there are some exciting early results. Some examples of tasks that involve graph data are predicting the toxicity of molecules, predicting the evolution of systems, or generating new plausible molecules.

*3D data*
Performing segmentation of data that can be represented in 3D, such as LiDAR point clouds in autonomous driving or CT scans for organ segmentation. Another example is estimating an object's six degrees of freedom, which can be helpful in robotics applications.

*Time series*
Analyzing stock prices or performing weather forecasting.

*Multimodal*
Some transformer models are designed to process or output multiple types of data (such as text, images, and audio) together. This opens up new possibilities, such as multimodal systems where you can speak, write, or provide pictures and have a single model to process them. Another example is visual question answering, where a model can answer questions about provided images.

# Project Time: Using LMs to Generate Text

We used the `generate()` method in "Generating Text" on page 20 to perform various decoding techniques. To better understand how it works under the hood, it's time to implement it ourselves. We'll use `generate()` as a reference but implement it from scratch.

Your goal is to fill the code in the following function. Rather than use `model .generate()`, the idea is to iteratively call `model()`, passing the previous tokens as input. You have to implement greedy search when `do_sample=False`, sampling when `do_sample=True`, and Top-K sampling when `do_sample=True` and `top_k` is not `None`. This will be a challenging task, so do not worry if you don't come up with a solution quickly. We suggest you begin implementing greedy search and then build on top of it:

```python
def generate(
    model, tokenizer, input_ids, max_length=50, do_sample=False, top_k=None
):
    """Generate a sequence without using model.generate()

    Args:
        model: The model to use for generation.
        tokenizer: The tokenizer to use for generation.
        input_ids: The input IDs
        max_length: The maximum length of the sequence.
        do_sample: Whether to use sampling.
        top_k: The number of tokens to sample from.
    """
    # Write your code here
    # Begin by the simplest approach, greedy decoding.
    # Then add sampling and finally top-k sampling.
```

# Summary

You now have learned to load and use transformers for various tasks. This chapter also covered how transformer models sequence data such as text and how this property lets them learn valuable representations that we can use to generate or classify new sequences. As the scale of these models increases, so do their capabilities—to the point where massive models with hundreds of billions of parameters can now perform many tasks previously thought impossible for computers.

We can pick powerful existing pretrained models and modify them for specific domains and use cases thanks to fine-tuning. The trend toward larger and more capable models has caused a shift in how people use them. Task-specific models are often outcompeted by general-purpose LLMs, and most people now interact with these models via APIs, hosted solutions, and local deployments or directly via slick chat-based user interfaces. At the same time, the release of large and powerful open-access models such as Llama has sparked a strong movement among researchers and practitioners to run high-quality models directly on consumer computers, resulting in privacy-first solutions. This trend extends beyond inference: novel training approaches that allow individuals to fine-tune these models without many computational resources have emerged in recent years. Chapter 6 explores this further and dives into both traditional and novel fine-tuning techniques.

Although we covered how transformers work and we'll dive into their training, exploring the internals of these models (for example, the math behind attention mechanisms) or how to pretrain a model from scratch is outside the scope of this book. Luckily for us, there are excellent resources to learn about this:

- "The Illustrated Transformer" (*https://oreil.ly/FL3cz*) by Jay Alammar is a beautiful visual guide that explains transformers in a detailed and intuitive way.

- We recommend reading *Natural Language Processing with Transformers* by Lewis Tunstall et al. (O'Reilly) if you want to dive deeper into the internals of fine-tuning these models for multiple specific tasks.

- Hugging Face has a free, open source course (*http://hf.co/course*) that teaches how to solve different NLP tasks.

If you want to dive more into the GPT family of models, we suggest reviewing the following papers:

*"Improving Language Understanding by Generative Pre-training" (https://oreil.ly/ ND5Bk)*
> This is the original GPT paper, published in 2018 by Alec Radford et al. It introduced the idea of using a transformer-based model pretrained on a large corpus of text to learn general language representations and then fine-tuning it on specific downstream tasks. The paper also showed that the GPT model achieved SOTA results on several natural language understanding benchmarks at the time.

*"Language Models Are Unsupervised Multitask Learners" (https://oreil.ly/m5bBi)*
> Published in 2019 by Alec Radford et al., this paper presented GPT-2, a transformer-based model with 1.5 billion parameters pretrained on a large corpus of web text called WebText. The paper also demonstrated that GPT-2 could perform well on various natural language tasks without fine-tuning, such as text generation, summarization, translation, reading comprehension, and common-sense reasoning. Finally, it discussed large-scale LMs' potential ethical and social implications.

*"Language Models Are Few-Shot Learners" (http://arxiv.org/abs/2005.14165)*
> Published in 2020 by Tom B. Brown and others, this paper shows that scaling up LMs dramatically improves their ability to perform new language tasks from only

a few examples or simple instructions without fine-tuning or gradient updates. The paper also presents GPT-3, an autoregressive LM with 175 billion parameters, which achieves strong performance on many NLP datasets and tasks.

# Exercises

1. What's the role of the attention mechanism in text generation?

2. In which cases would a character-based tokenizer be preferred?

3. What happens if you use a tokenizer different from the one used with the model?

4. What's the risk of using `no_repeat_ngram_size` when doing generation? (Hint: Think of city names.)

5. What would happen if you combine beam search and sampling?

6. Imagine you're using an LLM that generates code in a code editor by doing sampling. What would be more convenient: a low temperature or a high temperature?

7. What's the importance of fine-tuning, and why is it different from zero-shot generation?

8. Explain the differences and applications of encoder, decoder, and encoder-decoder transformers.

You can find the solutions to these exercises and the following challenges in the book's GitHub repository (*https://oreil.ly/handsonGenAIcode*).

# Challenges

1. *Summarization.* Use a summarization model (you can use `pipeline("summarization")`) to generate summaries of a paragraph. How does it compare with the results of using zero-shot? Can it be beaten by providing few-shot examples?

2. *Sentiment analysis.* In the zero-shot supplementary material, we calculate some metrics using zero-shot classification. Explore using the `distilbert-base-uncased-finetuned-sst-2-english` encoder model that can do sentiment analysis. What results do you get?

3. *Semantic search.* Let's build an FAQ system! Sentence transformers are powerful models that can measure semantic text similarity. While the transformer encoder usually outputs an embedding for each token, sentence transformers output an embedding for the whole input text, allowing us to determine if two texts have similar meanings based on their similarity score. Let's look at a simple example using the *sentence_transformers* library:

```
from sentence_transformers import SentenceTransformer, util

sentences = ["I'm happy", "I'm full of happiness"]
model = SentenceTransformer("sentence-transformers/all-MiniLM-L6-v2")

# Compute embedding for both lists
embedding_1 = model.encode(sentences[0], convert_to_tensor=True)
embedding_2 = model.encode(sentences[1], convert_to_tensor=True)

util.pytorch_cos_sim(embedding_1, embedding_2)

tensor([[0.6003]], device='cuda:0')
```

Write a list of five questions and answers about a topic. Your goal will be to build a system that, given a new question, can give the user the most likely answer. How can we use sentence transformers to solve this? The supplementary material (*https://oreil.ly/handsonGenAIcode*) contains the solution, but, although challenging, we suggest that you try it first before looking there.

A powerful technique called *retrieval-augmented generation* (RAG) combines text generation and embeddings to retrieve relevant documents. Appendix C shows an end-to-end example of how to build a minimal RAG pipeline. Before that, we suggest reading Chapter 6, which introduces fine-tuning and how to use it to adapt models to specific tasks.

# References

Brown, Tom B., et al. "Language Models Are Few-Shot Learners." arXiv, July 22, 2020. *http://arxiv.org/abs/2005.14165*.

Devlin, Jacob, et al. "BERT: Pre-Training of Deep Bidirectional Transformers for Language Understanding." arXiv, May 24, 2019. *http://arxiv.org/abs/1810.04805*.

Dosovitskiy, Alexey, et al. "An Image Is Worth 16x16 Words: Transformers for Image Recognition at Scale." arXiv, June 3, 2021. *http://arxiv.org/abs/2010.11929*.

Fourrier, Clémentine. "Introduction to Graph Machine Learning." Hugging Face blog, January 3, 2023. *https://oreil.ly/TK9vt*.

Gao, Leo, et al. "Scaling and Evaluating Sparse Autoencoders." arXiv, June 6, 2024. *https://arxiv.org/abs/2406.04093*.

Holtzman, Ari, et al. "The Curious Case of Neural Text Degeneration." arXiv, February 14, 2020. *http://arxiv.org/abs/1904.09751*.

Howard, Jeremy, and Sebastian Ruder. "Universal Language Model Fine-Tuning for Text Classification." arXiv, May 23, 2018. *http://arxiv.org/abs/1801.06146*.

Lan, Tian. "Generating Human-Level Text with Contrastive Search in Transformers 👻." Hugging Face blog, November 8, 2022. *https://oreil.ly/VFc42.*

Lewis, Mike, et al. "BART: Denoising Sequence-to-Sequence Pre-training for Natural Language Generation, Translation, and Comprehension." arXiv, October 29, 2019. *http://arxiv.org/abs/1910.13461.*

Radford, Alec, et al. "Improving Language Understanding by Generative Pre-training." *OpenAI Blog*, June 11, 2018. *https://oreil.ly/ND5Bk.*

Radford, Alec, et al. "Language Models Are Unsupervised Multitask Learners." *OpenAI Blog* 1, no. 8 (2019): 9. *https://oreil.ly/m5bBi.*

Raffel, Colin, et al. "Exploring the Limits of Transfer Learning with a Unified Text-to-Text Transformer." arXiv, July 28, 2020. *http://arxiv.org/abs/1910.10683.*

Vaswani, Ashish, et al. "Attention Is All You Need." arXiv, June 12, 2017. *https://arxiv.org/abs/1706.03762.*

Yang, Jingfeng, et al. "Harnessing the Power of LLMs in Practice: A Survey on ChatGPT and Beyond." arXiv, April 27, 2023. *http://arxiv.org/abs/2304.13712.*

# CHAPTER 3

# Compressing and Representing Information

This chapter introduces ML models and techniques to learn efficient data representations for tasks involving images, videos, or text. Why are efficient representations important? We want to reduce the amount of information we need to store and process while keeping the essential characteristics of the data. Rich representations enable training models specialized on particular tasks, and making the representations compact reduces the computational requirements to train and work with data-intensive models. For example, training on a vector embedding of an image can be more efficient and expressive than doing it directly on its pixels.

Traditional compression methods like ZIP or JPEG focus on specific data types and use handcrafted algorithms to reduce file sizes. While these methods are effective for their intended purposes, they lack the flexibility and adaptability of learned compression techniques. ZIP, for instance, excels at lossless compression of general data by identifying and encoding repetitive patterns. On the other hand, JPEG is designed specifically for image compression and achieves significant size reduction by discarding less noticeable visual information. However, these traditional methods don't learn from the data they compress and can't automatically adapt to different types of content or optimize for specific tasks beyond size reduction. This is where ML models can be useful.

We'll begin by exploring AutoEncoders, a family of ML models that consist of an encoder that "compresses" data and a decoder that reconstructs it just by using the representation. The encoder learns the essential features of the data it needs to focus on, which allows the decoder to reverse the transformations, as shown in the left panel of Figure 3-1. This training approach is a way to build compressors automatically without relying on handcrafted algorithms. Compressing information (even in a lossy way) is helpful in itself, but there are a few other interesting things we can do once we have a compact dataset representation.

If our system is correctly trained and the decoder can recover the original from the representations, it means that the learned representations have captured the essential information. Therefore, operating on the representations is equivalent to working with the originals but requires much less memory and computing. This is one of the key design aspects of models such as Stable Diffusion—as we'll see in Chapter 5, we can generate and manipulate large images, but most of the computation happens in the smaller *latent space* where representations reside.

Because the learned representations capture the essential information, we can split the encoder and decoder after the AutoEncoder is trained and use the encoder as a feature extraction component. Adding a small network on top of the encoder's outputs, as represented in the center panel of Figure 3-1, allows us to train the model for different tasks, such as text or image classification. These small networks don't operate on the whole input image but on the essential characteristics obtained by the encoder.

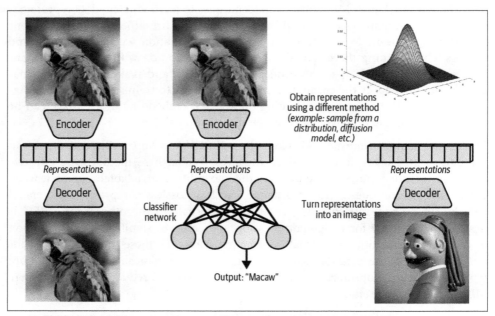

*Figure 3-1. Efficient data representation methods (left) can be used for other tasks, such as classification (middle), or to generate new content (right)*

We can also encode different data types to the same latent space representations. As we saw in Chapter 2, sequence-to-sequence LMs use an encoder-decoder architecture to perform a wide variety of tasks, such as translation or summarization. Although there are more details to consider when designing such systems, one key insight is that the encoder's job is to capture the essential features that carry enough semantic information about the input text. This works across modalities too: the job of an image-captioning model, for example, is to translate image representations to textual descriptions, using a latent space as the internal working data.

A final example of the use of AutoEncoders is for generative modeling (right panel of Figure 3-1). After we have trained the encoder-decoder pair, we can throw away the encoder and generate new data by sampling from a random distribution in the latent space. This is the base of Variational AutoEncoders (or VAEs). We'll see an example of how it's done in the second section of this chapter.

We'll use image data to showcase how AutoEncoders and VAEs work, but the techniques can be applied to any data, not just images. The final section of this chapter examines how multimodal representation learning systems, such as CLIP, bridge the gap between text and images and can be used for very interesting use cases such as semantic search, data filtering, text-to-image generation, and more.

# AutoEncoders

AutoEncoders consist of two models stitched together—namely, an encoder and a decoder, schematically represented in Figure 3-2. Both models are trained together with the objective that the encoder produces intermediate representations, which the decoder then uses to regenerate the input data. If training succeeds, the AutoEncoder learns to extract key features from the input data.

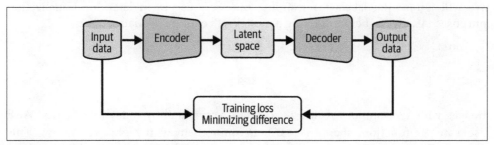

*Figure 3-2. AutoEncoder architecture*

## Preparing the Data

In this section, we'll build a simple AutoEncoder using the MNIST dataset. *MNIST* is a classical dataset consisting of 70,000 low-resolution (28 × 28) black-and-white images of handwritten numerical digits. We'll download it from the redistribution of the dataset hosted on Hugging Face (*https://oreil.ly/_8IgI*). To download it, we'll use a library called *datasets* (*https://oreil.ly/VxsPo*), which provides a unified API to access thousands of datasets for any type of data. Details about how it works are not important now; just note that it will take care of downloading and caching for subsequent use. It provides two dataset splits—a `train` set with 60,000 images and a `test` dataset with the remaining 10,000 images:

```
from datasets import load_dataset

mnist = load_dataset("mnist")

mnist

DatasetDict({
    train: Dataset({
        features: ['image', 'label'],
        num_rows: 60000
    })
    test: Dataset({
        features: ['image', 'label'],
        num_rows: 10000
    })
})
```

As you can see, the dataset contains a column called `image`, with the handwritten images, and `label`, which contains the number represented by the image. As we're going to train an AutoEncoder to compress and reconstruct the image, we don't really need the label data at all: we'll feed batches of random samples to the encoder, and the decoder's job will be to regenerate images that resemble the inputs. Because the input data has everything required to train without relying on external annotated information, AutoEncoder training is an example of a *self-supervised* learning process.

We will ignore the labels for training, but we'll use them later for visualization purposes. As always, before training a model, let's explore the dataset:

```
mnist["train"]["image"][1]
```

Images with a resolution of just 28 × 28 are very small by today's standards. We'll use a helper function, `show_images()`, to show them with higher resolution. This function is based on Python's *matplotlib* library, which by default uses a high-contrast color palette to represent monochrome image data:

```
from genaibook.core import import show_images

show_images(mnist["train"]["image"][:4])
```

Because the originals are black-and-white, we'll configure *matplotlib* to just use gray colors instead. We choose "reversed gray" (gray_r) to get black numbers on a white background. Note that the originals are the other way around (pixels with number data are white, while the background is all zeros, which means black color):

```
import matplotlib as mpl

mpl.rcParams["image.cmap"] = "gray_r"

show_images(mnist["train"]["image"][:4])
```

In the following example, we'll convert the images to PyTorch tensors and shuffle the training dataset. We'll use `ToTensor()`, from the *torchvision* library,[1] to convert the input pixels, in the [0, 255] range, to PyTorch tensors, from 0 to 1. We don't apply any other manipulations. For convenience, `show_images()` can also draw tensors representing images.

```
from torchvision import transforms


def mnist_to_tensor(samples):
    t = transforms.ToTensor()
    samples["image"] = [t(image) for image in samples["image"]]
    return samples

mnist = mnist.with_transform(mnist_to_tensor)
mnist["train"] = mnist["train"].shuffle(seed=1337)
```

Let's check out a single image from the dataset and confirm that the input pixels range from 0 to 1:

```
x = mnist["train"]["image"][0]
x.min(), x.max()

(tensor(0.), tensor(1.))

show_images(mnist["train"]["image"][0])
```

With the following code, we now create a PyTorch `DataLoader` to prepare the training data. Because training an AutoEncoder is a self-supervised process, we'll work with the `image` column of the dataset and ignore the labels. Later, we'll return and use the labels to visualize results. A `DataLoader` is an abstraction whose primary mission is to collate inputs, which means gathering and combining individual samples into training batches with the same shape. In our case, all images have the same size, and therefore, all tensors have the same shape, so the `DataLoader` will concatenate them together. In more complicated cases, `DataLoaders` may need to deal with irregular input shapes by using strategies such as padding or truncation.

---

1 As we'll see later, the *torchvision* library `transforms` is a collection of common image transformation, conversion, augmentation, and manipulation routines.

```
from torch.utils.data import DataLoader

bs = 64
train_dataloader = DataLoader(mnist["train"]["image"], batch_size=bs)
```

## Modeling the Encoder

First, we'll create a model definition for the encoder part of the AutoEncoder. Because we are working with image data, a natural choice is to use convolutional layers, which are good at capturing image features. We could consider many other alternatives for this problem: linear layers, transformer blocks, use of residual skip connections, etc. We'll use a simple convolutional encoder that is based on a convolutional AutoEncoder implementation (*https://oreil.ly/og_9i*) from the excellent *pythae* library. This is a great starting point for exploration!

 *Convolutional layers* are a collection of small 2D filters applied repeatedly to different regions of the input image. These filters can detect patterns such as lines or circular areas. Traditionally, 2D filters have been used in digital image processing, where they are carefully handcrafted to match specific features in input images. The main difference with convolutional layers is that the filters are not prepared beforehand—instead, convolutional layers *learn them* as part of the training process of the network. By stacking multiple convolutional layers, the model can progressively extract more abstract features from the input image, learning filters that effectively resolve the task. There's a thrilling field of interpretation and explainability that aims to visualize and understand the internal workings of model layers, and it's been shown that filters learned by neural networks sometimes resemble classic filters designed manually to detect edges, colors, or contours.

For an in-depth look at CNNs, we recommend Chapter 13 of *Deep Learning for Coders with fastai and PyTorch* by Jeremy Howard and Sylvain Gugger (O'Reilly).

Because we will stack several convolutional layers, we'll write a simple helper function, conv_block(), to create them. Our conv_block() helper makes a 2D convolution, then appends a batch normalization layer and a nonlinearity (we'll use the ReLU activation function for this example). During training, batch normalization uses the mean and standard deviation of the current batch to normalize input data so that it remains within a predictable range, which most of the time results in smoother and faster training.[2]

---

2 For an in-depth discussion of these and many other design choices, as well as an excellent and practical overview of deep learning, we recommend *Deep Learning for Coders with fastai and PyTorch*.

Let's implement the function:

```python
from torch import nn


def conv_block(in_channels, out_channels, kernel_size=4, stride=2, padding=1):
    return nn.Sequential(
        nn.Conv2d(
            in_channels,
            out_channels,
            kernel_size=kernel_size,
            stride=stride,
            padding=padding,
        ),
        nn.BatchNorm2d(out_channels),
        nn.ReLU(),
    )
```

As described, the encoder implementation will be a sequence of convolutional layers. Each layer progressively reduces the image resolution while it increases the number of channels of the representations to 1,024. Finally, we'll append a linear layer at the end to create 16-dimensional vector representations. The comments in the `forward()` method show how the shape of the input data is transformed as it travels through the layers:

```python
class Encoder(nn.Module):
    def __init__(self, in_channels):
        super().__init__()
        self.conv1 = conv_block(in_channels, 128)
        self.conv2 = conv_block(128, 256)
        self.conv3 = conv_block(256, 512)
        self.conv4 = conv_block(512, 1024)
        self.linear = nn.Linear(1024, 16)

    def forward(self, x):
        x = self.conv1(x)  # (batch size, 128, 14, 14)
        x = self.conv2(x)  # (bs, 256, 7, 7)
        x = self.conv3(x)  # (bs, 512, 3, 3)
        x = self.conv4(x)  # (bs, 1024, 1, 1)
        # Keep batch dimension when flattening
        x = self.linear(x.flatten(start_dim=1))  # (bs, 16)
        return x
```

Let's verify that we can run our input images through the encoder. They have a `[1, 28, 28]` shape because they contain only one channel of (black or white) pixel data. However, note that we coded our encoder in a general way; we could use it for three-channel images as well:

```python
mnist["train"]["image"][0].shape

torch.Size([1, 28, 28])
```

Let's select and put a single image inside a batch, creating a new dimension with PyTorch's None indexing. We also need to set the encoder in eval mode. This mode configures the model for inference instead of training. If we don't do this, the last BatchNorm2d layer will fail because it will receive a tensor with shape [1, 1024, 1, 1], and it can't compute the mean and standard deviation of a single sample:[3]

```
in_channels = 1

x = mnist["train"]["image"][0][None, :]
encoder = Encoder(in_channels).eval()

encoded = encoder(x)
encoded.shape

torch.Size([1, 16])
```

The encoder model works! It converts $28 \times 28$ images (784 pixels each) into vectors with just 16 numbers. If we can train it effectively, the representations computed by the encoder will have much lower dimensionality than the original pixel data.

Of course, the representations are currently meaningless, as the model is yet to be trained:

```
encoded

tensor([[-0.0145, -0.0318, -0.0109,  0.0080,
         -0.0218,  0.0305,  0.0183, -0.0294,
          0.0075,  0.0178, -0.0161, -0.0018,
          0.0208, -0.0079,  0.0215,  0.0101]],
       grad_fn=<AddmmBackward0>)
```

Let's see if it can handle a batch of 64 images:

```
batch = next(iter(train_dataloader))
encoded = Encoder(in_channels=1)(batch)
batch.shape, encoded.shape

(torch.Size([64, 1, 28, 28]), torch.Size([64, 16]))
```

This completes our Encoder model, which transforms images to intermediate representations. Let's move to the Decoder now.

---

3 In eval mode, BatchNorm2d applies the mean and standard deviation learned from all the mini batches during training. Since we haven't trained the model yet, this will be random data, but we are interested only in seeing if the model definition works. During actual training, we use a batch size larger than one, and BatchNorm2d will work fine.

# Decoder

The decoder begins with the *latent* representation obtained by the encoder (vectors with 16 dimensions) and turns them into images of the original size.

The decoder architecture does not have to be the reverse of the encoder's; it can be anything that "understands" the encoder representations and is able to translate them to images. In our case, we'll create a more or less symmetrical network to the encoder: we'll apply transposed convolutions to increase the resolution while decreasing the number of channels until we reach our desired output resolution of 28 × 28 pixels.[4]

We'll prepend the transposed convolutions with a linear layer to create tensors of 16,384 (1024 × 4 × 4) pixels. This layer will be reshaped to a 4 × 4 resolution ([1024,4,4]), which will be the input to the first transposed convolution. From there, we progressively reduce the channels and increase the resolution until we reach the original image shape. There are other ways to achieve the same; remember that the input is a flat vector with 16 channels, and the output must consist of 1 channel and 28 × 28 pixels.

Here's our `Decoder` implementation:

```
def conv_transpose_block(
    in_channels,
    out_channels,
    kernel_size=3,
    stride=2,
    padding=1,
    output_padding=0,
    with_act=True,
):
    modules = [
        nn.ConvTranspose2d(
            in_channels,
            out_channels,
            kernel_size=kernel_size,
            stride=stride,
            padding=padding,
            output_padding=output_padding,
        ),
    ]
    if with_act:  # Controlling this will be handy later
        modules.append(nn.BatchNorm2d(out_channels))
```

---

4 A transposed convolution works just like a convolution, but instead of applying it to the 2D input data, it is applied to an enlarged version of it (the 2D input is filled with zeros between the rows and the columns). This results in an output 2D matrix that is larger than the input after the filter is applied. Aqeel Anwar's blog post "What Is Transposed Convolutional Layer?" (*https://oreil.ly/blQzh*) shows excellent visualizations of how convolutions and transposed convolutions work.

```
            modules.append(nn.ReLU())
        return nn.Sequential(*modules)

class Decoder(nn.Module):
    def __init__(self, out_channels):
        super().__init__()

        self.linear = nn.Linear(
            16, 1024 * 4 * 4
        )  # note it's reshaped in forward
        self.t_conv1 = conv_transpose_block(1024, 512)
        self.t_conv2 = conv_transpose_block(512, 256, output_padding=1)
        self.t_conv3 = conv_transpose_block(256, out_channels, output_padding=1)

    def forward(self, x):
        bs = x.shape[0]
        x = self.linear(x)   # (bs, 1024*4*4)
        x = x.reshape((bs, 1024, 4, 4))   # (bs, 1024, 4, 4)
        x = self.t_conv1(x)   # (bs, 512, 7, 7)
        x = self.t_conv2(x)   # (bs, 256, 14, 14)
        x = self.t_conv3(x)   # (bs, 1, 28, 28)
        return x

decoded_batch = Decoder(x.shape[0])(encoded)
decoded_batch.shape

torch.Size([64, 1, 28, 28])
```

# Training

So far, we have created the `Encoder`, which reduces the dimensionality of the input images, and the `Decoder`, which expands low-dimensional latent to the original image resolution. In addition to being initialized with random weights, these two components are completely unconnected at the moment. We need to train them together so that they both understand the same latent representations.

To do so, we'll create an `AutoEncoder` model that passes the input data through the encoder and the decoder in sequence. We'll train it to minimize the difference between the decoded image at the output and the original image we supplied as input. If we are successful, the output images will resemble the inputs.

This process is useful as it allows data compression, but it becomes even more interesting when we realize that we can use the two components separately after training. This will enable us to do many exciting things in the following chapters. For example, we can use the encoder to convert arbitrary images to more-compressed representations, which can be used as inputs by other models. We can also use the decoder to generate new images that resemble the ones from the training dataset.

Excited? Let's get started on training our AutoEncoder:

```python
class AutoEncoder(nn.Module):
    def __init__(self, in_channels):
        super().__init__()
        self.encoder = Encoder(in_channels)
        self.decoder = Decoder(in_channels)

    def encode(self, x):
        return self.encoder(x)

    def decode(self, x):
        return self.decoder(x)

    def forward(self, x):
        return self.decode(self.encode(x))

model = AutoEncoder(1)
```

We can use the *torchsummary* library to print a summary of the model, which shows the number of parameters and the output shape of each layer. This is a useful tool to check if the model is correctly defined and to understand the model's architecture:

```python
import torchsummary

torchsummary.summary(model, input_size=(1, 28, 28), device="cpu")
```

```
----------------------------------------------------------------
        Layer (type)               Output Shape         Param #
================================================================
            Conv2d-1          [-1, 128, 14, 14]           2,176
       BatchNorm2d-2          [-1, 128, 14, 14]             256
              ReLU-3          [-1, 128, 14, 14]               0
            Conv2d-4           [-1, 256, 7, 7]          524,544
       BatchNorm2d-5           [-1, 256, 7, 7]             512
              ReLU-6           [-1, 256, 7, 7]               0
            Conv2d-7           [-1, 512, 3, 3]        2,097,664
       BatchNorm2d-8           [-1, 512, 3, 3]           1,024
              ReLU-9           [-1, 512, 3, 3]               0
           Conv2d-10          [-1, 1024, 1, 1]        8,389,632
      BatchNorm2d-11          [-1, 1024, 1, 1]           2,048
             ReLU-12          [-1, 1024, 1, 1]               0
           Linear-13                  [-1, 16]          16,400
          Encoder-14                  [-1, 16]               0
           Linear-15               [-1, 16384]         278,528
  ConvTranspose2d-16           [-1, 512, 7, 7]        4,719,104
      BatchNorm2d-17           [-1, 512, 7, 7]           1,024
             ReLU-18           [-1, 512, 7, 7]               0
  ConvTranspose2d-19         [-1, 256, 14, 14]        1,179,904
      BatchNorm2d-20         [-1, 256, 14, 14]             512
             ReLU-21         [-1, 256, 14, 14]               0
  ConvTranspose2d-22           [-1, 1, 28, 28]           2,305
      BatchNorm2d-23           [-1, 1, 28, 28]               2
```

```
           ReLU-24              [-1, 1, 28, 28]              0
        Decoder-25              [-1, 1, 28, 28]              0
================================================================
Total params: 17,215,635
Trainable params: 17,215,635
Non-trainable params: 0
----------------------------------------------------------------
Input size (MB): 0.00
Forward/backward pass size (MB): 2.86
Params size (MB): 65.67
Estimated Total Size (MB): 68.54
----------------------------------------------------------------
```

In the code that follows, we create a simple training loop that repeatedly goes through the training data and uses a constant learning rate. To focus on the essentials, we won't bother running validations on the test set (but you are encouraged to do it to practice!). We use the popular *tqdm* library for progress display, but we won't describe it here for the sake of brevity; we'll see more examples in other chapters. It's not necessary to understand everything that's going on; just pay attention to the high-level operations:

1. Load a batch from the `DataLoader`.
2. Get the model predictions.
3. Calculate the loss with respect to the original images.
4. Perform an optimizer step to update the model weights.

```python
import torch
from matplotlib import pyplot as plt
from torch.nn import functional as F
from tqdm.notebook import tqdm, trange

from genaibook.core import get_device

num_epochs = 10
lr = 1e-4

device = get_device()
model = model.to(device)
optimizer = torch.optim.AdamW(model.parameters(), lr=lr, eps=1e-5)

losses = []  # List to store the loss values for plotting
for _ in (progress := trange(num_epochs, desc="Training")):
    for _, batch in (
        inner := tqdm(enumerate(train_dataloader), total=len(train_dataloader))
    ):
        batch = batch.to(device)

        # Pass through the model and obtain reconstructed images
        preds = model(batch)
```

```
    # Compare the prediction with the original images
    loss = F.mse_loss(preds, batch)

    # Display loss and store for plotting
    inner.set_postfix(loss=f"{loss.cpu().item():.3f}")
    losses.append(loss.item())

    # Update the model parameters with the optimizer based on this loss
    loss.backward()
    optimizer.step()
    optimizer.zero_grad()
progress.set_postfix(loss=f"{loss.cpu().item():.3f}", lr=f"{lr:.0e}")
```

Let's plot the loss curve to see how the training went:

```
plt.plot(losses)
plt.xlabel("Step")
plt.ylabel("Loss")
plt.title("AutoEncoder - Training Loss Curve")
plt.show()
```

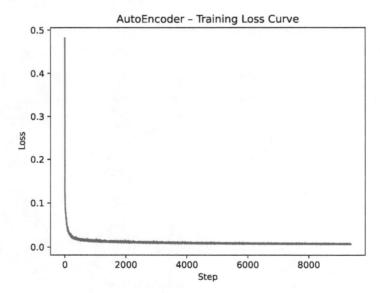

We didn't perform validation during the training loop, but we can see how the AutoEncoder fares with the test set. Training with visual data is a great way to learn and iterate, as we can see the final results and judge for ourselves.

We'll create a batch with 16 samples from the test set, pass them through the trained encoder and decoder, and display the reconstructions. Let's begin creating the evaluation `DataLoader`:

```
eval_bs = 16
eval_dataloader = DataLoader(mnist["test"]["image"], batch_size=eval_bs)
```

We'll use `model.eval()` to put the model in evaluation mode (in our case, it will disable `BatchNorm` updates) and the `inference_mode` context manager to turn off gradient computation:

```
model.eval()
with torch.inference_mode():
    eval_batch = next(iter(eval_dataloader))
    predicted = model(eval_batch.to(device)).cpu()
```

Now that we have the predictions, let's display the original images and their reconstructions:

```
batch_vs_preds = torch.cat((eval_batch, predicted))
show_images(batch_vs_preds, imsize=1, nrows=2)
```

7 2 / 0 4 / 4 9 5 9 0 6 9 0 / 5
7 2 / 0 4 / 4 9 5 9 0 6 9 0 / 5

The results shown here, with the first line of images representing the original MNIST images and the second line of images representing reconstructions from our AutoEncoder, look pretty good! Remember that the numbers in the second row are approximations of the originals obtained by the decoder from concise vector representations.

At this point, we suggest ensuring you understand the concepts just introduced. We also recommend trying to get better reconstruction results. Here are some experiment ideas:

- Progressively decrease the learning rate.
- Try different batch sizes.
- Use a sigmoid function at the decoder's end to encourage the final pixel values to be either black or white. Note that our input data is between 0 and 1, so the sigmoid output must match that range.
- Play with the network depth or topology.

We also suggest experimenting with the training loop by adding and logging the evaluation loss during training.

# Exploring the Latent Space

One important hyperparameter of the AutoEncoder is the number of dimensions we use to represent the encoded inputs. We arbitrarily chose 16, and our results show that this seems enough to represent the wide variety of hand-drawn numbers in the MNIST dataset.

For our next experiment, we will use just two dimensions to represent the vectors in the latent space. We'll force the encoder to squeeze as much information as possible about input images into just two float numbers, and we'll figure out if this is enough to recover the inputs. In addition, using two dimensions is very convenient for visualization. After training our new model, we can draw some interesting plots in 2D space that will help us gain additional intuition.

We'll slightly refactor our code with the following changes:

- We include the dimensionality of the latent space as a hyperparameter.
- We use a container (nn.Sequential) for the convolution layers to make it easier to adjust the network depth if we want to experiment with that later.
- We replace the activation after the final decoder convolution with a sigmoid function. We want to encourage the decoder to produce pixels that are either black or white, and a sigmoid activation function is better suited than ReLU for that purpose. This is because the sigmoid function squashes the output to the range (0, 1), the same range as pixels in the images.

This can also be an excellent time to put our training loop inside a function.

 Don't try to create code with many options and parameters from the start. It's better to start with the simplest working code you can write and progressively make it richer as needed (and *if* required).

Figure 3-3 shows a plot of the ReLU versus the sigmoid function. By using sigmoid as the activation function, we ensure that the output after each layer lies within the range (0, 1), the same range the input images use. This is not strictly necessary for the network to learn; we are trying to help it because we know our desired output range.

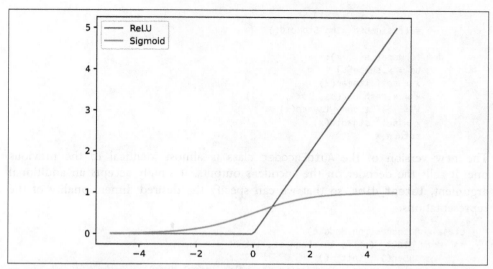

*Figure 3-3. Activation functions: ReLU versus Sigmoid*

The refactored code with these changes looks like this:

```python
class Encoder(nn.Module):
    def __init__(self, in_channels, latent_dims):
        super().__init__()

        self.conv_layers = nn.Sequential(
            conv_block(in_channels, 128),
            conv_block(128, 256),
            conv_block(256, 512),
            conv_block(512, 1024),
        )
        self.linear = nn.Linear(1024, latent_dims)

    def forward(self, x):
        bs = x.shape[0]
        x = self.conv_layers(x)
        x = self.linear(x.reshape(bs, -1))
        return x

class Decoder(nn.Module):
    def __init__(self, out_channels, latent_dims):
        super().__init__()

        self.linear = nn.Linear(latent_dims, 1024 * 4 * 4)
        self.t_conv_layers = nn.Sequential(
            conv_transpose_block(1024, 512),
            conv_transpose_block(512, 256, output_padding=1),
            conv_transpose_block(
                256, out_channels, output_padding=1, with_act=False
            ),
        )
```

```
    )
    self.sigmoid = nn.Sigmoid()

def forward(self, x):
    bs = x.shape[0]
    x = self.linear(x)
    x = x.reshape((bs, 1024, 4, 4))
    x = self.t_conv_layers(x)
    x = self.sigmoid(x)
    return x
```

The new version of the AutoEncoder class is almost identical to the previous one: it calls the decoder on the encoder's outputs. It simply accepts an additional argument, latent_dims, so that we can specify the desired dimensionality of the representations:

```
class AutoEncoder(nn.Module):
    def __init__(self, in_channels, latent_dims):
        super().__init__()
        self.encoder = Encoder(in_channels, latent_dims)
        self.decoder = Decoder(in_channels, latent_dims)

    def encode(self, x):
        return self.encoder(x)

    def decode(self, x):
        return self.decoder(x)

    def forward(self, x):
        return self.decode(self.encode(x))
```

The training loop is the same as before, but we put it inside a function to reuse it and call it whenever needed:

```
def train(model, num_epochs=10, lr=1e-4):
    optimizer = torch.optim.AdamW(model.parameters(), lr=lr, eps=1e-5)

    model.train()  # Put model in training mode
    losses = []
    for _ in (progress := trange(num_epochs, desc="Training")):
        for _, batch in (
            inner := tqdm(
                enumerate(train_dataloader), total=len(train_dataloader)
            )
        ):
            batch = batch.to(device)

            # Pass through the model and obtain another set of images
            preds = model(batch)

            # Compare the prediction with the original images
            loss = F.mse_loss(preds, batch)
```

```
        # Display loss and store for plotting
        inner.set_postfix(loss=f"{loss.cpu().item():.3f}")
        losses.append(loss.item())

        # Update the model parameters with the optimizer based on this loss
        loss.backward()
        optimizer.step()
        optimizer.zero_grad()
      progress.set_postfix(loss=f"{loss.cpu().item():.3f}", lr=f"{lr:.0e}")
    return losses
```

We create and train an AutoEncoder with just two latent variables:

```
ae_model = AutoEncoder(in_channels=1, latent_dims=2)
ae_model.to(device)

losses = train(ae_model)

plt.plot(losses)
plt.xlabel("Step")
plt.ylabel("Loss")
plt.title("Training Loss Curve (two latent dimensions)")
plt.show()
```

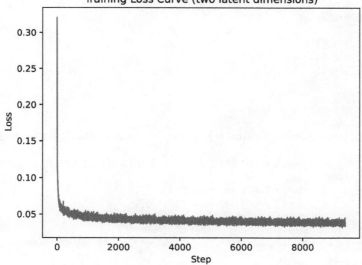

Let's once again load the trained model and look at some reconstructions:

```
ae_model.eval()
with torch.inference_mode():
    eval_batch = next(iter(eval_dataloader))
    predicted = ae_model(eval_batch.to(device)).cpu()
```

```
batch_vs_preds = torch.cat((eval_batch, predicted))
show_images(batch_vs_preds, imsize=1, nrows=2)
```

7 2 / 0 4 / 4 9 5 9 0 6 9 0 1 5
7 2 / 0 4 / 7 9 9 9 7 0 6 9 0 1 6

The results are not quite as good as before, but remember, we now use just *two* floats to represent a 28 × 28 handwritten image. We see some confusion with the 4s, the 5s, and the 9s, but overall, the recovered images are very similar to the input ones!

## Visualizing the Latent Space

We used just two dimensions for the latent space to visualize its structure easily. Let's now represent all the encoded vectors from the test dataset, using the `label` column to assign different colors to each class. The first value of the encoded vectors will be displayed on the x-axis, and the second value will be represented on the y-axis:

```
images_labels_dataloader = DataLoader(mnist["test"], batch_size=512)

import pandas as pd

df = pd.DataFrame(
    {
        "x": [],
        "y": [],
        "label": [],
    }
)

for batch in tqdm(
    iter(images_labels_dataloader), total=len(images_labels_dataloader)
):
    encoded = ae_model.encode(batch["image"].to(device)).cpu()
    new_items = {
        "x": [t.item() for t in encoded[:, 0]],
        "y": [t.item() for t in encoded[:, 1]],
        "label": batch["label"],
    }
    df = pd.concat([df, pd.DataFrame(new_items)], ignore_index=True)

plt.figure(figsize=(10, 8))

for label in range(10):
    points = df[df["label"] == label]
    plt.scatter(points["x"], points["y"], label=label, marker=".")

plt.legend();
```

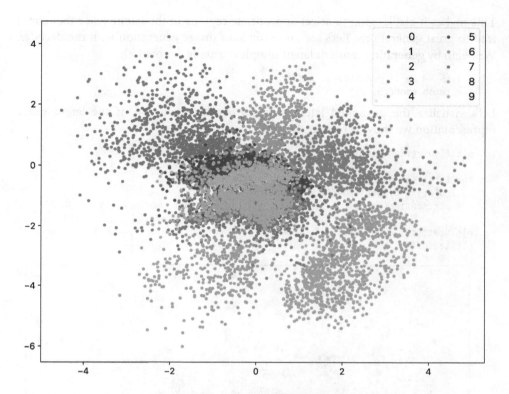

The AutoEncoder has done a good job at separating different areas of the latent space for the various images in our dataset. Note, for example, how images representing the number 0 (dark blue dots) are distant from the representations of 1s (orange dots). Remember that no information about the image labels was used during training, but even so, data points were automatically grouped in different regions according to their visual features. However, this process took place in an entirely unconstrained way, so there is no guarantee about the shape or structure of the latent space.

Therefore, the latent space is rich enough to capture the relevant image features in our dataset, but it's still not clear how we can use it for generative purposes. Ideally, to generate new images similar to the ones in MNIST, we'd want to discard the encoder and supply random samples from the latent space to the decoder. However, we can see some issues in the plot:

- The space taken by the representation is spread out in all directions.
- There are many overlaps at the center and big regions of empty space.
- The plot is nonsymmetric: negative values in the y-axis are used more than positive ones.

This makes it challenging to select appropriate regions in the latent space that could lead to great generations. Let's see an example of image generation with the decoder. We begin by generating random latent samples (usually denoted z):

```
N = 16  # We'll generate 16 points
z = torch.rand((N, 2)) * 8 - 4
```

Let's visualize the generated latent samples overlayed on top of the latent space representation we showed before:

```
plt.figure(figsize=(10, 8))

for label in range(10):
    points = df[df["label"] == label]
    plt.scatter(points["x"], points["y"], label=label, marker=".")

plt.scatter(z[:, 0], z[:, 1], label="z", marker="s", color="black")
plt.legend();
```

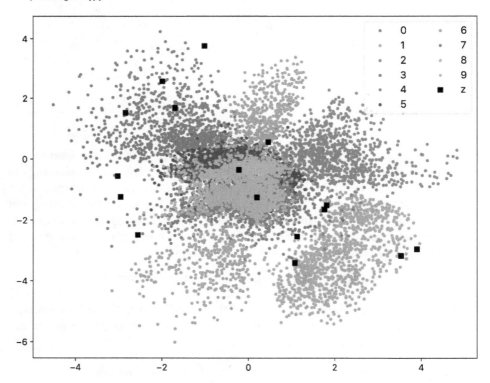

Finally, let's ask the decoder to generate images from the latent samples we just created:

```
ae_decoded = ae_model.decode(z.to(device))
show_images(ae_decoded.cpu(), imsize=1, nrows=1, suptitle="AutoEncoder")
```

AutoEncoder

The generated images are reasonable in the places where the samples are close to one of the regions carved by the model in the latent space, but they are much less convincing when they lie outside those areas. In addition, note that some numbers will be overrepresented because their assigned regions in latent space are larger.

The next section discusses how we can use a different type of AutoEncoder to impose some order in latent space and how this can make generation easier.

Before moving on, here are some (progressively more challenging) exercises that you can tackle now (or at the end of the chapter) to reinforce your understanding of the concepts:

1. How well does generation work if the model is trained with 16 latent dimensions?

2. Train the model again with the same parameters we used (just run the code shown in the chapter) but with different random number initialization,[5] and visualize the latent space. Chances are that the shapes and structure are different. Is this something you would expect? Why?

3. How good are the image features extracted by the encoder? Discard the decoder part of the AutoEncoder and build a number classifier on top of the encoder. You can, for example, train a couple of linear layers with a nonlinearity between them. The final linear layer should output a vector with 10 dimensions representing the 10 labels in the dataset. Train only these layers without updating the weights of the encoder. What accuracy can you get? How does the model with 16 latent dimensions compare to the one with just two?

---

5 You can use `torch.manual_seed(num)` to specify a seed.

# Variational AutoEncoders

In the previous section, we explored how a simple AutoEncoder can learn efficient representations of the input data in a lower-dimensional latent space. The AutoEncoder can faithfully *encode* any sample and recover (or *decode*) it later. This works great for feature extraction or data representation but is not well suited for generating new samples.

As discussed before, the reason is that the AutoEncoder is not incentivized to separate the representations into consistent portions of the latent space. As we saw, representations of similar inputs are usually clustered close together, but there's a significant amount of overlap and empty space, as well as substantial variability in the amount of latent space dedicated to each class. If we choose a random point in the latent space and pass it through the decoder, we can't faithfully predict what result will come up.

Variational AutoEncoders (VAEs) address this by learning a probability distribution for each feature in the latent space. Instead of mapping inputs to specific points, VAEs represent each feature with a Gaussian distribution,[6] capturing the variability of that feature within the data.

Consider, for example, a dataset consisting of images of multiple breeds of dogs and cats. We don't know what features will be extracted by the encoder, but we could imagine that some could be used to represent characteristics such as furry patches, eyes, ears, legs, or tails. These may have a great degree of overlap among all the images in the dataset (all these animals have two ears, four legs, and a tail), but there's also variability in how ears look in dogs versus how they look in cats. Our "ear" feature could be represented by a Gaussian distribution that covers all this variability, with the mean of the distribution representing the average shape of an animal ear. If we move away from the mean in different directions, we'll get a continuous and homogeneous transition toward different ear shapes that may appear in various breeds.

This approach, conceptually represented in Figure 3-4, creates a more structured latent space, where sampling from these distributions allows us to generate new, plausible instances. Just as with AutoEncoders, class information is typically not used in VAEs.[7] Let's see how we can code and train them.

---

6 A Gaussian distribution, also called *normal distribution*, has a bell-shaped curve with most values clustered around the mean and fewer values at the extremes.

7 A family of VAEs called *conditional VAEs* (C-VAEs) uses class information to further separate distributions in latent space while still keeping Gaussian representation of the features. This makes it easier to generate samples resembling the specific class we're interested in.

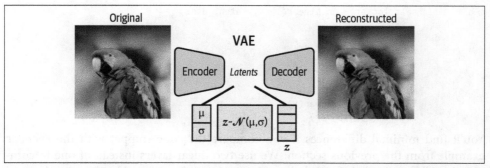

*Figure 3-4. VAEs learn Gaussian representations of the features and describe them through their means and variances. Points z in the latent space are sampled from the predicted Gaussian distributions.*

## VAE Encoders and Decoders

VAE encoders are very similar to the basic encoders in the previous section. In our example, we used a few convolutional layers and a linear layer to project to the desired size of the latent representation.

To create our first VAE encoder, we'll use the same architecture. The only difference is that, instead of a linear layer to predict the latent space of an image, we want to use linear layers to learn the distribution. A distribution is characterized by two parameters, the mean and the variance, so we'll need two linear layers:

- One of the linear layers will represent the *mean* of the distribution we are trying to learn.

- The other linear layer will learn the *variance* of the distribution.[8]

In terms of code, this is what our first VAE encoder looks like:

```python
class VAEEncoder(nn.Module):
    def __init__(self, in_channels, latent_dims):
        super().__init__()

        self.conv_layers = nn.Sequential(
            conv_block(in_channels, 128),
            conv_block(128, 256),
            conv_block(256, 512),
            conv_block(512, 1024),
        )

        # Define fully connected layers for mean and log-variance
        self.mu = nn.Linear(1024, latent_dims)
```

---

8  Actually, not really the variance, as we'll see shortly.

```
        self.logvar = nn.Linear(1024, latent_dims)

    def forward(self, x):
        bs = x.shape[0]
        x = self.conv_layers(x)
        x = x.reshape(bs, -1)
        mu = self.mu(x)
        logvar = self.logvar(x)
        return (mu, logvar)
```

You'll find minimal differences if you compare the code snippet with the Encoder example from the previous section. We use two linear layers instead of one to compute two different values from the same representation extracted by the convolutional layers, and we return those two values in the forward() method.

The purpose of these two computed values is to represent the mean and the variance of a probability distribution. However, they are initially just two identical linear layers. The challenge is to ensure that they learn to represent what we intend—mean and variance—during the training process, as we'll show.

Before that, note that the computed value mu represents the mean, and logvar represents the logarithm of the variance. We use mu for the mean after the Greek letter $\mu$, frequently used in math notation to represent the mean of a normal distribution. The reason for using logvar rather than directly outputting the variance is primarily numerical stability, as we'll explain later.

How about the decoder? It turns out we don't need to make any changes to it. The difference between a VAE and a simple AutoEncoder lies in the way we find a point in latent space to represent an input item, but the mission of the decoder is the same: given a point in latent space (z), show the pixels whose encoded representation is most similar to z. In the case of the AutoEncoder, z is a linear projection of the features extracted by the convolutional layers. When we use a VAE encoder, we obtain a normal distribution, and then we *sample* from that distribution to obtain z. Therefore, we can use the same Decoder class we used in the previous section, but we do need to modify the model to *sample* from the distribution.

## Sampling from the Encoder Distribution

Our updated VAE encoder returns the mean and variance of a normal distribution that tries to match the input data representations. To obtain a decoded output, we must sample from that distribution, as shown in the following snippet:

```
class VAE(nn.Module):
    def __init__(self, in_channels, latent_dims):
        super().__init__()
        self.encoder = VAEEncoder(in_channels, latent_dims) ❶
        self.decoder = Decoder(in_channels, latent_dims)
```

```python
def encode(self, x):
    # Returns mu, log_var
    return self.encoder(x)

def decode(self, z):
    return self.decoder(z)

def forward(self, x):
    # Obtain parameters of the normal (Gaussian) distribution
    mu, logvar = self.encode(x)  ❷

    # Sample from the distribution
    std = torch.exp(0.5 * logvar)  ❸
    z = self.sample(mu, std)  ❹

    # Decode the latent point to pixel space
    reconstructed = self.decode(z)  ❺

    # Return the reconstructed image, and also the mu and logvar
    # so we can compute a distribution loss
    return reconstructed, mu, logvar  ❻

def sample(self, mu, std):
    # Reparametrization trick
    # Sample from N(0, I), translate and scale
    eps = torch.randn_like(std)  ❼
    return mu + eps * std
```

❶ We use `latent_dims` dimensions to represent the mean and log variance of the distributions.

❷ The encoder computes two variables now: mean and log variance.

❸ Compute the standard deviation from the log variance.

❹ Sample from the distribution by using the computed mean and standard deviation.

❺ The decoder converts the sample to an image.

❻ We return not only the reconstructed image but also the mean and the log variance.

❼ Reparametrization trick: sample from a standard normal distribution and then translate and scale.

So far, we've appealed to intuition to explain how VAEs work. If you allow us a brief detour into a couple of statistical concepts, we can quickly review the preceding code while trying to be more precise in terminology. Feel free to skip this section or come back to it later. It's not necessary to understand it to use or train VAEs, but it may help if you want to dive deeper and read papers about the topic.

First, note that we use multidimensional Gaussian distributions, not just real-valued 1D normal curves. In this VAE encoder example, we use latent_dims for both the mean and the variance. We could use an arbitrary number of dimensions, like the 16 we used for our first MNIST AutoEncoder, or 2 for easier visualization. A real-valued (1D) normal distribution is denoted as $\mathcal{N}(\mu, \sigma^2)$ and is defined by two magnitudes: $\mu$, the mean of the distribution, and $\sigma$, the *standard deviation*, which is the square root of the *variance* $\sigma^2$.

One useful characteristic of normal distributions is that all of them can be expressed in terms of the *standard* normal distribution, whose mean is 0 and variance is 1, by translating and scaling it:

$$\mathcal{N}(\mu, \sigma^2) = \mu + \sigma \mathcal{N}(0, 1)$$

This means that to obtain a sample from an arbitrary normal distribution $\mathcal{N}(\mu, \sigma^2)$, we can instead sample from $\mathcal{N}(0, 1)$, then multiply by $\sigma$ and add $\mu$. This is called *reparametrization* and will be quite helpful when we look into diffusion models.

Multidimensional Gaussian distributions are called *multivariate*. They can still be defined by two parameters, with the difference that $\mu$ is a vector and $\sigma$ (the covariance matrix, now denoted with $\Sigma$) is a matrix. Hence, the distribution is defined as $\mathcal{N}(\mu, \Sigma)$. If the distribution is independent in all dimensions, meaning each variable is uncorrelated with the others and has the same variance, it is called *isotropic*. In an isotropic multivariate Gaussian distribution, the covariance matrix $\Sigma$ is a diagonal matrix where all the items in the diagonal are equal and can be expressed as $\sigma^2 \mathbf{I}$, where $\mathbf{I}$ is the identity matrix. The standard multivariate Gaussian is then expressed as $\mathcal{N}(0, \mathbf{I})$.

Our preceding VAE example models a multivariate, isotropic Gaussian distribution, as there's no reason to think that sample coordinates depend on each other (and it's simpler!). This means we can use the so-called reparametrization trick to sample from the *standard* Gaussian, then translate and scale to obtain the latent space vector we'll decode.

The reparametrization trick is not used just for convenience—it's a crucial ingredient for training. When we use the expression mu + eps * std, where eps is a sample from the standard Gaussian, the gradients with respect to the model inputs are independent of the stochastic process (sampling from a distribution) and can, therefore, be computed. This makes it possible to train the model with the familiar gradient descent methods we follow to train any neural network.

Speaking of stability, our model predicts the *log* of the variance instead of the variance to increase numerical stability and facilitate training. Mathematically, it makes no difference to compute one or the other. In practice, we know the variance is always a positive number, usually close to 0. However, there's no reason for the model to produce positive and small values when we start training. Furthermore, numbers are represented in floating-point format, which makes it difficult to discriminate values very close together. By taking the *log*, we get two benefits:

- We expand the range of acceptable values to −∞, so the model has a lot more latitude to express the results with floating-point values.
- We ensure that the variance is always positive, because it's the exponential of the `logvar`.

 Gaussian distributions are frequently used in many other areas of ML, sometimes for convenience because their mathematical characteristics are well-known. In Chapter 4, we'll explore their use to model the noise corruption, which is an essential part of diffusion models.

## Training the VAE

The key to training the VAE is the loss function. In "AutoEncoders" on page 57, the loss function we used measured the difference between the reconstructed and original images. We still want the reconstructed images to resemble the originals as much as possible, but we now introduce a second factor to the loss to impose the VAE constraint we've been talking about: we want the features to (more or less) follow a Gaussian distribution.

The way we achieve that goal is by using *Kullback–Leibler divergence*, also known as *relative entropy*, between the distributions. Kullback–Leibler divergence, or KL divergence (KLD), is a way to measure how much a probability distribution differs from another one. In the case of multivariate isotropic Gaussian distributions, it can be shown that KLD can be computed as follows:

$$D_{KL}[\mathcal{N}(\mu, \sigma^2) || \mathcal{N}(0, 1)] = -\frac{1}{2}\sum\left(1 + log(\sigma^2) - \mu^2 - \sigma^2\right)$$

To combine the two loss factors, we create a loss function called `vae_loss()` that receives the original images and the outputs from the encoder and does the following:[9]

- Computes the reconstruction loss as the mean squared error (MSE) between the pixels generated by the decoder and the original images. This loss factor is identical to the one we used to train AutoEncoders.

- Computes the KLD term following the equation we just presented.

- Adds them together. We could assign more importance to one or the other to balance reconstruction fidelity and conformance to a Gaussian distribution. We'll sum them for now, but playing with this balance is a great experiment to try.

The loss function returns three values: the total loss, the reconstruction loss, and the KLD term. We need only the total loss for training, but we keep track of the others for visualization and analysis:

```python
def vae_loss(batch, reconstructed, mu, logvar):
    bs = batch.shape[0]

    # Reconstruction loss from the pixels - 1 per image
    reconstruction_loss = F.mse_loss(
        reconstructed.reshape(bs, -1),
        batch.reshape(bs, -1),
        reduction="none",
    ).sum(dim=-1)

    # KL-divergence loss, per input image
    kl_loss = -0.5 * torch.sum(1 + logvar - mu.pow(2) - logvar.exp(), dim=-1)

    # Combine both losses and get the mean across images
    loss = (reconstruction_loss + kl_loss).mean(dim=0)

    return (loss, reconstruction_loss, kl_loss)
```

Now that we've defined the loss, we can proceed to train the model. We'll use the total loss to update the model weights, but we'll also keep track of the reconstruction loss and the KLD term to understand how the model is learning:

```python
def train_vae(model, num_epochs=10, lr=1e-4):
    model = model.to(device)
    losses = {
        "loss": [],
        "reconstruction_loss": [],
        "kl_loss": [],
    }
```

---

9 Remember that the VAE encoder returns not only the reconstructed images but also the mean and the log variance of the distributions.

```
        model.train()
        optimizer = torch.optim.AdamW(model.parameters(), lr=lr, eps=1e-5)
        for _ in (progress := trange(num_epochs, desc="Training")):
            for _, batch in (
                inner := tqdm(
                    enumerate(train_dataloader), total=len(train_dataloader)
                )
            ):
                batch = batch.to(device)

                # Pass through the model
                reconstructed, mu, logvar = model(batch)

                # Compute the losses
                loss, reconstruction_loss, kl_loss = vae_loss(
                    batch, reconstructed, mu, logvar
                )

                # Display loss and store for plotting
                inner.set_postfix(loss=f"{loss.cpu().item():.3f}")
                losses["loss"].append(loss.item())
                losses["reconstruction_loss"].append(
                    reconstruction_loss.mean().item()
                )
                losses["kl_loss"].append(kl_loss.mean().item())

                # Update model parameters based on the total loss
                optimizer.zero_grad()
                loss.backward()
                optimizer.step()
            progress.set_postfix(loss=f"{loss.cpu().item():.3f}", lr=f"{lr:.0e}")
        return losses
    vae_model = VAE(in_channels=1, latent_dims=2)
    losses = train_vae(vae_model, num_epochs=10, lr=1e-4)
```

Let's analyze the three loss terms we stored during training:

*Reconstruction loss*
  Measures how much the output images resemble the originals

*KLD*
  Measures how well the features follow a Gaussian distribution

*Total loss*
  The addition of the two previous losses

Let's now plot the loss components while training a VAE. The total loss is the sum of the reconstruction loss plus the KL term:

```
for k, v in losses.items():
    plt.plot(v, label=k)
plt.legend();
```

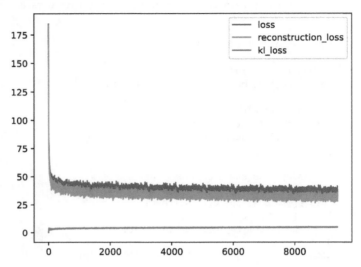

Even though the total loss was taken as the sum of the two losses, it is dominated, in this case, by the reconstruction loss because its magnitude is much larger than KLD. Let's plot the loss components separately to see how they evolve during training, as shown in Figure 3-5.

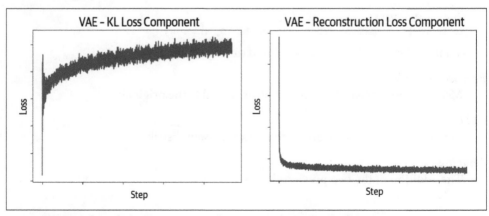

*Figure 3-5. KL loss and reconstruction loss components during VAE training*

Note that the KL loss plot has a peculiar form: it spikes at the beginning of training, then decreases, then slowly *increases* again. Why does that happen? We think these are, conceptually, the phases KLD goes through in training:

- When training starts, the VAE encoder and decoder are initialized with random weights, and the model knows nothing about the input data. Therefore, the outputs resemble a random distribution, and the KLD is very low.

- When the network has seen just a few batches of data, the reconstructions will be low-quality but not random anymore, and KLD spikes.

- Still in the early training stages, the model knows just enough to represent the average characteristics of the input data. The KLD term drives the model to produce outputs that get closer and closer to a Gaussian distribution, decreasing the KLD loss.

- As the encoder and decoder learn to produce more-faithful representations, it becomes harder to improve quality while still matching a Gaussian distribution. The reconstruction loss dominates, and KLD increases, but there's a balance between the two. If we increased the importance of KLD in the loss term, we could achieve better Gaussian conformance, but the cost would be worse pixel representations.

Let's reconstruct some images and visualize the results of VAE reconstructions from MNIST samples:

```
vae_model.eval()
with torch.inference_mode():
    eval_batch = next(iter(eval_dataloader))
    predicted, mu, logvar = (v.cpu() for v in vae_model(eval_batch.to(device)))

batch_vs_preds = torch.cat((eval_batch, predicted))
show_images(batch_vs_preds, imsize=1, nrows=2)
```

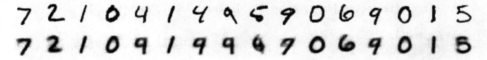

Visual results are worse than in the AutoEncoder case because the model not only has to learn how to encode the input images but is also constrained in terms of trying to avoid diverging too much from a normal distribution. Let's explore what happened after we added this new goal.

If we plot the means of the standard distribution encoded by the model for the test set, we obtain a slightly better-behaved result than in the AutoEncoder case, as shown in the following plot. Results are now better centered around zero and don't get as far away as in the AutoEncoder case. Areas taken by the different classes are of similar size, although there's still overlap between similar-looking numbers:

```
df = pd.DataFrame(
    {
        "x": [],
        "y": [],
        "label": [],
    }
)

for batch in tqdm(
    iter(images_labels_dataloader), total=len(images_labels_dataloader)
):
    mu, _ = vae_model.encode(batch["image"].to(device))
    mu = mu.to("cpu")
    new_items = {
        "x": [t.item() for t in mu[:, 0]],
        "y": [t.item() for t in mu[:, 1]],
        "label": batch["label"],
    }
    df = pd.concat([df, pd.DataFrame(new_items)], ignore_index=True)

plt.figure(figsize=(10, 8))

for label in range(10):
    points = df[df["label"] == label]
    plt.scatter(points["x"], points["y"], label=label, marker=".")

plt.legend();
```

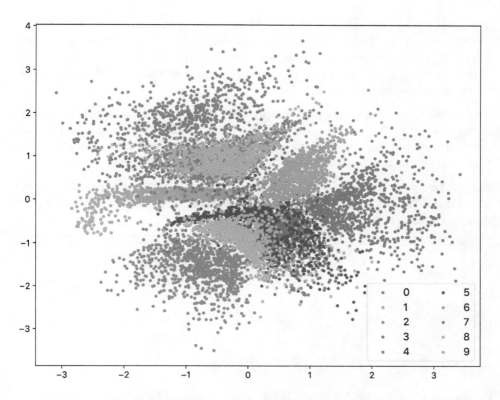

The main advantage of trying to fit the encoder to a normal distribution is that we should now be able to sample random data from the distribution and, hopefully, obtain images that resemble our input dataset. Let's see how it works for both the AutoEncoder and the VAE:

```
z = torch.normal(0, 1, size=(10, 2))
ae_decoded = ae_model.decode(z.to(device))
vae_decoded = vae_model.decode(z.to(device))

show_images(ae_decoded.cpu(), imsize=1, nrows=1)
show_images(vae_decoded.cpu(), imsize=1, nrows=1)
```

We sample pure random data from a normal distribution and then use the Auto-Encoder (top row) and VAE (bottom row) decoders to display how those points would be reconstructed. Of course, we will see different reconstructions, as the AutoEncoder and VAE were trained separately, and they allocated different portions of the latent space to each class.

The results from the VAE are more number-like than those of the AutoEncoder. This is because the VAE training process encouraged the encoder to not veer away too much from a normal distribution, while the AutoEncoder had no such restriction. Can you run the sampling code a few times and observe it yourself?

A fun exercise is to show how representations morph as we travel in 2D through latent space. We can fix a vertical line at $x = -0.8$, as done in Figure 3-6, and explore different points on this line.

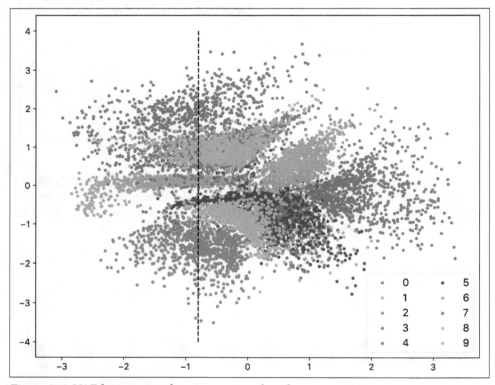

*Figure 3-6. VAE latent space focusing on samples where $x = -0.8$*

If we select points from y = -2 to y = 2, we see that the reconstructions match the latent space areas that represent various numbers:

```python
import numpy as np

with torch.inference_mode():
    inputs = []
    for y in np.linspace(-2, 2, 10):
        inputs.append([-0.8, y])
    z = torch.tensor(inputs, dtype=torch.float32).to(device)
    decoded = vae_model.decode(z)
show_images(decoded.cpu(), imsize=1, nrows=1)
```

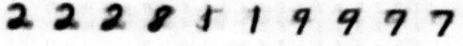

Let's expand the idea of exploring the latent space to a 2D grid. This is a visual representation of what the model learned, and it's interesting to see that transitions are not too crazy![10]

```python
inputs = []
for x in np.linspace(-2, 2, 20):
    for y in np.linspace(-2, 2, 20):
        inputs.append([x, y])
z = torch.tensor(inputs, dtype=torch.float32).to(device)
decoded = vae_model.to(device).decode(z)

show_images(decoded.cpu(), imsize=0.4, nrows=20)
```

---

10 This is a rather crude way to show the *learned manifold* of the model. For a better way to display this result and additional experiments, we recommend the pytorch-mnist-vae GitHub repo (*https://oreil.ly/IyBnn*) by Jackie Loong.

Once again, here are some exercises to dive into these topics:

1. When we trained the VAE, we added the reconstruction and KL divergence losses. However, both have different scales. What will happen if we give more importance to one versus the other? Can you run a few experiments and explain the results?

2. The VAE we explored in this section uses only two dimensions to represent the distribution's mean and the *logvar*. Can you repeat a similar exploration using 16 dimensions?

3. Humans are trained to look at faces and easily identify unrealistic features. Can you train an AutoEncoder and a VAE for a dataset containing faces and analyze the results? You can start with the Frey Face dataset (*https://oreil.ly/Vxiln*) that was used in the VAE paper—it's a homogenous set of monochrome images of faces from the same person sporting different facial expressions. If you want to be more ambitious, you can try your hand at the CelebFaces Attributes dataset (*https://oreil.ly/R75gg*), easily usable from the Hugging Face Hub (*https://oreil.ly/mnpbI*). Another interesting example is the Oxford pets dataset (*https://oreil.ly/rKMkI*), also available on the Hugging Face Hub (*https://oreil.ly/oz8hw*).

## VAEs for Generative Modeling

Training an encoder constrained to be close to a distribution is a key insight into VAEs and one of the cornerstones of generative modeling. With AutoEncoder, we could learn efficient representations of a dataset. Still, there was no guarantee that the latent space learned by the model would help us generate new data that resembled the original. By aiming to learn a distribution, VAEs allow us to generate plausible new images, simply starting from random points in the latent space. Diffusion models take this idea of sampling from random noise a step further, by incorporating iterative refinement to the process. We'll discuss them at length in future chapters.

# CLIP

So far, we've focused on image data. With Contrastive Language-Image Pre-training (CLIP), we'll steer away from AutoEncoder/VAE methods and explore a different technique to match images with text. The process is similar in the sense that we aim to create rich representations from the input data, but the method is different, and, more importantly, it can deal with both images and text at once.

Our dataset now consists of two *modalities*: images and text captions describing those images. Given that training data, the goal of CLIP is to create a model that measures how accurately a text describes the contents of an image for an arbitrary text-image pair that we supply. The key, as usual, is the loss function we use.

## Contrastive Loss

CLIP was introduced by OpenAI (*https://oreil.ly/Anejl*) in 2021. It was part of the tools developed to create the initial DALL·E (*https://oreil.ly/4DUf7*), an impressive text-to-image model that took the world by storm. Even though DALL·E was not made open source (the model weights remain private), CLIP was. This was extraordinary news, as the ability to relate images with text enables quite a few tricks. CLIP and CLIP-like models have since become indispensable tools in the generative landscape.

CLIP uses a loss function called *contrastive loss*. The way it works is shown schematically in Figure 3-7. The training dataset consists of millions of images with their associated descriptions or captions. For each image-caption pair, we encode the image by using any image encoder to obtain an *embedding vector* in the encoder's latent space. Each of the figure's $I_1$, $I_2$, ..., $I_N$ boxes represents embedding vectors for different images. The text is also encoded, usually with a transformer model like the ones we saw in Chapter 2. Crucially, we use encoders such that the dimensions of the embedding vectors of images and text are the same. This way, we can calculate the inner product (or dot product) between the text and image embeddings to determine how close they are.

Training progresses by supplying a lot of image-text pairs in the same batch. We compute the dot products of all the image embeddings in the batch with all the text embeddings in the same batch and try to maximize the product of the items originally from the same pair (i.e., the blue diagonal in the image) while minimizing the rest. This way, texts and images that are *similar* will be represented by vectors close in the latent space, while different concepts will be far away in other regions.

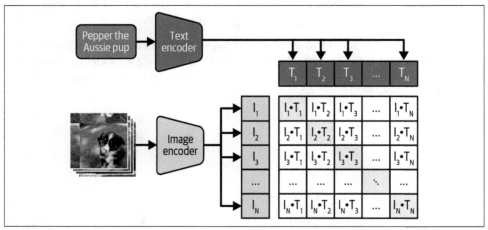

*Figure 3-7. CLIP (adapted from an image by OpenAI (https://oreil.ly/5UQ25))*

## Why Use the Dot Product?

If you don't remember or haven't studied calculus before, an important relationship that holds in vector spaces is as follows:

$$A \cdot B = |A||B| \cos(\theta)$$

This means that the dot product between two vectors is the same as the product of the lengths of the two vectors multiplied by the angle between them. This can be shown using the law of cosines (*https://oreil.ly/t7d65*) from Euclidean geometry and the definition of dot product as $A \cdot B = \sum_{n=1}^{N} a_i b_i$. In our brief discussion, we didn't mention that the vector embeddings are normalized to unit length; therefore, their dot product is the angle between the vectors. This is called *cosine similarity*, and it measures the proximity between two vectors. Even though the vectors have many dimensions, the dot product is just a scalar (i.e., a real number) that can be used as a similarity score.

Training a CLIP model requires huge amounts of data and lots of compute. The original CLIP models released by OpenAI used a proprietary dataset of 400 million image-text pairs and large batch sizes of 32,000 pairs. Since then, there have been multiple efforts to train CLIP or CLIP-like models, including support for additional modalities such as audio:

*OpenCLIP (https://oreil.ly/Hkjbj)*
  An open implementation of CLIP. It was used to train several models with different datasets, image resolutions, and model sizes.

*CLAP (Contrastive Language-Audio Pretraining) (https://oreil.ly/wCGgZ)*
  Allows obtaining representations of audio rather than images. This can be used to train models that generate audio, as we'll explore in Chapter 9.

## Using CLIP, Step-by-Step

We'll now use pretrained CLIP models to gain intuition about how they work and see a few examples of what they can be used for. In the following example, we use clip-vit-large-patch14 (*https://oreil.ly/KIIqC*), one of the OpenAI CLIP models. It uses a Vision Transformer (ViT) as the image encoder (other versions exist that use the ResNet convolutional architecture). Larger and smaller versions exist as well; you can experiment with a few to see how they work on your hardware in terms of speed, memory, and quality.

Consider the photo in Figure 3-8, a royalty-free resource from Pixabay showing an adorable lion cub looking at us from behind a tree branch. Let's see how we can use it with CLIP.

*Figure 3-8. Photo of a cute lion cub behind a branch*

So far we've used *transformers* only to load text models, but we can also use them to work with other modalities. Just as we used GPT2LMHeadModel in the previous chapter, we can use CLIPModel. Let's try it out:

```
import requests
from PIL import Image
from transformers import CLIPModel, CLIPProcessor

from genaibook.core import SampleURL

clip = CLIPModel.from_pretrained("openai/clip-vit-large-patch14").to(device)
processor = CLIPProcessor.from_pretrained("openai/clip-vit-large-patch14")

url = SampleURL.LionExample
image = Image.open(requests.get(url, stream=True).raw)
```

The CLIP model we loaded, clip, contains two components: a vision model to encode images and a text model to encode text. CLIPProcessor, which you can think of as the tokenizer equivalent, prepares input data to match the preprocessing steps used during model training: image resizing, normalization, etc. This is essential to ensure that the inputs we provide for inference have the same characteristics as the data the model saw when it was trained. Let's process the image first:

```
image_inputs = processor(images=image, return_tensors="pt")
pixel_values = image_inputs["pixel_values"]
pixel_values.shape, pixel_values.min(), pixel_values.max()
```

```
(torch.Size([1, 3, 224, 224]), tensor(-1.7923), tensor(2.0179))
```

The image has been resized to a square of 224 pixels × 224 pixels and normalized.
You can examine the image processor for the full set of applied transformations. Note
that the strategy used for resizing is to center-crop (i.e., select a square-sized block
around the center of the image and then downscale it to 224 × 224). This method cuts
the left and right portions from landscape images or the top and bottom bands from
images with a portrait aspect ratio. Be mindful that this may result in information loss
if some of the subjects you want to examine are in those areas:

```
processor.image_processor
```

```
CLIPImageProcessor {
  "crop_size": {
    "height": 224,
    "width": 224
  },
  "do_center_crop": true,
  "do_convert_rgb": true,
  "do_normalize": true,
  "do_rescale": true,
  "do_resize": true,
  "image_mean": [
    0.48145466,
    0.4578275,
    0.40821073
  ],
  "image_processor_type": "CLIPImageProcessor",
  "image_std": [
    0.26862954,
    0.26130258,
    0.27577711
  ],
  "resample": 3,
  "rescale_factor": 0.00392156862745098,
  "size": {
    "shortest_edge": 224
  }
}
```

Let's verify that our lion cub photo can survive a center crop:

```
width, height = image.size
crop_length = min(image.size)

left = (width - crop_length) / 2
top = (height - crop_length) / 2
right = (width + crop_length) / 2
bottom = (height + crop_length) / 2
```

```
cropped = image.crop((left, top, right, bottom))
cropped
```

The subject in our photo is fully preserved. Depending on your data, you may need to crop the source images before passing them to the processor to ensure the subject is visible.

We'll now get the embedding vector from the preprocessed image. We use the vision model stored inside the `clip` instance to do that. This subcomponent is sometimes called the *vision tower*:

```
with torch.inference_mode():
    output = clip.vision_model(pixel_values.to(device))
image_embeddings = output.pooler_output
image_embeddings.shape

torch.Size([1, 1024])
```

The vision model returns a dictionary with the last hidden states and the pooler output. This vector with shape `[1, 1024]` represents the result of the encoding process. Let's now turn our attention to the language portion of the model. We'll follow a similar process to get the embeddings for two text prompts: "a photo of a lion" and "a photo of a zebra". Our end goal is to compare the cosine similarity between the image embeddings and each prompt embedding. Hopefully, the lion description should match the image better!

```
prompts = [
    "a photo of a lion",
    "a photo of a zebra",
]

# Padding makes sure all inputs have the same length
text_inputs = processor(text=prompts, return_tensors="pt", padding=True)

{'attention_mask': tensor([[1, 1, 1, 1, 1, 1, 1],
        [1, 1, 1, 1, 1, 1, 1]]),
 'input_ids': tensor([[49406,   320,  1125,   539,   320,  5567, 49407],
        [49406,   320,  1125,   539,   320, 22548, 49407]])}
```

Text processing tokenizes the input strings just as in the previous chapter. We can now pass the tokenized text inputs through the *language tower* part of the model to get the prompt embeddings:

```
text_inputs = {k: v.to(device) for k, v in text_inputs.items()}

with torch.inference_mode():
    text_output = clip.text_model(**text_inputs)
text_embeddings = text_output.pooler_output
text_embeddings.shape
```

```
torch.Size([2, 768])
```

We get two vectors in the output by using a batch of two input prompts. However, each vector has 768 dimensions, while the embeddings from the image have 1,024 dimensions. Remember that to compute the dot product of two vectors, they have to have the same number of dimensions, and we insisted in the introduction to this section that both the text encoder and the image encoder must produce embeddings with the same dimensionality. There's an additional step we didn't mention before. Instead of selecting encoder models that produce the same dimensions, we can take arbitrary text and image encoders and compute a projection to vectors with the same dimensionality. These projections were learned during the CLIP training process and are also part of the clip model wrapper we downloaded before.

In this case, the learned projections are just linear layers that map their inputs to vectors with 768 dimensions. There's a projection for the text encoder and a different one for the vision part of the model:

```
print(clip.text_projection)
print(clip.visual_projection)
```

```
Linear(in_features=768, out_features=768, bias=False)
Linear(in_features=1024, out_features=768, bias=False)
```

```
with torch.inference_mode():
    text_embeddings = clip.text_projection(text_embeddings)
    image_embeddings = clip.visual_projection(image_embeddings)
text_embeddings.shape, image_embeddings.shape
```

```
(torch.Size([2, 768]), torch.Size([1, 768]))
```

We are almost ready to compute the cosine similarities. We just need to remember to use normalized vectors with unit norms, which we achieve by scaling our embeddings and dividing by their respective norms. We can then compute the two dot products at once by using matrix multiplication:

```
text_embeddings = text_embeddings / text_embeddings.norm(
    p=2, dim=-1, keepdim=True
)
image_embeddings = image_embeddings / image_embeddings.norm(
    p=2, dim=-1, keepdim=True
)

similarities = torch.matmul(text_embeddings, image_embeddings.T)
similarities
```

```
tensor([[0.2171],
        [0.1888]], device='cuda:0')
```

During training, these cosine similarities were interpreted as the logits to be fed to a cross-entropy loss classifier that predicts the label for each image-text pair. Since CLIP training used 32-sized batches, labels are each one of the 32,768 positions in the batch. If you refer again to the CLIP image at the beginning of the section, once the model has been trained, the cross-entropy process will select "class" $T_1$ for $I_1$, class $T_2$ for $I_2$, and so on.

There's a final detail, though. Because the vectors are normalized, logits can lie only within the range [-1, 1], which, because of floating-point format limitations, may not have enough dynamic range to expressively capture the categorical probability distributions of the 32K items. The authors used a learnable *temperature* parameter to scale the logits to have a wider range. However, they also clipped this scale value to a maximum of 100 for numerical stability. In all the training runs, they found that the scale always reached the maximum value of 100. Therefore, CLIP inference uses a scale factor of 100 before interpreting the logits as probabilities.

Let's apply that correction to our previous code snippet, and then we can convert the scaled similarity logits to probabilities. These probabilities represent how confident the model is that the image corresponds to one of the two text captions we used:

```
similarities = 100 * torch.matmul(text_embeddings, image_embeddings.T)
similarities.softmax(dim=0).cpu()
```

```
tensor([[0.9441],
        [0.0559]])
```

The model matches the prompt "a photo of a lion" with the image with a confidence of 94.4%.

## Zero-Shot Image Classification with CLIP

The process we followed in the previous section is a detailed walk-through of the steps needed to implement a *zero-shot classification task* with CLIP. Fortunately, software libraries such as *transformers* or *OpenCLIP* provide higher layers of abstraction that make the process much easier.

---

### Why Is This Called Zero-Shot Classification?

Classification is one of the quintessential ML problems: given a data point and a set of predefined classes, estimate the probability that the point corresponds to one of the classes. According to this definition, the set of classes must be fixed in advance, so the model we train will know only about these classes and nothing else. The ImageNet dataset, for example, contains images from 20,000 classes. For years, the ImageNet Large Scale Visual Recognition Challenge (ILSVRC) was a test benchmark for Computer Vision systems, with the goal of classifying objects belonging to *just 1,000* of the ImageNet classes. In 2012, a deep CNN known as AlexNet easily won that year's challenge, and this started a revolution where accuracy figures increased year after year as newer and better deep learning models were designed.

Zero-shot classification refers to the capability of a model to correctly classify data without having been trained explicitly for the classes we are asking for. In Chapter 2, we saw an example of zero-shot sentiment classification using LMs, and the previous section is another prime demonstration of this capability. CLIP was trained to match image-caption pairs, but we can leverage this behavior for classification if we construct captions that could reasonably describe the images we want to classify. For example, if we want to classify cats versus dogs, our prompts can be "A photo of a cat" and "A photo of a dog". CLIP will match the best prompt for the image we supply, giving us the classification result we're after.

---

Let's replicate the example in the previous section with a higher-level *transformers* API. We load the CLIP model, processor, and test image the same way we did before:

```
clip = CLIPModel.from_pretrained("openai/clip-vit-large-patch14").to(device)
processor = CLIPProcessor.from_pretrained("openai/clip-vit-large-patch14")

image = Image.open(requests.get(SampleURL.LionExample, stream=True).raw)
```

We can leverage the processor to compute the inputs for both the image and the text prompts simultaneously. We can also conveniently invoke the CLIP model with the full set of inputs to retrieve the logits—or scaled cosine similarities—between the image and each prompt. Let's use a few more prompts to make things more fun:

```
prompts = [
    "a photo of a lion",
    "a photo of a zebra",
```

```
        "a photo of a cat",
        "a photo of an adorable lion cub",
        "a puppy",
        "a lion behind a branch",
]
inputs = processor(
    text=prompts, images=image, return_tensors="pt", padding=True
)
inputs = {k: v.to(device) for k, v in inputs.items()}

outputs = clip(**inputs)
logits_per_image = outputs.logits_per_image
probabilities = logits_per_image.softmax(dim=1)

probabilities = probabilities[0].cpu().detach().tolist()

for prob, prompt in sorted(zip(probabilities, prompts), reverse=True):
    print(f"{100*prob: =2.0f}%: {prompt}")

89%: a photo of an adorable lion cub
 9%: a lion behind a branch
 2%: a photo of a lion
 0%: a photo of a zebra
 0%: a photo of a cat
 0%: a puppy
```

Similarly, we can supply multiple images and prompts in the same input batch and get all classification probabilities simultaneously. Feel free to explore and adapt to your use case.

## Zero-Shot Image-Classification Pipeline

Now that you know how CLIP works and how to use it for zero-shot image classification, we can use an even higher-level API for simplicity and convenience. We'll use the `pipeline` abstraction, which we already presented in Chapter 1. In that case, we demonstrated how to use it for the text-classification task, but we can also apply it for many other tasks, including zero-shot image classification.

To instantiate a pipeline, we simply give it the task name (`zero-shot-image-classification`, in this case) and the model we want to use:

```
from transformers import pipeline

classifier = pipeline(
    "zero-shot-image-classification",
    model="openai/clip-vit-large-patch14",
    device=device,
)
```

The pipeline takes care of all the details for us: tokenization, image preprocessing, and logits postprocessing. We just need to invoke the pipeline instance with the image we want to classify and a set of candidate labels. The pipeline returns a dictionary, conveniently sorted by score, containing all the scores associated to the labels we provided:

```
scores = classifier(
    image,
    candidate_labels=prompts,
    hypothesis_template="{}",
)
```

The `hypothesis_template` is a Python format string that is applied to each candidate label to build the text prompt for classification. If we omit the `hypothesis_template` argument, the pipeline will automatically use `"This is a photo of a \{}"`, which is appropriate to format class labels indicated by their name, such as "cat" or "lion". Since we already built prompts that work well with CLIP, we use `"{}"` to use our labels untouched:

```
[{'label': 'a photo of an adorable lion cub',
  'score': 0.886413037776947},
 {'label': 'a lion behind a branch', 'score': 0.09321863204240799},
 {'label': 'a photo of a lion', 'score': 0.018809959292411804},
 {'label': 'a photo of a zebra', 'score': 0.0011134858941659331},
 {'label': 'a photo of a cat', 'score': 0.0004198708338662982},
 {'label': 'a puppy', 'score': 2.4912407752708532e-05}]
```

## CLIP Use Cases

The original use case that CLIP was designed to solve is zero-shot image classification. The results are impressive: CLIP achieves performance similar to models trained for ImageNet classification, without ever using the ImageNet labels during training. As a consequence, performance remains equally strong on many other datasets, with no need for fine-tuning them, as you can read in the original blog post (*https://oreil.ly/Anejl*).

The previous sections have shown that the basis for solving zero-shot image classification is the ability to compute the similarity between an arbitrary image and a text prompt, and this is possible because both the image and the text embeddings capture the essential semantics of the data. The *way* CLIP works has enabled the community to use it for many tasks, not just zero-shot classification.

Being able to compute the *similarity between text and images* enables applications such as *semantic search*, which makes it possible to search for photos based on natural-language descriptions of their contents or find images similar to an example image we provide. Applications of these techniques exist in multiple domains, including consumer hardware (such as phones), medical systems, fashion, and others. In Chapter 2, we proposed a similar challenge, but it is constrained to textual data: building an FAQ system by computing similarities between the embedding outputs of an LM. At the end of this chapter, we propose a challenge using CLIP for semantic search.

CLIP can also be used to obtain *rich embeddings* for downstream tasks. For example, some text-to-image models use CLIP to obtain semantically rich representations of the prompts supplied by the user.

CLIP was also adopted as an essential tool for generative use cases. The CLIP Guidance method, developed by Ryan Murdock (*https://oreil.ly/BR17d*), Katherine Crowson (*https://oreil.ly/LDL_B*), and others, uses CLIP as a loss to guide model gradients toward the desired representation (expressed with a prompt). This method spawned a creative explosion in the generative art community. Later, CLIP conditioning became essential in models such as Stable Diffusion, which we'll explore in Chapter 5.

CLIP scoring capabilities have also been used to filter and score massive datasets of image-caption pairs, such as LAION (*https://oreil.ly/-UcPE*), crawled from Internet sources. Relying on CLIP allows dataset creators to select pairs where the similarity between the image and the caption yields a high score and discard the others. This has made it possible to build and refine datasets in the order of billions of items, which can be used to build better models that can refine datasets even more precisely. So meta!

## Alternatives to CLIP

Because CLIP is extensively used in industry and research, there has been much activity around the ideas presented in the model and how to make them better, faster, or adapted to other tasks. A significant effort has been made to make CLIP fully open source and reproducible. The OpenCLIP repository (*https://oreil.ly/Hkjbj*) provides open source code to implement CLIP and a number of architecture variants. Using the OpenCLIP codebase and the huge LAION dataset we mentioned in the previous section, the LAION team trained very powerful CLIP models of various sizes and made all the checkpoints available for everyone to use.

Recent research has shown that better text understanding can lead to better text-image models. BLIP (*https://arxiv.org/abs/2201.12086*), CoCa (*https://arxiv.org/abs/2205.01917*), and CapPa (*https://arxiv.org/abs/2306.07915*) demonstrate that the captioning task (generate a detailed description of what an image represents) can produce models that are capable of generating excellent image representations and solve a wide range of vision-language tasks. In parallel research, the use of a different loss function (sigmoid loss used in SigLIP (*https://arxiv.org/abs/2303.15343*), instead of softmax normalization) can make training easier and alleviate CLIP's problem of requiring huge batch sizes to train effectively.

Another promising direction is building smaller, faster models that can run on personal computers and mobile devices. This is the case with Apple's MobileCLIP (*https://arxiv.org/abs/2311.17049*), which achieves the performance of OpenAI's CLIP models with much smaller (and faster) models. Another Apple effort, Data Filtering Networks (*https://arxiv.org/abs/2309.17425*), aims to improve the quality of text-image datasets and also trained several CLIP variants (*https://oreil.ly/PFghl*) with those datasets.

As you'll see throughout the rest of this book, CLIP is an essential component of image-generation systems. This healthy research on more robust, capable, and faster CLIP-like models makes us very optimistic about the future.

# Project Time: Semantic Image Search

A fun project is building a semantic search engine for your photos. When you are done, you should be able to look for photos in your library by simply describing their contents (for example: "dog jumping into the water on a hot summer day" or "woman with umbrella walking down a busy street"), instead of trying to remember where in your collection those photos are stored. You can also use any other image dataset you like, but using content that means something to you will be rewarding and allow you to evaluate how well the system works. It may also make you want to think of ideas for improvement or share them with your family.

These are some suggested steps to tackle the project:

1. Choose a text-image model, such as CLIP, that can produce embeddings for both images and text descriptions. You can explore other alternatives, but CLIP should be a good start. Choose a family of models with multiple-size variants that you can easily replace with one another. This way, you can use a small model to iterate faster while working and see how much performance increases when you use a larger model.

2. Find a good number of photos and copy them all to a folder on your computer. Several hundred or a thousand photos should be fine.

3. Write a loop to create embeddings from your photos by using the model you chose:

    a. Read the photos from disk, crop and/or resize them so that they are the same size, and create a batch. You can use a PyTorch `DataLoader`, as we did in the training loops in this chapter. For preprocessing, you may do it manually with `torchvision.transforms`, or you can leverage the model's built-in preprocessor if it exists. Choose a batch size that fits your hardware.

b. Run each batch of images through the image portion of the CLIP model. Use inference mode (no gradients need to be computed, as you won't be training anything).

c. Get the embeddings from the output and save them to disk. You'll get a multidimensional vector for each image file. You can convert them to *numpy* arrays and write them all into the same file. Don't forget to store the names or paths to the original photos; you'll need them to retrieve the photos later.

4. At this point, you have an array of vectors in *numpy* format. You can now use the text portion of the model to run queries:

a. Write a function that receives an input prompt and generates an embedding vector using the text *tower* of the model.

b. Compute the cosine similarity between that vector and *all the vectors in the image embedding table*. If you have enough RAM, you can do it by simply using PyTorch's `matmul` operation.

c. Sort the outputs and select the top ones.

d. Find the images associated with the top scores and visualize them. Do they match the prompt you used?

Bonus tasks:

- Can you try to find images that *look similar* to another image? (That is, semantic search based on an input image, not a text description.)

- If you have a lot of photos, you may have trouble computing the scores. How could you solve this problem? Are there any frameworks or services that help with this? How many photos does it take to reach the limits of your computer?

- Pretrained models don't know anything about the subjects that appear in your photos. What could you do to be able to search by personal names or places?

- If you are adventurous, you can use MobileCLIP to run the search engine on your phone. This is a big challenge in itself; don't underestimate the effort!

# Summary

This chapter showed how learning compressed representations from input data is a way to capture the dataset's essential characteristics and how those representations can be effectively used for many additional downstream tasks. We started this exploration by looking at a classical system, the AutoEncoder, whose goal is to encode input samples into a latent space of reduced dimensionality and then recover the original data points from the latent representations.

By splitting the AutoEncoder into two components—the encoder and the decoder—we can imagine new applications beyond reconstruction. The encoder, for example, can be used as a feature extractor. Because it learned the essential features of the input dataset, we can use it to train other systems, such as classifiers, whose input data are latent representations. We also explored the idea of using the decoder for generative purposes. If the latent space is a representation of the original dataset, can we move to arbitrary points there and see what outputs we get? AutoEncoders, however, have some limitations for this task because of how they are trained.

The VAE is a special kind of AutoEncoder that tries to achieve "better-behaved" representations in latent space. By trying to make latent features match a probability distribution, we can sample from the desired distribution to obtain new random latent features. If we feed those features to the decoder, we can generate data points that look like they came from the original dataset. This is a crucial result for generative applications. Exploring this further, the fact that the latent space is a compact representation of the data is an essential idea behind generative systems such as Stable Diffusion. As we'll see in more detail in Chapter 5, we can conduct computation in the latent space that represents images rather than on the raw image data. This has enabled the training of high-quality image-generation systems that can run fast and efficiently on consumer hardware.

The final section of the chapter focused on CLIP, a highly influential model developed and published by OpenAI that encodes image and text data into the same latent space. New tricks are possible with CLIP that were pretty hard problems to solve. For example, given an image and a few sentences, we can measure which sentence matches the image better. Conversely, given a caption and a few image candidates, we can select the image that best matches the caption. CLIP was published as part of OpenAI's DALL·E image-generation project (which was not published itself), and it spawned a revolution in generative research. CLIP-like models are key components of Stable Diffusion and other text-to-image models, but they are used for many other applications: natural-language image retrieval, semantic search, extracting images that are similar based on content or style, and a lot more.

All of this came about from the initial realization that learning how to compress data is equivalent to learning about the data. Many variations on these concepts use different types of data extraction and representation techniques: CNNs, transformers, or combining the best of both with systems like VQGAN. We just offered a glimpse of the motivations and ideas behind these foundational blocks with the hope that they will be useful for navigating this rich and fascinating space.

# Exercises

Most of these exercises are the same ones we proposed during the chapter, compiled here for your convenience. Depending on your learning style, you may like to work on them as you go through the chapter, or you may try them all after a first read:

1. How does generation work if the AutoEncoder model is trained with 16 latent dimensions? Can you compare generations between the model with 16 latent dimensions and the one with just 2?

2. Train the model again with the same parameters we used (just run the code shown in the chapter) but with different random number initialization, and visualize the latent space. Chances are that the shapes and structure are different. Is this something you would expect? Why?

3. How good are the image features extracted by the encoder? Explore it by training a number classifier on top of the encoder.

4. When we trained the VAE, we added the reconstruction and KL divergence losses. However, both have different scales. What will happen if we give more importance to one versus the other? Can you run a few experiments and explain the results?

5. The VAE we trained uses only two dimensions to represent the mean and the *logvar* of the distribution. Can you repeat a similar exploration using 16 dimensions?

You can find the solutions to these exercises and the following challenges in the book's GitHub repository (*https://oreil.ly/handsonGenAIcode*).

# Challenges

1. *BLIP-2 for search.* The hands-on project on semantic image search is quite challenging, but here's another idea. Can you use the BLIP-2 model (*https://oreil.ly/e_CpT*) for similarity tasks, just as we did with CLIP in this chapter? How would you go about it, and how does it compare with CLIP? What other tasks can you solve with BLIP-2?

2. *Train your own AutoEncoder or VAE.* Humans are trained to look at faces and easily identify unrealistic features. Can you try to train an AutoEncoder and a VAE for a dataset containing faces, and see what the results look like? You can start with the Frey Face dataset (*https://oreil.ly/Vxiln*) that was used in the VAE paper—it's a homogenous set of monochrome faces from the same person sporting different facial expressions. If you want to be more ambitious, you can try your hand at the CelebFaces Attributes dataset (*https://oreil.ly/R75gg*), also hosted on the Hugging Face Hub (*https://oreil.ly/mnpbI*). Another interesting

example could be to try the Oxford pets dataset (*https://oreil.ly/rKMkI*), also available on the Hub (*https://oreil.ly/oz8hw*).

# References

Chollet, François. "Variational AutoEncoder." Keras implementation of a VAE. April 24, 2024. *https://oreil.ly/TShML*.

Clément, Chadebec. *pythae* library GitHub repository. 2022. *https://oreil.ly/XUGjo*.

Ermon, Stefano, et al. "The Variational Auto-Encoder." In course notes for *CS 228 - Probabilistic Graphical Models*. *https://oreil.ly/pc0EP*.

Esser, Patrick, Robin Rombach, and Bjorn Ommer. "Taming Transformers for High-Resolution Image Synthesis." arXiv, June 23, 2021, *https://arxiv.org/abs/2012.09841*.

Fang, Alex, et al. "Data Filtering Networks." arXiv, November 6, 2023. *https://arxiv.org/abs/2309.17425*.

Floret, François. *Deep Learning* course materials (2024 version). *https://oreil.ly/Csb_F*. Revised VAE handouts (PDF) at *https://oreil.ly/456Vq*.

Foster, David. Chapter 3, "Variational Autoencoders." In *Generative Deep Learning*, 2nd edition. O'Reilly, 2023. *https://oreil.ly/TH2aO*.

Howard, Jeremy, and Sylvain Gugger. *Deep Learning for Coders with fastai & PyTorch*. O'Reilly, 2020. *https://oreil.ly/n1M6C*.

Kingma, Diederik P., and Max Welling. "Auto-Encoding Variational Bayes." arXiv, December 10, 2022. *https://arxiv.org/abs/1312.6114*.

LAION (various authors). "Large Scale OpenCLIP Trained on LAION-2B." LAION blog, September 15, 2022. *https://oreil.ly/FBlmH*.

Li, Junnan, et al. "BLIP: Bootstrapping Language-Image Pre-training for Unified Vision-Language Understanding and Generation." arXiv, February 15, 2022. *https://arxiv.org/abs/2201.12086*.

Li, Junnan, et al. "BLIP-2: Bootstrapping Language-Image Pre-training with Frozen Image Encoders and Large Language Models." arXiv, June 15, 2023. *https://arxiv.org/abs/2301.12597*.

Loong, Jackie. Variational Auto-Encoder for MNIST GitHub repository. *https://oreil.ly/-IRhy*.

Maucher, Johannes. "Animations of Convolution and Deconvolution." In *Intro and Overview Machine Learning* lecture notes, 2022. *https://oreil.ly/KL8VU*.

ML Foundations (various authors). OpenCLIP GitHub repository. *https://oreil.ly/Hkjbj*.

PyTorch team. PyTorch VAE example in the PyTorch GitHub repository, January 2017. *https://oreil.ly/ZchyF*.

Radford, Alec, et al. "Learning Transferable Visual Models From Natural Language Supervision." arXiv, February 26, 2021. *https://arxiv.org/abs/2103.00020.*

Stanford University. "Convolutional Layer." In course notes for *CS231n Convolutional Neural Networks for Visual Recognition*, November 2022. *https://oreil.ly/Ohh6z.*

Tschannen, Michael, et al. "Image Captioners Are Scalable Vision Learners Too." arXiv, December 21, 2023. *https://arxiv.org/abs/2306.07915.*

Vasu, Pavan Kumar Anasosalu, et al. "MobileCLIP: Fast Image-Text Models through Multi-Modal Reinforced Training." arXiv, April 1, 2024. *https://arxiv.org/abs/2311.17049.* Code repository at *https://oreil.ly/DmtWF.*

Whitaker, Jonathan. "A Deep Dive into OpenCLIP from OpenAI." *W&B Fully Connected*, November 7, 2022. *https://oreil.ly/9SSo1.*

Yanagisawa, Chiaki. "Conv2d and ConvTransposed2d." PowerPoint presentation, February 19, 2021. *https://oreil.ly/JEEl0.*

Yu, Jiahui, et al. "Coca: Contrastive Captioners Are Image-Text Foundation Models." arXiv, June 14, 2022. *https://arxiv.org/abs/2205.01917.*

Zhai, Xiaohua, et al. "Sigmoid Loss for Language Image Pre-Training." arXiv, September 27, 2023. *https://arxiv.org/abs/2303.15343.*

# CHAPTER 4

# Diffusion Models

The field of image generation became widely popular with Ian Goodfellow's introduction of Generative Adversarial Nets (GANs) in 2014. The key ideas of GANs led to a big family of models that could quickly generate high-quality images. However, despite their success, GANs posed challenges, requiring many parameters and help to generalize effectively. These limitations sparked parallel research endeavors, leading to the exploration of diffusion models—a class of models that would redefine the landscape of high-quality, flexible image generation.

In late 2020, a little-known class of models called *diffusion models* began causing a stir in the ML world. Researchers figured out how to use these diffusion models to generate higher-quality images than those produced by GANs. A flurry of papers followed, proposing improvements and modifications that pushed the quality up even further. By late 2021, models like GLIDE showcased incredible results on text-to-image tasks. Just a few months later, these models had entered the mainstream with tools like DALL·E 2 and Stable Diffusion. These models made it easy for anyone to generate images just by typing in a text description of what they wanted to see.

In this chapter, we will dig into how these models work. We'll outline the key insights that make them so powerful, generate images with existing models to get a feel for how they work, and then train our own to deepen this understanding further. The field is still rapidly evolving, but the topics covered here should give you a solid foundation to build on, which will be extended further in Chapters 5, 7, and 8.

The high-level idea of diffusion models is that they receive images blurred with noise and learn to denoise them, outputting a clear image. When diffusion models are trained, the dataset contains images with different amounts of noise (even when the input is pure noise). In inference, we can begin with pure noise, and the model will generate an image that matches the training distribution. The model does multiple iterations to accomplish this, correcting itself and leading to impressively high-quality generations.

# The Key Insight: Iterative Refinement

So, what is it that makes diffusion models so powerful? Previous techniques, such as VAEs or GANs, generate their final output via a single forward pass of the model. This means the model must get everything right on the first try. If it makes a mistake, it can't go back and fix it. Diffusion models, on the other hand, generate their output by iterating over many steps.[1] This *iterative refinement* allows the model to correct mistakes in previous steps and gradually improve the output. To illustrate this, Figure 4-1 shows an example of a diffusion model in action.

*Figure 4-1. Progressive denoising process*

We can load a pretrained diffusion model using the Hugging Face *diffusers* library. The library provides a high-level pipeline that can be used to create images directly. We'll load the ddpm-celebahq-256 model (*https://oreil.ly/AoJQf*), one of the first shared diffusion models for image generation. This model was trained with the CelebA-HQ dataset, a then-popular dataset of high-quality images of celebrities, so it will generate images that look like they came from that dataset. We'll use this model to generate an image from noise:

```
import torch
from diffusers import DDPMPipeline

from genaibook.core import get_device

# Set the device to use our GPU or CPU
device = get_device()

# Load the pipeline
image_pipe = DDPMPipeline.from_pretrained("google/ddpm-celebahq-256")
image_pipe.to(device)
```

---

1 There's a lot of research about reducing the number of diffusion steps in inference; please check Challenge 2 in "Challenges" on page 147 for an initial glimpse into the area.

```
# Sample an image
image_pipe().images[0]
```

The pipeline does not show us what happens under the hood, so let's dive into its internals. If you run the code, you will notice that generation took 1,000 steps. This diffusion pipeline has to go through 1,000 refinement steps (and forward passes) to get to the final image. This is one of the major drawbacks of the vanilla diffusion models compared to the GANs—they require many steps to generate high-quality images, making the models slow at inference time.

We can re-create this *sampling* process step-by-step to understand better what is happening under the hood. At the beginning of the diffusion process, we initialize our sample x with a batch of four random images (in other words, we sample some random noise). We'll run 30 steps to progressively denoise the input images and end up with a sample from the real distribution.

Let's generate some images! On the left side of the following image, you can see the input at a given step (beginning with the random noise). You can see the model's prediction for the final images on the right. The results of the first row are not particularly good. Instead of jumping right to that final predicted image in a given diffusion step, we only modify the input x (shown on the left) by a small amount in the direction of the prediction. We then feed this new, slightly better x through the model again for the next step, hopefully resulting in a slightly improved prediction, which can be used to update x a little more, and so on. With enough steps, the model can produce some impressively realistic images:

```
from genaibook.core import import plot_noise_and_denoise

# The random starting point is a batch of 4 images
# Each image is 3-channel (RGB) 256x256 pixel image
image = torch.randn(4, 3, 256, 256).to(device)

# Set the specific number of diffusion steps
image_pipe.scheduler.set_timesteps(num_inference_steps=30)
```

```
# Loop through the sampling timesteps
for i, t in enumerate(image_pipe.scheduler.timesteps):
    # Get the prediction given the current sample x and the timestep t
    # As we're running inference, we don't need to calculate gradients,
    # so we can use torch.inference_mode().
    with torch.inference_mode():
        # We need to pass in the timestep t so that the model knows what
        # timestep it's currently at. We'll learn more about this in the
        # coming sections.
        noise_pred = image_pipe.unet(image, t)["sample"]

    # Calculate what the updated x should look like with the scheduler
    scheduler_output = image_pipe.scheduler.step(noise_pred, t, image)

    # Update x
    image = scheduler_output.prev_sample

    # Occasionally display both x and the predicted denoised images
    if i % 10 == 0 or i == len(image_pipe.scheduler.timesteps) - 1:
        plot_noise_and_denoise(scheduler_output, i)
```

Don't worry if that chunk of code looks intimidating—we'll explain how this all works throughout this chapter. Focus on the idea for now.

This core idea of learning how to iteratively refine a noisy input can be applied to a wide range of tasks. This chapter will focus on unconditional image generation, generating images that resemble the training data distribution. For example, we can train an unconditional image-generation model with a dataset of butterflies so that it can also generate new, high-quality images. This model would not be able to create images different from the distribution of its training dataset, so don't expect it to generate dinosaurs.

In Chapter 5, we'll do a deep dive into diffusion models conditioned on text, but we can do many other things. Diffusion models have been applied to audio, video, text, 3D objects, protein structures, and other domains. While most implementations use some variant of the denoising approach we'll cover here, emerging approaches that apply different types of "corruption" (always combined with iterative refinement) may move the field beyond the current focus on denoising diffusion.

## Training a Diffusion Model

In this section, we're going to train a diffusion model from scratch to gain a better understanding of how they work. We'll start by using components from the *diffusers* library. As the chapter progresses, we'll gradually demystify how each component works. Training a diffusion model is relatively straightforward compared to other generative models. To train a model, we repeatedly do the following:

1. Load some images from the training data.
2. Add noise in different amounts. Remember, we want the model to do a good job estimating how to "fix" (denoise) both extremely noisy images and images that are close to perfect, so we want a dataset with diverse amounts of noise.
3. Feed the noisy versions of the inputs into the model.
4. Evaluate how well the model does at denoising these inputs.
5. Use this information to update the model weights.

To generate new images with a trained model, we begin with a completely random input and repeatedly feed it through the model, updating the input on each iteration by a small amount based on the model prediction. As we'll see, several sampling methods streamline this process to generate good images with as few steps as possible.

# The Data

For this example, we'll use a dataset of images from the Hugging Face Hub—specifically, a collection of 1,000 butterfly pictures (*https://oreil.ly/HTDlA*).[2] Later on, in "Project Time: Train Your Diffusion Model" on page 145, you will see how to use your own data. Let's load the butterflies dataset:

```
from datasets import load_dataset

dataset = load_dataset("huggan/smithsonian_butterflies_subset", split="train")
```

We must prepare the data before using it to train a model. Images are typically represented as a grid of pixels. Unlike in the previous chapter, where we used grayscale images, these images are in color. Each pixel is represented with color values between 0 and 255 for each of the three color channels (red, green, and blue). To process these and make them ready for training, we do the following:

1. Resize them to a fixed size. This is necessary because the model expects all images to have the same dimensions.

2. (Optional) Add some augmentation by randomly flipping them horizontally, making the model more robust and allowing us to train with more data. Augmentation (Figure 4-2) is a common practice in Computer Vision tasks, as it helps the model generalize better to unseen data. Flipping is just one technique of augmentation with image data. Other techniques are translating, scaling, and rotating.

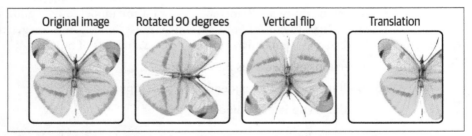

*Figure 4-2. Augmentation creates more data from the training dataset, improving generalization*

3. Convert them to a PyTorch tensor (representing the color values as floats between 0 and 1). Model inputs must always be formatted as multidimensional matrices, or tensors.

---

2 This is a subset of a dataset compiled by Ceyda Cinarel with butterflies extracted from the Smithsonian Institute.

4. Normalize them to have a mean of 0, with values between −1 and 1. This is a common practice in training deep learning models, as it helps the model learn faster and more effectively.

We can define these transformations by using `torchvision.transforms`:[3]

```
from torchvision import transforms

image_size = 64

# Define transformations
preprocess = transforms.Compose(
    [
        transforms.Resize((image_size, image_size)),  # Resize
        transforms.RandomHorizontalFlip(),  # Randomly flip (data augmentation)
        transforms.ToTensor(),  # Convert to tensor (0, 1)
        transforms.Normalize([0.5], [0.5]),  # Map to (-1, 1)
    ]
)
```

The *datasets* library provides a convenient method, `set_transform()`, which allows us to specify transformations that will be applied on the fly as the data is used. Finally, we can wrap the dataset with a `DataLoader`, a loading utility that makes it easy to iterate over batches of data, simplifying our training code:

```
def transform(examples):
    examples = [preprocess(image) for image in examples["image"]]
    return {"images": examples}


dataset.set_transform(transform)
batch_size = 16

train_dataloader = torch.utils.data.DataLoader(
    dataset, batch_size=batch_size, shuffle=True
)
```

We can check that this worked by loading a batch and inspecting the images. Here's an example batch from the training set:[4]

```
from genaibook.core import import show_images

batch = next(iter(train_dataloader))
```

---

3 *torchvision* is a PyTorch library that provides a wide range of tools for working with images. In the book, we'll use this library only for data preprocessing transformations.

4 We used images larger than 64 × 64 to print beautiful butterflies in the book instead of pixelated ones.

```
# When we normalized, we mapped (0, 1) to (-1, 1)
# Now we map back to (0, 1) for display
show_images(batch["images"][:8] * 0.5 + 0.5)
```

## Adding Noise

How do we gradually corrupt our data? The most common approach is to add noise
to the images. We will add different amounts of noise to the training data, as the goal
is to train a robust model to denoise no matter how much noise is in the input. The
amount of noise we add is controlled by a noise schedule, which is a critical aspect of
diffusion models. Different papers and approaches tackle this in different ways.

For now, let's explore one common approach in action based on the DDPM paper
(*http://arxiv.org/abs/2006.11239*). In *diffusers*, adding noise is handled by a class called
a Scheduler, which takes in a batch of images and a list of timesteps and determines
how to create the noisy versions of those images. We'll explore the math behind this
later in the chapter, but for now, let's see how it works in practice. The following code
snippet applies increasingly larger amounts of noise to each one of the input images:

```
from diffusers import DDPMScheduler

# We'll learn about beta_start and beta_end in the next sections
scheduler = DDPMScheduler(
    num_train_timesteps=1000, beta_start=0.001, beta_end=0.02
)

# Create a tensor with 8 evenly spaced values from 0 to 999
timesteps = torch.linspace(0, 999, 8).long()

# We load 8 images from the dataset and
# add increasing amounts of noise to them
x = batch["images"][:8]
```

```
noise = torch.rand_like(x)
noised_x = scheduler.add_noise(x, noise, timesteps)
show_images((noised_x * 0.5 + 0.5).clip(0, 1))
```

During training, we'll pick the timesteps at random. The scheduler takes some parameters (`beta_start` and `beta_end`), which it uses to determine how much noise should be present for a given timestep. We will cover schedulers in more detail in "In Depth: Noise Schedules" on page 126.

## The UNet

The *UNet* is a CNN invented for tasks such as image segmentation, where the desired output has the same shape as the input. For example, UNets are used in medical imaging to segment different anatomical structures.

As shown in Figure 4-3, the UNet consists of a series of *downsampling* layers that reduce the spatial size of the input, followed by a series of *upsampling* layers that increase the spatial extent of the input again. The downsampling layers are typically followed by skip connections that connect the downsampling layers' outputs to the upsampling layers' inputs. This allows the upsampling layers to incorporate finer details from earlier layers, preserving important high-resolution information during the denoising process.

The UNet architecture used in the *diffusers* library is more advanced than the original UNet proposed in 2015 (*http://arxiv.org/abs/1505.04597*), with additions like attention and residual blocks. We'll take a closer look later, but the key idea here is that it can take in an input and produce a prediction that is the same shape. In diffusion models, the input can be a noisy image, and the output can be the predicted noise. With this information, we can now denoise the input image.

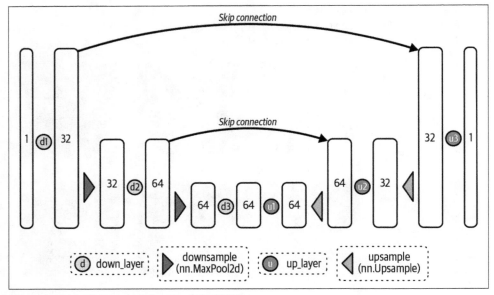

*Figure 4-3. Architecture of a simplified UNet*

Here's how we might create a UNet and feed our batch of noisy images through it:

```python
from diffusers import UNet2DModel

model = UNet2DModel(
    in_channels=3,   # 3 channels for RGB images
    sample_size=64,  # Specify our input size
    # The number of channels per block affects the model size
    block_out_channels=(64, 128, 256, 512),
    down_block_types=(
        "DownBlock2D",
        "DownBlock2D",
        "AttnDownBlock2D",
        "AttnDownBlock2D",
    ),
    up_block_types=("AttnUpBlock2D", "AttnUpBlock2D", "UpBlock2D", "UpBlock2D"),
).to(device)

# Pass a batch of data through to make sure it works
with torch.inference_mode():
    out = model(noised_x.to(device), timestep=timesteps.to(device)).sample

print(noised_x.shape)
print(out.shape)

torch.Size([8, 3, 64, 64])
torch.Size([8, 3, 64, 64])
```

Note that the output is the same shape as the input, which is exactly what we want.

# Training

Now that we have our data and model ready, let's train it. For each training step, we do the following:

1. Load a batch of images.

2. Add noise to the images. The amount of noise added depends on a specified number of timesteps: the more timesteps, the more noise. As mentioned, we want our model to denoise images with little noise and images with lots of noise. To achieve this, we'll add random amounts of noise, so we'll pick a random number of timesteps.

3. Feed the noisy images into the model.

4. Calculate the loss using MSE. MSE is a common loss function for regression tasks, including the UNet model's noise prediction. It measures the average squared difference between predicted and true values, penalizing larger errors more. In the UNet model, MSE is calculated between predicted and actual noise, helping the model generate more realistic images by minimizing the loss. This is called the noise or epsilon objective.

5. Backpropagate the loss and update the model weights with the optimizer.

Here's what all of that looks like in code. Training will take a while, so this is a great moment to pause, review the chapter's content, or get some food:

```python
from torch.nn import functional as F

num_epochs = 50  # How many runs through the data should we do?
lr = 1e-4  # What learning rate should we use
optimizer = torch.optim.AdamW(model.parameters(), lr=lr)
losses = []  # Somewhere to store the loss values for later plotting

# Train the model (this takes a while)
for epoch in range(num_epochs):
    for batch in train_dataloader:
        # Load the input images
        clean_images = batch["images"].to(device)

        # Sample noise to add to the images
        noise = torch.randn(clean_images.shape).to(device)

        # Sample a random timestep for each image
        timesteps = torch.randint(
            0,
            scheduler.config.num_train_timesteps,
            (clean_images.shape[0],),
            device=device,
        ).long()
```

```
# Add noise to the clean images according
# to the noise magnitude at each timestep
noisy_images = scheduler.add_noise(clean_images, noise, timesteps)

# Get the model prediction for the noise
# The model also uses the timestep as an input
# for additional conditioning
noise_pred = model(noisy_images, timesteps, return_dict=False)[0]

# Compare the prediction with the actual noise
loss = F.mse_loss(noise_pred, noise)

# Store the loss for later plotting
losses.append(loss.item())

# Update the model parameters with the optimizer based on this loss
loss.backward()
optimizer.step()
optimizer.zero_grad()
```

Now that the model is trained, let's plot the training loss:

```
from matplotlib import pyplot as plt

plt.subplots(1, 2, figsize=(12, 4))

plt.subplot(1, 2, 1)
plt.plot(losses)
plt.title("Training loss")
plt.xlabel("Training step")

plt.subplot(1, 2, 2)
plt.plot(range(400, len(losses)), losses[400:])
plt.title("Training loss from step 400")
plt.xlabel("Training step");
```

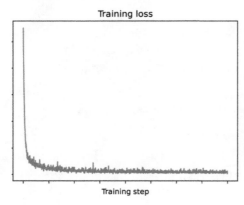

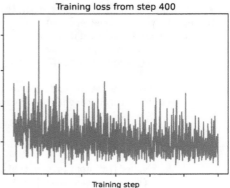

The loss curve on the left shows all the steps, while that on the right skips the first 400 steps. The loss curve trends downward as the model learns to denoise the images. The curve is somewhat noisy—the loss is not very stable. This is because each iteration uses different numbers of noising time steps. It is hard to tell whether this model will be good at generating samples by looking at the MSE of the noise predictions, so let's move on to the next section and see how well it does.

## Sampling

Now that we have a model, let's do inference and generate some images. The *diffusers* library uses the idea of pipelines to bundle together all the components needed to generate samples with a diffusion model. We can use a pipeline to test the UNet we just trained; a few generations are shown as follows:[5]

```
pipeline = DDPMPipeline(unet=model, scheduler=scheduler)
ims = pipeline(batch_size=4).images
show_images(ims, nrows=1)
```

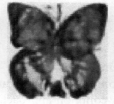

Offloading the job of creating samples to the pipeline doesn't show us what is going on under the hood. So, let's do a simple sampling loop showing how the model gradually refines the input image based on the code in the pipeline's `call()` method:

```
# Random starting point (4 random images):
sample = torch.randn(4, 3, 64, 64).to(device)

for t in scheduler.timesteps:
    # Get the model prediction
    with torch.inference_mode():
        noise_pred = model(sample, t)["sample"]

    # Update sample with step
    sample = scheduler.step(noise_pred, t, sample).prev_sample

show_images(sample.clip(-1, 1) * 0.5 + 0.5, nrows=1)
```

---

5 The images were generated by the model we trained at a resolution of 64 × 64 and upscaled, so they'll look pixelated.

This is the same code we used at the beginning of the chapter to illustrate the idea of iterative refinement, but now you better understand what is happening here. If you look at the implementation of the DDPMPipeline in the *diffusers* library, you'll see that the logic closely resembles our implementation in the previous snippet.

We start with a completely random input, which the model then refines in a series of steps. Each step is a small update to the input based on the model's prediction for the noise at that timestep. We're still abstracting away some complexity behind the call to pipeline.scheduler.step(); later, we will dive deeper into different sampling methods and how they work.

## Evaluation

Evaluating generative models is complex—it's a subjective task in nature. For example, given an input prompt "image of a cat with sunglasses", there are many potential correct generations. A common approach is to combine qualitative evaluation (e.g., by having humans compare generations) and quantitative metrics, which provide a framework for evaluation but don't necessarily correspond to high image quality.

Fréchet Inception Distance (FID) scores can evaluate generative model performance. FID scores compare how similar two image datasets are. Using a pretrained neural network (an example is shown in Figure 4-4), they measure how closely generated samples match real samples by comparing statistics between feature maps extracted from both datasets. The lower the score, the better the quality and realism of generated images produced by a given model. FID scores are popular because of their ability to provide an "objective" comparison metric for different types of generative networks without relying on human judgment.

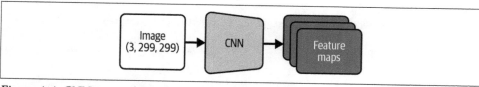

*Figure 4-4. CNN network used to extract feature maps from images*

As convenient as FID scores are, there are important caveats to be aware of (which might be true for other evaluation metrics as well):

- FID scores are designed to compare two distributions. Because of this, it assumes that we have access to a source dataset for comparison. A second issue is that you cannot calculate the FID score of a single generation. If we have one image, there's no way to calculate its FID score.

- The FID score for a given model depends on the number of samples used to calculate it, so when comparing models, we need to make sure both reported scores are calculated using the same number of samples. The common practice is to use 50,000 samples for this purpose, although to save time, you may evaluate a smaller number during development and do the complete evaluation only after you're ready to publish the results.

- The FID can be sensitive to many factors. For example, a different number of inference steps will lead to a very different FID. The scheduler (DDPM in this case) will also affect the FID.

- When calculating the FID, images are resized to 299 × 299 images. This makes it less useful as a metric for extremely low- or high-resolution images. There are also minor differences between how resizing is handled by different deep learning frameworks, which can result in slight differences in the FID score.

- The network used as a feature extractor for FID is typically a model trained on the ImageNet classification task.[6] When generating images in a different domain, the features learned by this model may be less useful. A more accurate approach is to first train a classification network on domain-specific data, making comparing scores between different papers and techniques harder. For now, the ImageNet model is the standard choice.

- If you save generated samples for later evaluation, the format and compression can affect the FID score. Avoid low-quality JPEG images where possible.

Even if you account for all these caveats, FID scores are just a rough measure of quality and do not perfectly capture the nuances of what makes images look more "real." The evaluation of generative models is an active research area. Standard metrics like Kernel Inception Distance (KID) and Inception Score share similar issues with FID. So, use these metrics to get an idea of how one model performs relative to another, but also look at the actual images generated by each model to get a better sense of how they compare.

---

6 ImageNet is one of the most popular Computer Vision benchmarks. It contains millions of images in thousands of categories, making it a popular dataset for training and benchmarking base models.

Image quality, as measured by FID or KID, is only one of the metrics we can use to evaluate the performance of text-to-image models. Efforts such as *Holistic Evaluation of Text-to-Image Models* (HEIM) (*https://oreil.ly/G-o44*) attempt to take into account additional desirable characteristics of text-to-image models, such as prompt adherence, originality, reasoning capabilities, multilingualism, absence of bias and toxicity, and others.

Human preference is still the gold standard for quality in what is ultimately a fairly subjective field. For example, the Parti Prompts dataset (*https://oreil.ly/GebH2*) contains 1,600 prompts of varying difficulties and categories and allows comparing text-to-image models such as the ones we'll explore in Chapter 5.[7]

# In Depth: Noise Schedules

In the preceding training example, one of the steps was to "add noise in different amounts." We achieved this by picking a random timestep between 0 and 1,000 and then relying on the scheduler to add the appropriate amount of noise. Likewise, during inference, we again relied on the scheduler to tell us which timesteps to use and how to move from one to the next, given the model predictions. Choosing how much noise to add is a crucial design decision that can drastically affect the performance of a given model. In this section, we'll see why this is the case and explore different approaches used in practice.

## Why Add Noise?

At the start of this chapter, we said that the key idea behind diffusion models is that of iterative refinement. During training, we *corrupt* an input by different amounts. During inference, we begin with a maximally corrupted input (that is, a pure noise image) and iteratively decorrupt it, expecting to end up with a nice final result eventually.

So far, we've focused on one specific kind of corruption: adding Gaussian noise. Gaussian noise is a type of noise that follows a normal distribution, which as we saw in Chapter 3, has most values around the mean and fewer values as we get further away.[8] One reason for this focus is the theoretical underpinnings of diffusion models, which assume the use of Gaussian noise—if we use a different corruption method, we are no longer technically doing diffusion.

---

7 For a practical deep dive into evaluating diffusion models, we suggest reviewing the *diffusers* library's "Evaluating Diffusion Models" documentation (*https://oreil.ly/KXujR*).

8 The Gaussian noise is added with `torch.rand_like()`.

However, the Cold Diffusion paper (*http://arxiv.org/abs/2208.09392*) demonstrated that we do not necessarily need to constrain ourselves to this method just for theoretical convenience. The authors showed (Figure 4-5) that a diffusion model–like approach works for many corruption methods. That means that rather than using noise, we can use other image transformations. For example, models such as Muse, MaskGIT, and Paella have used random token masking or replacement as equivalent corruption methods.

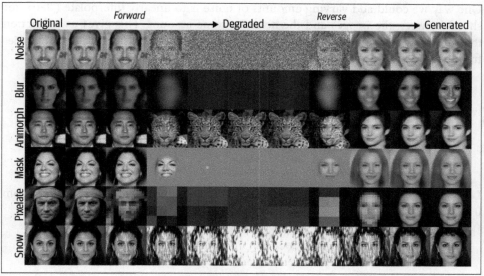

*Figure 4-5. The general principles of diffusion work for other types of corruption, not just Gaussian noise (adapted from an image in the Cold Diffusion paper (https:// arxiv.org/pdf/2208.09392))*

Nonetheless, adding noise remains the most popular approach for several reasons:

- We can easily control the amount of noise added, giving a smooth transition from "perfect" to "completely corrupted." This is not the case for something like reducing the resolution of an image, which may result in "discrete" transitions.

- We can have many valid random starting points for inference, unlike some methods, which may have only a limited number of possible initial (fully corrupted) states, such as a completely black image or a single-pixel image.

So, for now, we'll add noise as our corruption method. Next, let's explore how we add noise to our images.

# Starting Simple

We have some images, x, and we'd like to add some random noise to them. We generate pure Gaussian noise of the same dimensions as the input images with `torch.rand_like()`:

```
x = next(iter(train_dataloader))["images"][:8]
noise = torch.rand_like(x)
```

One way we could add varying amounts of noise is to linearly interpolate ("lerp" for short) between the images and the noise by some amount. This gives us a function that smoothly transitions from the original image x to pure noise as the amount varies from 0 to 1:

```
def corrupt(x, noise, amount):
    # Reshape amount so it works correctly with the original data
    amount = amount.view(-1, 1, 1, 1)  # make sure it's broadcastable

    # Blend the original data and noise based on the amount
    return (
        x * (1 - amount) + noise * amount
    )  # equivalent to x.lerp(noise, amount)
```

Let's see this in action on a batch of data, with the amount of noise varying from 0 to 1:

```
amount = torch.linspace(0, 1, 8)
noised_x = corrupt(x, noise, amount)
show_images(noised_x * 0.5 + 0.5)
```

---

This is doing what we want: smoothly transitioning from the original image to pure noise. We've created a noise schedule with the *continuous time* approach, where we represent the full path on a time scale from 0 to 1. Other approaches use a *discrete time* approach, with a large integer number of *timesteps* used to define the noise scheduler. We can wrap our function into a class that converts from continuous time to discrete timesteps and adds noise appropriately:

```python
class SimpleScheduler:
    def __init__(self):
        self.num_train_timesteps = 1000

    def add_noise(self, x, noise, timesteps):
        amount = timesteps / self.num_train_timesteps
        return corrupt(x, noise, amount)


scheduler = SimpleScheduler()
timesteps = torch.linspace(0, 999, 8).long()
noised_x = scheduler.add_noise(x, noise, timesteps)
show_images(noised_x * 0.5 + 0.5)
```

Now we have something we can directly compare to the schedulers used in the *diffusers* library, such as the DDPMScheduler we used during training. Let's see how it compares:

```python
scheduler = DDPMScheduler(beta_end=0.01)
timesteps = torch.linspace(0, 999, 8).long()
noised_x = scheduler.add_noise(x, noise, timesteps)
show_images((noised_x * 0.5 + 0.5).clip(0, 1))
```

If you compare the results from our scheduler with those of `DDPMScheduler`, you may notice that they are not exactly the same, but they're similar enough to explore training the model with our noise scheduler.

## The Math

Let's dive into the underlying math that explains how noise is added to the original images. One thing to remember is that there are many notations and approaches in the literature. For example, in some papers, the noise schedule is parametrized continuously, so `t` runs from 0 (no noise) to 1 (fully corrupted), as we did in our `corrupt` function. Other papers use a discrete time approach in which the timesteps are integers and run from 0 to a large number `T`, typically 1,000. It is possible to convert between these two approaches the way we did with our `SimpleScheduler` class—make sure you're consistent when comparing different models. We'll stick with the discrete time approach here.

A good place to start for going deeper into the math is the DDPM paper or the "Annotated Diffusion Model" blog post (*https://oreil.ly/mFHxe*). If you feel this section is too dense, it's OK to focus on the high-level concepts and come back to the math later on.

Let's kick things off by defining how to do a single noise step to go from timestep $t - 1$ to timestep $t$. As mentioned earlier, the idea is to add Gaussian noise ($\epsilon$). The noise has unit variance, which controls the spread of the noise values. By adding this noise to the previous step's image, we gradually corrupt the original image, which is a key part of the diffusion model's training process:

$$\mathbf{x}_t = \mathbf{x}_{t-1} + \epsilon$$

To control the amount of noise added at each step, let's introduce $\beta_t$. This parameter is defined for all timesteps $t$ and specifies how much noise should be added at each step. In other words, $\mathbf{x}_t$ is a mix of $\mathbf{x}_{t-1}$ and some random noise scaled by $\beta_t$. This allows us to gradually increase the amount of noise added to the image as we move through the timesteps, which is a key part of the diffusion model's training process:

$$\mathbf{x}_t = \sqrt{1 - \beta_t}\mathbf{x}_{t-1} + \sqrt{\beta_t}\epsilon$$

We can further define the noise addition process as a distribution, where the noisy $\mathbf{x}_t$ has a mean $\sqrt{1 - \beta_t}\mathbf{x}_{t-1}$ and a variance of $\beta_t$. This distribution helps us model the noise addition process more accurately. This is what the formula looks like in distribution form:

$$q(\mathbf{x}_t | \mathbf{x}_{t-1}) = \mathcal{N}\left(\mathbf{x}_t; \sqrt{1 - \beta_t}\mathbf{x}_{t-1}, \beta_t\mathbf{I}\right)$$

We've now defined a distribution to sample $x$ conditioned on the previous value. To get the noisy input at timestep $t$, we could begin at $t = 0$ and repeatedly apply this single step, which would be very inefficient. Instead, we can find a formula to move to any timestep $t$ in one go by doing the *reparameterization trick*. The idea is to precompute the noise schedule, which is defined by the $\beta_t$ values. We can then define $\alpha_t = 1 - \beta_t$ and $\bar{\alpha}$ as the cumulative product of all the $\alpha$ values up to time $t$, which can be expressed as $\bar{\alpha}_t := \Pi_{s=1}^{t}\alpha_s$. Using these tools and notation, we can redefine the distribution and how to sample at a particular time. The new distribution, $q(\mathbf{x}_t | \mathbf{x}_{t-1})$, has a mean of $\bar{\alpha}_t\mathbf{x}_{t-1}$ and a variance of $(1 - \bar{\alpha}_t)\mathbf{I}$:

$$q(\mathbf{x}_t | \mathbf{x}_{t-1}) = \mathcal{N}(\mathbf{x}_t; \bar{\alpha}_t\mathbf{x}_{t-1}, (1 - \bar{\alpha}_t)\mathbf{I})$$

Exploring this reparameterization trick is part of the challenges at the end of the chapter. We can now sample a noisy image at timestep $t$ by using the following formula:

$$x_t = \sqrt{\bar{\alpha}_t}x_0 + \sqrt{1 - \bar{\alpha}_t}\epsilon$$

The equation for $x_t$ shows that the noisy input at timestep $t$ is a combination of the original image $x_0$ (scaled by $\sqrt{\bar{\alpha}_t}$) and $\epsilon$ (scaled by $\sqrt{1 - \bar{\alpha}_t}$). Note that we can now calculate a sample directly without looping over all previous timesteps, making it much more efficient for training diffusion models.

In the *diffusers* library, the $\bar{\alpha}$ values are stored in `scheduler.alphas_cumprod`. Knowing this, we can plot the scaling factors for the original image $x_0$ and the noise $\epsilon$ across the different timesteps for a given scheduler. The *diffusers* library allows us to control the beta values by defining its initial value (`beta_start`), final value (`beta_end`), and how the values will step, for example, linearly (`beta_schedule="linear"`). The following plot for the `DDPMScheduler` describes the amount of noise (orange line) added to the input image (blue line). We can see that the noise is scaled up more as we have more timesteps, as expected:

```
from genaibook.core import plot_scheduler
```

```
plot_scheduler(
    DDPMScheduler(beta_start=0.001, beta_end=0.02, beta_schedule="linear")
)
```

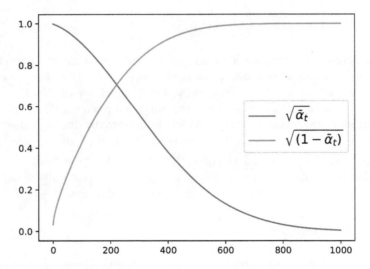

Our `SimpleScheduler` just linearly mixes between the original image and noise, as we can see if we plot the scaling factors (equivalent to $\sqrt{\bar{\alpha}_t}$ and $\sqrt{(1 - \bar{\alpha}_t)}$ in the DDPM case):

```
plot_scheduler(SimpleScheduler())
```

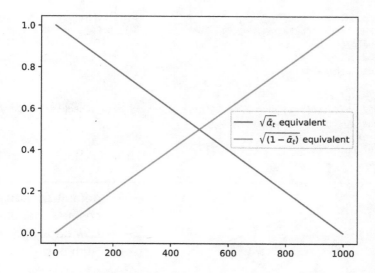

A good noise schedule will ensure the model sees a mix of images at different noise levels. The best choice will differ based on the training data. Visualizing a few more options, note the following:

- Setting `beta_end` too low means we never completely corrupt the image, so the model will never see anything like the random noise used as a starting point for inference.

- Setting `beta_end` extremely high means that most of the timesteps are spent on almost complete noise, resulting in poor training performance.

- Different beta schedules give different curves. The cosine schedule is popular, as it smoothly transitions from the original image to the noise.

Let's visualize the comparison of different `DDPMScheduler` schedulers, varying hyperparameters and $\beta$ schedules, with the following plot:

```
fig, (ax) = plt.subplots(1, 1, figsize=(8, 5))
plot_scheduler(
    DDPMScheduler(beta_schedule="linear"),
    label="default schedule",
    ax=ax,
    plot_both=False,
)
plot_scheduler(
    DDPMScheduler(beta_schedule="squaredcos_cap_v2"),
    label="cosine schedule",
    ax=ax,
    plot_both=False,
)
```

```
plot_scheduler(
    DDPMScheduler(beta_start=0.001, beta_end=0.003, beta_schedule="linear"),
    label="Low beta_end",
    ax=ax,
    plot_both=False,
)
plot_scheduler(
    DDPMScheduler(beta_start=0.001, beta_end=0.1, beta_schedule="linear"),
    label="High beta_end",
    ax=ax,
    plot_both=False,
)
```

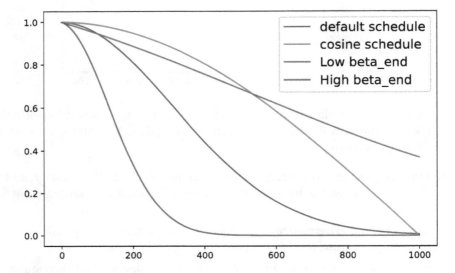

 All the schedules shown here are called *variance preserving* (VP), meaning that the variance of the model input is kept close to 1 across the entire schedule. You may also encounter *variance exploding* (VE), formulations where noise is added to the original image in different amounts (resulting in high-variance inputs). Our `SimpleScheduler` is almost a VP schedule, but the variance is not quite preserved because of the linear interpolation.

The importance of exposing the model to a good mix of noised images—including pure noise, which is the initial state for inference—was explored in a paper titled "Common Diffusion Noise Schedules and Sample Steps Are Flawed" (*https://arxiv.org/abs/2305.08891*), which showed that some diffusion models were not able to generate images too bright or too dark because the training schedule didn't cover all states. As with many diffusion-related topics, a constant stream of new papers is exploring the topic of noise schedules, so by the time you read this, there will likely be an extensive collection of options to try out.[9]

## Effect of Input Resolution and Scaling

One aspect of noise schedules that has mostly been overlooked until recently is the effect of the input size and scaling. Many papers test potential schedulers on small-scale datasets and at low resolution and then use the best-performing scheduler to train their final models on larger images. The problem with this can be seen if we add the same amount of noise to two images of different sizes, as shown in Figure 4-6.

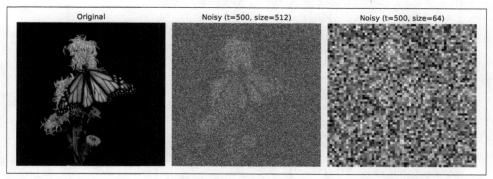

*Figure 4-6. Applying the same amount of input noise to images with different resolutions*

Images at high resolution tend to contain a lot of redundant information. This means that even if a single pixel is obscured by noise, the surrounding pixels have enough information to reconstruct the original image. This is different for low-resolution images, where a single pixel can contain a lot of useful information. Adding the same amount of noise to a low-resolution image will result in a much more corrupted image than adding the equivalent amount of noise to a high-resolution image.

Two independent papers from early 2023 thoroughly investigated this effect. Each used the new insights to train models capable of generating high-resolution outputs without requiring any of the tricks that have previously been necessary. Simple diffusion (*http://arxiv.org/abs/2301.11093*) introduced a method for adjusting the noise schedule based on the input size, allowing a schedule optimized on low-resolution images to be appropriately modified for a new target resolution. The other paper (*http://arxiv.org/abs/2301.10972*) performed similar experiments and noted another critical variable: input scaling. That is, how do we represent our images? If the images are represented as floats between 0 and 1, they will have a lower variance than the

---

9 The *diffusers* documentation page on schedulers (*https://oreil.ly/EFrxh*) can be a good place to get started with the multiple schedulers variants.

noise (typically unit variance). Thus, the signal-to-noise ratio will be lower for a given noise level than if the images were represented as floats between −1 and 1 (which we used in the preceding training example) or something else. Scaling the input images shifts the signal-to-noise ratio, so modifying this scaling is another way to adjust when training on larger images. This paper, in fact, recommends input scaling as an easy way to adapt training for different image sizes. It is also possible to adjust the noise schedule depending on the resolution, but then it's more difficult to find the optimal schedule because several hyperparameters are involved. Here we see the effect of input scaling:

```python
import numpy as np
from genaibook.core import load_image, SampleURL

scheduler = DDPMScheduler(beta_end=0.05, beta_schedule="scaled_linear")
image = load_image(
    SampleURL.DogExample,
    size=((512, 512)),
    return_tensor=True,
)

t = torch.tensor(300)  # The timestep we're noising to
scales = np.linspace(0.1, 1.0, 4)

images = [image]
noise = torch.randn_like(image)
for b in reversed(scales):
    noised = (
        scheduler.add_noise(b * (image * 2 - 1), noise, t).clip(-1, 1) * 0.5
        + 0.5
    )
    images.append(noised)

show_images(
    images[1:],
    nrows=1,
    titles=[f"Scale: {b}" for b in reversed(scales)],
    figsize=(15, 5),
)
```

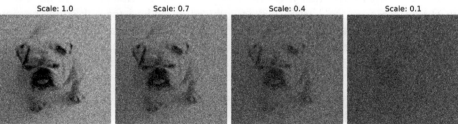

All the images have the same input noise applied, corresponding to step t=300, but we multiply the input image by different scale factors. The noise is more noticeable as the scale affects the image more. The scale also decreases the dynamic range (or variance), resulting in darker-looking inputs.[10]

# In Depth: UNets and Alternatives

Let's address the actual model that makes the all-important predictions. To recap, this model must be capable of taking in a noisy image and outputting its noise, hence enabling denoising the input image. This requires a model that can take in an image of arbitrary size and output an image of the same size. Furthermore, the model should be able to make precise predictions at the pixel level while capturing higher-level information about the image. A popular approach is to use an architecture called a UNet. UNets were invented in 2015 for medical image segmentation and have since become a popular choice for various image-related tasks.

Like the AutoEncoders and VAEs we looked at in the previous chapter, UNets are made up of a series of *downsampling* and *upsampling* blocks. The downsampling blocks are responsible for reducing the image size, while the upsampling blocks are responsible for increasing the image size. The downsampling blocks typically comprise a series of convolutional layers, followed by a pooling or downsampling layer.[11] The upsampling blocks generally include a series of convolutional layers, followed by an upsampling or transposed convolution layer. The transposed convolution layer is a particular type of convolutional layer that increases the size of the image rather than reducing it.

Regular AutoEncoders and VAE are not good choices for this task because they are less capable of making precise predictions at the pixel level since they must reconstruct the images from the low-dimensional latent space. In a UNet, the downsampling and upsampling blocks are connected by *skip connections*, which allow information to flow directly from the downsampling blocks to the upsampling blocks. This allows the model to make precise predictions at the pixel level while also capturing higher-level information about the image as a whole.

---

10 In this regime, input images are normalized before being passed to the model to not reduce variance so drastically.

11 *Pooling* is the method to choose the information to preserve when downsampling the output from a previous layer. Common strategies include *average pooling*, which reduces a patch to its average value, or *max pooling*, which selects the maximum value in a given patch. Pooling is applied independently to all the channels of the input tensor.

## A Simple UNet

To better understand the structure of a UNet, let's build a simple one from scratch. Figure 4-7 shows the architecture diagram of a basic UNET.

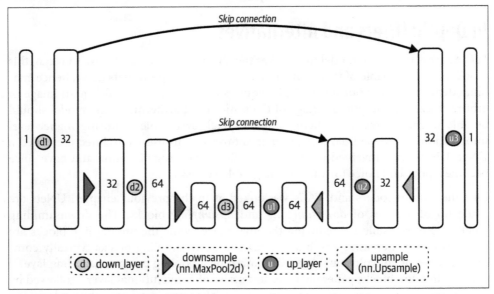

*Figure 4-7. Architecture of a basic UNet*

We'll design a UNet that works with single-channel images (e.g., grayscale images), which we could use to build a diffusion model for datasets such as MNIST. We'll use three layers in the downsampling path and another three in the upsampling path. Each layer consists of a convolution followed by an activation function and an upsampling or downsampling step, depending on whether they are in the encoding or decoding path. The skip connections, as mentioned, directly connect the downsampling blocks to the upsampling ones. There are multiple ways to implement the skip connections.

One approach, which we'll use here, is to add the output of the downsampling block to the input of the corresponding upsampling block. Another method is concatenating the downsampling block's output to the upsampling block's input. We could even add some additional layers in the skip connections.

Let's keep things simple for now with the initial approach. Here's what this network looks like in code:

```python
from torch import nn


class BasicUNet(nn.Module):
    """A minimal UNet implementation."""

    def __init__(self, in_channels=1, out_channels=1):
        super().__init__()
        self.down_layers = nn.ModuleList(
            [
                nn.Conv2d(in_channels, 32, kernel_size=5, padding=2),
                nn.Conv2d(32, 64, kernel_size=5, padding=2),
                nn.Conv2d(64, 64, kernel_size=5, padding=2),
            ]
        )
        self.up_layers = nn.ModuleList(
            [
                nn.Conv2d(64, 64, kernel_size=5, padding=2),
                nn.Conv2d(64, 32, kernel_size=5, padding=2),
                nn.Conv2d(32, out_channels, kernel_size=5, padding=2),
            ]
        )

        # Use the SiLU activation function, which has been shown to work well
        # due to different properties (smoothness, non-monotonicity, etc.).
        self.act = nn.SiLU()
        self.downscale = nn.MaxPool2d(2)
        self.upscale = nn.Upsample(scale_factor=2)

    def forward(self, x):
        h = []
        for i, l in enumerate(self.down_layers):
            x = self.act(l(x))
            if i < 2:  # For all but the third (final) down layer:
                h.append(x)  # Storing output for skip connection
                x = self.downscale(x)  # Downscale ready for the next layer

        for i, l in enumerate(self.up_layers):
            if i > 0:  # For all except the first up layer
                x = self.upscale(x)  # Upscale
                x += h.pop()  # Fetching stored output (skip connection)
            x = self.act(l(x))

        return x
```

If you take a grayscale input image of shape (1, 28, 28), the path through the model would be as follows:

1. The image goes through the downscaling block. The first layer, a 2D convolution with 32 filters, will make it of shape [32, 28, 28].

2. The image is then downscaled with max pooling, making it of shape [32, 14, 14]. The MNIST dataset contains white numbers drawn on a black background (where black is represented by the number zero). We choose max pooling to select the largest values in a region and thus focus on the brightest pixels.[12]

3. The image goes through the second downscaling block. The second layer, a 2D convolution with 64 filters, will make it of shape [64, 14, 14].

4. After another downscaling, the shape is [64, 7, 7].

5. There is a third layer in the downscaling block, but no downscaling this time because we are already using very small 7 × 7 blocks. This will keep the shape of [64, 7, 7].

6. We do the same process but in inverse, upscaling to [64, 14, 14], [32, 14, 14], and finally [1, 28, 28].

A diffusion model trained with this architecture on MNIST produces the samples shown in Figure 4-8 (code included in the supplementary material (*https://oreil.ly/ handsonGenAIcode*) but omitted here for brevity).

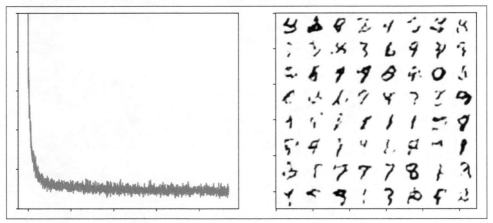

*Figure 4-8. Loss and generations of a basic UNet*

---

12 For visualization purposes, we show MNIST as black numbers on a white background, but the training dataset uses the opposite.

# Improving the UNet

This simple UNet works for this relatively easy task. How can we handle more-complex data? Here are some options:

*Add more parameters*
> This can be accomplished by using multiple convolutional layers in each block, using a larger number of filters in each convolutional layer, or making the network deeper.

*Add normalization, such as batch normalization*
> Batch normalization can help the model learn more quickly and reliably by ensuring that the outputs of each layer are centered around 0 and have a standard deviation of 1.

*Add regularization, such as dropout*
> Dropout helps prevent overfitting to the training data, which is essential when working with smaller datasets.

*Add attention*
> Introducing self-attention layers allows the model to focus on different parts of the image at different times, which can help the UNet learn more-complex functions. Adding transformer-like attention layers also lets us increase the number of learnable parameters. The downside is that attention layers are much more expensive to compute than regular convolutional layers at higher resolutions, so we typically use them only at lower resolutions (e.g., the lower-resolution blocks in the UNet).

For comparison, Figure 4-9 shows the results on MNIST when using the UNet implementation in the *diffusers* library, which features the aforementioned improvements.

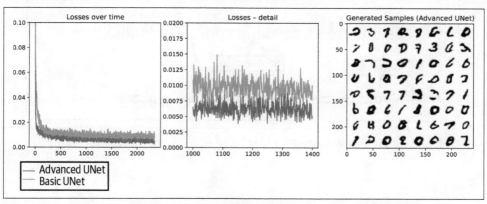

*Figure 4-9. Loss and generations from the diffusers UNet, with several improvements over the basic architecture*

## Alternative Architectures

More recently, several alternative architectures have been proposed for diffusion models (Figure 4-10).

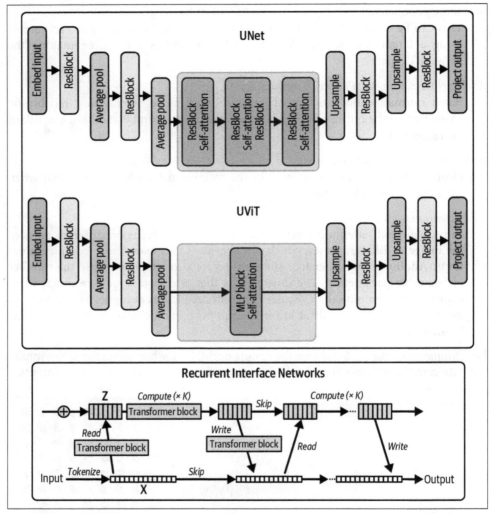

*Figure 4-10. Comparison of UNet with UViT and RIN*

These architectures include the following:

*Transformers*

The Diffusion Transformers paper (*http://arxiv.org/abs/2212.09748*) showed that a transformer-based architecture can train a diffusion model with excellent results. However, the compute and memory requirements of the transformer architecture remain a challenge for very high resolutions.

*UViT*

The UViT architecture from the Simple Diffusion paper aims to get the best of both worlds by replacing the middle layers of the UNet with a large stack of transformer blocks. A key insight of this paper is that focusing most of the compute at the lower-resolution blocks of the UNet allows for more efficient training of high-resolution diffusion models. For very high resolutions, they do some additional preprocessing using something called a wavelet transform to reduce the spatial resolution of the input image while keeping as much information as possible through additional channels, again reducing the amount of compute spent on the higher spatial resolutions.

*Recurrent Interface Networks (RINs)*

The RIN paper (*http://arxiv.org/abs/2212.11972*) takes a similar approach, first mapping the high-resolution inputs to a more manageable and lower-dimensional latent representation, which is then processed by a stack of transformer blocks before being decoded back out to an image. Additionally, the RIN paper introduces the idea of *recurrence*, where information is passed to the model from the previous processing step. This can benefit the iterative improvement that diffusion models are designed to perform.

Some high-quality diffusion transformer models include Flux, Stable Diffusion 3, PixArt-Σ, and the text-to-video Sora. It remains to be seen whether transformer-based approaches completely supplant UNets as the go-to architecture for diffusion models or whether hybrid approaches like the UViT and RIN architectures will be the most effective.

# In Depth: Diffusion Objectives

We've discussed diffusion models taking a noisy input and learning to denoise it. At first glance, you might assume that the network's natural prediction target is the image's denoised version, which we'll call x0. However, we compared the model prediction in the code with the unit-variance noise used to create the noisy version (often called the epsilon objective, eps). The two appear mathematically identical since if we know the noise and the timestep, we can derive x0, and vice versa. While this is true, the objective choice has some subtle effects on how large the loss is at different timesteps and, thus, which noise levels the model learns best to denoise.

Predicting noise is easier for the model than directly predicting the target data. This is because the noise follows a known distribution at each step, and predicting the difference between two steps is often simpler than predicting the absolute values of the target data.

To gain some intuition, let's visualize some different objectives across different timesteps. The input image and the random noise in Figure 4-11 are the same (first two rows in the illustration), but the noised images in the third row have different amounts of added noise depending on the timestep.

*Figure 4-11. Comparing `eps` versus `x0` versus `v` objectives: `eps` tries to predict the noise added at each timestep, `x0` predicts the denoised image, and `v` uses a mixture of the two*

At extremely low noise levels, the `x0` objective is trivially easy (the noised image is almost the same as the input), while predicting the noise accurately is almost impossible. Likewise, at extremely high noise levels, the `eps` objective is straightforward (the noised image is almost equal to the pure noise added), while predicting the denoised image accurately is almost impossible. If we use the `x0` objective, our training will put less weight on lower noise levels.

Neither case is ideal, and so additional objectives have been introduced that have the model predict a mix of `x0` and `eps` at different timesteps. The velocity (`v`) objective, shown in the last row of the illustration, is one such objective, which is defined as $v = \sqrt{\bar{\alpha}} \cdot \epsilon + \sqrt{1 - \bar{\alpha}} \cdot x_0$. The `eps` objective remains one of the most preferred approaches, but it's important to be aware of its disadvantages and the existence of other objectives.

 A group of researchers at NVIDIA worked to unify the different formulations of diffusion models into a consistent framework with a clear separation of design choices. This allowed them to identify changes in the sampling and training processes, resulting in better performance, leading to what is known as k-diffusion. If you're interested in learning more about the different objectives, scalings, and nuances of the diffusion model formulations, we recommend reading the EDM paper (*http://arxiv.org/abs/2206.00364*) for a more in-depth discussion.

## Project Time: Train Your Diffusion Model

OK, that's enough theory. It's now time for you to train your unconditional diffusion model. As before, you'll train a model to generate new images. The main challenge of this project will be creating or finding a good dataset you can use for this.

In case you want to use an existing dataset, a good starting point is to filter for image-classification datasets (*https://oreil.ly/AF8QV*) on the Hugging Face Hub and pick one of your liking. One of the main questions you will want to answer is which part of the dataset you want to use for training. Will you use the whole dataset, as before, so that the model generates digits? Or will you use a specific class (e.g., cats, so that we get a cats expert model)? Or will you use a subset of the dataset (e.g., only images with a certain resolution)?

If you want to upload a new dataset instead, the first step will be to find and access the data. To share a dataset, the most straightforward approach is to use the Image-Folder feature (*https://oreil.ly/RV4Bh*) of the *datasets* library. You can then upload the dataset to the Hugging Face Hub and use it in your project.

Once you have the data, think about the preprocessing steps, the model definition, and the training loop. You can use the code from the chapter as a starting point and modify it to fit your dataset.

## Summary

We started the chapter using high-level pipelines to run inference of diffusion models. We ended up training our diffusion model from scratch and diving into each component. Let's do a brief recap.

The goal is to train a model, usually a UNet, that receives noisy images as input and can predict the noise part of that image. When training our model, we add noise in different magnitudes according to a random number of timesteps. One of the challenges we saw was that to add noise at a high number of steps, 900, for example, we would need to do a high number of noise iterations. To fix this, we use the reparameterization trick, which allows us to obtain the noisy input at a specific timestep directly. The model is trained to minimize the difference between the noise predictions and the actual input noise. For inference, we do an iterative refinement process in which the model refines the initial random input. Rather than keeping the final prediction of a single diffusion step, we iteratively modify the input x by a small amount in the direction of that prediction. This, of course, is one of the reasons doing inference with diffusion models tends to be slow and becomes one of its main disadvantages compared to models like GANs.

The diffusion world is fast-moving, so many advances exist (e.g., the scheduler, the model, the training techniques, and so on). This chapter focused on foundations that will allow us to jump to conditional generation (e.g., generating an image conditioned on an input prompt) and provide a background for you to dive deeper into the diffusion world. Some of the readings through this chapter can help you dive deeper.

For additional readings, we suggest reviewing the following:

- The "Annotated Diffusion Model" blog post (*https://oreil.ly/mFHxe*), which does a technical write-up of the DDPM paper
- Lilian Weng's write-up (*https://oreil.ly/ZEVF4*), which is excellent for a deeper dive into the math
- The "Denoising Diffusion Probabilistic Models" paper (*https://arxiv.org/abs/2006.11239*) itself
- Karras's work on unifying the formulations of diffusion models (*http://arxiv.org/abs/2206.00364*)
- "Simple Diffusion: End-to-End Diffusion for High Resolution Images" (*https://arxiv.org/abs/2301.11093*), which explains how to adjust the sample schedule for different sizes

## Exercises

1. Explain the diffusion inference algorithm.
2. What's the role of the noise scheduler?
3. When creating a training dataset of images, which characteristics are important to watch?
4. Why do we randomly flip training images?
5. How can we evaluate the generations of diffusion models?
6. How do the values of `beta_end` impact the diffusion process?

7. Why do we use UNets rather than VAEs as the main model for diffusion?

8. What benefits and challenges are faced when incorporating techniques from transformers (like attention layers or a transformer-based architecture) to diffusion?

You can find the solutions to these exercises and the following challenges in the book's GitHub repository (*https://oreil.ly/handsonGenAIcode*).

# Challenges

1. *Reparameterization trick.* Show that

$$\mathbf{x}_t = \sqrt{1 - \beta_t}\mathbf{x}_{t-1} + \sqrt{\beta_t}\epsilon$$

is equivalent to

$$\mathbf{x}_t = \sqrt{\overline{\alpha}_t}\mathbf{x}_0 + \sqrt{1 - \overline{\alpha}_t}\epsilon$$

Note that this is not a trivial example and is not required to use diffusion models. We recommend reviewing "A Beginner's Guide to Diffusion Models: Understanding the Basics and Beyond" (*https://oreil.ly/m3SET*) for guidance. An important thing to know is how to merge two Gaussians: if you have two Gaussians with different variance, $\mathcal{N}(\mu_1, \sigma_1^2)$ and $\mathcal{N}(\mu_2, \sigma_2^2)$, the resulting Gaussian is $\mathcal{N}(\mu_1 + \mu_2, \sigma_1^2 + \sigma_2^2)$.

2. *DDIM scheduler.* This chapter uses the DDPM scheduler, sometimes requiring hundreds or thousands of steps to achieve high-quality results. Recent research has explored achieving good generations with as few steps as possible, down to even one or two. The *diffusers* library contains multiple schedulers such as the DDIMScheduler from the "Denoising Diffusion Implicit Models" paper (*https://arxiv.org/abs/2010.02502*). Create some images using the DDIMScheduler. This chapter's sampling section required 1,000 steps with the DDPMScheduler. How many steps are required for you to generate images with similar quality? Experiment switching the scheduler for google/ddpm-celebahq-256 and compare both schedulers.

# References

Bansal, Arpit, et al. "Cold Diffusion: Inverting Arbitrary Image Transforms Without Noise." arXiv, August 19, 2022. *http://arxiv.org/abs/2208.09392*.

Chen, Ting. "On the Importance of Noise Scheduling for Diffusion Models." arXiv, May 21, 2023. *http://arxiv.org/abs/2301.10972*.

Ho, Jonathan, et al. "Denoising Diffusion Probabilistic Models." arXiv, December 16, 2020. *http://arxiv.org/abs/2006.11239*.

Hoogeboom, Emiel, et al. "Simple Diffusion: End-to-End Diffusion for High Resolution Images." arXiv, December 12, 2023. *http://arxiv.org/abs/2301.11093*.

Jabri, Allan, et al. "Scalable Adaptive Computation for Iterative Generation." arXiv, June 13 2023. *http://arxiv.org/abs/2212.11972*.

Karras, Tero, et al. "Elucidating the Design Space of Diffusion-Based Generative Models." arXiv, October 11, 2022. *http://arxiv.org/abs/2206.00364*.

Lee, Tony, et al. "Holistic Evaluation of Text-to-Image Models." arXiv, November 7, 2023. *https://arxiv.org/abs/2311.04287*.

Lin, Shanchuan, et al. "Common Diffusion Noise Schedules and Sample Steps Are Flawed." arXiv, January 23, 2024. *https://arxiv.org/abs/2305.08891*.

Peebles, William, and Saining Xie. "Scalable Diffusion Models with Transformers." arXiv, March 2, 2023. *http://arxiv.org/abs/2212.09748*.

Rogge, Niels, and Kashif Rasul. "The Annotated Diffusion Model." Hugging Face blog, June 7, 2022. *https://oreil.ly/mFHxe*.

Ronneberger, Olaf, et al. "U-Net: Convolutional Networks for Biomedical Image Segmentation." arXiv, May 18, 2015. *http://arxiv.org/abs/1505.04597*.

Song, Jiaming, et al. "Denoising Diffusion Implicit Models." arXiv, October 5, 2022. *https://arxiv.org/abs/2010.02502*.

# CHAPTER 5

# Stable Diffusion and Conditional Generation

In the previous chapter, we introduced diffusion models and the underlying idea of iterative refinement. By the end of the chapter, we could generate images, but training the model was time-consuming, and we had no control over the generated images. In this chapter, we'll see how to go from this to text-conditioned models that can efficiently generate images based on text descriptions, with a model called Stable Diffusion as a case study. Before we get to Stable Diffusionable Diffusion, though, we'll look at how conditional models work and review some of the innovations that led to the text-to-image models we have today.

## Adding Control: Conditional Diffusion Models

Before we tackle the challenge of generating images from text descriptions, let's start with something slightly easier. We'll explore how we can steer our model outputs toward specific types or classes of images. We can use a method called *conditioning*, where the idea is to ask the model to generate not just any image but an image belonging to a predefined class. In this context, conditioning refers to guiding the model's output by providing additional information, such as a label or prompt, during the generation process.

Model conditioning is a simple but effective concept. We'll start from the diffusion model we used in Chapter 4 and introduce a few changes. First, rather than using the butterflies dataset, we'll switch to a dataset that has classes. We'll use Fashion MNIST, a dataset with thousands of images of clothes associated with labels from 10 classes. Then, crucially, we'll provide the model with two inputs: (1) the images, just as before, along with (2) the class label each image belongs to. By doing so, we expect the model to learn the associations between images and labels, helping it understand the distinctive features of sweaters, boots, and other clothing items.

Note that we are not interested in solving a classification problem—we don't want the model to tell us which class the image belongs to. We still want it to perform the same task as in Chapter 4: please generate plausible images that look like they came from this dataset. The only difference is that we are giving it additional information about those images. We'll use the same loss function and training strategy, as it's the same task as before.

## Preparing the Data

We need a dataset with distinct groups of images. Datasets intended for Computer Vision classification tasks are ideal for this purpose. We could start with something like the ImageNet dataset, which contains millions of images across 1,000 classes. However, training models on this dataset would take an extremely long time. When approaching a new problem, starting with a smaller dataset is a good idea to ensure everything works as expected. This keeps the feedback loop short so that we can iterate quickly and ensure we're on the right track.

We could choose MNIST for this example, as in Chapter 4. To make things just a little bit different, we'll choose Fashion MNIST instead. Fashion MNIST, developed and made open source by Zalando (*https://oreil.ly/9q640*), is a replacement for MNIST that shares similar characteristics: a compact size, black-and-white images, and 10 classes. The main difference is that classes correspond to different types of clothing instead of being digits, and the images contain more detail than simple handwritten digits.

Just as in Chapter 3, we'll need to configure *matplotlib* to use reversed gray colors to match the Fashion MNIST dataset. Let's check out some examples:

```
import matplotlib as mpl
from datasets import load_dataset

from genaibook.core import show_images

mpl.rcParams["image.cmap"] = "gray_r"


fashion_mnist = load_dataset("fashion_mnist")
clothes = fashion_mnist["train"]["image"][:8]
classes = fashion_mnist["train"]["label"][:8]
show_images(clothes, titles=classes, figsize=(4, 2.5))
```

So class 0 corresponds to a t-shirt, 2 is a sweater, and 9 is a boot.[1] We prepare our dataset and `DataLoader` similarly to how we did it in Chapter 4, with the main difference that we'll also include the class information as input. Instead of resizing as we did in Chapter 4, we'll pad our image inputs (28 × 28 pixels) to 32 × 32. This will preserve the original image quality, which will help the UNet make higher-quality predictions.[2] Padding helps avoid issues where the operations might crop out or distort edge information:

```python
import torch
from torchvision import transforms

preprocess = transforms.Compose(
    [
        transforms.RandomHorizontalFlip(),  # Randomly flip (data augmentation)
        transforms.ToTensor(),  # Convert to tensor (0, 1)
        transforms.Pad(2),  # Add 2 pixels on all sides
        transforms.Normalize([0.5], [0.5]),  # Map to (-1, 1)
    ]
) ❶


def transform(examples):  ❷
    images = [preprocess(image) for image in examples["image"]]
    return {"images": images, "labels": examples["label"]}  ❸


train_dataset = fashion_mnist["train"].with_transform(transform)  ❹

train_dataloader = torch.utils.data.DataLoader(
    train_dataset, batch_size=256, shuffle=True
) ❺
```

---

1 A list of the 10 categories in Fashion MNIST can be found online (*https://oreil.ly/28Wrg*).

2 In Chapter 4, we resized the butterfly images as they were very large (512 × 283). We resized them to be smaller to speed up training. In this section, our images are small and don't require resizing, but we pad them to 32 × 32 to use powers of 2, which usually play better with the cascaded UNet layers.

❶ Define a series of transformations (flipping, converting to tensor, padding, and normalizing) that will be applied to the images in the dataset.

❷ Process a batch of images using the transformations.

❸ Return a dictionary containing the processed images and their corresponding labels.

❹ Load the dataset's train split. By using `with_transform`, you ensure that items are returned after applying the transformation.

❺ Create a `DataLoader` that will build the batches and shuffle the data, simplifying our code.

## Creating a Class-Conditioned Model

The `UNet` from the *diffusers* library allows for providing custom conditioning information. Here, we create a similar model to the one we used in Chapter 4, but we add a `num_class_embeds` argument to the `UNet` constructor. This argument tells the model we'd like to use class labels as additional conditioning. We'll use 10 as that's the number of classes in Fashion MNIST:

```python
from diffusers import UNet2DModel

model = UNet2DModel(
    in_channels=1,  # 1 channel for grayscale images
    out_channels=1,
    sample_size=32,
    block_out_channels=(32, 64, 128, 256),
    num_class_embeds=10,  # Enable class conditioning
)
```

To make predictions with this model, we must pass in the class labels as additional inputs to the `forward()` method:

```python
x = torch.randn((1, 1, 32, 32))
with torch.inference_mode():
    out = model(x, timestep=7, class_labels=torch.tensor([2])).sample
out.shape

torch.Size([1, 1, 32, 32])
```

We also pass something else to the model as conditioning: the timestep. That's right, even the model from Chapter 4 can be considered a conditional diffusion model. We condition it on the timestep, expecting that knowing how far we are in the diffusion process will help it generate more-realistic images.

Internally, the timestep and the class label are turned into embeddings that the model uses during its forward pass. At multiple stages throughout the UNet, these embeddings are projected onto a dimension that matches the number of channels in a given layer. The embeddings are then added to the outputs of that layer. This means the conditioning information is fed to every block of the UNet, giving the model ample opportunity to learn how to use it effectively.

Embeddings are effective in diffusion models because they provide a compact and dense representation of conditioning information, such as timesteps and class labels, which the model can easily integrate throughout the UNet architecture. The flexibility of embeddings also allows for effective handling of different types of conditioning inputs, whether they are continuous (like timesteps), categorical (like class labels), or even text based (like prompts).

## Training the Model

Adding noise works just as well on grayscale images as on the butterflies from Chapter 4. Let's look at the impact of noise as we do more noising timesteps:

```python
from diffusers import DDPMScheduler

scheduler = DDPMScheduler(
    num_train_timesteps=1000, beta_start=0.001, beta_end=0.02
)
timesteps = torch.linspace(0, 999, 8).long()
batch = next(iter(train_dataloader))

# We load 8 images from the dataset and
# add increasing amounts of noise to them
x = batch["images"][0].expand([8, 1, 32, 32])
noise = torch.rand_like(x)
noised_x = scheduler.add_noise(x, noise, timesteps)
show_images((noised_x * 0.5 + 0.5).clip(0, 1))
```

Our training loop will be almost the same as in Chapter 4, except that we now pass the class labels for conditioning. Note that this is just additional information for the model, but it doesn't affect how we define our loss function in any way. We'll also use *tqdm* to display progress bars during training.

This is a great moment to kick off the training and get a tea, coffee, or drink of your choice. Do not be intimidated by the following code: it's similar to what we've done with unconditional generation. We strongly suggest looking at this code side by side with the code in the previous chapter. Can you find all differences?[3]

The script does the following:

1. Loads a batch of images and their corresponding labels (using `train_dataloader` and *tqdm* to iterate through it)

2. Adds noise to the images based on their timestep (using `scheduler .add_noise()`)

3. Feeds the noisy images into the model, alongside the class labels for conditioning (using `model()`)

4. Calculates the loss

5. Backpropagates the loss and updates the model weights with the optimizer

---

3 Different number of epochs and learning rate, a different epsilon for AdamW, usage of *tqdm* for data loading, loading labels, and passing the labels to the model. The most important part, the conditioning, is a two-line diff.

```python
from torch.nn import functional as F
from tqdm import tqdm

from genaibook.core import get_device

# Initialize the scheduler
scheduler = DDPMScheduler(
    num_train_timesteps=1000, beta_start=0.0001, beta_end=0.02
)

num_epochs = 25
lr = 3e-4
optimizer = torch.optim.AdamW(model.parameters(), lr=lr, eps=1e-5)
losses = []  # To store loss values for plotting

device = get_device()
model = model.to(device)

# Train the model (this takes a while!)
for epoch in (progress := tqdm(range(num_epochs))):
    for step, batch in (
        inner := tqdm(
            enumerate(train_dataloader),
            position=0,
            leave=True,
            total=len(train_dataloader),
        )
    ):
        # Load the input images and classes
        clean_images = batch["images"].to(device)
        class_labels = batch["labels"].to(device)

        # Sample noise to add to the images
        noise = torch.randn(clean_images.shape).to(device)

        # Sample a random timestep for each image
        timesteps = torch.randint(
            0,
            scheduler.config.num_train_timesteps,
            (clean_images.shape[0],),
            device=device,
        ).long()

        # Add noise to the clean images according
        # to the noise magnitude at each timestep
        noisy_images = scheduler.add_noise(clean_images, noise, timesteps)

        # Get the model prediction for the noise
        # Note the use of class_labels
        noise_pred = model(
            noisy_images,
            timesteps,
```

```
        class_labels=class_labels,
        return_dict=False,
    )[0]

    # Compare the prediction with the actual noise
    loss = F.mse_loss(noise_pred, noise)

    # Update loss display
    inner.set_postfix(loss=f"{loss.cpu().item():.3f}")

    # Store the loss for later plotting
    losses.append(loss.item())

    # Backward pass and optimization
    loss.backward()
    optimizer.step()
    optimizer.zero_grad()
```

Once the training is complete, we can plot the training loss to see how the model performed:

```
import matplotlib.pyplot as plt

plt.plot(losses)
```

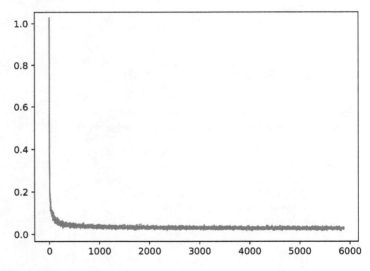

# Sampling

We now have a model that expects two inputs when making predictions: the image and the class label. We can create samples by beginning with random noise and then iteratively denoising, passing in whatever class label we'd like to generate:

```python
def generate_from_class(class_to_generate, n_samples=8):
    sample = torch.randn(n_samples, 1, 32, 32).to(device)
    class_labels = [class_to_generate] * n_samples
    class_labels = torch.tensor(class_labels).to(device)

    for _, t in tqdm(enumerate(scheduler.timesteps)):
        # Get model prediction
        with torch.inference_mode():
            noise_pred = model(sample, t, class_labels=class_labels).sample

        # Update sample with step
        sample = scheduler.step(noise_pred, t, sample).prev_sample

    return sample.clip(-1, 1) * 0.5 + 0.5
```

We can generate some t-shirts (class 0):

```python
images = generate_from_class(0)
show_images(images, nrows=2)
```

Now, we can generate some sneakers (class 7):

```python
images = generate_from_class(7)
show_images(images, nrows=2)
```

Or, finally, we can generate some boots (class 9):

```
images = generate_from_class(9)
show_images(images, nrows=2)
```

As you can see, the generated images still contain some noise. They could get better if we explored the model architecture, did hyperparameter tuning, and trained for longer. In any case, it's amazing that the model learned the shapes of different types of clothing and realized that shape 9 looks different than shape 0 just by sending this information alongside the training data. To put it slightly differently, the model is used to seeing the number 9 accompanying boots. When we ask it to generate an image and provide the 9, it responds with a boot.

# Improving Efficiency: Latent Diffusion

Now that we can train a conditional model, we just need to scale it up and condition it on text instead of class labels…right? Right? Well, not quite. As image size grows, so does the computational power required to work with those images. This is especially pronounced in self-attention, where the amount of operations grows quadratically with the number of inputs. A 128 × 128 image has four times as many pixels as a 64 × 64 image, requiring 16 times the memory and computing in a self-attention layer. This is a problem for anyone who'd like to generate high-resolution images.

Latent Diffusion tries to mitigate this issue by using a separate Variational Auto-Encoder (Figure 5-1). As we saw in Chapter 2, VAEs can compress images to a smaller spatial dimension. The rationale is that images tend to contain a large amount of redundant information. Given enough training data, a VAE can learn to produce a much smaller representation of an input image and then reconstruct the image with high fidelity based on this small latent representation. The VAE used in Stable Diffusion takes in three-channel images and produces a four-channel latent representation with a reduction factor of 8 for each spatial dimension. A 512 × 512 input image (3 × 512 × 512 = 786,432 values) will be compressed down to a 4 × 64 × 64 latent (16,384 values).

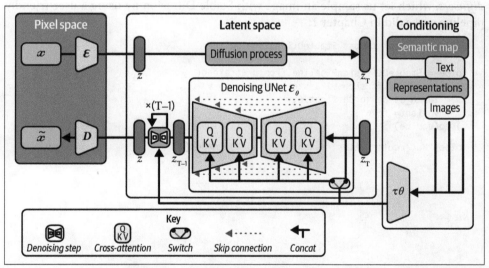

*Figure 5-1. The Latent Diffusion process. Note the VAE encoder and decoder on the left for translating between pixel and latent space.*

By applying the diffusion process on these smaller latent representations rather than on full-resolution images, we can get many of the benefits that would come from using smaller images (lower memory usage, fewer layers needed in the UNet, faster generation times, etc.) and still decode the result back to a high-resolution image once we're ready to view it. This innovation dramatically lowers the cost to train and run these models. The paper that introduced this idea, "Latent Diffusion Models" (*http://arxiv.org/abs/2112.10752*), demonstrated the power of this technique by training models conditioned on segmentation maps, class labels, and text. The impressive results led to further collaboration between the authors and partners such as LAION, StabilityAI, RunwayML, and EleutherAI to train a more powerful model version, which became Stable Diffusion.[4]

## Stable Diffusion: Components in Depth

Stable Diffusion is a Latent Diffusion model that can generate images conditioned on text prompts. It can also be used to do many other things, such as modifying images, which you'll learn more about in Chapter 9.

Thanks to its popularity, hundreds of websites and apps let you use it to create images with no technical knowledge required. It's also very well supported by libraries like *diffusers*, which let us sample an image with Stable Diffusion by using a user-friendly pipeline as we did in Chapter 1:

```
from diffusers import StableDiffusionPipeline

pipe = StableDiffusionPipeline.from_pretrained(
    "stable-diffusion-v1-5/stable-diffusion-v1-5",
    torch_dtype=torch.float16,
    variant="fp16",
).to(device)

pipe("Watercolor illustration of a rose").images[0]
```

---

4 LAION and EleutherAI are nonprofit organizations focused on open ML. StabilityAI is one of the companies that has pushed the most for open access ML. RunwayML is a company building AI-powered tools for creative applications.

This section will explore all the components that make this possible.

 Just as *diffusers* has `StableDiffusionPipeline`, it also provides access to dozens of other models from different families (Würstchen, AuraFlow, Flux, etc.). Additionally, it offers similar pipelines for other tasks, such as inpainting (`StableDiffusionInpaint`) and super-resolution (`StableDiffusionLatentUpscale`). Chapter 8 further explores some of these models and pipelines. We'll first focus on understanding the whole Stable Diffusion pipeline.

## The Text Encoder

So, how does Stable Diffusion understand text? Earlier on, we explained how feeding additional information to the UNet allows us to have some control over the types of images generated. Given a noisy version of an image, the model is tasked with predicting the denoised version based on additional clues such as a class label. In the case of Stable Diffusion, the additional clue is the text prompt. At inference time, we feed in the description of an image we'd like to generate and some pure noise as a starting point, and the model does its best to denoise the random input into something that matches the caption.

For this to work, we need to create a numeric representation of the text that captures relevant information about what it describes. To accomplish this, we'll use a *text encoder* that turns an input string into text embeddings, which are then fed into the UNet along with the timestep and the noisy latents, as shown in Figure 5-2.

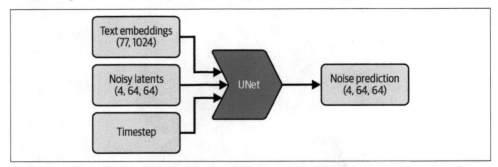

*Figure 5-2. The UNet can be conditioned on multiple inputs, such as the timestep, the class label, or the text embeddings*

To do this, Stable Diffusion leverages a pretrained transformer model based on CLIP, introduced in Chapter 3. The text encoder is a transformer model that takes in a sequence of tokens and produces a vector for each token, as can be seen in Figure 5-3. In the case of the first versions of Stable Diffusion (Stable Diffusion 1 to 1.5), where they used the original CLIP from OpenAI, the text encoder maps to a 768-dimensional vector. As the original dataset of CLIP is unknown, the community trained an open source version called OpenCLIP. Stable Diffusion 2 uses the text encoder from OpenCLIP, which generates 1,024-dimensional vectors for each token.

Instead of combining the vectors of all tokens into a single representation, we keep them separate and use them as conditioning for the UNet. This allows the UNet to use the information in each token separately rather than just the overall meaning of the prompt. Because we're extracting these text embeddings from the internal representation of the CLIP model, they are often called the *encoder hidden states*. Let's dive deeper into how the text encoder works under the hood. This is the same process as that for the encoder models we discussed in Chapter 2.

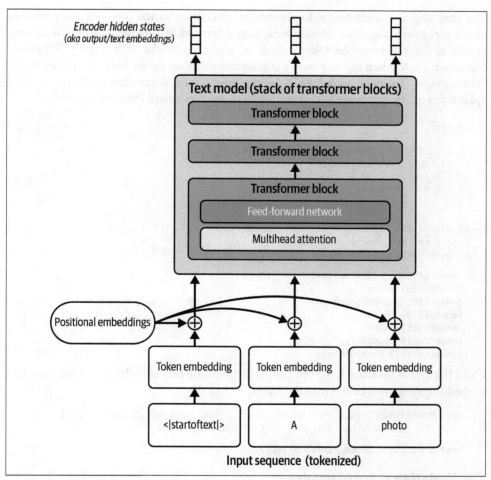

*Figure 5-3. The text-encoding process transforms the input prompt into a set of text embeddings (the encoder hidden states), which can then be fed in as conditioning to the UNet*

The first step to encode text is to perform tokenization, which converts a sequence of characters into a sequence of numbers, as you learned in Chapter 2. In the following example, we see how the tokenization of a phrase works with Stable Diffusion's tokenizer. Each token in the prompt is assigned a unique token number (for example, "photograph" happens to be 8853 in the tokenizer's vocabulary). There are also special tokens that provide additional context, such as where the sentence ends:

```
prompt = "A photograph of a puppy"

# Turn the text into a sequence of tokens:
text_input = pipe.tokenizer(
    prompt,
    return_tensors="pt",
)

# Output each token and its corresponding ID
for t in text_input["input_ids"][0]:
    print(t, pipe.tokenizer.decoder.get(int(t)))
tensor(49406) <|startoftext|>
tensor(320) a</w>
tensor(8853) photograph</w>
tensor(539) of</w>
tensor(320) a</w>
tensor(6829) puppy</w>
tensor(49407) <|endoftext|>
```

Once the text is tokenized, we can pass it through the text encoder to get the final text embeddings that will be fed into the UNet:

```
text_embeddings = pipe.text_encoder(text_input.input_ids.to(device))[0]
print("Text embeddings shape:", text_embeddings.shape)

Text embeddings shape: torch.Size([1, 77, 768])
```

## The Variational AutoEncoder

The VAE is tasked with compressing images into a smaller latent representation and reconstructing them again. The VAE, shown in Figure 5-4, is a crucial component of the Stable Diffusion model and is truly impressive. We won't go into the training details here, but in addition to the usual reconstruction loss and KL divergence described in Chapter 3, the VAE uses an additional patch-based discriminator loss to help the model generate plausible details and textures. This helps avoid the slightly blurry outputs typical in previous VAEs. Like the text encoder, the VAE is usually trained separately and used as a frozen component during the diffusion model training and sampling process.

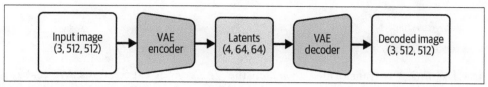

*Figure 5-4. The VAE architecture*

Let's load an image and see what it looks like after being compressed and decompressed by the VAE. First, let's check out the original image:

```python
from genaibook.core import import load_image, show_image, SampleURL


im = load_image(
    SampleURL.LlamaExample,
    size=(512, 512),
)
show_image(im);
```

Now, let's pass the image through the VAE:

```python
with torch.inference_mode():
    # Process image
    tensor_im = transforms.ToTensor()(im).unsqueeze(0).to(device) * 2 - 1  ❶
    tensor_im = tensor_im.half()  ❷

    # Encode the image
    latent = pipe.vae.encode(tensor_im)  ❸

    # Sample from the latent distribution
    latents = latent.latent_dist.sample()  ❹
    latents = latents * 0.18215  ❺
```

```
latents.shape

torch.Size([1, 4, 64, 64])
```

❶ The image is transformed to match the VAE's input expectations. We make it a tensor and add a dimension with `unsqueeze(0)` to make it a batch of size 1. Finally, we normalize the image to the range [−1, 1] to match the VAE's input range.

❷ The image is converted from `float32` to `float16`, because we loaded the pipeline with `torch.float16` precision.

❸ The image is passed through the VAE's encoder. As discussed in Chapter 3, VAEs output a distribution from which we can sample.

❹ We can access the distribution object produced by the VAE encoder to generate a sample from it.

❺ Scale the latent vector by a fixed size of 0.18215. The Stable Diffusion authors introduced this scaling factor of 0.18215 to ensure that the latent space has a variance close to 1, matching the approximate scale of the noise added during the diffusion process. It can be accessed in `vae.config.scaling_factor`.

The original image is a three-channel image of size 512 × 512 (786,432 values). The VAE compresses this image into a four-channel latent representation of size 64 × 64 (16,384 values). We can plot each of the channels in the latent representation:

```
show_images(
    [l for l in latents[0]],
    titles=[f"Channel {i}" for i in range(latents.shape[1])],
    ncols=4,
)
```

Channel 0 | Channel 1 | Channel 2 | Channel 3

  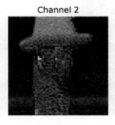 

Now that we've encoded the image into a latent representation, we can decode it back into an image. In an ideal world, the decoded image would be identical to the original image. In practice, the VAE can potentially introduce some noise and artifacts. Let's see how the decoded image looks:

```
with torch.inference_mode():
    image = pipe.vae.decode(latents / 0.18215).sample
image = (image / 2 + 0.5).clamp(0, 1)
show_image(image[0].float())
```

When generating images from scratch, we create a random set of latents as the starting point. We iteratively refine these noisy latents to generate a sample, and then the VAE decoder is used to decode these final latents into an image we can view. The encoder is used only if we'd like to start the process from an existing image, which is something we'll explore in Chapter 8.

## The UNet

The UNet used in Stable Diffusion is similar to the one in Chapter 4 for generating images. Instead of taking in a three-channel image as the input, we take in a four-channel latent. The timestep embedding is fed the same way as the class conditioning in the example at the start of this chapter. But this UNet also needs to accept the text embeddings as additional conditioning. Scattered throughout the UNet are cross-attention layers. Each spatial location in the UNet can attend to different tokens in the text conditioning, bringing in relevant information from the prompt. Figure 5-5 shows how this text conditioning (as well as the timestep-based conditioning) is fed in at different points.

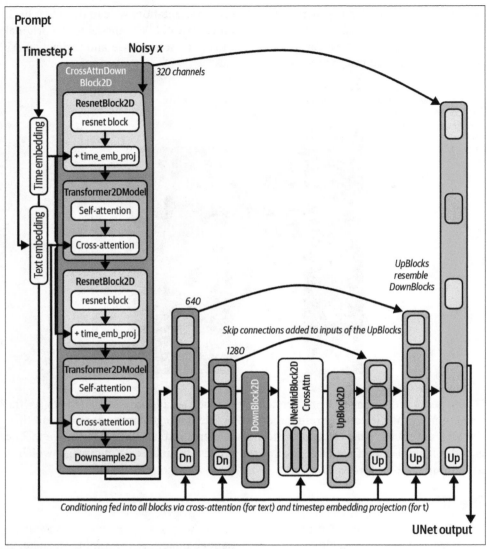

*Figure 5-5. Conditioned UNet architecture*

At the left in Figure 5-5, you can find the model inputs: the noisy $x$, which would be the four-channel latent in this case. The timestep and prompt are also fed to the model (in the form of embeddings) at different points of the architecture. As with all previous UNets, the model has a series of layers that downsample the input and then upsample it back to the original size. The network also has skip connections that allow the model to access information from earlier blocks.

The UNet for Stable Diffusion versions 1 and 2 has around 860 million parameters. The UNet in the more recent Stable Diffusion XL (SDXL) (*http://arxiv.org/abs/2307.01952*) has even more, at about 2.6 billion, and it uses additional conditioning information.

## Stable Diffusion XL

During the summer of 2023, a new and better version of Stable Diffusion was released: Stable Diffusion XL. It uses the same principles described in this chapter, with various improvements across all system components. Some of the most exciting changes are as follows:

*A larger text encoder to capture better prompt representations*
It uses the output from two text encoders and concatenates the embeddings.

*Condition on everything*
In addition to the timestep (which carries information about the amount of noise) and the text embeddings, SDXL uses the following additional conditioning signals:

*Original image size*
Instead of discarding small images in the training set (they account for almost 40% of the total training data used to train SDXL), small images are upscaled and used during training. However, the model also receives information about the image sizes it's receiving. This way, it learns that upscaling artifacts are not supposed to be part of large images and is encouraged to produce better quality during inference.

*Cropping coordinates*
Input images are usually randomly cropped during training because all the images in a batch must have the same size. Random crops may produce undesired effects, such as cutting subject heads or completely removing subjects from the image, even though they may be described in the text prompt. After the model is trained, if we request an uncropped image (by setting the crop coordinates to (0, 0)), the model is more likely to produce subjects centered in the frame.

*Target aspect ratio*
> After initial pretraining on square images, SDXL was fine-tuned on various aspect ratios, and the information about the original aspect ratio was used as another conditioning signal. As in the other conditioning cases, this enables the generation of much more realistic landscape and portrait images with fewer artifacts than before.

*Larger resolution*
> SDXL is designed to produce images with a resolution of 1,024 × 1,024 pixels (or nonsquare images with a total number of pixels of approximately $1,024^2$). Like the aspect ratio, this feature was achieved during a fine-tuning phase.

*The UNet is about three times as large*
> The cross-attention context is larger to account for the increase in the amount of conditioning.

*Improved VAE*
> It uses the same architecture as the original Stable Diffusion, but it's trained on a larger batch size and uses the exponential moving average (EMA) technique to update the weights.

*Refiner model*
> In addition to the base model, SDXL includes an additional *refiner* model that works on the same latent space as the base model. However, this model was trained on high-quality images only during the first 20% of the noise schedule. This means that it knows how to take an image with a small amount of noise and create high-quality textures and details.

Other researchers and the open source community had already explored many of these techniques, thanks to the original Stable Diffusion being open source. SDXL combines many of these ideas to achieve an impressive improvement in image quality (see Figure 5-6), with the cost of running the model being slower and using more memory.

*Figure 5-6. Image generated with SDXL*

## FLUX, SD3, and Video

The development in the diffusion models space doesn't show a sign of slowdown. In June 2024, Stability AI released Stable Diffusion 3 (*https://oreil.ly/BtzKD*), and in August 2024, Black Forest Labs released the Flux family of models (*https://oreil.ly/C73d8*). The principles behind these models are the same as those you learned in this chapter. However, they contain a different type of scheduler (rectified flow matching schedulers) and a different architecture: a diffusion transformer (*https://arxiv.org/abs/2212.09748*) instead of the UNet.[5]

Both model families are available in various sizes and support different resolutions, and they have improved prompt understanding and text-rendering capabilities. The same architecture is also scalable to support video generation. CogVideoX (*https://arxiv.org/abs/2408.06072*) is a family of models that apply those ideas to the video-generation space. These models demonstrate that the principles we covered (conditioning, in particular) are great general tools to guide the behavior of generative models and that open source releases can make exploration faster.

---

5 For more information, check out "Scaling Rectified Flow Transformers for High-Resolution Image Synthesis" (*https://arxiv.org/abs/2403.03206*) by Patrick Esser et al.

# Classifier-Free Guidance

Despite all the efforts to make the text conditioning as helpful as possible, the model still tends to default to relying primarily on the noisy input image rather than the prompt when making its predictions. In a way, this makes sense: many captions are only loosely related to their associated images, so the model learns not to rely too heavily on the descriptions. However, this is undesirable when generating new images: if the model doesn't follow the prompt, we may get images that don't relate to our description.

To mitigate this, we introduce *guidance*. Guidance is any method that provides more control over the sampling process. One option we could apply is to modify the loss function to favor a specific direction. For example, if we wanted to bias the generations toward a particular color, we could change the loss function to measure how far we are, on average, from the target color. Another alternative is to use models, such as CLIP or a classifier, to evaluate the result and include their loss signal as part of the generation process. For example, using CLIP, we could compare the difference between the prompt text and the generated image embeddings and guide the diffusion process to minimize this difference. "Exercises" on page 181 shows how to use this technique.

Another alternative is to use a trick called *classifier-free guidance* (CFG), which combines the generations of conditional and unconditional diffusion models. During training, text conditioning is sometimes kept blank, forcing the model to learn to denoise images with no text information whatsoever (unconditional generation). Then, we make two predictions at inference time: one with the text prompt as conditioning and one without. We can then use the difference between these two predictions to create a final combined prediction that pushes even further in the direction indicated by the text-conditioned prediction according to a scaling factor (the guidance scale), hopefully resulting in an image that better matches the prompt.

To incorporate the guidance, we can modify the noise prediction by doing something like `noise_pred = noise_pred_uncond + guidance_scale * (noise_pred_text - noise_pred_uncond)`. This small change works surprisingly well and allows us to have much better control of the generations. We'll dive into the implementation details later in the chapter, but let's take a look at how to use it. Check out the results of the prompt "An oil painting of a collie in a top hat" with CFG scale 1, 2, 4, and 12 (left to right in the output image):

```
images = []
prompt = "An oil painting of a collie in a top hat"
for guidance_scale in [1, 2, 4, 12]:
    torch.manual_seed(0)
    image = pipe(prompt, guidance_scale=guidance_scale).images[0]
    images.append(image)
```

```
from genaibook.core import image_grid

image_grid(images, 1, 4)
```

As you can see, higher values result in images that better match the description, but going too high may start to oversaturate the image. Google's Imagen paper (*https:// arxiv.org/abs/2205.11487*) found that this was because the in-progress predictions were exceeding the [-1, 1] bounds the model was trained with. Because the diffusion model runs iteratively, it has to deal with inputs whose values had not been seen during training, which can result in excessive saturation, posterization, and even generation failures. They proposed a method called *dynamic thresholding* to contain values within range and greatly improve quality at high CFG scales.

## Putting It All Together: Annotated Sampling Loop

Now that you know what each component does, let's combine them to generate an image without relying on the pipeline. Here are the settings we'll use:

```
# Some settings
prompt = [
    "Acrylic palette knife painting of a flower"
] # What we want to generate
height = 512  # default height of Stable Diffusion
width = 512  # default width of Stable Diffusion
num_inference_steps = 30  # Number of denoising steps
guidance_scale = 7.5  # Scale for classifier-free guidance
seed = 42  # Seed for random number generator
```

The first step is to encode the text prompt "Acrylic palette knife painting of a flower". Because we plan to do CFG, we'll create two sets of text embeddings: one with the prompt embedding and one representing an empty string, which is the unconditional input. Although we'll go with unconditional input here, this setup provides lots of flexibility. For example, we can do the following:

*Encode a negative prompt instead of the empty string*
    Adding a negative prompt allows us to guide the model in avoiding going in a certain direction. In Exercise 6 of this chapter, you'll play with negative prompts.

*Combine multiple prompts with different weights*

Prompt weighting allows us to emphasize or deemphasize certain parts of a prompt. You'll learn more about prompt weighting in Chapter 8.

Let's implement creation of the text embeddings:

```
# Tokenize the input
text_input = pipe.tokenizer(
    prompt,
    padding="max_length",   # Pad to max length to ensure inputs have same shape
    return_tensors="pt",
)

# Do the same for the unconditional input (a blank string)
uncond_input = pipe.tokenizer(
    "",
    padding="max_length",
    return_tensors="pt",
)

# Feed both embeddings through the text encoder
with torch.inference_mode():
    text_embeddings = pipe.text_encoder(text_input.input_ids.to(device))[0]
    uncond_embeddings = pipe.text_encoder(uncond_input.input_ids.to(device))[0]

# Concatenate the two sets of text embeddings embeddings
text_embeddings = torch.cat([uncond_embeddings, text_embeddings])
```

Next, we create our random initial latents and set up the scheduler to use the desired number of inference steps:

```
# Prepare the scheduler
pipe.scheduler.set_timesteps(num_inference_steps)

# Prepare the random starting latents
latents = (
    torch.randn(
        (1, pipe.unet.config.in_channels, height // 8, width // 8),
    )
    .to(device)
    .half()
)
latents = latents * pipe.scheduler.init_noise_sigma
```

Now we loop through the sampling steps, getting the model prediction at each stage and using this to update the latents:

```
for t in pipe.scheduler.timesteps:
    # Create two copies of the latents to match the two
    # text embeddings (unconditional and conditional)
    latent_input = torch.cat([latents] * 2)
    latent_input = pipe.scheduler.scale_model_input(latent_input, t)
```

```
# Predict noise residuals for both unconditional and conditional latents
with torch.inference_mode():
    noise_pred = pipe.unet(
        latent_input, t, encoder_hidden_states=text_embeddings
    ).sample

# Split the prediction into unconditional and conditional versions
noise_pred_uncond, noise_pred_text = noise_pred.chunk(2)

# Perform classifier-free guidance
noise_pred = noise_pred_uncond + guidance_scale * (
    noise_pred_text - noise_pred_uncond
)

# Update latents for the next timestep
latents = pipe.scheduler.step(noise_pred, t, latents).prev_sample
```

Notice the CFG step. Our final noise prediction is `noise_pred_uncond + guid` `ance_scale * (noise_pred_text - noise_pred_uncond)`, pushing the prediction away from the unconditional prediction and toward the prediction based on the prompt. Try changing the guidance scale to explore how this affects the output.

By the end of the loop, the latents should represent a plausible image that matches the prompt. The final step is to decode the latents into an image by using the VAE so that we can see the result:

```
# Scale and decode the image latents with the VAE
latents = 1 / pipe.vae.config.scaling_factor * latents
with torch.inference_mode():
    image = pipe.vae.decode(latents).sample
image = (image / 2 + 0.5).clamp(0, 1)

show_image(image[0].float());
```

If you explore the source code for the `StableDiffusionPipeline`, you'll notice that the preceding code closely matches the `call()` method used by the pipeline. Hopefully, this annotated version shows that nothing too magical is happening behind the scenes. Use this as a reference when we encounter additional pipelines that add tricks to this foundation.

## Open Data, Open Models

The LAION-5B dataset (*https://oreil.ly/F3ReL*) comprised over 5 billion image URLs and their respective associated captions (image-caption pairs). The dataset was created by first taking all image URLs found in CommonCrawl (*https://oreil.ly/zPMOu*) (an open repository of web-crawled data, similar to how Google indexes the internet for its search) and then using CLIP to keep only the image-caption pairs with high similarity between text and image.

This dataset was created by and for the open ML community, which saw the need for an open-access dataset of this kind. Before the LAION initiative, only a handful of research labs at large companies had access to image-text pair datasets. These organizations kept their datasets' details to themselves, making their results impossible to validate or replicate. By creating a publicly available source of URL and caption indexes, LAION enabled a wave of smaller communities and organizations to train models and perform research that would otherwise have been impossible.

The first Latent Diffusion model was one such model, trained on a previous version of the LAION dataset with 400 million image-text pairs by CompVis.[6] The release of the LAION-trained Latent Diffusion model marked the first time a robust text-to-image model was available for the entire research community.

The success of Latent Diffusion showed the potential of this approach, which was realized by the follow-up work, Stable Diffusion. Training a model like Stable Diffusion required a significant amount of GPU time. Even leveraging the freely available LAION dataset, only a few could afford the GPU-hours investment. This is why the public release of the model weights and code was such a big deal: it marked the first time a powerful text-to-image model with similar capabilities to the best closed-source alternatives was available to all.

Stable Diffusion's public availability has made it the go-to choice for researchers and developers exploring this technology over the past years. Hundreds of papers build upon the base model, adding new capabilities or finding innovative ways to improve its speed and quality. Apart from research papers, a diverse community not necessarily from an ML background has been hacking with the models to enable new

---

6 At the time, the Computer Vision Group at Heidelberg University. Currently, it is a research group at LMU Munich (*https://oreil.ly/-N_g8*).

creative workflows, optimize for faster inference, and so much more (see Figure 5-7). Innumerable startups have found ways to integrate these rapidly improving tools into their products, spawning an entire ecosystem of new applications.

*Figure 5-7. Creativity has been exploding in the text-to-image space*

The months after the introduction of Stable Diffusion demonstrated the impact of openly sharing these technologies, with many further quality improvements and customization techniques that we will explore in Chapters 7 and 8. Stable Diffusion was competitive in quality with the commercial alternatives of the time, such as DALL·E and Midjourney, and thousands of people have spent their time improving it and building upon that open foundation. We hope this example encourages others to follow suit and share their work with the open source community in the future.

 Apart from being used to train Stable Diffusion, LAION-5B has been used by many other research efforts. One example is Open-CLIP, an effort from the LAION community to train high-quality (SOTA) open source CLIP models and replicate similar quality to the original one. A high-quality open source CLIP model benefits many tasks, such as image retrieval and zero-shot image classification. Having transparency in the data used to train the model also enables researching the impact of scaling up the models, correctly reproducing results, and making research more accessible.

## Challenges and the Sunset of LAION-5B

However, the huge success of text-to-image generative models and downstream commercial applications based on such models have raised concerns about the data source and content in those datasets.

Because the dataset comprises links to images crawled from the internet, it contains millions of URLs pointing to images that may contain copyrighted material, such as photographs, works of art, comics, and illustrations. Research has found that such a dataset also includes private sensitive information (*https://oreil.ly/tpSih*), such as personally identifiable medical imagery, that was publicly available online.

Using such a dataset to train generative AI models can also inject the model with the capability of producing content that reinforces or exacerbates societal biases (*http://arxiv.org/abs/2303.11408*), and they can be used to produce explicit adult content. Additionally, these models can frequently produce content that is very close to the training data, which can lead to the generation of content extremely similar to copyrighted material. However, those open models are trained on open datasets, so such biases and problematic content can be studied, analyzed, and mitigated (*http://arxiv.org/abs/2211.05105*).

More recent research (*https://oreil.ly/OdyqI*) shows that the LAION-2B dataset, having been scraped from the internet, failed to filter out explicitly illegal material regarding violence and child safety, which led to the dataset deactivation.

## Alternatives

With the deactivation of LAION datasets on the grounds of child safety, open alternatives such as COYO-700M (*https://oreil.ly/pVG1d*) and DataComp-1B (*https://oreil.ly/nyYLs*) fill the void as open datasets that follow a similar formula of internet-level scraping of images. Although they don't contain content that would lead to their immediate deactivation, they still contain the same challenges of biases, copyrighted material, and personal rights that were brought up in the previous section. Common-Canvas (*https://oreil.ly/Qzq0k*) is a smaller scale (70 million image-text pairs) dataset but contains exclusively openly Creative Commons licensed images.

## Fair and Commercial Use

While some countries have fair-use exceptions regarding copyright law for research usage, and others have precedents that seem favorable regarding using scraped data to train ML models, what happens when a research model trained on such materials is used commercially and at scale for generative AI? This complex subject is currently being litigated in courts in multiple jurisdictions in the United States and Europe, with angles that relate to copyright law, fair use for research applications, privacy, the economic impact of AI tools on creative jobs, and others. We don't claim to have an answer for such complex matters, but such a legal gray area is moving the research and open source community away from using open datasets; for Stable Diffusion XL, the dataset used to train it was not disclosed, despite the open source model weights.

The construction of a new large-scale text-image dataset that puts consent, safety, and licensing at the center stage would also be an excellent resource for the research and open source communities and legal certainty for commercial downstream applications. The CommonCanvas datasets show a path in this direction.

# Project Time: Build an Interactive ML Demo with Gradio

Until now, we've focused on running transformer and diffusion models using open source libraries. This gives us lots of flexibility and control over the models but also requires much work to set up and run. The reality is that most people don't know how to code but might be interested in exploring models and their capabilities.

In this project, we'll build a simple ML demo that allows users to generate images from text prompts by using Stable Diffusion. Demos allow you to easily showcase a model to a broad audience and make your work and research more accessible.

There are many ways to build ML demos. You could use HTML, JavaScript, and CSS. However, this requires some web development experience and is not a straightforward process. Alternatively, open source libraries such as *streamlit* (*https://streamlit.io/*) and *gradio* (*https://oreil.ly/bBo5a*) make it easy to build interactive ML demos using Python. We'll use *gradio* in this chapter, which is a very simple and minimal library.

The *gradio* library can be run anywhere—in a Python IDE, Jupyter notebook, Google Colab, or a cloud environment such as Hugging Face Spaces. The easiest way to build *gradio* demos is using its `Interface` class, which has three key aspects:

inputs
> The expected input types of the demo, such as text prompts or images

outputs
> The expected output types of the demo, such as generated images

fn
> The function that will be called when the user interacts with the demo. This is where the magic happens. You can run any code here, including running models with *transformers* or *diffusers*.

Let's look at an example:

```
import gradio as gr


def greet(name):
    return "Hello " + name


demo = gr.Interface(fn=greet, inputs="text", outputs="text")

demo.launch()
```

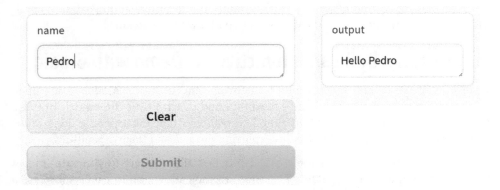

Now it's your turn! Build a simple demo that allows users to generate images from text prompts by using Stable Diffusion. You can use the code from the previous section as a starting point. Once you get a demo running, we suggest adding more features to make it interactive and fun. For example, you could do the following:

- Add a slider to control the guidance scale.
- Add an additional text field to add a negative prompt.
- Add a title and a description so that users understand what the demo is about.

If you need help, remember to look at the official documentation (*https://oreil.ly/3YkzU*) and the quick start guide (*https://oreil.ly/dkoZ3*).

# Summary

This chapter showed how *conditioning* gives us new ways to control the images generated by diffusion models. We've seen how a text encoder can condition a diffusion model on a text prompt, enabling powerful text-to-image capabilities. And we've explored how all of this comes together in the Stable Diffusion model by digging into the sampling loop and seeing how the different components work together.

In Chapter 7, you'll learn how to fine-tune Stable Diffusion to add new knowledge or capabilities to the model. For example, you'll see how, by showing pictures of your pet, Stable Diffusion can learn the concept of "your pet" and generate novel images in new scenarios, such as "your pet on the moon".

Later, in Chapter 8, we'll show some of the capabilities we can add to diffusion models to take them beyond simple image generation. For example, we'll explore inpainting, which allows us to mask a part of the image and then fill that part. Chapter 8 also explores techniques to edit images based on a prompt.

# Exercises

1. How does the training process of a class-conditioned diffusion model differ from a nonconditioned model, particularly in terms of the input data and the loss function used?

2. How does the timestep embedding influence the quality and evolution of the images during the diffusion process?

3. Explain the difference between Latent Diffusion and normal diffusion. What are the trade-offs of using Latent Diffusion?

4. How is the text prompt incorporated into the model?

5. What is the difference between model-based and classifier-free guidance? What is the benefit of classifier-free guidance?

6. What is the effect of using a negative prompt? Experiment with it using `pipe(…, negative_prompt="")`. How are you able to guide the image generation using Stable Diffusion?

7. Let's say you want to remove white hats from any generated image. How can you use negative prompts for this? First try implementing this using the high-level pipeline. Then, try adapting the end-to-end inference example. (Hint: It requires only modifying the random part of the classifier-free conditioning.)

8. What happens in SDXL if you use `(256, 256)` instead of `(1024, 1024)` as the "original size" conditioning signal? What happens if you use crop coordinates other than `(0, 0)`? Can you explain why?

You can find the solutions to these exercises and the following challenge in the book's GitHub repository (*https://oreil.ly/handsonGenAIcode*).

# Challenge

*Blue guidance.* Let's say we want to bias generated images to a specific color, such as blue. How can we do that? The first step is to define a conditioning function we'd like to minimize, which, in this case, will be a color loss:

```python
def color_loss(images, target_color=(0.1, 0.5, 0.9)):
    """Given a target color (R, G, B) return a loss for how far away on
    average the images' pixels are from that color."""
    # Map target color to (-1, 1)
    target = torch.tensor(target_color).to(images.device) * 2 - 1

    # Get shape right to work with the images (b, c, h, w)
    target = target[None, :, None, None]
```

```
# Mean absolute difference between the image pixels and the target color
error = torch.abs(images - target).mean()
return error
```

Given this loss function, write a sampling loop (no training is needed) that modifies x in the direction of the loss function.[7]

# References

Esser, Patrick, et al. "Scaling Rectified Flow Transformers for High-Resolution Image Synthesis." arXiv, March 5, 2024. *https://arxiv.org/abs/2403.03206.*

Ho, Jonathan, and Tim Salimans. "Classifier-Free Diffusion Guidance." arXiv, July 25, 2022. *http://arxiv.org/abs/2207.12598.*

Luccioni, Alexandra Sasha, et al. "Stable Bias: Analyzing Societal Representations in Diffusion Models." arXiv, March 20, 2023. *http://arxiv.org/abs/2303.11408.*

Peebles, William, and Saining Xie. "Scalable Diffusion Models with Transformers." arXiv, December 19, 2023. *https://arxiv.org/abs/2212.09748.*

Podell, Dustin, et al. "SDXL: Improving Latent Diffusion Models for High-Resolution Image Synthesis." arXiv, July 4, 2023. *http://arxiv.org/abs/2307.01952.*

Rombach, Robin, et al. "High-Resolution Image Synthesis with Latent Diffusion Models." arXiv, April 13, 2022. *http://arxiv.org/abs/2112.10752.*

Saharia, Chitwan, et al. "Photorealistic Text-to-Image Diffusion Models with Deep Language Understanding." *Advances in Neural Information Processing Systems* 35 (2022): 36479–36494. arXiv, May 24, 2022. *https://arxiv.org/abs/2205.11487.*

Schramowski, Patrick, et al. "Safe Latent Diffusion: Mitigating Inappropriate Degeneration in Diffusion Models." arXiv, April 26, 2023. *http://arxiv.org/abs/2211.05105.*

Schuhmann, Christoph, et al. "LAION-5B: An Open Large-Scale Dataset for Training Next Generation Image-Text Models." arXiv, October 15, 2022. *http://arxiv.org/abs/2210.08402.*

Xiao, Han, et al. "Fashion-MNIST: A Novel Image Dataset for Benchmarking Machine Learning Algorithms." arXiv, September 15, 2017. *http://arxiv.org/abs/1708.07747.*

Yang, Zhuoyi, et al. "CogVideoX: Text-to-Video Diffusion Models with an Expert Transformer." arXiv, August 12, 2024. *https://arxiv.org/abs/2408.06072.*

---

7 To simplify things, we recommend using the unconditional `DDPMPipeline` from Chapter 4.

# PART II

# Transfer Learning for Generative Models

# CHAPTER 6

# Fine-Tuning Language Models

In Chapter 2, we explored how LMs work and how to use them for tasks such as text generation and sequence classification. We saw that LMs could be helpful in many tasks without further training, thanks to proper prompting and the zero-shot capabilities of these models. We also explored some of the hundreds of thousands of pretrained models by the community. In this chapter, we'll discuss how we can improve the performance of LMs on specific tasks by fine-tuning them on our data.

While pretrained models showcase remarkable capabilities, their general-purpose training may not be suited for certain tasks or domains. Fine-tuning is frequently used to tailor the model's understanding to the nuances of their dataset or task. For instance, in the field of medical research, an LM pretrained on general web text will not perform great out of the box, so we can fine-tune it on a dataset of medical literature to enhance its ability to generate relevant medical text or assist in information extraction from healthcare documents. Another example is for making conversational models. Although large pretrained models can generate coherent text, they usually don't work well for generating high-quality conversational text or following instructions. We can fine-tune this model on a dataset with everyday conversations and informal language structures, adapting the model to output engaging, conversational text, as the one you would expect in interfaces such as ChatGPT.

The goal of this chapter is to build strong foundations in fine-tuning LLMs, and hence, we'll cover the following:

- Classifying the topic of a text using a fine-tuned encoder model
- Understanding the role of encoder-based models in the modern LLM era

- Generating text in a particular style using a decoder model
- Solving multiple tasks with a single model via instruction fine-tuning
- Parameter-efficient fine-tuning techniques that allow us to train models with smaller GPUs
- Techniques that will allow us to run inference of the models with less compute

# Classifying Text

Before jumping into the land of generative models, it's a good idea to understand the general flow of fine-tuning a pretrained model. We'll begin with sequence classification, where a model assigns a class to a given input. Sequence classification is one of the classical ML problems. With it, you can tackle challenges such as spam detection, sentiment recognition, intent classification, and fake content detection, among many others. Although it's a simple task that people frequently solve via prompting a general-purpose LM, it's a good starting point to understand the fine-tuning process and the steps involved.

We'll fine-tune a model to classify the topic of short news article abstracts. As we'll find out soon, fine-tuning requires much less compute and data than training a model from scratch. The usual process is as follows (Figure 6-1):

1. Identify a dataset for the task.
2. Define which model type is needed (encoder, decoder, or encoder-decoder).
3. Select a good base model that meets your requirements.
4. Preprocess the dataset.
5. Define evaluation metrics.
6. Train the model.
7. Share.

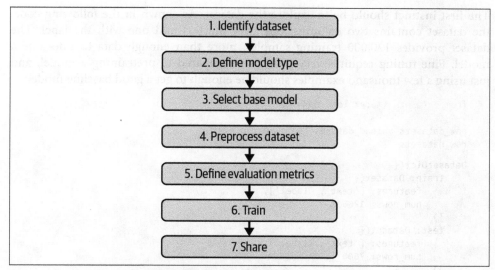

*Figure 6-1. The usual steps of a fine-tuning workflow*

## Identify a Dataset

Our goal is to adapt a general-purpose pretrained LM to work as a text classifier, and we need to teach it the categories it needs to detect. This leads to us needing a labeled dataset for sequence classification. Depending on your task and use case, you can use a public or private dataset (e.g., a dataset from your company). Some good places to find public datasets are Hugging Face Datasets (*https://oreil.ly/uMGkw*), Kaggle (*https://oreil.ly/All2r*), Zenodo (*https://zenodo.org/*), and Google Dataset Search (*https://oreil.ly/sukKP*). With hundreds of thousands of datasets out there, we need help finding a suitable dataset for our use case. One approach can be to filter for text-classification datasets (*https://oreil.ly/36JyT*) on Hugging Face.

Among the most downloaded datasets is the AG News dataset (*https://oreil.ly/uPJHa*), a well-known noncommercial dataset used for benchmarking text-classification models and researching data mining, information retrieval, and data streaming.

 Sometimes you will want to share a dataset with the community. To do that, you can upload it as a dataset repository. The *datasets* library has out-of-the-box support for common data types (audio, images, text, CSV, JSON, pandas DataFrames, etc.).

The first instinct should be to explore the dataset. As shown in the following code, the dataset contains two columns: one with the text and one with the label. The dataset provides 120,000 training samples, more than enough data to fine-tune a model. Fine-tuning requires very little data compared to pretraining a model, and just using a few thousand examples should be enough to get a good baseline model:

```
from datasets import load_dataset

raw_datasets = load_dataset("fancyzhx/ag_news")
raw_datasets

DatasetDict({
    train: Dataset({
        features: ['text', 'label'],
        num_rows: 120000
    })
    test: Dataset({
        features: ['text', 'label'],
        num_rows: 7600
    })
})
```

Let's explore how a specific example looks:

```
raw_train_dataset = raw_datasets["train"]
raw_train_dataset[0]

{'label': 2,
 'text': 'Wall St. Bears Claw Back Into the Black (Reuters) Reuters '
         "- Short-sellers, Wall Street's dwindling\\band of "
         "'ultra-cynics, are seeing green again.'}
```

The first sample contains the text and a label, which is...2? To which class does 2 refer? To figure this out, we can inspect the dataset features and its label field:

```
print(raw_train_dataset.features)

{'label': ClassLabel(names=['World',
                            'Sports',
                            'Business',
                            'Sci/Tech'],
                     id=None),
  'text': Value(dtype='string', id=None)}
```

So a label of 0 means news about the world, 1 about sports, 2 about business, and 3 about science and tech. With this figured out, let's decide which model to use.

# Define Which Model Type to Use

Let's recap Chapter 2. We can use one of three types of transformers, depending on which type of task we're trying to solve:

*Encoder models*
> They obtain rich semantic representations from sequences, capturing the meaning of the input, which can be used for various tasks relying on the input's semantic information (e.g., identifying entities in the text or classifying the sequence). A small network can be added on top of these embeddings to train for a specific downstream task.

*Decoder models*
> These models are designed to generate new sequences, such as text. They take an input (often an embedding or context) and produce coherent output sequences, making them ideal for text-generation tasks.

*Encoder-decoder models*
> These models are well suited for tasks that require transforming an input sequence into a different output sequence, such as machine translation or summarization. The encoder processes the input while the decoder generates the corresponding output.

Considering the task of topic classification for short news article abstracts, we have three possible approaches:

*1. Zero or few-shot learning*
> We can use a high-quality pretrained model, explain the task (e.g., "classify into these four categories"), and let the model do the rest. This approach does not require any fine-tuning and is very common nowadays with powerful pretrained models—a single model can solve many tasks by formulating them as text-generation problems.

*2. Text-generation model*
> Fine-tune a text-generation model to generate the label (e.g., "business") given an input news article. We could use either a decoder or an encoder-decoder model here.

*3. Encoder model with classification head*
> Fine-tune an encoder model by adding a simple classification network (called *head*) to the embeddings. This approach provides a specialized and efficient model tailored to our use case, making it a favorable choice for our topic-classification task.

Based on the preceding, we'll choose the third approach.

## Select a Good Base Model

We require a model that:

- Has an encoder-based architecture
- Is small enough that we can fine-tune in a few minutes on a GPU
- Has solid pretraining results
- Can process short sequences of text

BERT, although old, is a great base encoder architecture for fine-tuning. Given that we want to train the model quickly and with little computing power, we can use DistilBERT (*https://arxiv.org/abs/1910.01108*), which is 40% smaller and 60% faster while retaining 97% of BERT capabilities. Given the base model, we can fine-tune it for multiple downstream tasks, such as answering questions or classifying text.

Apart from the original BERT and DistilBERT, many other models can be used as base models for fine-tuning. We won't dive into each of them, but knowing they exist is important. Some examples are RoBERTa, ALBERT, Electra, DeBERTa, Longformer, LuKE, MobileBERT, and Reformer. Each model has its own training procedure and builds upon the original BERT model. Which one to choose depends on your specific requirements, but using DistilBERT is a good starting point given our computing requirements. DeBERTa (*https://oreil.ly/VZMrc*) is among the SOTA at the time of writing.

## Preprocess the Dataset

As explained in Chapter 2, each LM comes with its tokenizer. To fine-tune Distil-BERT, we must ensure that the whole dataset is tokenized with the same tokenizer that was used to pretrain the model. We can use `AutoTokenizer` to load the appropriate one, and then we can define a function that will tokenize a batch of samples. The *transformers* library expects all inputs in a batch to be the same length: by adding `padding=True`, we add zeros to the samples so that they all have the same size as the longest input sample.

It's important to note that transformer models have a maximum context size—the maximum number of tokens an LM can use when making predictions. For Distil-BERT, this limit is 512 tokens, so don't try to use it for entire books. Fortunately, most of our samples are small abstracts, but some may still exceed this token limit. To handle this, we can use `truncation=True`, which will truncate all samples to fit within the model's context length. However, this approach comes with a trade-off: truncating the text means that some potentially useful information might be lost.

Handling long contexts with transformers is an active research area. For scenarios involving encoder-based models and long contexts, you can try out several strategies:

- Use a specialized long-context transformer model, such as Longformer.
- Divide the text into smaller segments and process them separately.
- Use a sliding window approach to process the text in chunks.
- Summarize the text as a preprocessing step, then feed the summary to the model.

Which strategy to pick depends on the task and model. For example, if you want to analyze the sentiment of a book, use chunking and analyze different parts of the book separately. If you want to classify the topic of a long article, you could summarize the article and then classify the summary.

 Although models come with an out-of-the-box context length, which refers to the number of tokens the model can consider at a time, techniques such as rotary embeddings allow us to use longer or even infinite context lengths. We'll discuss more about this later on.

Let's tokenize two samples to inspect the output:

```
from transformers import AutoTokenizer

checkpoint = "distilbert-base-uncased"
tokenizer = AutoTokenizer.from_pretrained(checkpoint)


def tokenize_function(batch):
    return tokenizer(
        batch["text"], truncation=True, padding=True, return_tensors="pt"
    )


tokenize_function(raw_train_dataset[:2])
{'attention_mask': tensor([[1, 1, 1, 1, 1, 1, 1, 1, 1, 1, 1, 1, 1, 1,
         1, 1, 1, 1, 1, 1, 1, 1, 1, 1, 1, 1, 1, 1, 1, 1, 1, 1, 1, 1,
         1, 1, 1, 1, 1, 1, 0, 0, 0, 0, 0, 0, 0, 0, 0, 0, 0, 0],
        [1, 1, 1, 1, 1, 1, 1, 1, 1, 1, 1, 1, 1, 1, 1, 1, 1, 1, 1, 1,
         1, 1, 1, 1, 1, 1, 1, 1, 1, 1, 1, 1, 1, 1, 1, 1, 1, 1, 1, 1,
         1, 1, 1, 1, 1, 1, 1, 1, 1, 1, 1, 1, 1]]),
 'input_ids': tensor([[  101,  2813,  2358,  1012,  6468, 15020,  2067,  2046,
          1996,  2304,  1006, 26665,  1007, 26665,  1011,  2460,
          1011, 19041,  1010,  2813,  2395,  1005,  1055,  1040,
         11101,  2989,  1032,  2316,  1997, 11087,  1011, 22330,
          8713,  2015,  1010,  2024,  3773,  2665,  2153,  1012,
           102,     0,     0,     0,     0,     0,     0,     0,
             0,     0,     0,     0,     0],
        [  101, 18431,  2571,  3504,  2646,  3293, 13395,  1006,
         26665,  1007, 26665,  1011,  2797,  5211,  3813, 18431,
          2571,  2177,  1010,  1032,  2029,  2038,  1037,  5891,
```

```
2005,  2437,  2092,  1011, 22313,  1998,  5681,  1032,
6801,  3248,  1999,  1996,  3639,  3068,  1010,  2038,
5168,  2872,  1032,  2049, 29475,  2006,  2178,  2112,
1997,  1996,  3006,  1012,   102]])}
```

In this example, `tokenize_function()` takes a batch of samples, tokenizes them using the DistilBERT tokenizer, and ensures uniform length by padding and truncating as needed. As you can check out, the first element was shorter than the second, so it has some additional tokens with an ID of 0 at the end. The zeros correspond to the [PAD] token, which will be ignored during inference. Note that the attention mask for this sample also has 0 at the end; this ensures that the model pays attention only to the actual tokens.

Now that you understand the tokenization, we can use the `map()` method to tokenize the whole dataset. This method applies a function to each element of the dataset in parallel:

```
tokenized_datasets = raw_datasets.map(tokenize_function, batched=True)
tokenized_datasets

DatasetDict({
    train: Dataset({
        features: ['text', 'label', 'input_ids', 'attention_mask'],
        num_rows: 120000
    })
    test: Dataset({
        features: ['text', 'label', 'input_ids', 'attention_mask'],
        num_rows: 7600
    })
})
```

## Define Evaluation Metrics

In addition to monitoring the loss during training, it's usually a good idea to define some downstream metrics to better evaluate and monitor the model's performance. We'll leverage the *evaluate* library, a handy tool with a standardized interface for various metrics. The choice of metrics depends on the task. For sequence classification, suitable candidates can be the following:

*Accuracy*
> Represents the proportion of correct predictions out of all predictions, providing a high-level overview of the model's overall performance. It's a good metric for balanced datasets and is easy to interpret. However, it can be misleading for imbalanced datasets.

*Precision*
> This is the ratio of correctly labeled positive instances to all instances predicted as positive. It helps us understand the accuracy of the model's positive predictions.

Precision should be used when the cost of false positives is high, such as spam detection.

*Recall*

This metric indicates the proportion of actual positive instances that were correctly predicted by the model. It reflects the model's ability to capture all positive instances, and it will be lower if there are many false negatives. Recall should be used when the cost of false negatives is high, such as in medical diagnosis.

*F1 score*

The F1 score is the harmonic mean of precision and recall,[1] offering a balanced measure that considers both false positives and false negatives and penalizes strong discrepancies between precision and recall. F1 is often used for imbalanced datasets and is a good default metric for classification tasks.

Metrics in *evaluate* provide a `description` attribute and a `compute()` method to obtain the metric given the labels and model predictions:

```
import evaluate

accuracy = evaluate.load("accuracy")
print(accuracy.description)
print(accuracy.compute(references=[0, 1, 0, 1], predictions=[1, 0, 0, 1]))

('Accuracy is the proportion of correct predictions among the total '
 'number of cases processed. It can be computed with:'
 'Accuracy = (TP + TN) / (TP + TN + FP + FN)'
 ' Where:'
 'TP: True positive'
 'TN: True negative'
 'FP: False positive'
 'FN: False negative')
{'accuracy': 0.5}
```

Let's define a `compute_metrics()` function that, given a prediction instance (which contains both the label and predictions), returns a dictionary with the accuracy and the F1 score. When we evaluate the model during the training, we will automatically use this function to monitor its progress:

```
f1_score = evaluate.load("f1")


def compute_metrics(pred):  ❶
    labels = pred.label_ids
    preds = pred.predictions.argmax(-1)  ❷
```

---

1 The *harmonic mean* is a type of average useful when dealing with ratios, as it gives more weight to lower values.

```
# Compute accuracy and F1 Score
acc_result = accuracy.compute(references=labels, predictions=preds)
acc = acc_result["accuracy"]  ❸

f1_result = f1_score.compute(
    references=labels, predictions=preds, average="weighted"
)
f1 = f1_result["f1"]  ❹

return {"accuracy": acc, "f1": f1}  ❺
```

❶ compute_metrics() expects an EvalPrediction instance. An EvalPrediction is a utility class used by the Trainer that contains the labels and model predictions for a sample.

❷ Use argmax to get the predicted class with the highest probability.

❸ Use the loaded accuracy to compute the accuracy score between labels and predictions. Recall that accuracy outputs a dictionary with the accuracy key.

❹ Repeat with the F1 score. As we have multiple classes, we use the weighted=True argument. This means that we calculate F1 for each class and then average them, weighted by the number of true instances for each class.

❺ Finally, return both metrics by building a dictionary.

## Train the Model

Time to train. Recall that DistilBERT is an encoder model. If we use the raw model as is, we'll get the embeddings, as we did in Chapter 2, so we cannot use this model directly. For classifying text sequences, we feed these embeddings to a classification head (see Figure 6-2). When fine-tuning, we won't use fixed embeddings: all the model parameters, the original weights, and the classification head are trainable. This requires the head to be differentiable and leads us to use a neural network on top of the base transformer. This head will take the embeddings as input and output class probabilities. Why do we train all the weights? By training all the parameters, we help make the embeddings more useful for this specific classification task.

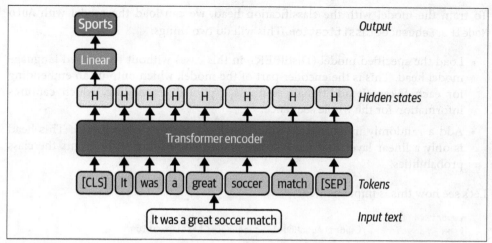

*Figure 6-2. BERT with a classification head. In practice, the embedding corresponding to CLS is used as the pooled embedding and can be used for classification tasks.*

Although we'll use a simple feed-forward network, we can use more-complex networks as the head or even classic models, such as Logistic Regression or Random Forests (in which case we use the model as a feature extractor and freeze the weights). Using a simple layer works well, is computationally efficient, and is the most common approach.

If you've done transfer learning in Computer Vision, you might be familiar with the concept of freezing the weights of the base model. This is frequently not done in NLP, as our goal is to make the internal language representations more useful for the downstream task. In Computer Vision, it's frequent to freeze some layers as the features learned by the base model are more general and useful for many tasks. For example, some layers capture generic features like edges or textures, which are broadly applicable across vision tasks. Whether to freeze or unfreeze layers depends on the context, including the dataset size, the amount of computing, and the similarity between the pretraining and fine-tuning tasks. Later in the chapter, you'll learn about a technique called adapters, which allow us to work with frozen LLMs.

To train the model with the classification head, we can load the model with `Auto ModelForSequenceClassification`. This will do two things:

- Load the specified model (DistilBERT in this case) without its masked language model head. This is the encoder part of the model, which outputs an embedding for each token. It additionally outputs a pooled embedding, which captures information for the whole sequence.

- Add a randomly initialized classification head on top of the model. This head is only a linear layer that receives the pooled embedding and outputs the class probabilities.

Let's see how this is implemented:

```
import torch
from transformers import AutoModelForSequenceClassification

from genaibook.core import get_device

device = get_device()
num_labels = 4
model = AutoModelForSequenceClassification.from_pretrained(
    checkpoint, num_labels=num_labels
).to(device)
```

```
('Some weights of DistilBertForSequenceClassification were not
 initialized from the model checkpoint at distilbert-base-uncased
 and are newly initialized: ["classifier.bias",
 "classifier.weight", "pre_classifier.bias",
 "pre_classifier.weight"]
 You should probably TRAIN this model on a down-stream task to be
 able to use it for predictions and inference.')
```

You will get a warning about some weights being newly initialized. This makes sense; we have a new head suitable for our classification task and need to train it.

With our model initialized, we can finally train it. We can take various approaches to train the model. If you're familiar with PyTorch, you can write your training loop. Alternatively, *transformers* provides a high-level class called `Trainer`, which streamlines much of the training loop complexity.

The first step before creating our `Trainer` is to define `TrainingArguments`, as shown in the following code example. `TrainingArguments` specifies the hyperparameters used for training, such as learning rate and weight decay, determining the number of samples per batch, setting evaluation intervals, and deciding whether we want to share our model with the ecosystem by pushing it to the Hub. We won't modify the hyperparameters, because the defaults provided by the `TrainingArguments` generally perform well. Still, we encourage you to explore and experiment with them. The `Trainer` class is a robust and flexible tool.[2]

```
from transformers import TrainingArguments

batch_size = 32  # You can change this if you have a big or small GPU
training_args = TrainingArguments(
    "classifier-chapter4",
    push_to_hub=True,  ❶
    num_train_epochs=2,  ❷
    eval_strategy="epoch",  ❸
    per_device_train_batch_size=batch_size,  ❹
    per_device_eval_batch_size=batch_size,
)
```

❶ Whether or not to push the model to the Hugging Face Hub every time the model is saved. You can change how often the model is saved with `save_strat egy`, which is done every few hundred steps by default.

❷ Total number of epochs to perform; an epoch is a full pass through the training data.

❸ When to evaluate the model on the validation set. It's done every 500 steps by default, but by specifying `epoch`, the evaluation happens at the end of each epoch.

❹ The batch size per core for training. You can reduce this if your GPU is running out of memory. Alternatively, you can use `auto_find_batch_size=True` to find the largest batch size that fits on your GPU.[3]

We now have all the pieces we need:

- A pretrained model with a proper head ready to be fine-tuned
- The training arguments
- A function that will compute metrics
- A training and evaluation dataset
- A tokenizer, which we add to ensure it's pushed with the model to the Hub

---

2 There are dozens of arguments you can modify. We suggest exploring the `Trainer` class documentation (*https://oreil.ly/5ocQU*) to understand all the options available.

3 A handy tool to estimate how much VRAM is needed to perform inference and training is the Model Memory Calculator (*https://oreil.ly/M2A2l*).

The AG News dataset contains 120,000 samples, more than we need to get good initial results. To make an initial quick training run, we'll use 10,000 samples, but feel free to play with this number—more data should yield better results. Note that we'll still evaluate with the whole test set:

```
from transformers import Trainer

# Shuffle the dataset and pick 10,000 examples for training
shuffled_dataset = tokenized_datasets["train"].shuffle(seed=42)
small_split = shuffled_dataset.select(range(10000))

# Initialize the Trainer
trainer = Trainer(
    model=model,
    args=training_args,
    compute_metrics=compute_metrics,
    train_dataset=small_split,
    eval_dataset=tokenized_datasets["test"],
    tokenizer=tokenizer,
)
```

With everything ready and the `Trainer` initialized, it's time to train:

```
trainer.train()
```

The training will report the loss, the evaluation metrics, and training speed details. Table 6-1 provides a summarized view.

*Table 6-1. Training and evaluation metrics for DistilBERT fine-tuning on the AG News dataset*

| Metric | Epoch 1 value | Epoch 2 value |
|---|---|---|
| eval_loss | 0.2624 | 0.2433 |
| eval_accuracy | 0.9117 | 0.9184 |
| eval_f1 | 0.9118 | 0.9183 |
| eval_runtime | 15.2709 | 14.5161 |
| eval_samples_per_second | 497.678 | 523.557 |
| eval_steps_per_second | 15.585 | 16.396 |
| train_runtime | - | 213.9327 |
| train_samples_per_second | - | 93.487 |
| train_steps_per_second | - | 2.926 |
| train_loss | - | 0.2714 |

Hopefully, that took just a little bit of time. The final evaluation accuracy and F1 score were close to 92%, which is OK, especially given we're using less than 10% of the available training data. The evaluation loss decreases between epochs, which is exactly what we were aiming for. If you want to share the final model for others to access, you need to make a call to push_to_hub at the end. You can find our model on the Hub (*https://oreil.ly/k5BP5*):

```
trainer.push_to_hub()
```

Although using the Trainer might appear like a black box, under the hood, it's just making regular PyTorch training loops as we did to train simple diffusion models in Chapter 3. Writing such a loop from scratch would look something like this:

```
from transformers import AdamW, get_scheduler

optimizer = AdamW(model.parameters(), lr=5e-5) ❶
lr_scheduler = get_scheduler("linear", ...) ❷

for epoch in range(num_epochs): ❸
    for batch in train_dataloader: ❹
        batch = {k: v.to(device) for k, v in batch.items()} ❺
        outputs = model(**batch)
        loss = outputs.loss ❻
        loss.backward()

        optimizer.step() ❼
        lr_scheduler.step()
        optimizer.zero_grad()
```

❶ The optimizer holds the current state of the model and will update the parameters based on the gradients.

❷ A learning rate scheduler that defines how the learning rate changes through training.

❸ Iterate over all data for a number of epochs.

❹ Iterate over all batches in the training data.

❺ Move the batch to the device and run the model.

❻ Compute the loss and backpropagate.

❼ Update the model parameters, adjust the learning rate, and reset the gradients to zero.

The Trainer takes care of this, from doing evaluations and predictions, pushing the models to the Hub, training on multiple GPUs, saving instant checkpoints, logging, and many other things.

If you pushed the model to the Hub, others can now access it using `AutoModel` or `pipeline()`. Let's try out an example:

```
# Use a pipeline as a high-level helper
from transformers import pipeline

pipe = pipeline(
    "text-classification",
    model="genaibook/classifier-chapter4",
    device=device,
)
pipe(
    """The soccer match between Spain and
Portugal ended in a terrible result for Portugal."""
)
[{'label': 'Sports', 'score': 0.8631355166435242}]
```

The prediction appears to be correct. On your first try, you might get `LABEL_1` instead of `Sports`. This is because the model doesn't have knowledge of the intrinsic label names. To update them, you can update the *config.json* file by adding the `id2label` and `label2id` mappings. This will make the predictions more human readable and interpretable.

Let's do a deep dive into the metrics. You can either use `Trainer.predict` or `pipe.predict` to get the predictions. The `Trainer.predict` method returns a `PredictionOutput` object, which contains the predictions, label IDs, and metrics, while `pipe.predict` returns a list of dictionaries with the predictions and the corresponding labels. Let's confirm that things make sense by looking at the first three sample texts with their corresponding predictions and labels. Running some samples through the network is always important to ensure that things work correctly:

```
# Get prediction for all samples
model_preds = pipe.predict(tokenized_datasets["test"]["text"])

# Get the dataset labels
references = tokenized_datasets["test"]["label"]

# Get the list of label names
label_names = raw_train_dataset.features["label"].names

# Print results of the first 3 samples
samples = 3
texts = tokenized_datasets["test"]["text"][:samples]
for pred, ref, text in zip(model_preds[:samples], references[:samples], texts):
    print(f"Predicted {pred['label']}; Actual {label_names[ref]};")
    print(text)

('Predicted Business; Actual Business; Fears for T N pension after '
 'talks Unions representing workers at Turner Newall say they are '
 "'disappointed' after talks with stricken parent firm Federal "
```

```
'Mogul.'
'\n'
'Predicted Sci/Tech; Actual Sci/Tech; The Race is On: Second '
'Private Team Sets Launch Date for Human Spaceflight (SPACE.com) '
'SPACE.com - TORONTO, Canada -- A second\team of rocketeers '
'competing for the  #36;10 million Ansari X Prize, a contest '
'for\\privately funded suborbital space flight, has officially '
'announced the first\\launch date for its manned rocket.'
'\n'
'Predicted Sci/Tech; Actual Sci/Tech; Ky. Company Wins Grant to '
'Study Peptides (AP) AP - A company founded by a chemistry '
'researcher at the University of Louisville won a grant to develop '
'a method of producing better peptides, which are short chains of '
'amino acids, the building blocks of proteins.')
```

The prediction is aligned with the reference, and the label makes sense. Let's now dive into the metrics.

In ML classification tasks, a confusion matrix serves as a table summarizing a model's performance, depicting counts of true positive, true negative, false positive, and false negative predictions. For multiclass classification, the matrix becomes a square with dimensions equal to the number of classes, where each cell represents the counts of instances for the combination of labels and predicted classes. Rows indicate actual (ground truth) classes, while columns indicate predicted classes. We can normalize the matrix so that each row adds up to 1, making it easier to interpret the model's performance across different classes. Analyzing this matrix provides insights into the model's strengths and weaknesses in distinguishing between specific classes.

We'll use *evaluate* to load and compute the confusion matrix and the Confusion MatrixDisplay from *sklearn* to visualize it. The confusion matrix will help us understand where the model is making mistakes and which classes are more challenging to predict. For example, by looking at the following confusion matrix, we can check that business articles are often mislabeled as sci/tech articles:

```python
import matplotlib.pyplot as plt
from sklearn.metrics import ConfusionMatrixDisplay

# Convert predicted labels to ids
label_to_id = {name: i for i, name in enumerate(label_names)}
pred_labels = [label_to_id[pred["label"]] for pred in model_preds]

# Compute confusion matrix
confusion_matrix = evaluate.load("confusion_matrix")
cm = confusion_matrix.compute(
    references=references, predictions=pred_labels, normalize="true"
)["confusion_matrix"]

# Plot the confusion matrix
fig, ax = plt.subplots(figsize=(6, 6))
disp = ConfusionMatrixDisplay(confusion_matrix=cm, display_labels=label_names)
```

```
disp.plot(cmap="Blues", values_format=".2f", ax=ax, colorbar=False)
plt.title("Normalized confusion matrix")
plt.show()
```

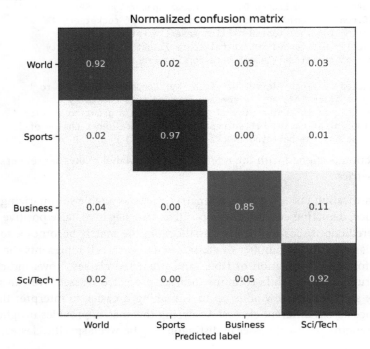

## Still Relevant?

Training an encoder model on text classification might appear almost quaint in the post-ChatGPT era. Can't we prompt a cheap model to "Classify the text into one of the following categories..."? While it is tough to beat the convenience of fast generalist models, in some cases small, custom classifiers prove helpful—particularly in applications where speed and efficiency are key.

For example, one domain in which these models shine is the preparation of training data for today's largest LLMs, which involves processing vast quantities of text. In the Llama 3 paper (*https://arxiv.org/abs/2407.21783*), the authors apply something they call "model-based quality filtering," in which a "quality classifier" is trained and then used to score documents for quality filtering. The authors state, "We use DistilRoberta to generate quality scores for each document for efficiency reasons." The training data for this quality model is predictions from Llama 2; it would have been extremely costly to use Llama 2 directly on the many trillions of tokens' worth of data that had to be filtered. A similar approach was used by the team behind Phi-3 (*https://arxiv.org/abs/2404.14219*), and by the FineWeb authors to curate the most educational content for their *FineWeb Edu* subset. The authors wrote an excellent blog post (*https://oreil.ly/ddh7Q*) on their recipes and the importance of quality filtering.

Another helpful use of small and fast encoder-based models is obtaining embeddings for retrieval systems, where the goal is to find the most similar documents to a given query. A final example of their usage is guardrailing, where you use a small model to check the input to a model to detect if it's malicious or to check the model's output to ensure it's not harmful. In all these cases, the speed and efficiency of a small model are key.

With all that said, today's trend is away from these small, specialized models and toward more-capable generalist models. Still, there is room for customization (hence this book), so let's discuss how we can apply a similar process to the one we've outlined to generate text: find (or create) a dataset, pick a model, define evaluation metrics, and train the model.

# Generating Text

We've just fine-tuned an encoder-based model for text classification. Now, let's dive into training a model for text generation. While in text classification, our labels are a list of discrete options (World, Sports, Business, and Sci/Tech), training and fine-tuning a generative model means doing the next token prediction task, where the labels are text outputs.

For instance, if our goal is to generate code, we can gather a substantial dataset of permissible code (such as The Stack (*https://oreil.ly/8F37c*)) and train a model from scratch. Although this is interesting, it would require a lot of compute to get decent results (leading to multiple training weeks or months).

Instead of training a model from scratch for open-ended text generation, we can fine-tune an existing model to generate text in a specific style. This approach allows us to benefit from the model's preexisting knowledge about the language, drastically reducing the need for extensive data and computing power. For example, you could employ a few hundred tweets to generate new ones in your distinctive writing style.

## With Labels or Without Labels?

With the next token prediction task, we do not need to explicitly label the data as we did for classification; the model will learn to predict the next token based on the input text. This has allowed us to build large-scale datasets from the web.

On the other hand, a new family of techniques, Reinforcement Learning with Human Feedback (RLHF), allows us to steer the model's output by providing feedback. This is particularly useful for conversational models, where you can provide preferences or corrections to the model's output. This is why many chatbots have a thumbs-up/thumbs-down button or provide side-by-side generated text for users to select the best one. Even then, preference optimization is just one component of the training process, and the model still needs to learn from data unsupervised. We'll discuss more about RLHF in Chapter 10.

Let's continue the news theme and fine-tune a model to generate news in a specific style, such as business news. We can use the same AG News dataset. Let's start by filtering all samples labeled as business (where the label is 2) and removing the unnecessary `label` column:

```
filtered_datasets = raw_datasets.filter(lambda example: example["label"] == 2)
filtered_datasets = filtered_datasets.remove_columns("label")
```

## Picking the Right Generative Model

The second question is which base model to use. As our goal is to do text generation, we need a decoder model. With thousands of models available, we need to choose one that fits our requirements. Let's discuss some of the key factors that might influence our decision:

*Model size*

Deploying a model with 60 billion parameters locally on your computer won't be practical. The choice of model size depends on factors like expected inference time, hardware capacity, and deployment requirements. Later in this chapter, we'll explore techniques that enable running models with more parameters using the same computing resources.

*Training data*

The performance of your fine-tuned model correlates with how closely the training data of the base model aligns with your inference data. For instance, fine-tuning a model to generate code in your codebase style is more effective when starting with a model pretrained on code. Consider the specificity of data sources, especially if not all models disclose their training data. Similarly, you will want to use something other than a predominantly English-based model for Korean text generation (such as multilingual or a Korean-trained model). Not all models disclose their data sources, which can make it challenging to identify this.

*Context length*

As discussed before, different models have different context length limits. For example, if the context length is 1,024, the model can use the last 1,024 tokens to make predictions. To generate long-form text, you will need a model with a large context length. We'll explore ways to work with longer contexts later in the book.

*License*

The licensing aspect is crucial when selecting a base model. Consider whether the model aligns with your usage requirements. Models may have commercial or noncommercial licenses, and there's a distinction between open source and open-access licenses. Understanding these licenses is essential to ensure compliance with legal and usage restrictions. For example, although some models may permit commercial use, they can specify permissive use cases and scenarios where the model should not be used. In other cases, the license may limit how the model's output can be used (e.g., prohibiting using the output of a model to train another model).

Assessing generation models remains a challenge, with various benchmarks evaluating specific aspects. Benchmarks such as ARC for science questions, HellaSwag for common sense inference, and others serve as proxies for different capabilities. The Hugging Face Open LLM Leaderboard (*https://oreil.ly/1huVO*) collects benchmark results for thousands of models and allows filtering according to model size and type. However, it's essential to note that these benchmarks are tools for systematic comparison, and the final model choice should always be based on its performance in your real-world task. Many of the benchmarks used in the Open LLM Leaderboard are not focused on conversation, and hence, they should not be used as the main criteria for picking a conversational model. The choice of model depends on your use case, and selecting a model based on a single metric is not recommended.

The Leaderboard considers a set of challenging benchmarks:[4]

*MMLU-Pro (knowledge)*

This is a knowledge dataset containing 12,000 multiple-choice questions. Each question includes a passage and 10 answer choices. The questions are about math, physics, economics, psychology, business, and more disciplines.

---

4 For a detailed explanation, refer to the Leaderboard blog post (*https://oreil.ly/cNFB-*).

*GPQA (complex knowledge)*

This is a small dataset of challenging, graduate-level, multiple-choice physics, chemistry, and biology questions. The questions are designed by domain experts (having or pursuing a PhD in the respective field) and are expected to be challenging even for nonexperts (skilled humans from other fields with access to the internet—the GP in GPQA stands for "Google-Proof").[5]

*MuSR (multistep reasoning)*

This contains complex problems with around a thousand words each, which presents challenges for short-context models. The problems can include murder mysteries, team allocation, and object placements.

*MATH (problem-solving)*

This contains over 12,000 problems from high-school math exams. There are different levels of difficulty, and the LLM Leaderboard uses only the hardest, level 5.

*BBH (mix)*

This benchmark contains a suite of 23 challenging tasks that require some multistep reasoning. The tasks cover algorithmic and arithmetic reasoning (e.g., Boolean expressions, geometric shapes, and navigation), natural language understanding (e.g., sarcasm detection and adjective ordering), world knowledge (e.g., understanding sports and recommending movies), and reasoning (translation error detection). This benchmark is correlated with human preference.

*IFEval (instruction-following)*

This dataset evaluates whether a model can follow instructions such as "mention the keyword Y at least three times" or "write in less than ten words".

Out of the six benchmarks used by the LLM Leaderboard, only IFEval is specifically targeted toward conversational models. We'll discuss conversational models later in the chapter. Our current goal is generating text in a specific style, so we'll focus on that. Table 6-2 shows a couple of popular open-access pretrained LLMs.

---

5 Nonexperts (having or pursuing a PhD in a field different than the question) answered the questions with unrestricted time and full access to the internet (except using LLMs). They were paid $10 for attempting to answer each question and a $30 bonus for answering correctly. On average, they spent 37 minutes per question and even then had a 34% accuracy!

*Table 6-2. A selection of popular open-access pretrained LLMs and their performance on the Open LLM Leaderboard*

| Model | Creator | Size | Training data | Open LLM performance | Context length | Vocab size | License |
|---|---|---|---|---|---|---|---|
| GPT-2 | OpenAI | 117M<br>380M<br>812M<br>1.6B | Unreleased<br>Up to 40 GB of text<br>from a web scrape | 6.51<br>5.81<br>5.48<br>4.98 | 1,024 | 50,257 | MIT |
| GPT-Neo | EleutherAI | 125M<br>1.3B<br>2.7B | The Pile<br>300B tokens<br>380B tokens<br>420B tokens | 4.38<br>5.33<br>6.34 | 2,048 | 50,257 | MIT |
| Falcon | TII UAE | 7B<br>11B<br>40B<br>180B | Partially released<br>Refined<br>Web built on top<br>of CommonCrawl<br>1.5T tokens<br>1T tokens<br>3.5T tokens | 5.1<br>13.78<br>11.33<br>N/A | 8,192 | 65,024 | Apache 2.0<br>(7B and<br>40B)<br>Custom<br>(11B and<br>180B) |
| Llama 2 | Meta | 7B<br>13B<br>70B | Unreleased<br>2T tokens | 8.72<br>10.99<br>18.25 | 4,096 | 32,000 | Custom |
| Llama 3 | Meta | 8B<br>70B | Unreleased<br>15T tokens | 13.41<br>26.37 | 8,192 | 128,256 | Custom |
| Llama 3.1 | Meta | 8B<br>70B<br>405B | Unreleased<br>15T tokens | 13.78<br>25.91<br>N/A | 131,072 | 128,256 | Custom |
| Mistral | Mistral | 7B | Unreleased | 14.5 | 8,192 | 32,000 | Apache 2.0 |
| Mixtral | Mistral | 8x7B<br>8X22B[a] | Unreleased | 19.23<br>25.49 | 32,768<br>65,536 | 32,000 | Apache 2.0 |
| Qwen 2 | Alibaba | 500M<br>1.5B<br>7B<br>72B | Unreleased | 7.06<br>10.32<br>23.66<br>35.13 | 131,072 | ~150,000 | Custom |
| Phi (1, 1.5, 2) | Microsoft | 1.42B<br>1.42B<br>2.78 | 54B tokens<br>150B tokens<br>1.4T tokens | 5.52<br>7.06<br>15.45 | 2,048 | 51,200 | MIT |

[a] What does "8x7B" mean in the "Mixtral" model? This means the model is a Mixture of Experts (MoE), a special model architecture you'll learn more about in Chapter 10. In short, it's a model with multiple smaller models, and an internal mechanism decides which models to use for each token. Comparing a number of parameters between MoE models and regular dense models is not straightforward, as you'll learn more about later.

This table is not exhaustive; there are many other open LLMs, such as Google Gemma, Mosaic MPT, and Cohere Command R+, and when this book is published, there will likely be many others. Similarly, this table does not cover code models. For those, you might want to review the Big Code Models Leaderboard (*https://oreil.ly/gZZ6v*), where you can find models such as CodeLlama (a popular model from Meta) and BigCode's model (a model trained with permissively licensed code).

Additionally, it's worth noting that this table is biased toward models trained on mostly English data. However, powerful Chinese models such as InternLM, ChatGLM, and Baichuan are also noteworthy contributors to the expanding landscape of pretrained LMs. This information serves as a guide on what to consider when choosing a model for experimentation rather than an exhaustive list of open source models.

## Training a Generative Model

Given that we want to do a quick training with very little data that can run in an environment without a powerful GPU, we'll fine-tune SmolLM's smallest variant. We encourage you to experiment with larger models and different datasets. Later in the chapter, we'll explore techniques for using larger models for inference and training.

Just as before, we'll begin by loading the model and the tokenizer. One particular thing about SmolLM is that it does not specify a padding token, but we require one when tokenizing, as it's used to ensure all samples have the same length. We can set the padding token to be the same as the end-of-text token:

```
from transformers import AutoModelForCausalLM

model_id = "HuggingFaceTB/SmolLM-135M"
tokenizer = AutoTokenizer.from_pretrained(model_id)
tokenizer.pad_token = (
    tokenizer.eos_token
) # Needed as SmolLM does not specify padding token.
model = AutoModelForCausalLM.from_pretrained(model_id).to(device)
```

We'll tokenize the dataset (but using SmolLM's tokenizer):

```
def tokenize_function(batch):
    return tokenizer(batch["text"], truncation=True)

tokenized_datasets = filtered_datasets.map(
    tokenize_function,
    batched=True,
    remove_columns=["text"], # We only need the input_ids and attention_mask
)

tokenized_datasets
```

```
DatasetDict({
    test: Dataset({
        features: ['input_ids', 'attention_mask'],
        num_rows: 1900
    })
    train: Dataset({
        features: ['input_ids', 'attention_mask'],
        num_rows: 30000
    })
})
```

In the topic classification example, we padded and truncated all samples to ensure they were the same length. Apart from doing it in the tokenization stage, we can do it using *data collators*. These utilities assemble samples into a batch. The *transformers* library provides some out-of-the-box collators for tasks (such as language modeling). The collator will dynamically pad the examples in a batch to the maximum length. Apart from the padding, the language-modeling collator structures the inputs for the language-modeling task, which is slightly more complex than before. In language modeling, we shift the inputs by one element and use that as a label. For example, if the input is "I love Hugging Face", the label is `love Hugging Face`. The model aims to predict the next token given the previous ones. In practice, the data collator will create a `label` column with a copy of the inputs. Later, the model will take care of shifting the inputs and labels.

The following code shows how to create the data collator for causal language modeling:

```
from transformers import DataCollatorForLanguageModeling

# mlm corresponds to masked language modeling
# and we set it to False as we are not training a masked language model
# but a causal language model
data_collator = DataCollatorForLanguageModeling(tokenizer=tokenizer, mlm=False)
```

Let's check out how this works for three samples. As shown here, each sample has a different length (37, 55, and 51):

```
samples = [tokenized_datasets["train"][i] for i in range(3)]

for sample in samples:
    print(f"input_ids shape: {len(sample['input_ids'])}")

input_ids shape: 37
input_ids shape: 55
input_ids shape: 51
```

Thanks to the collator, the samples are padded to the maximum length in the batch (55) and a `label` column is added:

```
out = data_collator(samples)
for key in out:
    print(f"{key} shape: {out[key].shape}")

input_ids shape: torch.Size([3, 55])
attention_mask shape: torch.Size([3, 55])
labels shape: torch.Size([3, 55])
```

Finally, we need to define the training arguments. By adjusting any of several key parameters of `TrainingArguments`, such as those that follow, we can exert some control over the model training:

*Weight decay*
> This regularization technique prevents model overfitting by adding a penalty term to the loss function. It discourages the learning algorithm from assigning large weights. Adjusting the weight decay parameter in `TrainingArguments` allows you to adjust this regularization effect, influencing the model's generalization capabilities.

*Learning rate*
> This key hyperparameter determines the optimization step size. In the context of `TrainingArguments`, you can specify the learning rate, influencing the convergence speed and stability of the training process. Careful tuning of the learning rate can significantly impact the model's generation quality.

*Learning-rate scheduler type*
> The learning-rate scheduler dictates how the learning rate evolves during training. Different tasks and model architectures may benefit from specific scheduling strategies. `TrainingArguments` provides options to define the learning-rate scheduler type, enabling you to experiment with various schedules such as constant learning rates, cosine annealing, or others.

In this example, we modify a few parameters to showcase this flexibility:

```
training_args = TrainingArguments(
    "business-news-generator",
    push_to_hub=True,
    per_device_train_batch_size=8,
    weight_decay=0.1,
    lr_scheduler_type="cosine",
    learning_rate=5e-4,
    num_train_epochs=2,
    eval_strategy="steps",
    eval_steps=200,
    logging_steps=200,
)
```

After all this setup, just as in the classification example, the final step is creating a `Trainer` instance with all the components. The main differences are that we're using a data collator this time and that we're using 5,000 samples:

```
trainer = Trainer(
    model=model,
    tokenizer=tokenizer,
    args=training_args,
    data_collator=data_collator,
    train_dataset=tokenized_datasets["train"].select(range(5000)),
    eval_dataset=tokenized_datasets["test"],
)

trainer.train()
```

Table 6-3 summarizes the training and evaluation loss during the fine-tuning process.

*Table 6-3. Training results for SmolLM fine-tuning on the AG News dataset*

| epoch | step | loss | grad _norm | learning _rate | eval _loss | eval _runtime | eval _samples _per _second | eval_steps _per_second |
|-------|------|------|-----------|----------------|-----------|---------------|---------------------------|------------------------|
| 0.32 | 200 | 3.2009 | 2.99705 | 0.0004690 | 3.31005 | 18.6024 | 102.137 | 12.794 |
| 0.64 | 400 | 2.8833 | 2.46037 | 0.0003839 | 3.21182 | 18.8513 | 100.789 | 12.625 |
| 0.96 | 600 | 2.7102 | 2.35531 | 0.0002656 | 3.09971 | 18.953 | 100.248 | 12.557 |
| 1.28 | 800 | 1.722 | 2.55815 | 0.0001435 | 3.24014 | 18.7631 | 101.262 | 12.684 |
| 1.6 | 1000 | 1.5371 | 1.89922 | 4.774e-05 | 3.224 | 18.7509 | 101.328 | 12.693 |
| 1.92 | 1200 | 1.4841 | 2.78178 | 1.971e-06 | 3.22884 | 18.5468 | 102.444 | 12.832 |

As before, let's push the model to the Hub:

```
trainer.push_to_hub()
```

Now we can use `pipeline()` and specify the task (`text-generation`) to load the model and run inference:

```
from transformers import pipeline

pipe = pipeline(
    "text-generation",
    model="genaibook/business-news-generator",
    device=device,
)
print(
    pipe("Q1", do_sample=True, temperature=0.1, max_new_tokens=30)[0][
        "generated_text"
    ]
)
```

```
print(
    pipe("Wall", do_sample=True, temperature=0.1, max_new_tokens=30)[0][
        "generated_text"
    ]
)
print(
    pipe("Google", do_sample=True, temperature=0.1, max_new_tokens=30)[0][
        "generated_text"
    ]
)

('Q1: China #39;s Airline Pilots Union Says Unions May Block Planes '
 '(Update1) China #39;s Air')
('Wall Street Seen Flat After Jobless Data  NEW YORK (Reuters) - '
 'Wall Street was expected to see a  slightly lower open on Friday')
('Google IPO Imminent Google #39;s long-awaited stock sale is '
 'imminent, and the company is already considering whether to sell '
 'its')
```

As you can notice, the generated text follows a similar structure to the AG News
business slice. However, the generated content may not always exhibit coherence,
which is fine considering that we used a small base model that doesn't have great
quality and used little training data. Using Mistral 7B or a very large model such as
the 70B variant of Llama 3.1 would no doubt yield much more coherent text while
preserving the same format.

## Instructions

In the first part of the chapter, we discussed fine-tuning an encoder-based model for
specific text-classification tasks such as topic classification. However, this approach
requires training a new model for each distinct task. If we encounter an unseen task,
such as identifying whether a text corresponds to spam, we won't have a pretrained
model readily available, and we'll need to fine-tune a model for it. This leads us to
explore other techniques, so let's briefly discuss the benefits, limitations, and uses of
different approaches:

*Fine-tuning multiple models*

> We can pick and fine-tune a base model for each task to build a specialized
> model. All the model weights are updated during fine-tuning, which implies that
> if we want to solve five different tasks, we'll end up with five model fine-tunes.

*Adapters*

We can freeze the base model and train a small auxiliary model called an adapter rather than modifying all the model weights. We would still need a different adapter for every new task, but they are significantly smaller, meaning we can easily have multiple without adding overhead. There's active research to manage hundreds or even thousands of adapters in production, and they are widely popular and used both by practitioners and in industry. You'll learn about adapters in the following section.

*Prompting*

As learned in the first chapter, we can use a robust pretrained model's zero-shot and few-shot capabilities to solve different tasks. With zero-shot, we write a prompt that explains a task in detail. With a few-shot approach, we add examples of solving the task and improving the model's performance. The performance of these capabilities hinges on the strength of the base model. A very strong model such as Llama 3.1 may yield impressive zero-shot results, which is great for tackling all kinds of tasks, such as writing those long emails or summarizing a book chapter.

*Supervised fine-tuning (SFT)*

SFT, also known as instruct-tuning, is an alternative and simple way to improve the zero-shot performance of LLMs.[6] Classical instruct-tuning formulates tasks as instructions such as, "Is the topic of this post business or sports?" or "Translate *how are you* to Spanish". This approach mainly involves constructing a dataset of instructions for many tasks and then fine-tuning a pretrained LM with this mixture of instruction datasets, as shown in Figure 6-3. Creating datasets for instruct-tuning is a task of manageable complexity; for instance, we could utilize AG News and structure the inputs and labels as instructions by building a prompt like this:

```
To which of the "World", "Sports, "Business" or "Sci/Tech" categories
does the text correspond to? Answer with a single word:

Text: Wall St. Bears Claw Back Into the Black (Reuters)
Reuters - Short-sellers, Wall Street's dwindling\\band of
ultra-cynics, are seeing green again.
```

---

6 Although originally called *instruct-tuning*, the community has settled on *supervised fine-tuning*, especially in the context of chat models after the InstructGPT paper.

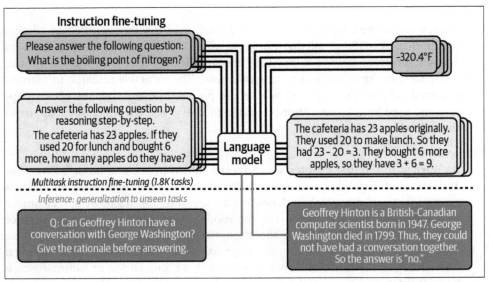

*Figure 6-3. With instruct-tuning, we can format many labeled datasets as generation tasks (adapted from an image in the Flan T5 paper (https://arxiv.org/abs/2210.11416))*

By building a large enough dataset of diverse instructions, we can end up with a general instruct-tuned model that can solve many tasks, even new ones, thanks to cross-task generalization. This idea is the foundation behind Flan, a model that can solve 62 tasks out of the box. This concept has been further expanded by the Flan T5 model (*https://arxiv.org/abs/2210.11416*), an open source family of instruct-tuned T5 models that can solve over 1,000 tasks. Something to note here is that the model is trained with input (instruction) and output (answer) texts; unlike the SmolLM fine-tune example, this is a supervised training technique. Instruct-tuning has been very popular with encoder-decoder architectures such as T5 or BART because of the input-output structure of the dataset. The idea has then been extended to most LLMs.

When should you use fine-tuning versus instruct-tuning versus prompt engineering? Once again, it depends on the task, available resources, desired experimentation speed, and more. Usually, fine-tuned models specific to a task or domain will perform better. On the other hand, they won't allow you to tackle tasks out of the box. Instruct-tune is more versatile, but defining the dataset and structure requires additional work. Prompt engineering is the most flexible approach for quick experimentation, as it won't require you to train a model out of the box. Still, it requires a more powerful base model, and there is limited control over the generation.

We won't build an end-to-end example of instruct-tuning as it's mostly a dataset task rather than a modeling task, but let's discuss some excellent papers if it's a topic you want to dive deeper into:

- The authors of "Finetuned Language Models Are Zero-Shot Learners" (February 2022) (*https://arxiv.org/abs/2109.01652*) train a model called Flan using instruction tuning and outperforming the base model's zero-shot performance and the few-shot performance of other models.

- After Flan, a new wave of dataset papers appeared. "Cross-Task Generalization via Natural Language Crowdsourcing Instructions" (March 2022) (*https://arxiv.org/abs/2104.08773*) introduces *Natural Instructions*, a dataset of 61 tasks with human instructions and 193,000 input-output pairs generated by mapping existing NLP datasets to a unified schema. The premise of doing this is that humans can follow instructions to solve novel problems by learning (in a supervised fashion) from instances of other tasks. The authors instruct-tuned BART, an encoder-decoder model, leading to a 19% gain in cross-task generalization compared to not using instructions. The more tasks the model is trained on, the better it performs.

- "Multitask Prompted Training Enables Zero-Shot Task Generalization" (March 2022) (*https://arxiv.org/abs/2110.08207*) follows a similar concept of unified data schemas for different tasks. The authors fine-tune T5 to build T0, an encoder-decoder model trained on a multitask mixture that generalizes to more tasks. One of the exciting highlights is that the more tasks represented in the data, the higher median performance the model achieves while not decreasing variability.

- This was later expanded with "Super-NaturalInstructions: Generalization via Declarative Instructions on 1600+ NLP Tasks" (October 2022) (*https://arxiv.org/abs/2204.07705*), a new dataset of over 1,600 tasks with 5 million examples. The difference in these projects is how the datasets were generated. T0 retroactively builds instructions based on already available task instances, while Natural Instructions had NLP researchers make instructions and crowd workers built dataset instances.

An alternative approach is to generate outputs by using LLMs:

- *Unnatural Instructions* (December 2022) (*https://arxiv.org/abs/2212.09689*) is a dataset of automatically generated examples based on seed examples and asking for a fourth. The dataset is augmented by asking the model to rephrase each instruction.

- *Self-Instruct* (May 2023) (*https://arxiv.org/abs/2212.10560*) bootstraps off the LMs' own generation. The idea is to have a model that generates the instruction, then the input (conditioned on the instruction), and finally the output.[7] Synthetically generated datasets tend to contain more noise. They can lead to

---

[7] In practice, this is more nuanced. The authors provided eight randomly sampled instructions and asked the model to generate more task instructions. The authors also removed duplicate and similar instructions.

a model that is less robust than a model trained with less but better-curated human-generated data.

- *LIMA* (May 2023) (*https://arxiv.org/abs/2305.11206*) is a much smaller English instruction dataset. Although it has only a thousand instances, the authors were able to fine-tune a robust Llama model. This was achieved thanks to a strong pretrained model and by very careful curation of training data.

These are just some of the massive explosion of instruct-tuned models. Flan-T5 is a fine-tuned T5 model using the FLAN dataset. Alpaca is a Llama fine-tuned on an instruction dataset generated by InstructGPT. WizardLM is a Llama instruct-tune on the Evol-Instruct dataset. ChatGLM2 is a fine-tuned bilingual model trained on English and Chinese instructions. We keep finding the same formula of combining a strong base model with a diverse dataset of instruction data (that can be human or model generated).

"Learning to Generate Task-Specific Adapters from Task Description" (June 2021) (*https://arxiv.org/abs/2101.00420*) is a different approach to improving generalization abilities. Rather than aiming for a general network for all tasks, the authors generate task-specific parameters called adapters. Although adapters have existed for years, their adoption has recently become widespread in natural language and image generation. In language models with billions of parameters, many people want to fine-tune for their domain or task. The next section is all about adapters.

To recap this section, the two main components for instruct-tuning are a robust base model and a high-quality instructions dataset. The quality of the instructions dataset is, unsurprisingly, key for the model. This dataset can be either synthetically generated (e.g., using self-instruct), manually generated, or a mix of both. Consistently, research has shown that the more tasks represented in the training data, the better the model is. Finally, the instruction template can impact the final performance a lot. Existing datasets end up trading off between quantity and diversity of tasks.

# A Quick Introduction to Adapters

Let's now dive into the fourth approach: adapters. So far, we've explored fine-tuning DistilBERT for text classification and SmolLM to generate text in our specific style. In both cases, all weights of the model were modified during fine-tuning. Fine-tuning is much more efficient than pretraining as we don't need too much data or compute power. However, as the trend of larger models keeps growing, doing traditional fine-tuning becomes infeasible on consumer hardware. Additionally, if we want to fine-tune an encoder model for different tasks, we'll end up with multiple models, multiplying the storage and compute requirements.

Welcome PEFT! *Parameter-efficient fine-tuning*, called *PEFT*, is a group of techniques that enable adapting the pretrained models without fine-tuning all the model parameters. Typically, we add a small number of extra parameters, called *adapters*, and then fine-tune them while freezing the original pretrained model. What effects does this have?

*Faster training and lower hardware requirements*
When doing traditional fine-tuning, we update many parameters. With PEFT, we update only the adapter, which has a small percentage of parameters compared to the base model. Hence, training is completed much faster and can be done with smaller GPUs.

*Lower storage costs*
After fine-tuning the model, we need to store only the adapter instead of the whole model for each fine-tuning. When some models can take over 100 GB to store, it won't scale well if each downstream model requires saving all the parameters again. An adapter could be 1% of the size of the original model. If we have 100 fine-tunes of a 100 GB model, traditional fine-tuning would take 10,000 GB of storage, while PEFT would take 200 GB (the original model and 100 adapters of 1 GB each).

*Comparable performance*
The performance of the PEFT models tends to be comparable to the performance of fully fine-tuned models.

*No latency hit*
As we'll discuss soon, after training, the adapter can be merged into the pretrained model, meaning the final size and inference latency will be the same.

This sounds too good to be true. How does it work? There are multiple PEFT methods. Among the most popular ones are prefix tuning, prompt tuning, and low-rank adaptation (LoRA), which we'll focus on in this chapter. LoRA represents the weight updates with two smaller matrices called *update matrices* using low-rank decomposition. Although this can be applied to all blocks in the transformer models, we usually apply them only to attention blocks.

*PEFT* is a simple library to use these techniques with *transformers* and *diffusers*. To start, let's discuss how to build an adapter of the SmolLM model from the previous section. In the case of LoRA, we can control multiple things, such as these:

*The rank* r
This controls the size of the update matrices. A larger rank allows the adapter to learn more-complex patterns but requires more parameters.

lora_alpha
This scales the update matrices. For example, if lora_alpha is 32 and r is 8, the gradient updates will be scaled by 4. This is similar to using a higher learning rate during training.

`lora_dropout`

    The dropout probability for LoRA layers, which can help with overfitting.

`task_type`

    The task type, such as `SEQ_CLS` (sequence classification) or `CAUSAL_LM` (causal language model). This will determine the adapter's architecture.

`use_dora`

    DoRA is a variant of LoRA that works particularly well to match the performance of full fine-tuning. We won't use it in this example, but it's good to know it exists.

The update matrix in LoRA isn't just any matrix. It's a special kind called a *low-rank matrix*. Imagine you have a huge matrix with lots of information. The idea behind low-rank matrices is to summarize it using fewer rows and columns without losing important information. For those interested in the (very high-level) math behind LoRA, the update matrix is represented with a low-rank decomposition, where $W_0$ is the original weight and $x$ is the input:

$$h = W_0 x + \Delta W = W_0 x + \frac{\alpha}{r} BA x$$

In LoRA, the update $\Delta W$ is expressed as the product of two low-rank matrices $B$ and $A$, with $B$ having fewer rows and $A$ having fewer columns than the original weight matrix. The scaling factor $\frac{\alpha}{r}$ controls the magnitude of this update. The dimensions of $B$ are $d \times r$ and the dimensions of $A$ are $r \times k$, where $d$ and $k$ are the rows and columns of the original weights, respectively.

Let's go into code. The first step is creating a configuration of a PEFT method:

```
from peft import LoraConfig, get_peft_model

peft_config = LoraConfig(
    r=8, lora_alpha=32, lora_dropout=0.05, task_type="CAUSAL_LM"
)

model = AutoModelForCausalLM.from_pretrained("HuggingFaceTB/SmolLM-135M")
peft_model = get_peft_model(model, peft_config)
peft_model.print_trainable_parameters()

trainable params: 460,800 || all params: 134,975,808 || trainable%: 0.3414
```

The initial model has almost 135 million parameters, but only about 460,000 would be trained. That's just 0.34% of the size of the original model. The idea behind PEFT is that we can train this small adapter and get similar performance to the model that's 300 times larger.

How does PEFT work under the hood? When you fine-tune a base model, you're updating all the layers. As discussed, LoRA approximates these update matrices with two smaller ones. For example, let's assume there's a single update matrix with 10,000 rows and 20,000 columns. That means it contains 200 million values. Let's assume we do LoRA with a rank of 8. The first matrix, $A$, would have 10,000 rows and 8 columns, while matrix $B$ would have 8 rows and 20,000 columns (to ensure the same input and output sizes). $A$ has 80,000 values and $B$ has 160,000. We went from 200 million values to 240,000 values. That's 800 times smaller! LoRA assumes that these matrices can approximate well enough the weight update matrices.[8]

We talked about the $r$ parameter. As mentioned, it controls the dimension of the LoRA matrices, which leads to a trade-off between capabilities and overfitting. A rank that is too high will lead to adapters that are too complex and prone to overfitting. A rank that is too low may result in underperformance because the model won't be able to capture enough complexity. The second key parameter is alpha, which controls how much the adapters impact the original model. A higher alpha gives more importance to the adapter. Picking the values of r and alpha depends on the problem and model. A good starting point for LLMs is to use a rank of 8 and consistently use an alpha twice as large as the rank.

After fine-tuning, we can merge the LoRA weights back into the original model, as shown in Figure 6-4. This means that the latency and the amount of compute needed to run inference with a model are exactly the same with or without a merged LoRA adapter:

$$\text{weight} = \text{weight} + \text{scaling} \times (B \times A)$$

---

8 This example is inspired by "Practical Tips for Finetuning LLMs Using LoRA (Low-Rank Adaptation)" by Sebastian Raschka (*https://oreil.ly/fsAqC*).

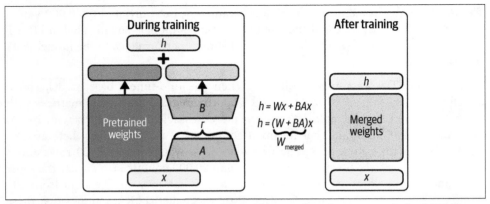

*Figure 6-4. LoRA reduces the number of trainable weights. Once trained, the LORA weights can be merged back into the original model.*

One exciting thing about LoRAs being so small is that they become very portable and practical for production. Imagine a use case in which the users expect a chatbot or an image generator to generate in 10 styles unknown by the initial model. Rather than fine-tuning the initial model 10 times and loading the models ad hoc, we can load and unload the adapter as needed. Recent techniques, such as LoRAX (*https://oreil.ly/ YCZei*), allow serving over a hundred fine-tuned adapters on a single GPU.

In some use cases, you might want to merge the adapters. Just as we updated a single adapter, we can keep doing so with multiple:

$$\text{weight} = \text{weight} + \text{scaling}_1 \times (B_1 \times A_1)$$
$$\text{weight} = \text{weight} + \text{scaling}_2 \times (B_2 \times A_2)$$
$$\text{weight} = \text{weight} + \text{scaling}_3 \times (B_3 \times A_3)$$

One last question is which parameters to update with LoRA. Using LoRA in more blocks often leads to slightly better performance at the expense of more extensive memory requirements during training, which may be a worthwhile trade-off and can be done with the `target_modules` parameter. We can use LoRA in the attention blocks for quick experimentation, which is usually the default of the *PEFT* library.[9] You can also use `target_modules="all-linear"` to choose all the linear modules, excluding the output blocks.

Although in this chapter we're focusing on text-generation fine-tuning, PEFT is widely used in other domains such as image generation (which we'll explore in Chapter 7), image segmentation, and more.

---

9 The default target modules depend on the model architecture.

# A Light Introduction to Quantization

PEFT allows us to fine-tune models with less compute and disk space. However, the size of the model during inference is not decreased. If you're doing inference of a model with 30 billion parameters, you will still need a powerful GPU to run it. For example, a 405B model such as Llama would require more than 8 A100 GPUs, which are pretty powerful and expensive (each one costs over $15,000). In this section, we'll discuss a technique that will allow us to run the models with smaller GPUs in a way that does not degrade their performance.

Each of those parameters has a data type or *precision* (see Figure 6-5). For example, the `float32` (FP32, also called full precision) type stores a float number with 32 bits. FP32 allows the representation of a wide range of numbers with high precision, which is important for pretraining models. In many cases, though, such a wide range is not required. In those cases, we can use `float16` (or FP16, also called half-precision). FP16 has less precision and a lower range of numbers (the largest number possible is 64,000), which introduces new risks: a model can overflow (if a number is not within the range of representable numbers). During inference, though, using FP16 is fine; the risks of half-precision are just significant during training. A third data type is brain floating-point, or `bfloat16`. BF16 uses 16 bits just like FP16, but allocates those bits in a different way in order to gain more precision for smaller numbers (like those typically found in neural network weights) while still covering the same total range as FP32.

Let's say we have a model of 7 billion parameters; 7 billion parameters, each being 32 bits, leads to 224 billion bits; 224 billion bits is 28 billion bytes, or ~26 GB. If we used half-precision, we would need only 13 GB. This is a significant reduction in memory usage, which can lead to faster inference and lower costs. Appendix B discusses memory requirements for different models and precisions.

Test your knowledge:

- How much memory would a 135M model in half-precision take?[10]
- How much memory would a 405B model in half-precision take?[11]

---

10 This would be ~260 MB, which is extremely light and can even run locally in a web browser.
11 This would be 405B × 16 ~ 800 GB. This would require at least two nodes with 8 A100 GPUs each.

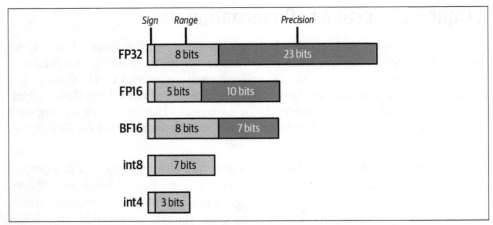

*Figure 6-5. How different precisions are represented*

Using full precision for training and inference usually leads to the best results, but it's significantly slower. For training, people have found ways to do mixed-precision training, which offers a significant speedup. In mixed-precision training, the weights are maintained in full precision as reference, but the operations are done in half-precision. The half-precision updates are used to update the full-precision weights.

The precision does not significantly impact inference, so we can load the model with half-precision. PyTorch loads all models in full precision by default, so we need to specify the type when loading a model by passing the `torch_dtype` if we want to use `float16` or `bfloat16`:

```
model = AutoModelForCausalLM.from_pretrained("gpt2", torch_dtype=torch.float16)
```

Loading the 7B model with 16 bits rather than 32 bits per parameter will require 13 GB of GPU for a 7B model, which might work well for some consumer GPUs; ~7B models such as Llama, Mistral, and Gemma have become popular solutions for consumer GPUs, but there are compelling models with even more parameters. For example, if we want to use a 32B model in half-precision, we would need a 64 GB GPU, far from any consumer GPU. Is there anything we can do to use these models?

Intuitively, we could think of naively reducing the range or the precision of the numbers to reach a quarter-precision (using a single byte, 8 bits per parameter). Unfortunately, doing so would lead to significant performance degradation. We can achieve quarter precision thanks to *8-bit quantization*. The idea behind 8-bit quantization techniques is to map a value from one type (e.g., fp16) into an `int8`, which would represent values in the [−127, 127] or [0, 256] range.

There are different 8-bit quantization techniques. Let's explore the simple *absmax quantization*. Given a vector, we first compute its maximum absolute value. We then divide 127 (the largest possible value) by this maximum value. This leads to a quantization factor—when we multiply the vector by this factor, we guarantee that the largest value will be 127. We can dequantize the array to retrieve the original numbers, but some information will be lost. This is better understood by running some code:

```python
import numpy as np


def scaling_factor(vector):
    # Get largest value of vector
    m = np.max(np.abs(vector))

    # Return scaling factor
    return 127 / m


array = [1.2, -0.5, -4.3, 1.2, -3.1, 0.8, 2.4, 5.4, 0.3]
alpha = scaling_factor(array)
quantized_array = np.round(alpha * np.array(array)).astype(np.int8)
dequantized_array = quantized_array / alpha

print(f"Scaling factor: {alpha}")
print(f"Quantized array: {quantized_array}")
print(f"Dequantized array: {dequantized_array}")
print(f"Difference: {array - dequantized_array}")

Scaling factor: 23.518518518518515
Quantized array: [  28  -12 -101   28  -73   19   56  127    7]
('Dequantized array: [ 1.19055118 -0.51023622 -4.29448819  1.19055118 '
 '-3.10393701  0.80787402  2.38110236  5.4         0.2976378 ]')
('Difference: [ 0.00944882  0.01023622 -0.00551181  0.00944882  0.00393701 '
 '-0.00787402  0.01889764  0.          0.0023622 ]')
```

These differences will lead to performance degradation. Because of this, classic quantization techniques have failed at scale with models of billions of parameters. *LLM.int8()* is a technique allowing us to do 8-bit quantization without degradation. The idea behind this technique is to extract outliers (i.e., values beyond certain bounds) and compute matrix multiplication of those outliers in FP16 while using int8 for the rest. This mixed-precision structure allows us to manage 99.9% of the values in 8-bit and 1% in full or half precision, and have no performance degradation.

What's the catch? The main goal of LLM.int8() is to reduce the requirement of huge GPUs to run model inference. Given the additional conversion overhead, doing inference will be slower (15–30% slower) than using fp16. One additional thing to note is that although all the GPUs from recent years provide tensor cores for int8, some older GPUs might not have good support for this.

The boundaries of low-precision inference are being pushed with new 4-bit and 2-bit quantization techniques. There are even explorations of using sub-1-bit quantization. Achieving quantization with no degradation is a research area of tremendous interest, given the trends of models becoming larger and larger. At the beginning of this section, we needed a 28 GB GPU to load a model with 7B parameters. We can now load the same model with 7 GB and no quality degradation at the cost of inference speed (but not too much).

The *transformers* library has integration with different quantization methods such as AWQ, GPTQ, and 4-bit and 8-bit with *bitsandbytes*.[12]

Loading the model in 8 bits is as easy as creating a `BitsAndBytesConfig` and specifying `load_in_8bit`. You can then pass this to the model when loading it:

```python
from transformers import BitsAndBytesConfig

quantization_config = BitsAndBytesConfig(load_in_8bit=True)
model = AutoModelForCausalLM.from_pretrained(
    "gpt2", quantization_config=quantization_config
)
```

Apart from quantization, we can do a couple of other things to work with very large models. One popular inference technique is called *offloading*, shown in Figure 6-6. If a model is too large to fit into your GPU, you can split it into multiple checkpoint shards, which are automatically handled by *transformers*. What benefits does it have? If a model is too large, we can load only the layers or shards that fit and offload the other operations into your CPU RAM, which is much slower. This allows us to work with any model size but at an inference speed cost that is not usable for many large models. If a model is so large that it won't fit into your CPU RAM, you can offload the model to disk, which is even slower but should allow you to work with any model size (as long as it fits your disk).

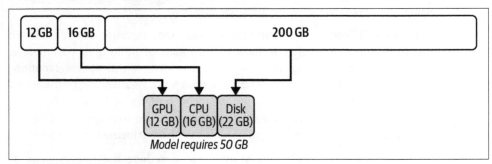

*Figure 6-6. Model offloading*

---

12 To learn more about model quantization techniques, we recommend reading the "Quantization" section (*https://oreil.ly/7XIKN*) of the *transformers* documentation.

# Putting It All Together

Let's review PEFT and quantization:

- PEFT allows us to fine-tune models using much less compute by adding adapters and freezing the base model weights. This accelerates training, given only a few weights are updatable.

- Quantization allows us to load a model by using fewer bits than those used for storage. This reduces the GPU requirements to load and run inference with a model.

Why not both? Let's imagine we train a model in 8 bits. Unfortunately, as discussed in the previous section, having high precision is important when pretraining or fine-tuning large models. On the other hand, PEFT freezes the base model and uses only a small adapter, so we could aim to use lower precision here while achieving the same performance.

*QLoRA* allows us to fine-tune large models with smaller GPUs. This technique is very similar to LoRA but with quantization. First, the base model is quantized into 4 bits and frozen. Then, the LoRA adapters (the two matrices) are added and kept in `bfloat16`. When fine-tuning, QLoRA uses the 4-bit storage base model and the half-precision 16-bit model to perform computations.

Loading a model in 4 bits just requires changing to the `load_in_4bit` parameter when you create the `BitsAndBytesConfig`. Let's try this with Mistral 7B, which is a solid base-model choice. Because this model is quite large compared to the previous ones, we'll also specify `device_map="auto"`. It will automatically try to fill all the space in your GPUs and then offload weights to the CPU if the model does not fit in the GPU (which would be much slower to run, but the model would still load).

One final detail before using Mistral: this model repository is *gated*, which means that the authors require explicit consent of their license terms. To use it, you have to visit the model page in Hugging Face (*https://oreil.ly/25rk2*) while being logged in to your account, read the license, and click the button to accept it if you agree to the terms. To access the model programmatically, as in the code snippet that follows, you have to be authenticated with the same account. The easiest way to do it is to install the *huggingface_hub* Python package (it comes with *transformers*) and run `huggingface-cli login` in a terminal session. You'll be asked for an access token that you can create on your Settings page (*https://oreil.ly/9zTFG*). If you are downloading the model from a Google Colab session, you can set up the `HF_TOKEN` secret and give permission to your notebook to use it.

```
quantization_config = BitsAndBytesConfig(load_in_4bit=True)

model = AutoModelForCausalLM.from_pretrained(
```

```
    "mistralai/Mistral-7B-v0.3",
    quantization_config=quantization_config,
    device_map="auto",
)
```

BitsAndBytesConfig allows more fine-grained control of the quantization techniques by using additional arguments to change the compute type, apply nested quantization, and more.

QLoRA is just a tool in our toolbox, not a golden bullet. It significantly reduces the GPU requirements while maintaining the same performance, but it also increases the training time it will take to train the model. All benefits of the PEFT section hold, making QLoRA a popular technique in the community to quickly fine-tune 7B models.

Let's do a QLoRA fine-tune to make a generative model that can do simple conversations. Let's go over each component:

*The base model*
    We'll use the Mistral model. Mistral is a very high-quality 7B model. We load the model with load_in_4bit and device_map="auto" to do 4-bit quantization.

*The dataset*
    We'll use the Guanaco dataset, which contains 10,000 high-quality conversations between humans and the OpenAssistant model.

*PEFT configuration*
    We'll specify a LoraConfig with good initial defaults: a rank (r) of 8 and alpha being double its value.

*Training arguments*
    Just as before, we can configure training parameters (such as how often to evaluate and how many epochs) as well as model hyperparameters (learning rate, weight decay, or number of epochs).

In the previous examples, we used the TrainingArguments and Trainer, two general-purpose tools from *transformers*. When fine-tuning an LLM for autoregressive techniques, the *trl* library's SFTConfig and SFTTrainer classes are useful tools. They are wrappers around the TrainingArguments and Trainer optimized for text generation. Their features include the following:

- Easy dataset loading and processing tools. Rather than having to process the dataset ourselves, we can use dataset_text_field to specify the field containing the training data. Additionally, we can use packing to concatenate multiple sequences, which is useful for efficient batch processing.

- Support for common prompt templates for conversations and instructions out of the box.

- The ability for you to directly pass any `PeftConfig` to the `SFTTrainer` to use PEFT techniques.

As before, we can pass the now quantized model and the dataset (we'll pass just 300 samples for fast training). `SFTTrainer` already comes with useful default collators and dataset utilities, so tokenizing and preprocessing the data is unnecessary:[13]

```python
from trl import SFTConfig, SFTTrainer

dataset = load_dataset("timdettmers/openassistant-guanaco", split="train")

peft_config = LoraConfig(
    r=8,
    lora_alpha=16,
    lora_dropout=0.05,
    task_type="CAUSAL_LM",
)

sft_config = SFTConfig(
    "fine_tune_e2e",
    push_to_hub=True,
    per_device_train_batch_size=8,
    weight_decay=0.1,
    lr_scheduler_type="cosine",
    learning_rate=5e-4,
    num_train_epochs=2,
    eval_strategy="steps",
    eval_steps=200,
    logging_steps=200,
    gradient_checkpointing=True,
    max_seq_length=512,
    # New parameters
    dataset_text_field="text",
    packing=True,
)

trainer = SFTTrainer(
    model,
    args=sft_config,
    train_dataset=dataset.select(range(300)),
    peft_config=peft_config,
)

trainer.train()

trainer.push_to_hub()
```

---

13 For more information, we recommend reviewing the *trl* documentation (*https://oreil.ly/27cdE*).

The preceding code might take about an hour or more to run. Remember, QLoRA leads to slower training as well.

While the model trains, it's a good opportunity to read more about the dataset. If you visit the dataset page (*https://oreil.ly/aARln*), you will notice it has the following format:

```
### Human: Can you write a short introduction ....### Assistant: "Monopsony"
refers to a market ..### Human: Now explain it to a dog
```

- Each turn begins with ### Human:, followed by a space, and then the human input.
- The model's response begins with ### Assistant:, followed by a space, and then the model's output.
- There can be many turns.

When you fine-tune a model for conversational tasks, it's common to have a *chat template*. All the details are essential. Adding a new line in the chat, removing a space, or having an additional # can degrade the model's generation. These expectations come from the training format that was used during training. Similarly, if a model is trained only with single-turn conversations, it will struggle to generate high-quality multiturn generations. Knowing the prompt format is important as we'll need to use it to generate high-quality conversations.

Once the training is done, let's proceed to using the model. When we pushed the model, we just pushed the adapter. Let's run inference with the model and the adapter:

```python
# We load the base model just as before
tokenizer = AutoTokenizer.from_pretrained("mistralai/Mistral-7B-v0.3")
model = AutoModelForCausalLM.from_pretrained(
    "mistralai/Mistral-7B-v0.3",
    torch_dtype=torch.float16,
    device_map="auto",
)

# You can load the adapter with `load_adapter`
model.load_adapter("genaibook/fine_tune_e2e")  # change with your adapter name

# Alternatively, you could just use `from_pretrained` with the adapter name and
# it will automatically take care of loading the base and adapter models.
# model = AutoModelForCausalLM.from_pretrained("genaibook/fine_tune_e2e"...

pipe = pipeline("text-generation", model=model, tokenizer=tokenizer)
pipe("### Human: Hello!### Assistant:", max_new_tokens=100)
```

The preceding code would output something like this:[14]

```
### Human: Hello
### Assistant: Hello! How can I help you?

### Human: I want to know how to make a website.
### Assistant: Sure! Here are some steps to help you get started...
```

Impressive, we just fine-tuned a 7B model to make it conversational without needing a huge GPU.

As conversational models became more common, Hugging Face *transformers* added a way for model creators to specify the `chat_template`. Thanks to this, end users don't need to worry so much about the prompt template and can instead focus on the content of the conversation. For example, you can simply pass the messages to the model, and the tokenizer will take care of formatting them automatically:

```python
pipe = pipeline(
    "text-generation", "HuggingFaceTB/SmolLM-135M-Instruct", device=device
)
messages = [
    {
        "role": "system",
        "content": """You are a friendly chatbot who always responds
        in the style of a pirate""",
    },
    {
        "role": "user",
        "content": "How many helicopters can a human eat in one sitting?",
    },
]
print(pipe(messages, max_new_tokens=128)[0]["generated_text"][-1])

{'content': 'The number of helicopters that can be eaten in one '
            'sitting depends on the number of people in the room. If '
            'there are 10 people, then there are 10 helicopters that '
            'can be eaten in one sitting. If there are 15 people, '
            'then there are 15 helicopters that can be eaten in one '
            'sitting. If there are 20 people, then there are 20 '
            'helicopters that can be eaten in one sitting.\n'
            '\n'
            'The number of helicopters that can be eaten in one '
            'sitting depends on the number of people in the room. If '
            'there are 10 people, then there are 10 helicopters',
    'role': 'assistant'}
```

---

14 We added a new line between human and assistant for readability, as well as an extra line between each turn.

If you just want to apply the chat template but not pass it to a model, you can use the `tokenizer.apply_chat_template()` method directly:

```python
tokenizer = AutoTokenizer.from_pretrained("HuggingFaceTB/SmolLM-135M-Instruct")

chat = [
    {"role": "user", "content": "Hello, how are you?"},
    {
        "role": "assistant",
        "content": "I'm doing great. How can I help you today?",
    },
    {
        "role": "user",
        "content": "I'd like to show off how chat templating works!",
    },
]

tokenizer.apply_chat_template(chat, tokenize=False)
```

We can use `print()` to get the full prompt, but take into account that the original string passed to the model contains characters such as \n to mark new lines:

```python
print(tokenizer.apply_chat_template(chat, tokenize=False))
```
```
<|im_start|>user
Hello, how are you?<|im_end|>
<|im_start|>assistant
I'm doing great. How can I help you today?<|im_end|>
<|im_start|>user
I'd like to show off how chat templating works!<|im_end|>
```

This will work for models where the `chat_template` is specified in *tokenizer _config.json*. To learn more about chat templates, we suggest reading the official documentation (*https://oreil.ly/qnikv*).

# A Deeper Dive into Evaluation

How can we evaluate the quality of the generated text? So far, we discussed popular benchmarks that evaluate general knowledge and reasoning, but you might wonder how to evaluate the quality of the generated text in a more general context. The first thing to differentiate is the evaluation of base models versus fine-tuned or chat models. The expectations are different for each, so we shouldn't evaluate them in exactly the same way. For example, we should not expect a base model to have instruct or chat capabilities out of the box, so evaluating it on these tasks would be unfair.[15]

---

15 This is changing recently. Some base models are adding instruction to their training data mixture, so they can follow basic instructions out of the box.

Let's begin discussing some ways to evaluate base models:

*Perplexity*

Perplexity measures how well an LM predicts a given dataset. A lower perplexity value indicates better performance and less uncertainty in generating text, suggesting that the model can predict the next word more accurately. Perplexity is particularly relevant during the training phase of base models, as it reflects the model's ability to learn effective probability distributions over word sequences.

*BLEU*

BLEU measures the similarity between the generated text and the reference text. It does so by calculating the proportions of n-grams in the generated text that are also present in the reference text. Given that BLEU heavily relies on exact n-gram matches, it can fail to capture the diversity of natural language and also lacks semantic understanding.

*ROUGE*

Similar to BLEU, ROUGE measures the overlap between two texts. However, ROUGE focuses on recall rather than precision, making it very useful for tasks such as summarization. However, it still lacks semantic understanding and tends to be biased toward longer outputs.

As you can see, evaluating base models is not straightforward. During training, loss and perplexity are usually tracked with the expectation that both decrease over time. ROUGE and BLEU are often used with datasets that have reference text. However, both metrics rely on exact matches and overlook semantic similarities, making them limited when evaluating more creative or diverse text generation.

A recent work, Urial (*https://arxiv.org/abs/2312.01552*), states that most of the gains we see in instruct-tuning actually come from the base model. The authors analyzed the token distribution shift between base and instruct-tuned models and found very little shift in the majority of tokens. The shifts that do occur are mostly stylistic, involving tokens like greetings and disclaimers expected in conversational models. This finding suggests that base models already possess much of the knowledge needed to follow instructions, highlighting the importance of pretraining. There's also potential for tuning-free methods (which don't require fine-tuning) to achieve similar performance to instruct-tuning, though this area is still under active research.

While these metrics provide a quantitative measure, qualitative evaluation, including human judgment, is also crucial to gauge the overall coherence and relevance of the generated text to the intended task. Quantitative metrics are useful for large-scale comparisons, but they might miss subtleties like fluency, creativity, or context appropriateness. This is where human evaluation shines. Balancing both quantitative and qualitative assessments ensures a more comprehensive evaluation of text-generation models.

For end-user generative models (such as chat models), one of the best things to do is play with the model. There are also popular arenas, such as LMSYS, where users interact with different anonymized models and pick the best results. The results are then aggregated in a leaderboard (*https://oreil.ly/L1L7Q*) that ranks the models, shown in Figure 6-7. These arenas are better than automated leaderboards as they reflect performance closer to real-world usage. Unfortunately, getting arena scores is expensive and, many times, not possible for a brand-new model. In such cases, benchmarks such as MT Bench, IFEval, EQ Bench, and AGIEval have some correlation to arena scores and hence can be useful to get a rough idea of how well a model will perform in the real world. New benchmarks are coming out frequently, so keeping current with the latest research is important.

| Arena | NEW: Arena (Vision) | Arena-Hard-Auto | Full Leaderboard |

Total #models: **133.** Total #votes: **1,717,800.** Last updated: 2024-08-22.

NEW! View leaderboard for different categories (e.g., coding, long user query)! This is still in preview and subject to change.

Code to recreate leaderboard tables and plots in this notebook. You can contribute your vote at chat.lmsys.org!

Category
Overall

Overall Questions
#models: **133 (100%)**   #votes: **1,717,800 (100%)**

| Rank* (UB) | Model | Arena Score | 95% CI | Votes | Organization | License |
|---|---|---|---|---|---|---|
| 1 | ChatGPT-4o-latest (2024-08-08) | 1317 | +5/-5 | 20885 | OpenAI | Proprietary |
| 2 | Gemini-1.5-Pro-Exp-0801 | 1298 | +4/-4 | 23232 | Google | Proprietary |
| 2 | Grok-2-08-13 | 1293 | +7/-6 | 6686 | xAI | Proprietary |
| 3 | GPT-4o-2024-05-13 | 1286 | +3/-3 | 80741 | OpenAI | Proprietary |
| 5 | GPT-4o-mini-2024-07-18 | 1275 | +5/-4 | 21621 | OpenAI | Proprietary |
| 5 | Claude 3.5 Sonnet | 1271 | +3/-3 | 51097 | Anthropic | Proprietary |
| 5 | Grok-2-Mini-08-13 | 1268 | +7/-7 | 7266 | xAI | Proprietary |
| 6 | Gemini Advanced App (2024-05-14) | 1267 | +4/-3 | 52136 | Google | Proprietary |
| 6 | Meta-Llama-3.1-405b-Instruct | 1266 | +4/-4 | 22312 | Meta | Llama 3.1 Community |
| 7 | GPT-4o-2024-08-06 | 1262 | +5/-5 | 13703 | OpenAI | Proprietary |

*Figure 6-7. This LMSYS leaderboard (https://oreil.ly/L1L7Q)*

Benchmarks, while valuable tools, also have their limitations. For instance, knowledge-based benchmarks often exhibit a US-centric bias, with questions about US history and law, as can be found in MMLU. Additionally, most of these benchmarks are English based, and few benchmarks are available for other languages. Some community efforts are underway to translate these benchmarks, but progress is slow and the translations may not be perfect. Furthermore, chat benchmarks (and often arenas as well) tend to focus more on single-turn conversations rather than multiturn conversations. Evaluating very long context models remains a challenge, particularly in a chat setting, and is an area that is yet to be resolved.

The most important takeaway is to test the model on the task you want to address. Benchmarks are useful for picking an initial base model for fine-tuning or general-purpose chat models, but they are not a substitute for real-world testing.

# Project Time: Retrieval-Augmented Generation

LLMs can use only information based on their context and the data used to train them. If you want to ask an LLM for information about a specific topic, it will know the answer only if it is part of its data. For example, if you try to ask Llama about new movies, it will struggle to provide accurate information.

Retrieval-augmented generation (RAG) is a technique in which the model can access information (e.g., paragraphs or documents) stored somewhere. With RAG, the LLM uses both the user input and the stored information to generate a response. This approach is powerful as it allows the model to access a large amount of information, which makes it easier to update than to retrain the model.

Unfortunately, there might be millions of documents, so you can't just pass all of them to the model. To solve this, we use an embedding model (such as the sentence transformers from Chapter 2) to encode each document into a vector, and we store these vectors (usually into something called a vector database). We then use a nearest neighbor search to find the documents most similar to the user input. Finally, we pass the user input and the retrieved documents to the LLM. This approach is compelling as it allows the model to access a large amount of information as needed.

Your goal is to build a pipeline as shown in Figure 6-8, in which:

1. The user inputs a question.
2. The pipeline retrieves the most similar documents to the question.
3. The pipeline passes the question and the retrieved documents to the LLM.
4. The pipeline generates a response.

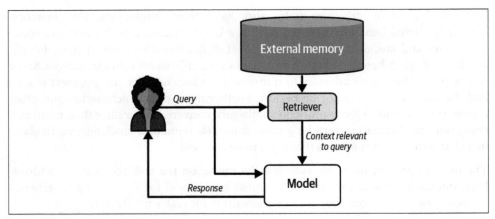

*Figure 6-8. A RAG pipeline*

You won't need to train any model for this task. For retrieval, we suggest using a *sentence_transformers* pretrained model. Feel free to use your favorite model, e.g., Mistral or Llama, for generations. Notice that Problems 1 and 2 were solved in Challenge 3 of Chapter 2, and Problems 3 and 4 were solved in this chapter. The goal is to put all these pieces together. You can use the following functions to guide you:

```python
def embed_documents(documents: List[str]):
    # Use a sentence transformer model to encode the documents

    # Store the documents somewhere

def retrieve_documents(query: str):
    # Use the stored documents to retrieve
    # the most similar documents to the query

def generate_response(query: str, documents: List[str]):
    # Use the LLM to generate a response

def pipeline(query: str):
    documents = retrieve_documents(query)
    response = generate_response(query, documents)
    return response
```

What documents to use? That's up to you, but we recommend beginning with a very minimal setup (i.e., pick 5–10 sentences or paragraphs, potentially crafted by yourself), and then you can scale up to more documents.

 Appendix C shows an end-to-end example of how to build a minimal RAG pipeline. We suggest trying to build the pipeline yourself first, and then check the appendix to see a complete example.

# Summary

This chapter explored techniques to fine-tune LLMs. We began by discussing traditional fine-tuning of encoder models for text classification. However, this approach can be used for other tasks, such as answering questions from a given text and identifying entities in a text. We then explored how to fine-tune a decoder model for text generation. We discussed the benefits and limitations of fine-tuning versus zero-shot or few-shot generation. We also examined how supervised fine-tuning can enable a generative model to solve multiple tasks out of the box.

Despite the power of these techniques, scaling them to the latest, increasingly larger models presents challenges. To address this, we explored using quantization to run inference with large models on smaller GPUs and discussed parameter-efficient fine-tuning (PEFT) techniques to fine-tune models with less computational and disk space requirements. By combining these techniques, we successfully fine-tuned a 7B model to make it conversational. With these foundations, you are equipped to fine-tune large models for your specific tasks.

While this chapter focused heavily on model architecture and fine-tuning techniques, it's important to remember that the success of these models also depends on the quality and diversity of the training data. It's not obvious to know how much data is needed: it depends on the model size, task complexity, and data quality. A few hundred high-quality training samples can often be more effective than thousands of low-quality ones.

For further readings, we suggest the following resources:

- To learn more about data, we recommend the FineWeb dataset blog post (*https://oreil.ly/ddh7Q*), a comprehensive introduction to a 15-trillion-token dataset, including an in-depth investigation on preprocessing, explanations on how to create high-quality web datasets, and how to create automatic annotations.

- Regarding evaluation, we suggest reading "Let's Talk About LLM Evaluation" (*https://oreil.ly/lC42O*), which presents a high-level overview of model evaluation and its challenges. We also recommend reading the Open LLM Leaderboard blog post (*https://oreil.ly/cNFB-*), which gives a comprehensive overview on community-centric model evaluation. Finally, Eugene Yan wrote an excellent blog post (*https://oreil.ly/JVlgq*) on the topic.

- To learn more about LoRA, we recommend reading "Practical Tips for Finetuning LLMs Using LoRA" (*https://oreil.ly/fsAqC*) as well as the QLoRA launch blog post (*https://oreil.ly/CbB9a*).

- To learn more about quantization, we recommend this visual guide to quantization (*https://oreil.ly/TINkA*) as well as *Hands-On Large Language Models* by Jay Alammar and Maarten Grootendorst (O'Reilly).

- To learn more about all the components used in a production LLM setup, we suggest the "Building a Generative AI Platform" blog post (*https://oreil.ly/l4R4h*).

## Exercises

1. What's the difference between base and fine-tuned models? What kind of model is a conversational one?

2. In which cases would you pick a base encoder model for fine-tuning?

3. Explain the differences between fine-tuning, instruct-tuning, and QLoRA.

4. Does using adapters lead to a larger model size?

5. How much GPU memory is needed to load a 70B model in half-precision, 8-bit quantization, and 4-bit quantization?

6. Why does QLoRA lead to slower training?

7. In which cases do we freeze the model weights during fine-tuning?

You can find the solutions to these exercises and the following challenge in the book's GitHub repository (*https://oreil.ly/handsonGenAIcode*).

## Challenge

*Image classification.* Although this chapter has focused on fine-tuning transformer models for NLP tasks, transformers can also be used for other modalities such as audio and Computer Vision. The goal of this challenge is to fine-tune a transformer model for image classification. We suggest the following:

- Use a pretrained ViT model such as google/vit-base-patch16-224-in21k (*https://oreil.ly/D174N*).

- Use a dataset of images and labels such as food101 (*https://oreil.ly/t4r_A*).

The logic will be almost the same, with some key differences such as using an `AutoImageProcessor` rather than an `AutoTokenizer`. We suggest looking into the documentation to guide you through the process.

# References

Abdin, Marah, et al. "Phi-3 Technical Report: A Highly Capable Language Model Locally on Your Phone." arXiv, August 30, 2024. *https://arxiv.org/abs/2404.14219.*

Belkada, Younes, and Tim Dettmers. "A Gentle Introduction to 8-bit Matrix Multiplication for Transformers at Scale Using Hugging Face Transformers, Accelerate and bitsandbytes." Hugging Face blog, August 17, 2022. *https://oreil.ly/FYVTE.*

Belkada, Younes, et al. "Making LLMs Even More Accessible with bitsandbytes, 4-bit Quantization and QLoRA." Hugging Face blog, May 24, 2023. *https://oreil.ly/CbB9a.*

Chung, Hyung Won, et al. "Scaling Instruction-Finetuned Language Models." arXiv, October 20, 2022. *https://arxiv.org/abs/2210.11416.*

Dettmers, Tim, et al. "LLM.int8(): 8-bit Matrix Multiplication for Transformers at Scale." arXiv, August 15, 2022. *https://arxiv.org/abs/2208.07339.*

Dubey, Abhimanyu, et al. "The Llama 3 Herd of Models." arXiv, August 15, 2024. *https://arxiv.org/abs/2407.21783.*

Honovich, Or, et al. "Unnatural Instructions: Tuning Language Models with (Almost) No Human Labor." arXiv, December 19, 2022. *https://arxiv.org/abs/2212.09689.*

Kocetkov, Denis, et al. "The Stack: 3 TB of Permissively Licensed Source Code." arXiv, November 20, 2022. *https://arxiv.org/abs/2211.15533.*

Lester, Brian, et al. "The Power of Scale for Parameter-Efficient Prompt Tuning." arXiv, September 2, 2021. *https://arxiv.org/abs/2104.08691.*

Li, Xiang Lisa, and Percy Liang. "Prefix-Tuning: Optimizing Continuous Prompts for Generation." arXiv, January 1, 2021. *https://arxiv.org/abs/2101.00190.*

Lin, Bill Yuchen, et al. "The Unlocking Spell on Base LLMs: Rethinking Alignment via In-Context Learning." arXiv, December 4, 2023. *https://arxiv.org/abs/2312.01552.*

Liu, Xiao, et al. "GPT Understands, Too." arXiv, October 25, 2023. *https://arxiv.org/abs/2103.10385.*

Mishra, Swaroop, et al. "Cross-Task Generalization via Natural Language Crowdsourcing Instructions." arXiv, March 14, 2022. *https://arxiv.org/abs/2104.08773.*

Sanh, Victor, et al. "DistilBERT, a Distilled Version of BERT: Smaller, Faster, Cheaper and Lighter." arXiv, March 1, 2020. *https://arxiv.org/abs/1910.01108.*

Sanh, Victor, et al. "Multitask Prompted Training Enables Zero-Shot Task Generalization." arXiv, March 17, 2022, *https://arxiv.org/abs/2110.08207.*

Wang, Yizhong, et al. "Self-Instruct: Aligning Language Models with Self-Generated Instructions." arXiv, May 25, 2023. *https://arxiv.org/abs/2212.10560.*

Wang, Yizhong, et al. "Super-NaturalInstructions: Generalization via Declarative Instructions on 1600+ NLP Tasks." arXiv, October 24, 2022. *https://arxiv.org/abs/2204.07705*.

Wei, Jason, et al. "Finetuned Language Models Are Zero-Shot Learners." arXiv, February 8, 2022. *https://arxiv.org/abs/2109.01652*.

Ye, Qinyuan, and Xiang Ren. "Learning to Generate Task-Specific Adapters from Task Description." arXiv, June 15, 2021. *https://arxiv.org/abs/2101.00420*.

Zhou, Chunting, et al. "LIMA: Less Is More for Alignment." arXiv, May 18, 2023. *https://arxiv.org/abs/2305.11206*.

# CHAPTER 7

# Fine-Tuning Stable Diffusion

In the previous chapter, we introduced how fine-tuning can teach LMs to write in a particular style or to learn concepts for a specific domain. We can apply the same principles to text-to-image models, allowing us to customize the models even with access to a single GPU (versus the multi-GPU nodes required to pretrain a model like Stable Diffusion).

In this chapter, we will use the base pretrained Stable Diffusion model you learned in Chapter 5 and extend it to learn styles and concepts it might not know about, such as the concept of "your pet" or a particular painting style. We will also learn how to give it new capabilities, such as inpainting and giving new conditions as inputs.

Rather than writing code from scratch here, we will look into understanding and running existing scripts created for fine-tuning the models in this section. For that, we recommend you clone the *diffusers* library, as most examples will be in the *examples* folder of the library:

```
git clone https://github.com/huggingface/diffusers.git
```

## Full Stable Diffusion Fine-Tuning

*Full model* is a qualifier to fine-tuning that emerged after the development of specific model customization techniques such as LoRA, Textual Inversion, and DreamBooth. Those techniques do not fully fine-tune the entire model, but rather either provide an efficient way for fine-tuning (as we learned with LoRAs for LLMs in Chapter 6) or provide novel ways to "teach" the model new concepts. We will discuss these techniques further in the chapter.

Before the emergence of such techniques, qualifiers such as *full model* didn't exist, as it was simply called fine-tuning. Fine-tuning in this context means further training the diffusion model—as you learned in Chapters 3 and 4—but with the goal to steer it toward specific knowledge you want to add. You could make Stable Diffusion learn a style or subject that you can't get via prompting or that was invented only after the model was released (see Figure 7-1). As the qualifier *full model* may imply, once the model gets fine-tuned, it will become good at the style or subject you introduced into it, and it may become specialized in producing primarily that type of content. This section will use a premade script to perform full fine-tuning. We are going to use the script *diffusers/examples/text_to_image/train_text_to_image.py* from the *diffusers* library.

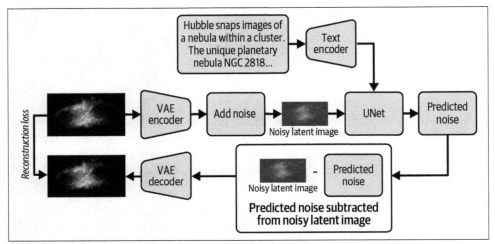

*Figure 7-1. Stable Diffusion fine-tuning architecture*

## Preparing the Dataset

The most important part of the dataset is quality. Filtering the dataset to keep only high-quality samples and removing low-quality examples can significantly affect the quality of your fine-tuning.

A relatively large dataset of 500+ images may be required for high-quality, full-model fine-tuning. Although this might sound like a lot, compared to the billions of images needed to train the entire Stable Diffusion model, having a dataset of hundreds of images is still a tiny fraction. In the specific model-customization techniques we will discuss further in the chapter, we will learn how to customize the model with as little as four images.

Back to the full model fine-tuning. As we steer a text-to-image model, we must show it a dataset containing images and the respective captions that describe those images, just as the model was shown during its pretraining training.

If you want inspiration, here are some examples:

- Renaissance paintings to make a Renaissance fine-tune
- Pictures of buildings in your favorite architectural style to make an architectural model
- A set of landscape photographs to fine-tune the model for generating realistic landscape scenes encompassing serene forests, majestic mountains, and tranquil lakeshores

 While we encourage exploration, fine-tuning and deploying for anything other than learning and educational purposes requires caution. If the images you are using are the style of an artist, the face of a person, or any material that holds intellectual property (IP) rights, asking the author or the IP holders whether you can do that not only is nice but could also be a legal requirement in your jurisdiction.

In our example, we will use Hubble Telescope imagery, which is put in the public domain by NASA six months after the images are taken. Creating a Hubble Telescope dataset and fine-tuning Stable Diffusion on Hubble imagery was pioneered by researcher Maxwell Weinzierl of the University of Texas at Dallas, who made the esa-hubble dataset (*https://oreil.ly/AtxyP*) and the Hubble Diffusion 1 and 2 models. For this example, we aim to re-create the Hubble Diffusion 1 model by fine-tuning Stable Diffusion v1.5 with the esa-hubble dataset.

The esa-hubble dataset was created by crawling images captured by the Hubble Telescope from the European Space Agency website. Thankfully, the captions describing the astronomical phenomena depicted in those images are also available, so both can be saved and put into a format compatible with the *datasets* library that can then be used for fine-tuning. How to collect the data (via web scraping or otherwise) is beyond the scope of this book, but you can look into tools such as Scrapy (*https://scrapy.org*) or Beautiful Soup (*https://oreil.ly/5a9Wr*) for web scraping in Python. Be mindful of each website's policy regarding crawling or scraping.

Once you have a dataset with image-text pairs, you can load them into the *datasets* library. The following section shows you how to do so. If you don't have your image dataset available, you can proceed with the provided esa-hubble dataset:

```
from datasets import load_dataset

dataset = load_dataset("imagefolder", data_dir="/path/to/folder")
```

`imagefolder` is a special mode for `load_dataset` that allows the loading of a directory of images and a metadata file containing the captions for each image. This mode requires you to have all your images in */path/to/folder* and a *metadata.csv* file containing the caption corresponding to each image. So your folder can have this structure:

```
folder/metadata.csv
folder/0001.png
folder/0002.png
folder/0003.png
```

And the *metadata.csv* file should look like this:

```
file_name,text
0001.png,This is a golden retriever playing with a ball
0002.png,A german shepherd
0003.png,One chihuahua
```

Once your dataset is loaded, you can push it to the Hugging Face Hub to share it with the community with a simple command:

```
dataset.push_to_hub("my-hf-username/my-incredible-dataset")
```

And you have your dataset saved and ready to fine-tune a model![1] In some cases, you have a perfect image dataset, but no human captions have been made for it. In these cases, you can use image-to-text captioning models to create captions that you can then use to fine-tune the model. Models such as BLIP-2 by Salesforce (*https://oreil.ly/pHzHH*) or Florence 2 by Microsoft (*https://oreil.ly/5rPi2*) are widely used for this task. To learn more, you can check the "Image-to-Text" task page (*https://oreil.ly/y8eOV*). If you don't have a dataset, don't worry; you can use the provided esa-hubble dataset.

## Fine-Tuning the Model

To fine-tune the model, we will need a dataset, as discussed in the previous section, as well as a training script and the weights of a pretrained model that we will be fine-tuning. Thankfully, we can easily set this up using the *diffusers* library, which provides example training scripts, and the *accelerate* library (for efficient training procedures, allowing training loops of PyTorch to work on multi-GPU, TPUs, or different precisions like `BF16`). This script is useful as it contains all the necessary code to efficiently train the UNet of Stable Diffusion while still giving control to the user with the exposed hyperparameters we will explore.

---

1 For more details on creating an image dataset with the *datasets* library, check out the "Create an Image Dataset" docs (*https://oreil.ly/wlPc7*).

You will need a GPU with at least 16 GB of VRAM to perform this fine-tuning or use services such as Google Colab Pro. The customization techniques we will learn about in this chapter allow for training on more modest GPUs or the free version of Google Colab.

You can follow along either by using your own dataset or by utilizing the esa-hubble dataset by Maxwell Weinzierl to follow along with replicating Hubble Diffusion.

To begin fine-tuning the model, you'll need to first clone the necessary training scripts from the *diffusers* repository:

```
git clone https://github.com/huggingface/diffusers.git
cd diffusers/examples/text_to_image/
```

Then, use the *train_text_to_image.py* script. For VRAM-constrained setups, we will use use_8bit_adam, which will require *bitsandbytes* and gradient_accumula tion_steps to use larger batch sizes than would typically fit in GPU memory:

```
accelerate launch train_text_to_image.py \
--pretrained_model_name_or_path="stable-diffusion-v1-5/stable-diffusion-v1-5" \
--dataset_name="Supermaxman/esa-hubble" \
--use_ema \
--mixed_precision="fp16" \
--resolution=512 \
--center_crop \
--random_flip \
--train_batch_size=1 \
--gradient_checkpointing \
--gradient_accumulation_steps=4 \
--use_8bit_adam \
--checkpointing_steps=1000 \
--num_train_epochs=50 \
--validation_prompts \
    "Hubble image of a colorful ringed nebula: \
A new vibrant ring-shaped nebula was imaged by the \
NASA/ESA Hubble Space Telescope." \
    "Pink-tinted plumes in the Large Magellanic Cloud: \
The aggressively pink plumes seen in this image are extremely uncommon, \
with purple-tinted currents and nebulous strands reaching out into \
the surrounding space." \
--validation_epochs 5 \
--learning_rate=1e-05 \
--output_dir="sd-hubble-model" \
--push_to_hub
```

Before we dig into the parameters, we suggest you run the script while you keep reading the chapter, as the training will take some time (one to three hours depending on your GPU). Then iterate the hyperparameters further after you've read through the entire chapter.

Going into detail on how the *train_text_to_image.py* script works under the hood is outside the scope of this book; however, the basics are the same as you learned in "Training a Diffusion Model" on page 115, where we covered the core concepts of training a diffusion model. The key steps involve preparing a dataset of images, defining a noise schedule, and creating a UNet model to predict noise. The training loop iteratively adds noise to clean images, has the model predict this noise, calculates loss between predicted and actual noise, and updates model weights via backpropagation. Here we are going to understand the key hyperparameters (which are the settings you set before starting to fine-tune your model), which are still very important; we are going to go over every setting in the preceding training script.

The most important concepts from this setup to learn are `learning_rate` and `num_train_epochs`:

`learning_rate`
: Denotes the amount by which the weights of your model are updated for each training step. If you aim for a higher learning rate, the optimization process for fine-tuning the model may not stabilize, while a too-low value may underfit, and your model may never learn. We recommend experimenting between 1e-04 (0.0001) and 1e-06 (0.000001).

`num_train_epochs`
: Denotes how many times your model will go through the entire dataset. It is normal for the model to need multiple passes over the dataset to learn a concept. Another way to set how many times the model will run the training loop is by setting up the `max_train_steps` variable, where you can set the exact amount of training steps the model will go through (even if it wraps up in the middle of an epoch).

We will also go over the other hyperparameters in less detail:

`use_ema`
: Denotes using the exponential moving average to train the model, which helps stabilize the model's training over epochs by averaging the weights.

`mixed_precision`
: Will train the model in mixed precision. If set to `FP16` as in the preceding code, all nontrainable weights, such as the VAE, will be cast to half-precision. These weights are used only for inference, so we don't need them in full precision. This will use less VRAM and speed up training.

`resolution`
: Specifies the image resolution for training. The images will then get resized based on parameters such as `center_crop` (if the images are larger than the target

resolution, they will get center-cropped) and `random_flip` (some images will get flipped during training for more robustness).

`train_batch_size`
Specifies how many examples are shown to the model simultaneously. The larger the batch size, the larger the VRAM requirement, but the lower the training time.

`gradient_checkpointing` *and* `gradient_accumulation_steps`
This enables users to fit training on less VRAM. Using `gradient_check pointing` trades gradient memory for some additional computation, whereas `gradient_accumulation_steps` allows the use of larger effective batches by accumulating results from several training mini-batches.

`use_8bit_adam`
Whether or not to use 8-bit Adam Optimizer from *bitsandbytes* to reduce the required GPU memory. This option makes training faster and uses less memory, with lower precision than `FP16` or `FP32` precision for the gradient accumulation (summing gradients over multiple mini-batches before updating the model weights).

`checkpointing_steps`
After how many training steps (batches the model saw) is a snapshot of the model saved? Saving intermediary models is useful if you set up a high number of `num_train_epochs` or `max_train_steps`. You may realize that the best-performing model is trained on 30 epochs, and the full 50 got overfit.

`validation_prompts`
Prompts that help you check how your model is doing during training. For every `validation_epochs` epoch, your model will generate the images with the `validation_prompts` prompts, and you can perceptually analyze how the model is learning.

`output_dir`
Local directory where the model will get saved.

`push_to_hub`
Whether to push your model to the Hugging Face Hub after it is trained.

The *train_text_to_image.py* training script has more parameters and settings (*https:// oreil.ly/FrlRX*). Stable Diffusion XL can also be fine-tuned similarly (*https://oreil.ly/ RigW5*). Once your model is trained and pushed to the Hub, you can run inference on it.

## Inference

Once fine-tuned, the model can be used for inference just like a regular Stable Diffusion model, as you learned in Chapter 5, but this time, the model to be loaded is a newly trained one. In case you don't have the compute to train the model, here's a model trained on the same Hubble dataset that you can try out: Supermaxman/hubble-diffusion-1 (*https://oreil.ly/7vGaM*). You can also share your model with others using the Hugging Face platform. Here's an output of the Hubble fine-tuned Stable Diffusion model:

```python
import torch
from diffusers import StableDiffusionPipeline

from genaibook.core import get_device

model_id = "Supermaxman/hubble-diffusion-1"
device = get_device()
pipe = StableDiffusionPipeline.from_pretrained(
    model_id,  # your-hf-username/your-finetuned-model
    torch_dtype=torch.float16,
).to(device)

prompt = (
    "Hubble reveals a cosmic dance of binary stars: In this stunning new image "
    "from the Hubble Space Telescope, a pair of binary stars orbit each other "
    "in a mesmerizing ballet of gravity and light. The interaction between "
    "these two stellar partners causes them to shine brighter, offering "
    "astronomers crucial insights into the mechanics of dual-star systems."
)

pipe(prompt).images[0]
```

As you play with the model, you may realize that it has become very good at generating images that could have come from the Hubble telescope (or whatever you have fine-tuned it for), as shown by the preceding image it generated. However, it became a specialist in that. If you prompt it to produce anything else, it will make either some galaxy-looking output or just gibberish. This is because with fine-tuning the full model, it experiences *catastrophic forgetting*, by which the entire model gets tuned toward the direction you steered it. Also, as mentioned before, you needed quite a few images to train it. Techniques such as DreamBooth and LoRA can help overcome these limitations.

# DreamBooth

DreamBooth (Figure 7-2) is a customization technique for fine-tuning Stable Diffusion that first appeared in the DreamBooth paper (*https://oreil.ly/hyTOd*) from Google Research. The DreamBooth technique works by fully fine-tuning the Stable Diffusion UNet with a few sample images that are associated with a trigger word. To preserve the previous knowledge of the model, it also uses sample images representative of the type of object we are fine-tuning, using a method called *prior preservation loss*. As we will explain further in this chapter, if we want to fine-tune a specific dog (our dog), we'll use images of the dog, but also *class* images of other dogs.

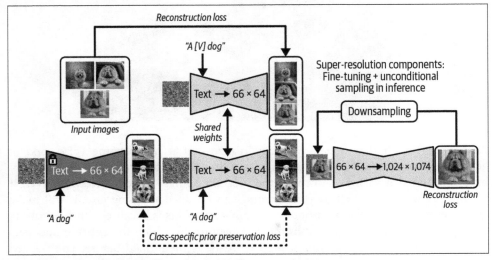

*Figure 7-2. The DreamBooth architecture flow*

DreamBooth brings in three exciting advancements when compared to full-model fine-tuning text-to-image diffusion models:

- Customizing a diffusion model by teaching it a new concept while retaining all the previous knowledge (avoiding the catastrophic forgetting property mentioned in the previous section). As shown in Figure 7-2, DreamBooth tunes a particular unique token or set of tokens toward a new concept being added. So, if you want to include your dog in the model, you can train it with the sentence a [T] dog, and every time you reference a [T] dog in your model, it will be able to do generations with the specific "dreamboothed" dog while keeping its characteristics. This can be achieved by utilizing the semantic knowledge the model already possesses (e.g., it "knows" what a dog is) with a novel class-specific prior preservation loss, allowing the model to keep that knowledge when generating the new concept. This combination allows for the creation of the subject in various scenes, poses, viewpoints, and lighting conditions that are not present in the reference images. Without a unique token, the model can mix in the new knowledge you are trying to train with an already existing concept associated with that token.

- Customizing a diffusion model with only 3–5 examples. Instead of using 500+ examples from full fine-tuning, the model can still learn and generalize well when given a small number of examples. This happens because the model can leverage its internal knowledge for the same class of content as the one you are aiming to customize (for example, a [T] dog contains the word "dog," which will then use the internal representations of dog from the model to then customize it to the specific dog in your image). A consequence of fewer examples is also fast training, as the model needs to process less.

- Writing a caption for each instance image that will be uploaded for the model to learn from, as we did for full fine-tuning, is compatible but optional, as using a token without captioning the images is sufficient for DreamBooth.

The DreamBooth technique in the original paper was applied to Google's proprietary diffusion model Imagen. However, open source community member Xavier Xiao adapted the technique to Stable Diffusion, and since then, many community implementations, such as the ones from TheLastBen and khoya-ss, emerged. The *diffusers* library also has DreamBooth training scripts.

Overall, through trial, error, and decentralized experience, community findings suggest the following:

- Three to five images typically suffice to train a common subject or style on Stable Diffusion.

- Using 8 to 20 images is more effective for training unique styles or rare objects.

- Prior preservation loss is beneficial for faces but may not be needed for other subjects or styles.

- Fine-tuning both the model's text encoder and UNet can produce good outcomes.

- Most of these insights have been incorporated into the community's training scripts.

We will use the script *diffusers/examples/dreambooth/train_dreambooth.py* from the *diffusers* library.

DreamBooth is not the first customization technique with the same goals. Textual Inversion (*https://oreil.ly/DdSxi*), based on the seminal paper "An Image Is Worth One Word" (*https://arxiv.org/abs/2208.01618*), showcases how to train a new embedding for the text encoder of the Stable Diffusion model to contain a new subject. The technique is still relevant, as the embeddings trained can be small (just a few kilobytes). However, there's a size versus quality trade-off, and DreamBooth's quality has made this technique dominant in the text-to-image community. Experiments with techniques combining Textual Inversion and DreamBooth (named Pivotal Tuning) have also shown good results. With DreamBooth, you need to find a unique trigger word. However, by utilizing Textual Inversion, we can create trigger words as new tokens, leading to better injection of new concepts.

## Preparing the Dataset

In general, 5 to 20 examples tend to be enough to train a new object or face. For styles, if the model is struggling to learn with that range, adding more examples can help. As captioning the images is not required for DreamBooth, all you have to do is have your training images in a folder of your preference that you can reference using the training code. For example, you can download the pictures of your pet.

For this example, we will train a model on the face of one of the authors. If you would like to follow along, feel free to train a model on your own face (or maybe a pet).

## Prior Preservation

With DreamBooth, you can optionally take advantage of a prior preservation class. This works by providing a prior preservation loss during training so that the model understands that it is generating elements of that same class. For example, when teaching the model your own face, having a collection of face images will help the model "understand" that the class you are trying to train are faces, so even though you provide few examples, it will be grounded on images of faces. If the model already has knowledge about the class you are going to create, you can even generate the prior images yourself (and the training code has a flag allowing you to do that) or upload them to a specific folder.

To enable prior preservation, you can configure a couple of parameters in the training script:

`with_prior_preservation`
    Whether to use prior preservation. If set to `True`, the model will generate images based on the `class_prompt` and `num_class_images` parameters. If you provide

a class_data_dir folder, images inside that folder will be used as class images instead.

class_prompt

When using prior preservation, the prompt describing the class of the generated sample images that will be used for training—for example, the face of a Brazilian man. It does *not* include the trigger word.

num_class_images

The number of class images to be generated. If you provide a class_data_dir folder, images inside that folder will be used as class images instead. If the folder has fewer images than num_class_images, the remaining ones will be generated by the class_prompt.

## DreamBoothing the Model

Just as with fine-tuning the entire model, the most important variables are learning_rate and num_train_epochs. A low learning rate followed by slowly incrementing the number of train epochs or steps can provide a good starting point to land on good quality. Another exploration route is fixing the number of train epochs or steps and increasing the learning rate. Both strategies can be combined to find the optimal hyperparameters.

Let's go over some parameters that are exclusive to DreamBooth:

instance_prompt

The prompt from which the model will attempt to learn the concept. Try to find a rare token or combination for your subject name and surround it with context, for example, in the style of mybtfuart, a photo of plstps, or an sckpto toy. The rare combination will be the trigger word for the particular instance you are fine-tuning.

train_text_encoder

Whether to train the text encoder as well. It can yield good results but consumes more VRAM. The reason training the text encoder together with the UNet may be useful is that you are also injecting knowledge about this new concept into the textual interpretation of the prompt.

with_prior_preservation

Whether to utilize prior preservation loss.

class_prompt *or* class_data_dir

A prompt to generate the class images for prior preservation. They will be taken from class_data_dir, if supplied. Otherwise, a few will be generated by the model by using the prompt specified in class_prompt.

`prior_loss_weight`

Controls the influence of the prior preservation loss on the model.

Let's use the *train_dreambooth.py* script to train a model on the face of one of the authors, as shown in Figure 7-3. If you want to follow along, feel free to train a model on your own face.

*Figure 7-3. Set of face images of "Apolinário Passos" for DreamBooth training*

```
accelerate launch train_dreambooth.py \
--pretrained_model_name_or_path="stable-diffusion-v1-5/stable-diffusion-v1-5"  \
--instance_data_dir="my-pictures" \
--instance_prompt="a photo of plstps" \ ❶
--resolution=512 \
--train_batch_size=1 \
--with_prior_preservation \
--class_prompt="an ultra realistic portrait of a man" \ ❷
--gradient_accumulation_steps=1 \
--train_text_encoder \
--learning_rate=5e-6 \
--num_train_epochs=100 \
--output_dir="myself-model" \
--push_to_hub
```

❶ `plstps` is a unique token for the model to learn the concept on.

❷ Here you can add a generic description of what you are training.

Once the model is trained, you can use it to generate new images. Let's explore how to do that.

## Inference

Even though the overall structure of the model is preserved and only the new token based on the `instance_prompt` is altered, the new DreamBooth model is still a full Stable Diffusion weight. Therefore, it can be loaded as such for inference:

```
model_id = "your-hf-profile/your-custom-dreambooth-model"
pipe = StableDiffusionPipeline.from_pretrained(
    model_id,
    torch_dtype=torch.float16,
).to(device)
```

```
prompt = "a photo of plstps speaking on a microphone"  ❶
pipe(prompt).images[0]
```

❶ Insert your instance prompt and some custom customization.

Figure 7-4 shows some results of the model trained on the face of one of the authors.

*Figure 7-4. Images generated by the model "DreamBoothed" on Apolinário's face*

# Training LoRAs

We have an issue with full fine-tuning and DreamBooth: once we finish tuning our model, we end up with new weights as large as the original Stable Diffusion model. This scenario is not ideal for sharing, hosting locally, stacking models, serving models in the cloud, and other downstream applications. For this, LoRA can be used (Figure 7-5), just as we did in Chapter 6 for LLMs.

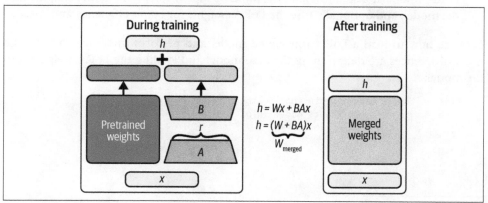

*Figure 7-5. LoRA architecture flow*

As discussed in Chapter 6, LoRAs allow freezing of the pretrained model weights and inject rank decomposition matrices, significantly reducing the number of parameters to be trained. The LoRA-trained ranks can also be shared as artifacts that can be merged into the model without additional inference latency.

Sounds great! But we are in the fine-tuning diffusion chapter, and the original LoRAs were focused on transformers. This is where Simo Ryu's Stable Diffusion LoRA GitHub repository (*https://oreil.ly/L3hEc*) comes into the picture. Realizing that LoRA rankings can be attached to the Stable Diffusion UNet and text encoder in the same way they can be added to transformers LLMs has now unlocked the power of LoRAs for diffusion models.

Once again, the *diffusers* library comes to the rescue, incorporating a script for LoRA training for both full-model fine-tuning and DreamBooth fine-tuning. Training a LoRA weight with *diffusers* is virtually the same as full model fine-tuning or Dream-Booth fine-tuning with *diffusers*, with some key differences:

- The dataset format is the same as the one used for full-model fine-tuning and DreamBooth fine-tuning.
- The training scripts are different, although the hyperparameters are the same. We will use *examples/text_to_image/train_text_to_image_lora.py* and *examples/dreambooth/train_dreambooth_lora.py* from the *diffusers* library.[2]
- For inference, the process involves loading the base model into the pipeline and then adding the LoRA adapter. This approach is convenient because it allows you to quickly load and switch between different LoRA adapters while keeping the same base model. For example, you can use a pretrained LoRA fine-tune shared by another user (you can find pretrained options on the Hugging Face Hub (*https://oreil.ly/3M8sI*)). The steps are: select the base model (the one the LoRA will be attached to), load the *diffusers* pipeline, load the LoRA weights into the model, and optionally fuse the LoRA weights for better efficiency and speed.

Let's see how to load a LoRA fine-tuned model and perform inference with it. The main differences are determining the base model and loading the LoRA weights into the model:

```
from diffusers import DiffusionPipeline
from huggingface_hub import model_info
```

---

2 LoRA trainer scripts such as Kohya (*https://oreil.ly/xIYPj*), TheLastBen (*https://oreil.ly/Yc1N5*), and Advanced LoRA Trainer (*https://oreil.ly/xsXSE*) built upon the *diffusers* scripts offer a lot more experimental functionality. Those are advanced but very well regarded by the community.

```python
# We'll use a classic hand drawn cartoon style
lora_model_id = "alvdansen/littletinies"

# Determine the base model
# This information is frequently in the model card
# It's "stabilityai/stable-diffusion-xl-base-1.0" in this case
info = model_info(lora_model_id)
base_model_id = info.card_data.base_model

# Load the base model
pipe = DiffusionPipeline.from_pretrained(
    base_model_id, torch_dtype=torch.float16
)
pipe = pipe.to(device)

# Add the LoRA to the model
pipe.load_lora_weights(lora_model_id)

# Merge the LoRA with the base model
pipe.fuse_lora()

image = pipe(
    "A llama drinking boba tea", num_inference_steps=25, guidance_scale=7.5
).images[0]
image
```

# Giving Stable Diffusion New Capabilities

Fine-tuning to teach the model new styles or subjects is incredible. But what if we could use fine-tuning to give Stable Diffusion more capabilities than usual? By fine-tuning with some special techniques, we can provide the model the capability of inpainting or include additional conditionings.

## Inpainting

Inpainting involves masking a specific area of an image that you would like to replace with something else. It is similar to image to image, with the difference that noise is added only to the masked area: the model denoises only that area, aiming to change or remove that item from the image while keeping the rest of the image intact.

It is possible to give inpainting capability to a pretrained text-to-image diffusion model by including additional input channels for the UNet. In the case of the inpainting specialist Stable Diffusion v1 model, they added ~400K steps by having five zeroed-out input channels for the UNet, with four for the encoded masked image and one for the mask itself. During training, synthetic masks are generated, with 25% of everything masked. As you have the ground truth of the image behind the mask, the model learns how to fill in the masked areas based on the prompt, becoming a powerful image-editing tool.

With more advanced models, such as Stable Diffusion XL, some inpainting capabilities come out of the box without further tuning, which made some people question whether a specialized fine-tuned model could improve this capability. However, SDXL specialist inpainting models (*https://oreil.ly/2XgEc*) were released with some extra capabilities, showing the potential for this technique even in bigger and more advanced models. While this technique is not accessible for training on domestic hardware, requiring full fine-tuning for hundreds of thousands of steps, the fine-tuned models are accessible and available to everyone. In the next chapter, we are going to explore inpainting in more depth (with code).

## Additional Inputs for Special Conditionings

Just as new input channels can be added to the UNet for the model to learn how to perform inpainting, other conditionings can be added. One example of this application was the Stable Diffusion 2 Depth (*https://oreil.ly/aZoEo*), a model resumed from `stable-diffusion-2-base` and fine-tuned for 200K steps with an extra input channel that processes both the user prompt and an image that contains a monocular depth (distance relative to the camera) prediction produced by MiDaS (*https://oreil.ly/5BbI3*). An example can be seen in Figure 7-6.

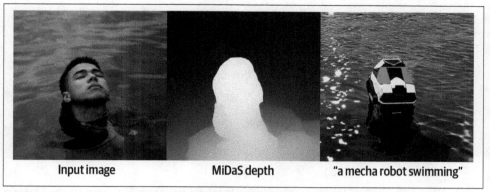

| Input image | MiDaS depth | "a mecha robot swimming" |

*Figure 7-6. Inference of Stable Diffusion 2 fine-tuned with MiDaS depth conditioning*

While this technique works well, fine-tuning the base model for hundreds or thousands of steps to get new conditioning limited this process to only a few companies and labs. However, techniques that append adaptors on top of the model, such as ControlNets, ControLoras, and T2I adaptors, emerged to make this process more efficient for training and inference; we are going to explore more of those creative text-to-image applications in the next chapter.

# Project Time: Train an SDXL DreamBooth LoRA by Yourself

Fine-tuning is a great way to bring more knowledge to text-to-image diffusion models, and as you learned in this chapter, DreamBooth allows for fine-tuning to happen with just a few example images, and LoRA training allows for small models and lower GPU usage when compared to fine-tuning the entire model. For this project, you will fine-tune a DreamBooth LoRA. After learning the basics of Dreambooth and LoRA, you can use *diffusers* more advanced scripts (*https://oreil.ly/xsXSE*). If you do not own a GPU with at least 16 GB of VRAM, we recommend using Google Colab (*https://oreil.ly/3ZIpB*) or Hugging Face Spaces (*https://oreil.ly/cgEOc*) for this project.

Your goal is to be able to prompt a new, not-yet-existing object or style into Stable Diffusion and have the model successfully generate a new image with it. This involves two steps:

1. Dataset creation:
   a. Find an object or style you want to include in the model. It could be a unique item you own (e.g., a wooden cat toy) or a style of furniture/paintings/rugs that you have in your house.
   b. Take a couple of pictures of these objects from different angles, in different backgrounds; around 3–8 pictures should suffice.

    c. Write a descriptive caption for each of the images, and use a unique token to describe your object (e.g., `cttoy`), for example:

- A photo of the front of a `cttoy`, white background

- A photo of the side of a `cttoy`, flowerpot in the background

    d. Either upload the dataset to the Hugging Face Datasets Hub (*https://oreil.ly/RV4Bh*) or keep it in a local folder.

2. Model training:

    a. Open any training script that suits you (based on the recommended ones or others you may find).

    b. Point the image folder to either the local folder or the Hugging Face Dataset you've created.

    c. Run the training. As explained earlier, you can experiment with `learning_rate`, `batch_size`, and other hyperparameters until you are satisfied with your LoRA. Refer to "Training LoRAs" on page 253 to learn how to load your trained LoRA into Stable Diffusion to test it out.

    d. With your `validation_prompts`, you can check how the samples are being generated during training. Once the model is trained, you can load it with `load_lora_weights` to understand how your model was trained.

## Summary

As training a big text-to-image model from scratch requires a significant amount of computing resources, fine-tuning steps in to enable single-GPU operations to customize preexisting models to produce what you need. In this chapter, you learned how fine-tuning diffusion models can lead to expanding knowledge and customization of the model for particular needs while retaining its overall knowledge. You learned how to do a full fine-tune, use DreamBooth for specific characters or styles, and use LoRA for efficiency. You also learned that fine-tuning diffusion models can give them new capabilities. Overall, fine-tuning is a powerful tool.

This chapter explored techniques for fine-tuning the Stable Diffusion model to teach it styles, subjects, or capabilities. Starting with full-model fine-tuning, you learned how to alter the model's behavior to generate images in a desired style or subject. We then moved to techniques like DreamBooth and LoRA, which allow for customization with fewer examples and less risk of catastrophic forgetting.

We also discussed the potential of fine-tuning to add new capabilities to the model, such as inpainting and special conditionings, expanding the utility of Stable Diffusion beyond its original configuration.

For additional readings, we suggest reviewing the following:

- "How to Fine Tune Stable Diffusion: How We Made the Text-to-Pokemon Model at Lambda" (*https://oreil.ly/-Vpcl*)
- "How I Train a LoRA: m3lt Style Training Overview" (*https://oreil.ly/oDuD6*)
- "Create an Infinite Icon Library by Fine-Tuning Stable Diffusion" (*https://oreil.ly/dEZPO*)
- Advanced diffusion training guide (*https://oreil.ly/xsXSE*)
- The DreamBooth paper itself (*https://arxiv.org/abs/2208.12242*)
- A lengthy introduction to LoRAs on diffusion models (*https://oreil.ly/zQZ-M*)

# Exercises

1. Explain the main differences between full-model fine-tuning and DreamBooth.
2. What are the advantages of using LoRA over full-model fine-tuning in terms of computational resources and model adaptability?
3. Why is it important to utilize a unique token when doing DreamBooth training?
4. Besides teaching new concepts, fine-tuning can also add new capabilities to the model. Cite two capabilities that the model can learn by applying fine-tuning techniques.
5. Discuss how the choice of hyperparameters affects the outcome of fine-tuning a diffusion model.
6. Describe the potential risks of fine-tuning text-to-image models on biased datasets.

You can find the solutions to these exercises and the following challenge in the book's GitHub repository (*https://oreil.ly/handsonGenAIcode*).

# Challenge

*LoRA versus full fine-tuning comparison.* Train a DreamBooth model with LoRA and full fine-tuning and compare the results. Try to modify the `rank` hyperparameter for the LoRA to see how much it affects the results.

# References

Gal, Rinon, et al. "An Image Is Worth One Word: Personalizing Text-to-Image Generation Using Textual Inversion." arXiv, August 2, 2022. *https://arxiv.org/abs/2208.01618*.

Hu, Edward J., et al. "LoRA: Low-Rank Adaptation of Large Language Models." arXiv, October 16, 2021. *https://arxiv.org/abs/2106.09685*.

Podell, Dustin, et al. "SDXL: Improving Latent Diffusion Models for High-Resolution Image Synthesis." arXiv, July 4, 2023. *http://arxiv.org/abs/2307.01952*.

Ruiz, Nataniel, et al. "DreamBooth: Fine Tuning Text-to-Image Diffusion Models for Subject-Driven Generation." arXiv, March 15, 2023. *https://arxiv.org/abs/2208.12242*.

Ryu, Simo. LoRA GitHub repository. 2022. *https://oreil.ly/L3hEc*.

# Going Further

# CHAPTER 8

# Creative Applications of Text-to-Image Models

This chapter presents creative applications that leverage text-to-image models and increase their capabilities beyond just using text to control generation. We will start with the most basic applications and then move on to more advanced ones.

## Image to Image

Even though generative text-to-image diffusion models like Stable Diffusion can produce images from text from a fully noised image, as you learned in Chapters 4 and 5, it is possible to start from an already existing image instead of a fully noised image. That is, add some noise to an initial image and have the model modify it partially by denoising it. This process is called *image to image*, as an image is transformed into another image based on how much it is noised and based on the text prompt.

With the *diffusers* library, we can load an image-to-image pipeline to load the class. As an example, let's explore how to use SDXL for this task. Here are the main differences:

- We use the `StableDiffusionXLImg2ImgPipeline` rather than the usual `Stable DiffusionXLPipeline`.
- We pass both a prompt and an initial image to the pipeline.

We can use either the `stabilityai/stable-diffusion-xl-base-1.0` (*https://oreil.ly/ kUqBY*) or the `stabilityai/stable-diffusion-xl-refiner-1.0` (*https://oreil.ly/ WqqsR*) model for applying our image-to-image refinements. The base model is recommended when you want to stylize your image or create new context from what is there. The refiner model, which specializes in working out fine details for the images, can be good if you want to refine or add details without many creative transformations to the image:

```
import torch
from diffusers import StableDiffusionXLImg2ImgPipeline
from genaibook.core import get_device

device = get_device()

# Load the pipeline
img2img_pipeline = StableDiffusionXLImg2ImgPipeline.from_pretrained(
    "stabilityai/stable-diffusion-xl-refiner-1.0",
    torch_dtype=torch.float16,
    variant="fp16",
)
```

Then, we can move the pipeline to our device (usually cuda for GPU). As some examples might require too much GPU, an alternative is to use img2img _pipeline.enable_model_cpu_offload(), which moves submodules to the GPU as needed. This will make inference slower but will allow you to run the model on a smaller GPU:

```
# Move the pipeline to the device
# Alternatively, img2img_pipeline.enable_model_cpu_offload()
img2img_pipeline.to(device)
```

Now that we have our pipeline, let's try an example:

```
from genaibook.core import SampleURL, load_image, image_grid

# Load the image
url = SampleURL.ToyAstronauts
init_image = load_image(url)

prompt = "Astronaut in a jungle, cold color palette, muted colors, detailed, 8k"

# Pass the prompt and the image through the pipeline
image = img2img_pipeline(prompt, image=init_image, strength=0.5).images[0]
image_grid([init_image, image], rows=1, cols=2)
```

Our StableDiffusionXLImg2ImgPipeline takes in the same inputs as the normal Stable Diffusion pipeline we've used so far, plus two extra parameters:

init_image
> The original image that we are going to modify.

strength
> How much noise we will add to the image. A strength of 0 will return the exact same image as no noise has been added. A strength of 1 will fully noise the image, ignoring it entirely and behaving like the regular text-to-image pipeline.

Check out the experiment in Figure 8-1, in which we took the same image and applied strengths between 0 and 1.

*Figure 8-1. Varying the denoising strength of an image from 0.1 to 1.0 with an image-to-image model*

# Inpainting

Inpainting is the process of filling in missing parts of an image based on the surrounding context. As we discussed in the previous chapter, it is possible to either use a model as it is for inpainting or fine-tune a text-to-image diffusion model to improve its inpainting capabilities.

Before we dive into the specifics of text-to-image diffusion models for inpainting, it's worth noting the distinction between this text-to-image generative approach and classical image-processing techniques for inpainting. Traditional methods typically rely on analyzing the surrounding pixels and using various algorithms to fill in the masked area based on local image statistics or patch-based sampling. While these classical approaches can be effective for simple backgrounds or small areas, they often struggle with complex textures or semantic understanding of the image content. In contrast, inpainting using text-to-image diffusion models offers several advantages. These models can understand and generate content based on both visual and semantic context, allowing for more coherent and creative results. However, ML methods generally require more computational resources.

Let's showcase how to perform inpainting and what creative applications it can leverage. As before, we can use a pipeline, `StableDiffusionXLInpaintPipeline`, to handle this:

```python
from diffusers import StableDiffusionXLInpaintPipeline

# Load the pipeline
inpaint_pipeline = StableDiffusionXLInpaintPipeline.from_pretrained(
    "stabilityai/stable-diffusion-xl-base-1.0",
    torch_dtype=torch.float16,
    variant="fp16",
).to(device)

img_url = SampleURL.DogBenchImage
mask_url = SampleURL.DogBenchMask

init_image = load_image(img_url).convert("RGB").resize((1024, 1024))
mask_image = load_image(mask_url).convert("RGB").resize((1024, 1024))

# Pass images and prompt through the pipeline
prompt = "A majestic tiger sitting on a bench"
image = inpaint_pipeline(
    prompt=prompt,
    image=init_image,
    mask_image=mask_image,
    num_inference_steps=50,
    strength=0.80,
    width=init_image.size[0],
    heigth=init_image.size[1],
).images[0]
```

In the resulting grid, the left panel denotes the source image, the middle panel denotes the mask image, and the right panel denotes the output image:

```python
image_grid([init_image, mask_image, image], rows=1, cols=3)
```

Some of the most important parameters that the `StableDiffusionXLInpaint` `Pipeline` takes in are as follows:

`init_image`
> The image that will be inpainted.

`mask_image`
> A binary color mask image. Black indicates the parts of the image that should remain the same, and white indicates where the image will be replaced with the generation.

`strength`
> The amount of noise we will add to the mask. Just like the strength for image to image, but applying only to the masked area. A strength of 0 will return the same image as if no noise has been added. A strength of 1 will fully noise the masked area, which is not the best scenario for smooth blending. Experiment with 0.6 to 0.8.

Apart from the base diffusion models, some models, such as `diffusers/stable-diffusion-xl-inpainting`, are fine-tuned to be specialized in inpainting. These models were fine-tuned explicitly for this task, which allows us to use a higher strength during inference.

# Prompt Weighting and Image Editing

As you learned in Chapter 4, diffusion models use transformer-like attention mechanisms that allow the model to focus flexibly on the most relevant parts of the input. Specifically, cross-attention is used to condition transformers inside the UNet layers with a text prompt to condition image generation.

However, you want more control over the generated image in some cases. For example, we may want to do the following:

- Modify how much weight is given to each word of a prompt by modifying the scale of the text embeddings.
- Combine multiple prompts to generate an image.
- Change the generations while keeping the structure for image editing.

For that purpose, "Prompt-to-Prompt Image Editing with Cross Attention Control" (*https://arxiv.org/abs/2208.01626*) introduced the idea of modifying the diffusion with the goal of obtaining steerability by modifying and controlling the cross-attention. That paper also has a nonofficial implementation for *diffusers* (*https://oreil.ly/wXPr_*).

Besides Prompt-to-Prompt, other techniques for editing generated images, such as Attend-and-Excite (*https://arxiv.org/abs/2301.13826*) and Semantic Guidance (*https://arxiv.org/abs/2301.12247*) emerged, both with official *diffusers* implementations. In this chapter, we will dive deeper into Semantic Guidance editing, as it balances steerability and edit quality.

## Prompt Weighting and Merging

The *compel* prompt enhancement library (*https://oreil.ly/eVTag*) implements key aspects of prompt weighting and merging and is easy to use with the *diffusers* library. It works by pre-processing the strings and enhancing the corresponding embeddings in the CLIP embedding space. As Stable Diffusion XL utilizes two text encoders, it adds complexity into the prompt weighting process. This complexity arises because the weighting must be harmonized between both encoders, and the output from the second text encoder needs to be pooled.[1] The *compel* library abstracts this complexity away.

Two simple ways to control the prompt are as follows:

- Increasing the weight with + signs after the word to give it more prominence in the image, modifying the scale of the text embedding. You can also decrease the weight with -. By adding multiple + and - signs, you can increase or decrease the weight of a word even more. Although we can reduce the prominence of a word, it may not always completely remove the concept from the image.

- Merge two prompts (by having them within brackets) and then specify the weight for each prompt.

Let's write some code. As usual, we begin by loading a pipeline:

```python
from diffusers import DiffusionPipeline

pipeline = DiffusionPipeline.from_pretrained(
    "stabilityai/stable-diffusion-xl-base-1.0",
    torch_dtype=torch.float16,
    variant="fp16",
).to(device)
```

---

1 Pooling involves converting the token embeddings into a single fixed-length embedding that reflects the entire sequence, just as we did with sentence embeddings.

We'll now initialize a `Compel` class, which requires providing the tokenizer and text encoders from the diffusion model. The class also requires specifying which text embedding will be pooled:

```python
from compel import Compel, ReturnedEmbeddingsType

# Use the penultimate CLIP layer as it is more expressive
embeddings_type = (
    ReturnedEmbeddingsType.PENULTIMATE_HIDDEN_STATES_NON_NORMALIZED
)
compel = Compel(
    tokenizer=[pipeline.tokenizer, pipeline.tokenizer_2],
    text_encoder=[pipeline.text_encoder, pipeline.text_encoder_2],
    returned_embeddings_type=embeddings_type,
    requires_pooled=[False, True],
)
```

Finally, we can generate images with different *compel*-enhanced prompts:

```python
from genaibook.core import image_grid

# Prepare the prompts
prompts = []
prompts.append("a humanoid robot eating pasta")
prompts.append(
    "a humanoid+++ robot eating pasta"
)  # make its humanoid characteristics a bit more pronounced
prompts.append(
    '["a humanoid robot eating pasta", "a van gogh painting"].and(0.8, 0.2)'
)  # make it van gogh!

images = []
for prompt in prompts:
    # Use the same seed across generations
    generator = torch.Generator(device=device).manual_seed(1)

    # The compel library returns both the conditioning vectors
    # and the pooled prompt embeds
    conditioning, pooled = compel(prompt)

    # We pass the conditioning and pooled prompt embeds to the pipeline
    image = pipeline(
        prompt_embeds=conditioning,
        pooled_prompt_embeds=pooled,
        num_inference_steps=30,
        generator=generator,
    ).images[0]
    images.append(image)
image_grid(images, rows=1, cols=3)
```

The + is equivalent to multiplying the prompt weight by 1.1, and the - is equivalent to a 0.9 multiplication. Besides using + and -, we can also weigh the tokens as follows: a robot eating (pasta)1.2. For more references in the *compel* library, check out its official reference guide (*https://oreil.ly/DES_7*).

## Editing Diffusion Images with Semantic Guidance

As mentioned, a few image-editing techniques exist for diffusion-generated images; while cross-attention control with Prompt-to-Prompt is a popular way to provide edits, Semantic Guidance (SEGA) allows for more fine-grained controls and precise edits.

SEGA operates by manipulating the model's noise estimates at each step of the reverse diffusion process. This dynamic noise adjustment allows SEGA to perform semantic edits in the latent space based on textual descriptions. By dynamically adjusting the predicted noise, SEGA ensures that the modification is steered toward the semantic direction derived from the text embeddings. The method calculates gradients of the text embeddings relative to the latent space, effectively guiding the image generation or modification toward the desired semantic outcomes. This process is achieved without needing to retrain or modify the original architecture of the model, allowing for dynamic and directed changes based solely on textual input.

Let's begin by showcasing the `SemanticStableDiffusionPipeline` to generate an image of a photo of the face of a man:

```
from diffusers import SemanticStableDiffusionPipeline

semantic_pipeline = SemanticStableDiffusionPipeline.from_pretrained(
    "CompVis/stable-diffusion-v1-4", torch_dtype=torch.float16, variant="fp16"
).to(device)

generator = torch.Generator(device=device).manual_seed(100)
out = semantic_pipeline(
    prompt="a photo of the face of a man",
    negative_prompt="low quality, deformed",
```

```
        generator=generator,
    )
    out.images[0]
```

As you'll see in the forthcoming examples, SEGA contains a few important parameters for its editing capabilities:

**edit_guidance_scale**
How strongly the model should follow the edits

**edit_warmup_steps**
How many denoising steps the model should start with before applying SEGA

**edit_threshold**
What percentage of the pixels of the original image should be preserved

**reverse_editing_direction**
Whether the edit should include (False) or remove (True) the concept

Let's guide the prompt in the direction of an editing_prompt to make the man smile, by adding "smiling, smile":

```
generator = torch.Generator(device=device).manual_seed(100)
out = semantic_pipeline(
    prompt="a photo of the face of a man",
    negative_prompt="low quality, deformed",
    editing_prompt="smiling, smile",
    edit_guidance_scale=4,
```

```
        edit_warmup_steps=10,
        edit_threshold=0.99,
        edit_momentum_scale=0.3,
        edit_mom_beta=0.6,
        reverse_editing_direction=False,
        generator=generator,
    )
    out.images[0]
```

Let's do another edit, this time to make the man wear glasses:

```
generator = torch.Generator(device=device).manual_seed(100)
out = semantic_pipeline(
    prompt="a photo of the face of a man",
    negative_prompt="low quality, deformed",
    editing_prompt="glasses, wearing glasses",
    reverse_editing_direction=False,
    edit_warmup_steps=10,
    edit_guidance_scale=4,
    edit_threshold=0.99,
    edit_momentum_scale=0.3,
    edit_mom_beta=0.6,
    generator=generator,
)
out.images[0]
```

Finally, let's do multiple edits simultaneously, as shown in the following code snippet. The only difference is that `editing_prompt` is now a list of prompts, and the key parameters (`edit_warmup_steps` and so on) must also be lists:

```python
generator = torch.Generator(device=device).manual_seed(100)
out = semantic_pipeline(
    prompt="a photo of the face of a man",
    negative_prompt="low quality, deformed",
    editing_prompt=[
        "smiling, smile",
        "glasses, wearing glasses",
    ],
    reverse_editing_direction=[False, False],
    edit_warmup_steps=[10, 10],
    edit_guidance_scale=[6, 6],
    edit_threshold=[0.99, 0.99],
    edit_momentum_scale=0.3,
    edit_mom_beta=0.6,
    generator=generator,
)
out.images[0]
```

## Real Image Editing via Inversion

Inversion is a technique for bringing a real image back into the latent space of a pretrained generative model. The technique showed promising results with GANs and was successfully implemented in guided diffusion models.

This allows us to answer a question you may have raised when learning about SEGA: "But what if we want to edit images from the real world instead?" One alternative is to use the image-to-image approach presented earlier. However, it can provide only very limited edits and does not always produce the expected results, as the results can change dramatically without much control. To solve that, we can combine a diffusion image-editing technique (such as Prompt-to-Prompt or SEGA) with an inversion technique to give more fine-grained editing.

The inversion process for guided diffusion models uses an *inversed scheduler* of a denoiser. The first denoiser with inversion introduced was DDIM Inverse (*https://oreil.ly/-W5z9*), which can predict samples from previous timesteps into the latent space by performing DDIM sampling in reverse order (starting with the real image and gradually adding noise to it). Then, when you denoise it, you have your original image as expected. By itself, this is not super-interesting; you've just used noisy latents to reconstruct an image you already had. However, inversion can become powerful if your goal is to provide edits to the image.

The most naive way to edit via inversion is to do the following:

1. Obtain the DDIM Inverse of a real prompt and a description (e.g., A photo of a horse in the field).

2. Modify the prompt to your target image (e.g., A photo of a zebra in the field).

3. Reconstruct the image with the modified prompt.

The results are shown in Figure 8-2.

*Figure 8-2. Editing with the DDIM Inversion technique (adapted from an image in "An Edit Friendly DDPM Noise Space: Inversion and Manipulations" (https://arxiv.org/abs/2304.06140))*

While these results are interesting, they aren't ideal for real image editing. More-advanced techniques, such as better inversions with DDPM Inversion with an edit-friendly noise space (*https://oreil.ly/XBqjc*), can provide better reconstructions but still cannot offer the broadest range of edits.

We can combine an inversion technique with editing techniques to provide a wide range of edits for real images. For example, "Null-text Inversion for Editing Real Images Using Guided Diffusion Models" (*https://arxiv.org/abs/2211.09794*) and LEDITS++ (*https://arxiv.org/abs/2311.16711*) utilize Prompt-to-Prompt and SEGA, respectively.

These techniques leverage the editing techniques you learned before, but instead of providing the edits in the latent space with an image that would be generated via a prompt, it happens in the latent space of the reconstruction of the image once it is inverted. Here, you will learn how to provide real-world image edits with LEDITS++, leveraging the already learned SEGA with inversion.

## Editing with LEDITS++

LEDITS++ combines two techniques you just learned: SEGA and inversion. It further implements a technique to ground your edit with the cross-attention and noise masks produced by the model. This combination allows us to edit real images with the same parameters we learned for SEGA.

LEDITS++ works as follows:

1. Apply inversion to bring the image we are interested in into a format the model can manipulate.

2. We decide our editing list with `editing_prompt` and the editing direction (whether to add or remove such concept) with `reverse_editing_direction`.

3. We apply the same `edit_guidance_scale` and `edit_threshold` we learned in SEGA for our edits.

Let's use the LEDITS++ pipeline:

```python
from diffusers import LEditsPPPipelineStableDiffusion

# Load the model as usual
pipe = LEditsPPPipelineStableDiffusion.from_pretrained(
    "stable-diffusion-v1-5/stable-diffusion-v1-5",
    torch_dtype=torch.float16,
    variant="fp16"
)
pipe.to(device)

image = load_image(SampleURL.ManInGlasses).convert("RGB")

# Invert the image, gradually adding noise to it so
# it can be denoised with modified directions,
# effectively providing an edit
pipe.invert(image=image, num_inversion_steps=50, skip=0.2)

# Edit the image with an editing prompt
edited_image = pipe(
    editing_prompt=["glasses"],
    # tell the model to remove the glasses by editing the direction
    reverse_editing_direction=[True],
    edit_guidance_scale=[1.5],
    edit_threshold=[0.95],
).images[0]

image_grid([image, edited_image], rows=1, cols=2)
```

## Real Image Editing via Instruction Fine-Tuning

Another way to provide real image editing for diffusion models is to fine-tune the model exclusively for this task. This approach was pioneered by the InstructPix2Pix paper (*https://oreil.ly/qKxf1*). Training requires a dataset of edit instruction pairs containing the original image, edit instructions, and the edited image.

The Stable Diffusion model is then appended with additional input channels to the first convolutional layer, allowing it to take in an image input. The model is trained with the same text-conditioning mechanism intended for captions in the original Stable Diffusion model, modified to take an edit instruction as its prompt (Figure 8-3).

Further trained and improved InstructPix2Pix models emerged after the publication of the original paper. The most prominent is CosXL Edit (*https://oreil.ly/See_0*) by Stability AI, trained on a variant Stable Diffusion XL to perform high-quality edits.

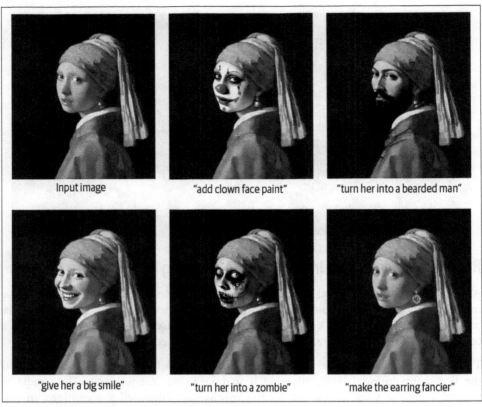

| | | |
|---|---|---|
| Input image | "add clown face paint" | "turn her into a bearded man" |
| "give her a big smile" | "turn her into a zombie" | "make the earring fancier" |

*Figure 8-3. Edits with the InstructPix2Pix technique*

The CosXL repository is *gated*, so visit the model page in Hugging Face (*https://oreil.ly/See_0*), read the license, and click the button to accept it if you agree to the terms. Run `huggingface-cli login` in a terminal session to log in. You'll be asked for an access token that you can create in your Settings page (*https://oreil.ly/9zTFG*). If you are downloading the model from a Google Colab session, you can set up a `HF_TOKEN` secret or environment variable and give permission to your notebook to use it. Here's an example edit done with CosXL:

```
from diffusers import (
    EDMEulerScheduler,
    StableDiffusionXLInstructPix2PixPipeline,
)
from huggingface_hub import hf_hub_download

edit_file = hf_hub_download(
    repo_id="stabilityai/cosxl", filename="cosxl_edit.safetensors"
)
```

```
# from_single_file loads a diffusion model from a single diffusers file
pipe_edit = StableDiffusionXLInstructPix2PixPipeline.from_single_file(
    edit_file, num_in_channels=8, is_cosxl_edit=True, torch_dtype=torch.float16
)

# The model was trained so that the EDMEulerScheduler
# is the correct noise scheduler for denoising
pipe_edit.scheduler = EDMEulerScheduler(
    sigma_min=0.002,
    sigma_max=120.0,
    sigma_data=1.0,
    prediction_type="v_prediction",
    sigma_schedule="exponential",
)
pipe_edit.to(device)

prompt = "make it a cloudy day"
image = load_image(SampleURL.Mountain)
edited_image = pipe_edit(
    prompt=prompt, image=image, num_inference_steps=20
).images[0]

image_grid([image, edited_image], rows=1, cols=2)
```

# ControlNet

*ControlNet* is a model for controlling image diffusion models by conditioning the model with additional conditions besides the text-prompt condition. The Control-Net models are trained over a trainable copy of the original model. Unlike direct fine-tuning, ControlNet preserves the original model completely and injects all the new conditions into this trainable copy of the original model. This allows for preserving the model's capabilities—even if your ControlNet is trained with relatively few samples.

The ControlNet models are trained to take in various conditions, two of which you see in Figure 8-4: `canny edges` and `human pose` (OpenPose). Besides those, there are also `depth maps`, `scribble`, `segmentation`, `lineart`, and more. Check out all the official Stable Diffusion v1-5 ControlNets on Hugging Face (*https://oreil.ly/q7-Rq*) and check out Hugging Face Models for community-trained ones (*https://oreil.ly/7JC4H*).

*Figure 8-4. ControlNet examples with image input, canny edges, and open pose conditionings, and the generated output*

ControlNet's versatility and efficiency make it a powerful tool for various image-generation and image-manipulation tasks. By allowing fine-grained control over the output while maintaining the original model's capabilities, ControlNet opens up new possibilities for creative and practical applications, as shown in Figure 8-5. For instance, it can be used in fields such as fashion design to visualize clothing on different body poses, in architecture to generate building designs based on rough sketches, or in film preproduction to quickly create storyboards from simple line drawings. The ability to use different types of control inputs, such as edges, pose estimations, or depth maps, provides creatives and developers with a flexible framework to guide the image-generation process according to their specific needs.

*Figure 8-5. Duck ControlNet Canny example*

We'll use an auxiliary library, *controlnet_aux* (*https://oreil.ly/Vjrv-*), to preprocess the input images into the desired condition format for the official pretrained ControlNet models. The *diffusers* library authors have also trained ControlNets for Stable Diffusion XL. You can find them in this Hugging Face collection (*https://oreil.ly/tYZu_*).

First, we load the main model with `StableDiffusionXLControlNetPipeline`. This pipeline also expects a `ControlNelModel` parameter with the model that provides additional conditioning to the UNet during denoising:

```
from diffusers import ControlNetModel, StableDiffusionXLControlNetPipeline

controlnet = ControlNetModel.from_pretrained(
    "diffusers/controlnet-depth-sdxl-1.0",
    torch_dtype=torch.float16,
    variant="fp16",
)

controlnet_pipeline = StableDiffusionXLControlNetPipeline.from_pretrained(
    "stabilityai/stable-diffusion-xl-base-1.0",
    controlnet=controlnet,
    torch_dtype=torch.float16,
    variant="fp16",
)
controlnet_pipeline.enable_model_cpu_offload()  # Optional, saves VRAM
controlnet_pipeline.to(device)
```

Then, we can use *controlnet_aux* to preprocess the image into the desired condition format. Here, we are using the `MidasDetector` preprocessing as it is a depth estimation model. This model takes in an image input and outputs an estimated depth map, which is exactly what we need to feed in for our `diffusers/controlnet-depth-sdxl-1.0` model:

```python
from controlnet_aux import MidasDetector
from PIL import Image

original_image = load_image(SampleURL.WomanSpeaking)
original_image = original_image.resize((1024, 1024))

# loads the MiDAS depth detector model
midas = MidasDetector.from_pretrained("lllyasviel/Annotators")

# Apply MiDAS depth detection
processed_image_midas = midas(original_image).resize(
    (1024, 1024), Image.BICUBIC
)
```

Finally, we can pass the prompt and the processed image to the pipeline to generate the new image. The `controlnet_conditioning_scale` will dictate how strongly the condition will influence the final result:

```python
image = controlnet_pipeline(
    "A colorful, ultra-realistic masked super hero singing a song",
    image=processed_image_midas,
    controlnet_conditioning_scale=0.4,
    num_inference_steps=30,
).images[0]
image_grid([original_image, processed_image_midas, image], rows=1, cols=3)
```

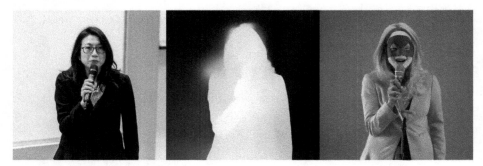

While training your ControlNets is outside the scope of this book, if you are interested in this subject, we recommend you check the Hugging Face blog's "Train Your ControlNet with diffusers" (*https://oreil.ly/TYKXl*).

# Image Prompting and Image Variations

Text prompts are great, but sometimes more is needed to express our intent to the model. Prompting diffusion models with images allows us to amplify our input range to the visual realm.

## Image Variations

To flourish our creativity, we sometimes need to look at something similar but different. That is the purpose of image variations: to take a given image and reinterpret it, providing a familiar yet different image generation. Let's explore two approaches—using CLIP image embeddings and IP-Adapter:

*Using CLIP image embeddings*

As you learned in Chapter 5, Stable Diffusion uses CLIP as its text encoder. Apart from the text encoder, CLIP can also be used to produce image embeddings. Some diffusion models were trained in such a way that they could use image embeddings as input to generate new image variations. That's the case of Karlo (*https://oreil.ly/WGWNf*) and Kandinsky (*https://oreil.ly/_NsIS*). For Stable Diffusion, this does not work out of the box. However, it can be achieved with fine-tuning. Stable Diffusion Image Variations (*https://oreil.ly/ZVOmp*) is a fine-tuned Stable Diffusion v1-5 model that accepts CLIP Image Embeddings as its inputs. You can try its demo on Hugging Face (*https://oreil.ly/fA2sU*).

*Using IP-Adapter*

Another approach that does not require fine-tuning the model is to utilize pretrained IP-Adapters (Image Prompt Adapters). These adapters allow prompting with images, allowing for image variations and a wide range of other use cases of image prompting, such as style transfer, subject identity preservation, and structure control.

As shown in Figure 8-6, IP-Adapter comprises two components: an encoder that extracts features from the image and decoupled cross-attention modules that get attached to the pretrained Stable Diffusion UNet.

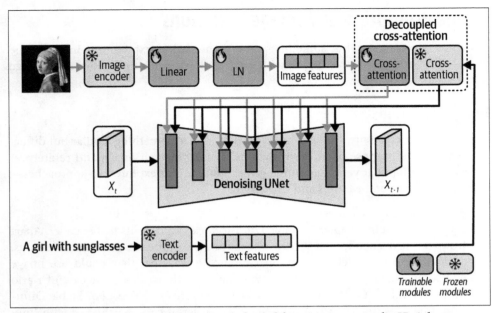

*Figure 8-6. The IP-Adapter architecture (adapted from an image in the IP-Adapter paper (https://arxiv.org/abs/2308.06721))*

Using IP-Adapter requires minimal changes over the base SDXL pipeline:

- Use `load_ip_adapter()` to load the IP-Adapter model.
- Specify the IP-Adapter scale with `set_ip_adapter_scale()`.

And that's it! To do image variations with IP-Adapter, we can provide the reference image and an empty prompt, and their results are as follows:

```python
from diffusers import StableDiffusionXLPipeline

sdxl_base_pipeline = StableDiffusionXLPipeline.from_pretrained(
    "stabilityai/stable-diffusion-xl-base-1.0",
    torch_dtype=torch.float16,
    variant="fp16",
)
sdxl_base_pipeline.to(device)

# We load the IP-Adapter too
sdxl_base_pipeline.load_ip_adapter(
    "h94/IP-Adapter", subfolder="sdxl_models", weight_name="ip-adapter_sdxl.bin"
)

# We can set the scale of how strong we
# want our IP-Adapter to impact our overall result
sdxl_base_pipeline.set_ip_adapter_scale(0.8)
```

```
image = load_image(SampleURL.ItemsVariation)
original_image = image.resize((1024, 1024))

# Create the image variation
generator = torch.Generator(device=device).manual_seed(1)
variation_image = sdxl_base_pipeline(
    prompt="",
    ip_adapter_image=original_image,
    num_inference_steps=25,
    generator=generator,
).images

image_grid([original_image, variation_image[0]], rows=1, cols=2)
```

With IP-Adapter, we generated a reinterpretation of our image (you can see that it removed the whipped cream—we can live with that!), which is really cool and enables fun use cases. However, IP-Adapter is way more powerful than what we've done so far. Image prompting can allow the combination of IP-Adapter with text prompting and the other controls you learned in this chapter.

## Image Prompting

IP-Adapter allows for more than just generating image variations. It allows you to utilize an image as one of the prompts, which enables you to apply techniques like style transfer and all the other techniques you learned in this chapter, adding an image prompt and a text prompt.

## Style transfer

While IP-Adapter works great out of the box with style transfer, the researchers behind the InstantStyle paper (*https://arxiv.org/abs/2404.02733*) realized that if IP-Adapter is applied to only certain blocks of the UNet of the Stable Diffusion model, it can affect exclusively the image style. The idea is that we can pass a prompt and a style image to the model, and the model will generate an image that follows the prompt but with the style of the style image. In this example, we are going to apply the style of the work by the Brazilian painter Tarsila do Amaral, "O Mamoeiro." The main differences are the scale of the IP-Adapter and the input prompt, which is no longer empty:

```python
# We load the model and the IP-Adapter, just as before
pipeline = StableDiffusionXLPipeline.from_pretrained(
    "stabilityai/stable-diffusion-xl-base-1.0", torch_dtype=torch.float16
).to(device)

# Load the IP-Adapter into the model
pipeline.load_ip_adapter(
    "h94/IP-Adapter", subfolder="sdxl_models", weight_name="ip-adapter_sdxl.bin"
)

# We are applying the IP-Adapter only to the mid block,
# which is where it should be mapped to the style in SDXL
scale = {"up": {"block_0": [0.0, 1.0, 0.0]}}
pipeline.set_ip_adapter_scale(scale)

image = load_image(SampleURL.Mamoeiro)
original_image = image.resize((1024, 1024))

# Run inference to generate the stylized image
generator = torch.Generator(device=device).manual_seed(0)
variation_image = pipeline(
    prompt="a cat inside of a box",
    ip_adapter_image=original_image,
    num_inference_steps=25,
    generator=generator,
).images

image_grid([original_image, variation_image[0]], rows=1, cols=2)
```

## Additional controls

Now, to wrap up this chapter, we can show how the multiple techniques we learn all composite together. We will add our IP-Adapter "O Mamoeiro" style to our previous example of the ControlNet masked singer:

```
controlnet = ControlNetModel.from_pretrained(
    "diffusers/controlnet-depth-sdxl-1.0", torch_dtype=torch.float16
)

# Load the ControlNet pipeline
controlnet_pipeline = StableDiffusionXLControlNetPipeline.from_pretrained(
    "stabilityai/stable-diffusion-xl-base-1.0",
    controlnet=controlnet,
    torch_dtype=torch.float16,
    variant="fp16",
)
controlnet_pipeline.to(device)

# Load the IP-Adapter
controlnet_pipeline.load_ip_adapter(
    "h94/IP-Adapter", subfolder="sdxl_models", weight_name="ip-adapter_sdxl.bin"
)
# We are applying the IP-Adapter only to the mid block,
# which is where it should be mapped to the style in SDXL
scale = {
    "up": {"block_0": [0.0, 1.0, 0.0]},
}
controlnet_pipeline.set_ip_adapter_scale(scale)

# Load the original image
original_image = load_image(SampleURL.WomanSpeaking)
original_image = original_image.resize((1024, 1024))
```

```
# Load the style image
style_image = load_image(SampleURL.Mamoeiro)
style_image = style_image.resize((1024, 1024))

# Apply the MiDAS depth estimation
processed_image_midas = midas(original_image).resize(
    (1024, 1024), Image.BICUBIC
)

image = controlnet_pipeline(
    "A masked super hero singing a song",
    image=processed_image_midas,
    ip_adapter_image=style_image,
    controlnet_conditioning_scale=0.5,
).images[0]
image_grid(
    [original_image, style_image, processed_image_midas, image], rows=1, cols=4
)
```

# Project Time: Your Creative Canvas

Now it's your creative canvas 🎨. In this chapter, we've provided multiple mechanisms for creative applications and expression. It's your time to exercise that now; your challenge in this chapter is to try to combine at least two techniques we presented here in your own creative ways—similarly to how we have created the masked superhero in the "memoirs" style. Here are some ideas to guide your creative journey:

- Use ControlNet canny edges to reimagine your living space with an IP-Adapter style applied from a reference you hold dear.

- Draw a rough sketch of a city on a piece of paper, take a picture, and apply image to image to turn that city into a Solarpunk utopia. Now use the style of this Solarpunk utopia generated by your sketch as a reference and create buildings, transportation systems, and inhabitants in your new city.

- Or find other ways to explore this latent space!

# Summary

In this chapter, we explored various creative applications that provide more control and extend the capabilities of text-to-image models with fine-grained controllability, increasing the range of inputs these models can take. As these techniques are composable and compatible with one another, we allow for complex creative pipelines and artistic processes to go beyond just inputting text and getting an image as an output. Using a combination of image transformations, variations, style, or structural image references, as well as finer-grained prompt control, artists and creative professionals can incorporate machine learning workflows into their toolbox.

However, going beyond generating images, especially when bringing real images into the latent space of the model, brings in new challenges. Key ethical concerns include misinformation, deception, and ownership. Making image editing accessible to everyone (and not only Adobe Photoshop specialists, for example) creates new opportunities and challenges, such as image manipulations that can be used to spread misinformation and deceive people with deepfakes or nonexistent content. The question of ownership is also key: artistic styles can be remixed, but the legal and ethical boundaries for when such remix is done fairly is still an open question. Mitigation strategies such as watermarking already exist in libraries like *diffusers*; however, there are more discussions to be held at a societal level about how to handle these new abilities ML gives us.

Nonetheless, the creative potential of these new models is an exciting development. When used ethically and responsibly, they will certainly empower creatives with tooling that goes beyond imagination.

For further readings, we suggest the following resources:

- "IP-Adapter: All You Need to Know" (*https://oreil.ly/yYsJo*)
- "Train Your ControlNet with diffusers" (*https://oreil.ly/TYKXl*)
- Diffusers inpainting guide (*https://oreil.ly/UQpgR*)
- "Instruction-tuning Stable Diffusion with InstructPix2Pix" (*https://oreil.ly/8lx5x*)
- The papers in "References" on page 290

# Exercises

1. Explain how inpainting differs from image-to-image transformation and provide an example of a practical application.

2. How can prompt weighting help overcome the limitations of the diffusion models?

3. What are the key differences between Prompt-to-Prompt editing and SEGA?

4. How does ControlNet enhance the capabilities of diffusion models? Give examples of conditions that can be used with ControlNet.

5. What is "Inversion" in the context of text-to-image models, and what does it allow us to do?

You can find the solutions to these exercises in the book's GitHub repository (*https://oreil.ly/handsonGenAIcode*).

# References

Brack, Manuel, et al. "LEDITS++: Limitless Image Editing Using Text-to-Image Models." arXiv, November 30, 2023. *http://arxiv.org/abs/2311.16711*.

Brack, Manuel, et al. "SEGA: Instructing Text-to-Image Models Using Semantic Guidance." arXiv, January 29, 2023. *http://arxiv.org/abs/2301.12247*.

Brooks, Tim, et al. "InstructPix2Pix: Learning to Follow Image Editing Instructions." arXiv, November 17, 2022. *https://arxiv.org/abs/2211.09800*.

Chefer, Hila, et al. "Attend-and-Excite: Attention-Based Semantic Guidance for Text-to-Image Diffusion Models." arXiv, January 31, 2023. *http://arxiv.org/abs/2301.13826*.

Hertz, Amir, et al. "Prompt-to-Prompt Image Editing with Cross Attention Control." arXiv, August 2, 2022. *http://arxiv.org/abs/2208.01626*.

Mokady, Ron, et al. "Null-Text Inversion for Editing Real Images Using Guided Diffusion Models." arXiv, November 17, 2022. *http://arxiv.org/abs/2211.09794*.

Podell, Dustin, et al. "SDXL: Improving Latent Diffusion Models for High-Resolution Image Synthesis." arXiv, July 4, 2023. *http://arxiv.org/abs/2307.01952*.

Wang, Haofan, et al. "InstantStyle: Free Lunch Towards Style-Preserving in Text-to-Image Generation." arXiv, April 4, 2024. *http://arxiv.org/abs/2404.02733*.

Ye, Hu, et al. "IP-Adapter: Text Compatible Image Prompt Adapter for Text-to-Image Diffusion Models." arXiv, August 14, 2023. *http://arxiv.org/abs/2308.06721*.

Zhang, Lvmin, et al. "Adding Conditional Control to Text-to-Image Diffusion Models." arXiv, February 11, 2023. *https://arxiv.org/abs/2302.05543*.

# CHAPTER 9

# Generating Audio

In Chapter 1, we caught a glimpse of the potential of audio generation with a transformers pipeline based on the MusicGen model by Meta. This chapter dives into generative audio, using both diffusion and transformer-based techniques, which will introduce a new set of exciting challenges and applications. Imagine if you could remove all background noise in real time during a call, if you could get high-quality transcriptions and summaries of conferences, or if a singer could regenerate their songs in other languages. You could even generate a theme of Mozart and Billie Eilish's compositions that gets a mariachi-infused twist. Well, that's the field's trajectory, exciting times ahead.

What kinds of things can we do with ML and audio? The two most common tasks are transcribing speech to text (automatic speech recognition, or ASR) and generating speech from text (text to speech). In ASR, a model receives as input audio of someone (or multiple people) speaking and outputs the corresponding text. For some models, the output captures additional information, such as which person is speaking or the times when somebody said something. ASR systems are widely used, from virtual speech assistants to caption generators. Thanks to many open-access models made available to the public in recent years, there has been exciting research on multilingualism and running the models directly on edge.

In text to speech (TTS), a model generates synthetic and, hopefully, realistic speech. As with ASR, in TTS there has been considerable interest in running models on-device as well as multilingualism. TTS also presents its own set of challenges, such as generating audios with multiple speakers, making the voices sound more natural, and bringing intonation, pauses, emotion markers, pitch control, accent, and other characteristics in the generations.

Although TTS and ASR are the most popular tasks, we can do a plethora of other things with ML and audio (some of which are shown in Figure 9-1):

*Text to audio*
> Text to speech can be generalized to text to audio (TTA), where, based on a prompt, a model can generate melodies, sound effects, and songs.

*Voice cloning*
> A person's voice, including tone, pitch, and prosody, is preserved to generate new sounds.

*Audio classification*
> The model classifies a provided audio. Typical examples are command recognition and speaker identification.

*Voice enhancement*
> The model removes noise from the audio and cleans the voice to be clearer.

*Audio translation*
> The model receives audio with a source language $X$ and outputs audio with a target language $Y$.

*Speaker diarization*
> The model identifies the speaker at a specific time.

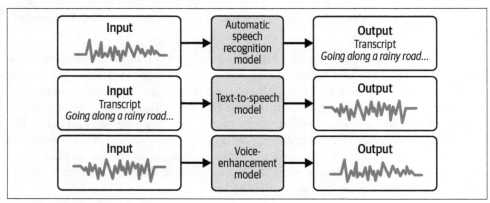

*Figure 9-1. Examples of audio tasks*

Audio-related tasks are challenging for multiple reasons. First, working with a raw audio signal is more complex and less intuitive than working with text. For many applications, audio models are expected to perform in real time or on-device, which can constrain model size and inference speed. For example, current diffusion models would be too slow if you wanted to use them for interactive translation. Finally, evaluating generative audio models can be challenging. How do you measure whether the quality of a song generated by a model is good?

We can use multiple tools and hundreds of open-access models and datasets for these tasks. *Common Voice (https://oreil.ly/AHfTa)*, a popular crowd-sourced dataset by the Mozilla Foundation, contains over 2,000 hours of audio files and their corresponding text in over a hundred languages. Many other popular audio datasets, such as LibriSpeech, VoxPopuli, and GigaSpeech, are also available, each with its own domain and use cases. Just as there are many open source datasets, we can also use many open-access models. This chapter will explore transformer-based models such as Meta's Wav2Vec2, OpenAI Whisper, Microsoft SpeechT5, and Suno Bark. We'll also explore exciting diffusion models that can generate songs, such as Stable Diffusion (but for songs), Dance Diffusion, and AudioLDM. Although jumping into another modality might be daunting, many of the tools we've collected in our generative journey are about to be used.

# Audio Data

To get started, we'll show how audio data is structured and how to use it. We'll explore the LibriSpeech dataset (*https://oreil.ly/Rw7-f*), which contains over 1,000 hours of books read out loud and is useful for training and evaluating speech-recognition systems. One of the first challenges with audio datasets is that they tend to be large, so loading all the data simultaneously might not be feasible. Audio datasets can quickly spawn terabytes of data and not fit in a hard drive.

We can use `load_dataset_builder()` to get a better overview of the dataset structure without loading all the data:

```
from datasets import load_dataset_builder

ds_builder = load_dataset_builder(
    "openslr/librispeech_asr", trust_remote_code=True
)
ds_builder.info.splits

{'test.clean': SplitInfo(name='test.clean',
                         num_bytes=368449831,
                         num_examples=2620,
                         shard_lengths=None,
                         dataset_name=None),
  'test.other': SplitInfo(name='test.other',
                         num_bytes=353231518,
                         num_examples=2939,
                         shard_lengths=None,
                         dataset_name=None),
 'train.clean.100': SplitInfo(name='train.clean.100',
                             num_bytes=6627791685,
                             num_examples=28539,
                             shard_lengths=None,
                             dataset_name=None),
 'train.clean.360': SplitInfo(name='train.clean.360',
```

```
                            num_bytes=23927767570,
                            num_examples=104014,
                            shard_lengths=None,
                            dataset_name=None),
    'train.other.500': SplitInfo(name='train.other.500',
                            num_bytes=31852502880,
                            num_examples=148688,
                            shard_lengths=None,
                            dataset_name=None),
    'validation.clean': SplitInfo(name='validation.clean',
                            num_bytes=359505691,
                            num_examples=2703,
                            shard_lengths=None,
                            dataset_name=None),
    'validation.other': SplitInfo(name='validation.other',
                            num_bytes=337213112,
                            num_examples=2864,
                            shard_lengths=None,
                            dataset_name=None)}
```

The dataset authors found that the size of the corpus made it impractical to work with it, so they decided to split it into subsets of 100, 360, and 500 hours. It makes sense as, after all, just the training data is over 60 GB. Without loading all this data, we can start looking into the features by using `.info.features`:

```
ds_builder.info.features
```

```
{'file': Value(dtype='string', id=None),
 'audio': Audio(sampling_rate=16000, mono=True, decode=True, id=None),
 'text': Value(dtype='string', id=None),
 'speaker_id': Value(dtype='int64', id=None),
 'chapter_id': Value(dtype='int64', id=None),
 'id': Value(dtype='string', id=None)}
```

The most valuable features are `text` and `audio`. We have all the data needed to build an initial speech-recognition pipeline with these two features: the audio and its corresponding transcription. Under the hood, each feature has a type. The `text` type, for example, is a `Value` feature, which contains the data type `string`. The `audio` type is an `Audio` feature, which contains the audio information. Just like images, audio can be represented with multiple channels. The `mono` attribute indicates whether the audio is mono (single channel, which provides a uniform sound experience) or stereo (two channels, which provide a sense of directionality). We'll discuss what `sampling_rate` and `decode` mean in the next section.

Given that the dataset is so large, we need to find ways to work with it efficiently. Rather than downloading the whole dataset and then using it, you can use `streaming` mode to load one example at a time, hence not consuming disk space and being able to use samples from the dataset as they are downloaded. When using `streaming` mode with the *datasets* library, we get an `IterableDataset`, which can be used as any Python iterator. Let's look at the first example of the 100-hour split:

```
from datasets import load_dataset

ds = load_dataset(
    "openslr/librispeech_asr",
    split="train.clean.360",
    streaming=True,
)
sample = next(iter(ds))
sample
{'audio': {'array': array([ 9.15527344e-05, 4.57763672e-04, 5.18798828e-04, ...,
       -4.57763672e-04, -5.49316406e-04, -4.88281250e-04]),
          'path': '1487-133273-0000.flac',
          'sampling_rate': 16000},
 'chapter_id': 133273,
 'file': '1487-133273-0000.flac',
 'id': '1487-133273-0000',
 'speaker_id': 1487,
 'text': 'THE SECOND IN IMPORTANCE IS AS FOLLOWS SOVEREIGNTY MAY BE '
         'DEFINED TO BE THE RIGHT OF MAKING LAWS IN FRANCE THE KING '
         'REALLY EXERCISES A PORTION OF THE SOVEREIGN POWER SINCE '
         'THE LAWS HAVE NO WEIGHT'}
```

The sample provides us with audio and the corresponding text. The `audio` entry is the feature type that contains the following:

- An `array` with the decoded audio data. Recall that the audio feature had `decode` set to `True`, which means that the audio is already decoded for you. Otherwise, the audio contains the bytes, and you need to decode it yourself.

- The `path` to the downloaded audio file.

- The data `sampling_rate`, which is essential for loading the audio properly.

If these concepts sound foreign to you, no worries. This is the perfect opportunity to learn what exactly audio is.

Audio is an infinite set of values over time. Computers can't work with continuous data, so we need to process the audio signal and have a digital discrete (finite) representation. To achieve this, we take many snapshots at a given second. That's called the *sampling rate*. For example, for this audio sample, we can find in the `audio` feature that the sampling rate is 16,000 (with the unit being Hertz). This means that 16,000 samples are taken in a given second. If we have an audio file of a minute, that's almost a million values—no wonder audio datasets are huge. Figure 9-2 shows an audio waveform sampled using a sampling rate of 6.

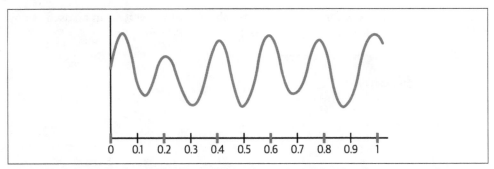

*Figure 9-2. In this waveform sampled using a sampling rate of 6, discretization happens at intervals 1/6th of a second apart*

The sampling rate is an essential parameter: when working with audio ML, we need to ensure that all the audio samples have the same sampling rate. The models are pretrained with data sampled at a specific rate, so when fine-tuning or running inference, you need to ensure to use the same sampling rate. Although some of the most popular audio datasets have a sampling rate of 16,000, this is only sometimes the case, so you must resample the data in the preprocessing stage:

```
array = sample["audio"]["array"]
sampling_rate = sample["audio"]["sampling_rate"]

# Let's get the first 5 seconds
array = array[: sampling_rate * 5]
print(f"Number of samples: {len(array)}. Values: {array}")

('Number of samples: 80000. Values: [9.15527344e-05 4.57763672e-04 '
 '5.18798828e-04 ... 7.05261230e-02\n'
 ' 5.92041016e-02 6.50329590e-02]')
```

Of course, we cannot print an audio file in the book, but you can run some code to listen to the audio. We can use the `IPython.display.Audio()` function for this. Alternatively, you can visit the official interactive demo (*https://oreil.ly/a5Yn_*) to listen to all the audio samples of the chapter. Let's listen to the first audio sample in the 100-hour split:

```
import IPython.display as ipd

ipd.Audio(data=array, rate=sampling_rate)
```

You might be wondering about `decode` and `mono` in the `Audio` feature. The `decode` attribute specifies whether the data should be decoded (returned as an array of floats) or not (returned as a bytes). The `mono` attribute specifies whether the audio is mono (one channel) or if there are multiple channels. We'll explore examples of these in the next sections.

# Waveforms

We just saw that we use a digital discrete representation of audio to be able to work with it. Under the hood, an audio is just an array of values. These arrays contain the information needed to train models for many tasks, so it's worth investing time in understanding the array before going into the applications.

What does the array represent? Each value in the array represents the amplitude, which describes the strength of the sound wave and is measured in decibels.[1] The amplitude tells us how loud a sound is relative to a reference value; 0 dB, the reference value, represents the lowest sound perceived by the human ear. Your breathing is around 10 dB, an intense concert could be 120 dB (starts getting painful), and the Krakatoa Eruption, a colossal volcano eruption in 1883, could be heard even 3,000 miles (4,800 kilometers) away with an estimated 310 dB, as shown in Figure 9-3.

*Figure 9-3. The amplitude of some sounds in the dB scale*

Amplitude is usually measured in decibels, but the array is frequently normalized, so the numbers are from –1 to 1. To visualize the audio, we can use a *waveform*, a plot of the amplitudes over time. Let's plot the waveform with *librosa*, a popular library for working with audio data:

```
import librosa.display

librosa.display.waveshow(array, sr=sampling_rate);
```

---

1 To be precise, vibrations produce changes in the air (or other mediums), which lead to sound. These vibrations cause a sound wave that leads to pressure changes in our ears.

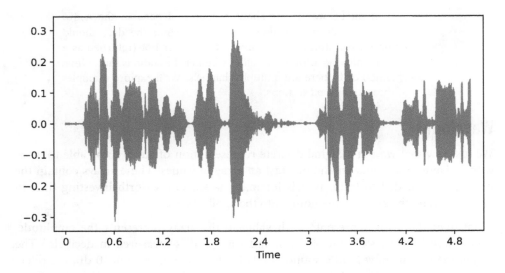

The waveform aids in doing the initial exploration of audio data. If you listen to the audio, you can identify that the first waves correspond to when the reader says, "the second in importance is as follows" followed by a short pause. More generally, waveforms are an intuitive way to identify irregularities in the audio and get an overall sense of the signal and its patterns.

## Spectrograms

Waveforms and spectrograms (Figure 9-4) are different ways to represent audio signals. This section explains what spectrograms are and when to use them.

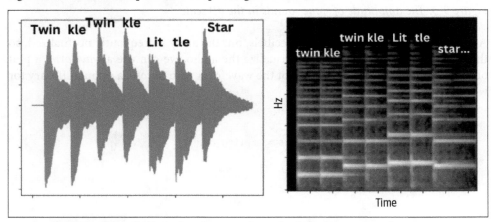

*Figure 9-4. Waveform (left) and mel spectrogram (right) representing the same audio clip*

Let's say we want to train a generative model to create a new sound or synthetic speech conditioned on an input audio. A straightforward approach might be to use the raw audio waveform as the model's input. Waveforms are a direct and intuitive representation of sound, containing all the information necessary to reproduce the original audio. You can easily verify this by listening to a few samples from a dataset, whether they include voices, music, or other sounds. So, if waveforms can accurately represent sound, why don't we use them to train our models?

The first challenge lies in the waveform's dimensionality. Although waveforms are one-dimensional, they consist of a very large number of data points. Each second of audio has tens of thousands of samples for the model to process, making it difficult to learn patterns and structures in the data. This high dimensionality makes it difficult for models to effectively learn patterns and structures in the data.

Additionally, our hearing system is very sensitive to small differences in attributes like pitch or timbre, which are related to the frequency characteristics of the sound. While these attributes are encoded in the waveform's shape, they are challenging to identify—even for humans—just by looking at the waveform. The most obvious information we can extract from a waveform is how amplitude changes over time, often called the *time domain*. However, attributes related to frequency, such as what makes a piano sound different from a violin, are much harder to discern from the waveform alone (Figure 9-5).

While it is possible to train a model using raw waveform data (as we'll explore later in this chapter), the sheer number of samples involved presents a significant challenge. For instance, one minute of audio at a sampling rate of 16,000 contains nearly a million samples. If we attempt to reduce this dimensionality by averaging or combining samples, we risk losing the nuanced differences that are crucial in the frequency domain. Even with a sampling rate of 16,000, which is adequate for voice, it's insufficient for high-quality music. There's a reason consumer audio standards, from CDs to streaming services, typically use a sampling rate of 44.1 kHz or higher.

Given these challenges, a more effective approach often involves converting the audio waveform into a different representation called a *spectrogram*. This compact visual representation depicts how the frequency and amplitude of sound change over time. By explicitly capturing frequency details, spectrograms provide a more structured and informative representation of the audio signal, which makes it easier for models to learn from. Spectrograms transform the problem from the time domain to the time-frequency domain, which is often more suitable for ML tasks involving audio. However, it is important to note that spectrograms are a lossy representation, meaning they do not retain all the information from the original waveform. Despite this, the loss is usually acceptable, as spectrograms preserve the most perceptually relevant features.

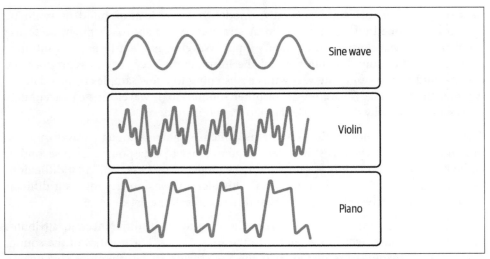

*Figure 9-5. The same note played by several instruments has the same pitch (frequency) and amplitude, but it sounds different because of the waveform's shape variations. A pure note is a perfect sine wave.*

Before we dive into spectrograms, let's look at frequencies. We'll plot four waves with the same amplitude ranges but varying frequencies:

```python
import numpy as np
from matplotlib import pyplot as plt


def plot_sine(freq):
    sr = 1000  # samples per second
    ts = 1.0 / sr  # sampling interval
    t = np.arange(0, 1, ts)  # time vector
    amplitude = np.sin(2 * np.pi * freq * t)

    plt.plot(t, amplitude)
    plt.title("Sine wave with frequency {}".format(freq))
    plt.xlabel("Time")


fig = plt.figure()

plt.subplot(2, 2, 1)
plot_sine(1)

plt.subplot(2, 2, 2)
plot_sine(2)

plt.subplot(2, 2, 3)
plot_sine(5)
```

```
plt.subplot(2, 2, 4)
plot_sine(30)

fig.tight_layout()
plt.show()
```

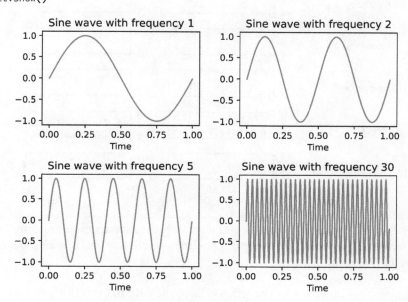

As you can observe, despite the waves sharing the same amplitude ranges, they exhibit different frequencies. While these are simple sine waves, real-world sounds are more complex. Typically, a sound will be a composition of multiple waves combined, each with its frequency and amplitude. Therefore, our first task is to break the sound wave into its multiple, simpler components. Why is this useful? This process allows us to extract valuable information that a model can leverage: How does the amplitude change over time at different frequencies? How can we decompose the sound? We employ Fourier Transforms (FT), a mathematical tool that enables decomposing a single function into multiple functions.[2]

Let's begin with some simple sinusoidal functions, as shown in Figure 9-6. In the first column, we have the sine functions. In the second column, we have a plot of the FT, which is the function in the frequency domain.

---

2 Explaining Fourier Transforms is outside the scope of the book. There are many educational resources for this such as 3Blue1Brown's video on the topic (*https://oreil.ly/rByYO*).

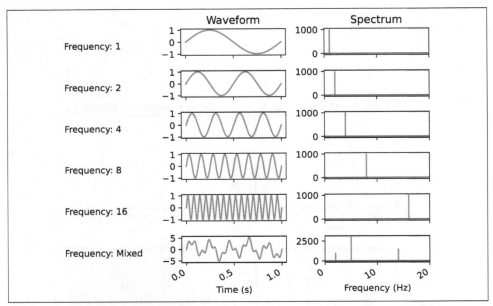

*Figure 9-6. Some sinusoidal functions and their frequency spectrums. Pure notes (sine waves) have a single peak at the sine period, whereas more-complex sounds show several peaks in the frequency domain.*

Let's analyze the top row. On the left, we have the original waveform—a sine wave with a one-cycle-per-second frequency. On the right, the FT plot depicts frequency on the x-axis and amplitude in the frequency domain on the y-axis. Observe the peak at 1, which aligns with the original waveform's frequency. The following rows show examples with different frequencies and share the same behavior: the FT plot peaks at the original waveform's frequency. The y-value is half the number of samples (in this example, the sampling rate is 2,000 and it is just one second, so we have 2,000 samples) multiplied by the amplitude in the original waveform amplitude (1 in the first five rows).[3]

Now, let's explore the last row—a more intriguing case. The waveform combines three distinct sinusoidal functions with varying amplitudes (1, 3, and 1.5) and frequencies (2, 5, and 14). It's hard to discern the composition just by looking at the waveform, so here's where the frequency domain is useful. In the frequency domain, we can observe three peaks corresponding to the original function's frequencies: 2, 5, and 14. Consequently, we can reverse-engineer and describe the initial waveform's three functions.

---

3 There are some nuances to this. When we calculate the FT of a real signal, its absolute value is symmetric. This leads to having a mirrored plot in the frequency domain. For explanation purposes, we plot the first half.

At a frequency of 2 Hz, the frequency domain amplitude (y-axis at the right) is 1,000. By performing 1,000 × 2 / 2,000, we end up with 1, the amplitude of the first sinusoidal function composing the waveform. Similarly, a frequency of 3 Hz yields a frequency domain amplitude of 3,000, and by doing 3,000 × 2 / 2,000, we end up with 3. The decomposed sine waves are depicted in Figure 9-7. FTs give us a mechanism that allows us to analyze complex waveforms and understand the frequencies that compose them. We've revealed hidden complexities within a sound, information that we thought wasn't there but is. This provides much more information and will be key to models that can transcribe speech or generate music.

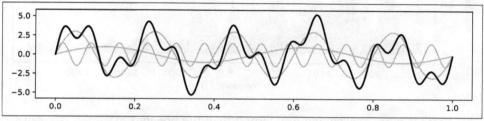

*Figure 9-7. A complex sound wave can be decomposed into sinusoidal frequencies by analyzing the spectrum representation*

What about the sound at the beginning of the chapter? As with the waveforms in Figure 9-7, the function can be broken into multiple sine functions with their amplitudes and frequencies. Let's look at its frequency domain plot:

```
# Compute the Fast Fourier Transform (FFT) of the input signal
X = np.fft.fft(array)

# Length of the FFT result (which is the same as the length of the input signal)
N = len(X)

# Calculate the frequency bins corresponding to the FFT result
n = np.arange(N)
T = N / sampling_rate
freq = n / T

# Plot the amplitude spectrum for the first 8000 frequency bins
# We could plot all the bins, but we would get a mirror image of the spectrum
plt.stem(freq[:8000], np.abs(X[:8000]), "b", markerfmt=" ", basefmt="-b")
plt.xlabel("Frequency (Hz)")
plt.ylabel("Amplitude in Frequency Domain")
plt.show()
```

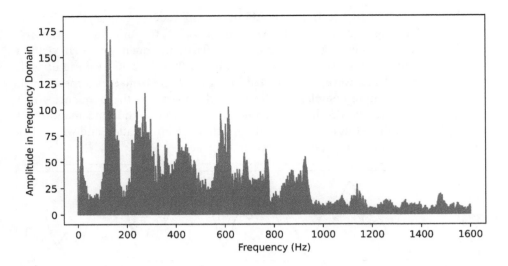

This audio is more challenging to interpret than the previous examples. We can see that most of the sound is in the 0–800 Hz range. We can also see that around 170 Hz, there are some loud noises. Although the plot is interesting, we lose information in the time domain. We don't know at what time we had sounds with specific frequencies. Waveforms have amplitude and time information, and FT plots have amplitude and frequency information. Can we combine the three at the same time?

Spectrograms plot how the frequency and amplitude of the signal change through time. They are informative tools that visualize time, frequency, and amplitude in a single plot. To create a spectrogram, we'll slide a window through the original waveform and compute the FT for that segment to capture how the frequencies change through time. The windows can then be stacked together to form the spectrogram. This approach of sliding a window through the audio is called Short-Time Fourier Transform.

With *librosa*, we can use `stft()` to obtain the Short-Time Fourier Transform. In addition to computing the spectrogram, we convert the amplitude to a decibel scale, which is logarithmic and much better for visualizing. Remember that the amplitude is the difference of sound pressure. Hence, the numerical range of sound pressure is very wide. By using a logarithmic scale, we limit the scale, make the plots more informative, and have information closer to the way humans perceive sound.

The decibel scale is logarithmic, meaning that each 10 dB increase corresponds to a tenfold increase in relative sound intensity. However, our perception of loudness does not align directly with these physical changes. While the decibel scale and our perception of loudness both follow logarithmic patterns, they do so differently. Specifically, a 10 dB increase in sound intensity is perceived by the human ear as roughly doubling the loudness, not tenfold. This difference arises because the human auditory system compresses changes in intensity into a more manageable range of perceived loudness.

Next, we'll look at the spectrogram of our example:

```
# Compute Short-Time Fourier Transform (STFT)
# We take the absolute value of the STFT to get the amplitude
# of each frequency bin.
D = np.abs(librosa.stft(array))

# Convert the ampltiude into decibels
# which is logarithmic.
S_db = librosa.amplitude_to_db(D, ref=np.max)

# Generate the spectrogram display
librosa.display.specshow(S_db, sr=sampling_rate, x_axis="time", y_axis="hz")
plt.colorbar(format="%+2.0f dB");
```

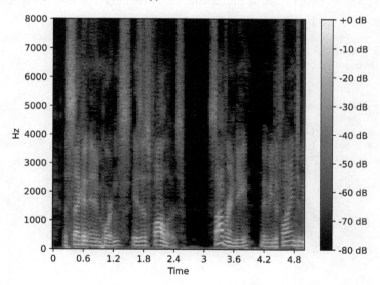

The x-axis is time, just as in the waveform. The y-axis shows the frequency (using Hertz, a linear unit), and the color represents the intensity (decibels) of the frequency at a given point. Areas in black represent areas with no energy (silence). As before, we can observe some noise in the first 2.4 seconds and the last 1.6 seconds. The loudest points happen at a low frequency (bright color and low value in the y-axis). This matches the waveform and the frequency domain plot, where we got a high amplitude at low frequencies.

 You might be wondering why we have negative decibel values. As we used `amplitude_to_db()` with a ref=np.max, the maximum value of the spectrogram is 0 dB. The rest of the values are relative to this maximum value. For example, a value of –20 dB means that the amplitude is 20 dB lower than the maximum value.

A popular spectrogram variation is called the mel spectrogram. While in a normal spectrogram, the unit for frequency is linear, the mel spectrogram uses a scale similar to how we (humans) perceive sound. Humans perceive audio logarithmically, meaning we're more sensitive to changes at low frequencies but less so at high frequencies. The difference between 500 and 1,000 Hz is much more noticeable than between 5,000 and 5,500. The *librosa* library once again offers a convenient method that computes the mel spectrogram. In the mel spectrogram, equal distances in the frequency (y-axis) have the same perceptual distance. Let's plot the mel spectrogram:

```
# Generate a Mel-scaled spectrogram from the audio signal.
# The result is a matrix where each element corresponds to the power
# of a frequency band (in the Mel scale) at a specific time.
S = librosa.feature.melspectrogram(y=array, sr=sampling_rate)

# We convert the power spectrogram to a decibel scale
S_dB = librosa.power_to_db(S, ref=np.max)

# Display the Mel-scaled spectrogram
librosa.display.specshow(S_dB, sr=sampling_rate, x_axis="time", y_axis="mel")
plt.colorbar(format="%+2.0f dB");
```

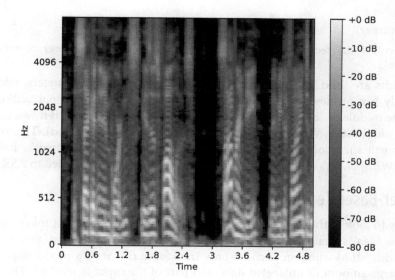

The mel spectrogram has similar patterns to the original, but we can notice some differences. First, the y-scale is not linear: the distance between 512 and 1,024 is the same as that between 2,048 and 4,096. Second, the areas with more energy (more decibels) in low frequency are much more noticeable in the mel spectrogram. This corresponds to how humans perceive sound.

Apart from being great visual representations to understand audio signals, spectrograms are commonly used directly by ML models. For example, a spectrogram of a song can be used as input to a model to classify its genre. Similarly, a model can receive some words as input and output a spectrogram representing the audio of a person speaking those words.

# Speech to Text with Transformer-Based Architectures

Let's now dive into ASR, the task of transcribing an audio file to text. As with many other tasks, we can use the *transformers* `pipeline()`, which conveniently takes care of all preprocessing and postprocessing and is a useful inference wrapper. Let's use the smallest variant of Whisper, a popular open source model released by OpenAI, to get an initial baseline:

```python
from transformers import pipeline

pipe = pipeline(
    "automatic-speech-recognition",
    model="openai/whisper-small",
    max_new_tokens=200,
```

```
)
pipe(array)
```

{'text': ' The second in importance is as follows. Sovereignty may be defined
to be'}

The results are solid for using a small version (244 million parameters, which can efficiently run on-device). More surprisingly, if you hear the original audio, it was cut in the middle of "be." Whisper can predict the entire word even if it was not completed. Additionally, Whisper predicted punctuation (e.g., the period). The following sections will shed some light on how models that perform ASR work. Before we explore Whisper, let's discuss how encoder-only models can be applied to ASR.

## Encoder-Based Techniques

One way to look at the ASR task is to think of it as we do about text token classification. The idea is analogous to using BERT in the NLP world. First, you pretrain a model with MLM using an encoder-only transformer; that is, a model is pretrained with a large amount of unlabeled data, and part of the input is masked. The model's objective is to predict which word should fill the mask. We can apply the same principle in audio. Rather than masking text, we mask audio (to be precise, the latent speech representation), and the model learns contextualized representations. Afterward, this model can be fine-tuned with labeled data on different audio tasks, such as speaker identification or ASR. Let's dive into achieving ASR with this idea.

The first challenge, which we already mentioned, is that an audio sample can be very long. A 30-second audio sample with a sample rate of 16 kHz will yield an array of 480,000 values. Using 480,000 values for a single input sample to the transformer encoder would require massive amounts of memory and computation. To mitigate this, one approach is to have a CNN as a feature encoder. The CNN will slide through the input data (the waveform) and output a latent speech representation. For example, assuming a window of 20 milliseconds sliding through 1 second of audio, we would end up with 50 latent representations (this assumes there are no overlapping windows; in CNN terms, we are using a stride of 20). These latent representations are then passed to a classical transformer encoder, which outputs embeddings for each of the 50 representations. During pretraining, spans of the latent representations are masked, and hence, the model learns to predict how to fill the missing parts.

A simple linear classification head is added to the encoder for ASR fine-tuning: the goal is that the classifier estimates the text that corresponds to each of the audio windows processed by the encoder. The number of classes that the model will classify is a design decision. We could decide to classify entire words, syllables, or just characters, but given we're using a window of 20 milliseconds, a single word would not fit in a window. Classifying characters appears to make a lot of sense in this context, and it has the additional benefit that we can keep a very small vocabulary. For example, for English, we can use a vocabulary of the 26 English characters plus some special tokens (e.g., a token for silence, a token for unknown, etc.). To keep a minimal vocabulary, we usually preprocess the text, uppercasing all of it and converting numbers to words (e.g., "14" to "fourteen").

In the first part of this chapter, we used spectrograms to capture the amplitude and frequency characteristics of the input data in a concise 2D visual representation. Now, we are exploring architectures that process the data differently, using CNNs to extract features directly from the waveform without converting it to a spectrogram. The choice between these approaches depends on factors like the specific task and the architecture's design.

As we'll discuss soon, some models take spectrograms as input, while others work directly with the raw waveform. Transformers, with their attention mechanisms, are particularly effective for handling sequential data, making it important to consider the temporal structure of the input.

Let's recap the whole flow to perform ASR with encoder-based models:

1. Raw audio data (1D array) representing the amplitudes is received.
2. Data is normalized to zero mean and univariance to standardize across different amplitudes.
3. A small CNN turns the audio into a latent representation. This reduces the length of the input sequence.
4. The representations are then passed to an encoder model, which outputs embeddings for each representation.
5. Each embedding is finally passed through a classifier, which predicts the corresponding character for each one.

The output of such a model would be something like the following:

```
CHAAAAAPTTERRRSSIXTEEEEENIMMMIIGHT...
```

Hmmm…that resembles a text, but obviously, it's not right. What's going on? If the sound of a character spreads over a period longer than a single window, it might appear multiple times in the output. Remember that the model does not know when each character happened during training, so it's impossible to align the audio with the text directly.

An approach to solve this, used initially for RNNs, is called Connectionist Temporal Classification (CTC). The idea behind using CTC in audio is to add the padding token (for visualization purposes, we'll use the character *), which helps as a boundary between groups of characters, and a separator token (/) that separates words. The model will learn to predict such tokens as well. During inference, the output might look as follows:

```
CHAAAAA*PTT*ERRR/SS*IX*T*EE*EEN/I/MMM*II*GHT
```

With this output, we can deduplicate by merging equal consecutive characters in the same group, resulting in our desired outcome.

```
CHAPTER SIXTEEN I MIGHT
```

All these ideas (using an encoder-only model, processing the waveform with a CNN, and using CTC to perform classification) form the foundation of encoder-based architectures such as Meta's Wav2Vec2 (2020) (*https://arxiv.org/abs/2006.11477*) and HuBERT (2021) (*https://arxiv.org/abs/2106.07447*). Wav2Vec2 is pretrained with Librispeech and LibriVox (both unlabeled datasets). It can be fine-tuned with just 10 minutes of labeled data to outperform models trained with significantly more data. This is very interesting as a base model can easily be tuned for specific domains or accents without much data. The downstream task being solved here is ASR, but the same pretrained model can be fine-tuned for other tasks, such as speaker recognition and language detection. The following code shows each step of running inference with Wav2Vec2 (note that you can also use `pipeline()` as a high-level API):

```python
import torch
from transformers import Wav2Vec2ForCTC, Wav2Vec2Processor

from genaibook.core import get_device

device = get_device()

# The Wav2Vec2Processor has the pre- and post-processing incorporated
wav2vec2_processor = Wav2Vec2Processor.from_pretrained(
    "facebook/wav2vec2-base-960h"
)
wav2vec2_model = Wav2Vec2ForCTC.from_pretrained(
    "facebook/wav2vec2-base-960h"
).to(device)

# Run forward pass, making sure to resample to 16kHz
inputs = wav2vec2_processor(
    array, sampling_rate=sampling_rate, return_tensors="pt"
)
with torch.inference_mode():
    outputs = wav2vec2_model(**inputs.to(device))

# Transcribe
predicted_ids = torch.argmax(outputs.logits, dim=-1)
transcription = wav2vec2_processor.batch_decode(predicted_ids)
print(transcription)

['THE SECOND IN IMPORTANCE IS AS FOLLOWS SOVEREIGNTY MAY BE DEFINED TO']
```

As the models are pretrained with data with a specific sampling rate, using audio with the same sampling rate is required during inference. You can achieve this by resampling the data (e.g., using `dataset.cast_column("audio", Audio(sampling_rate=16_000)))` or specifying the `sampling_rate` in the `processor`, as done in the preceding snippet.

HuBERT follows the same concept of pretraining to learn useful latent representations but changes the training process to use the original MLM objective of BERT.[4] While Wav2Vec2 predicts characters, HuBERT processes the waveform with clustering techniques to learn discrete hidden speech units, which can be seen as equivalent to tokens in NLP. The model predicts these hidden units in the second stage at randomly masked locations.

Note that Wav2Vec2 and HuBERT work only for English. A few weeks after the Wav2Vec2 release, Meta released XLSR-53, which has the same architecture as Wav2Vec2 but was pretrained on 56,000 hours of speech in 53 languages. XLSR learns speech units common to several languages. Hence, languages with little digital data can still get decent results. In 2021, Meta released XLS-R (*https://arxiv.org/abs/2111.09296*) (yes, it's different from XLSR), a 2-billion-parameter model trained with a similar setup, but using nearly 10 times as much unlabeled data (436,000 hours) from 128 languages.

It is important to note that these models are acoustic: their outputs are based purely on the sound of the input and lack inherent language information. For example, the model might frequently misspell words, output things that are not words, or confuse homophones (e.g., "bear" versus "bare"). An approach to mitigate this is to incorporate language information during the generation phase.

Typically, in the classification stage, we compute `argmax(logits)` to predict the most likely character. However, another approach is to introduce a language model that can predict the most likely word given the sequence of characters. An n-gram model is a type of language model that predicts the likelihood of a word based on the $n - 1$ previous words in a given text corpus. For instance, a bigram model ($n = 2$) considers pairs of words, while a trigram model ($n = 3$) considers triplets. This probabilistic model helps in understanding the context and structure of the language, and it can be very small and efficient. A full-fledged transformer-based language model, like the ones in Chapter 2, can also be used. However, n-grams achieve most of the quality improvements these models would, at a fraction of the cost in compute, memory, and inference time.

---

4 Diving into the specifics of their training losses and architectures is outside the book's scope, but we suggest reviewing the papers for those interested.

The n-gram score can be added to beam search to generate the *k* most probable text sequences. By integrating an LM into beam search, we can enhance the decoding process. The beam search evaluates both the acoustic and language model scores, which helps correct misspellings and filter out nonsensical words. This combined approach significantly improves the accuracy and coherence of the generated text.

 You might want to increase the probabilities of certain words (e.g., if some words are not in the language model or you need to boost domain-specific data). To do this, you can count the number of hot words in the output and increase the probability.

## Encoder-Decoder Techniques

Using encoder models with a CTC head is one of the most popular approaches for ASR. As discussed, acoustic models might generate spelling errors, for which an n-gram model needs to be incorporated. These challenges lead to the exploration of encoder-decoder architectures.

We can formulate the ASR problem as a sequence-to-sequence problem rather than a classification problem. This is what Whisper, the open source model we introduced at the beginning of this section, does. Unlike Wav2Vec2 or HuBERT, Whisper (Figure 9-8) was trained in a supervised setting with a massive amount of labeled data: over 680,000 hours of audio with corresponding text. For comparison, Wav2Vec2 was trained on less than 60,000 hours of unlabeled data. About one-third of the data is multilingual, which enables Whisper to perform ASR for 96 languages. Given that the model is trained with labeled data, Whisper learns a speech-to-text mapping directly during pretraining, without requiring fine-tuning. Another Whisper peculiarity is that it's trained to operate without an attention mask: it can directly infer where to ignore the inputs.

How can we do inference? Whisper, unlike Wav2Vec2, operates with spectrograms. We begin by padding and/or truncating a batch of audio samples to ensure uniform input length, converting them into log-mel spectrograms, and processing the outputs by using a CNN before passing them to the encoder. The encoder output is then passed to the decoder, which predicts the next token, one at a time, in an autoregressive way (just as models like Llama do) until the end token is generated. While the encoder-decoder architecture may be slower than encoder-only approaches, Whisper can handle long audio samples, can predict punctuation, and does not require an additional LM during inference.

In encoder-only models, incorporating an LM is necessary to address spelling errors generated by acoustic models, often requiring the use of an external n-gram model. In Whisper's case, the decoder serves a dual purpose: generating text transcriptions while also functioning as an LM.[5] Why does the decoder operate as an LM? By learning to predict the next token in the transcription sequence based on contextual information from the encoder, Whisper eliminates the need for an external LM during inference.

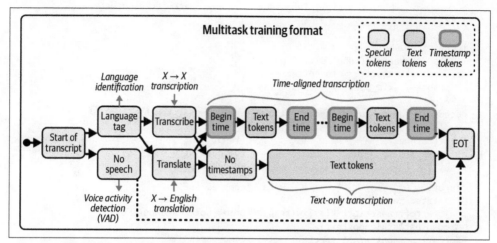

*Figure 9-8. Whisper training is modeled in a sequence-to-sequence fashion on a wide variety of tasks, including translation, transcription, multilingual speech recognition, and others. Special tokens are used to identify the task, language, and interesting points in the data, conditioning the model to perform the desired operation. (Adapted from an image in the Whisper paper (https://arxiv.org/pdf/2212.04356).)*

Whisper uses a specific sequence format, so looking at Figure 9-8 is essential to understand its generation. Special tokens are used to indicate the language or task, and thus guide the model toward the desired output. This is akin to the conditioning methods we covered in previous chapters. Some of the most important tokens are as follows:

- The speech begins with a `start of transcript` token.
- If the language is not English, there is a `language tag` token (e.g., `hi` for Hindi).
- With the language tag, we can perform language identification, transcription, or translate to English.
- If there's a `no speech` token, Whisper is used for voice-activity detection.

---

5 When the system incorporates the language model internally, it's called *deep fusion*. In the case of CTC with n-gram, the LM is external, and we call it *shallow fusion*.

Let's look at an example in Spanish with its corresponding format:

```
from transformers import WhisperTokenizer

tokenizer = WhisperTokenizer.from_pretrained(
    "openai/whisper-small", language="Spanish", task="transcribe"
) ❶

input_str = "Hola, ¿cómo estás?"
labels = tokenizer(input_str).input_ids ❷
decoded_with_special = tokenizer.decode(
    labels, skip_special_tokens=False
) ❸
decoded_str = tokenizer.decode(labels, skip_special_tokens=True) ❹

print(f"Input:                    {input_str}")
print(f"Formatted input w/ special:    {decoded_with_special}")
print(f"Formatted input w/out special: {decoded_str}")

'Input:                    Hola, ¿cómo estás?'
'Formatted input w/ special:    '
'<|startoftranscript|><|es|><|transcribe|><|notimestamps|>Hola, '
'¿cómo estás?<|endoftext|>'
'Formatted input w/out special: Hola, ¿cómo estás?'
```

❶ Load the pretrained tokenizer. As Whisper requires adding some tokens, such as the language ID token and the task identifier, we need to specify the language and task parameters.

❷ Tokenize the input string.

❸ Decode the token IDs back to the original string, but including the special tokens.

❹ Decode the token IDs back to the original string, but excluding the special tokens.

Creating transcriptions with Whisper is not too different from using Wav2Vec2:

1. We use the processor to prepare the audio for the model's expected format. In this case, mel spectrograms are extracted from the raw speech and then processed to be ready to be consumed by the model.

2. The model generates the token IDs corresponding to the transcription.

3. The processor decodes the IDs and converts them into human-readable strings.

OpenAI released nine Whisper variants, ranging from 39 million to 1.5 billion parameters, with model checkpoints for multilingual and English-only setups. In this example, we'll use the intermediate, small, multilingual model, which can run with 2 GB of GPU memory and is six times faster than the largest model.

 New models, such as the second and third versions of the large model, keep being released. Additionally, the Distil Whisper project (*https://oreil.ly/C6OwW*) has achieved the development of high-quality, smaller variants of the original models, up to six times faster and 49% smaller.

```
from transformers import WhisperForConditionalGeneration, WhisperProcessor

whisper_processor = WhisperProcessor.from_pretrained("openai/whisper-small")
whisper_model = WhisperForConditionalGeneration.from_pretrained(
    "openai/whisper-small"
).to(device)

inputs = whisper_processor(
    array, sampling_rate=sampling_rate, return_tensors="pt"
)
with torch.inference_mode():
    generated_ids = whisper_model.generate(**inputs.to(device))

transcription = whisper_processor.batch_decode(
    generated_ids, skip_special_tokens=False
)[0]
print(transcription)

('<|startoftranscript|><|en|><|transcribe|><|notimestamps|> The '
 'second in importance is as follows. Sovereignty may be defined to '
 'be<|endoftext|>')
```

This is a good opportunity to dive into `WhisperProcessor` (*https://oreil.ly/I4IDB*). To better understand the preceding code, we suggest the following:

- Review its documentation.
- Determine the two components of the processor.
- Identify and examine the processor's outputs (`inputs` in the preceding code).

## From Model to Pipeline

In the previous sections, you learned about different architectures and approaches to performing ASR. However, there are still three challenges to tackle when using them in production use cases:

*Long audio transcription*
 The first limitation is that transformers usually have a finite input length they can handle. Wav2vec2, for example, uses attention, which has a quadratic com-

plexity. Whisper does not have an attention mechanism, but it's designed to work with audios of 30 seconds and will truncate longer ones. A simple approach to solve this is chunking: chunk/split audios into shorter samples, run inference on them, and then reconstruct the output. Although efficient, this can lead to poor quality around the chunking border. To solve this, we can do chunking with strides, which means we would have overlapping chunks and then chain them. The result will not be the same as what the model would have predicted on the full-length audio, but the results should be close. We can batch the chunks and run them through the model in parallel, hence being more efficient than transcribing the whole audio file sequentially. Both chunking and chunk batching can quickly be done using the `chunk_length_s` and `batch_size` parameters of an ASR `pipeline`.

*Live inference*

Performing live ASR is desirable for many applications. Now that you have learned to chunk, we can use the model with small chunks (e.g., 5 seconds) and a 1-second stride. Making live inference with CTC models will be faster as it's a single-pass architecture compared to those incorporating decoders. Although Whisper would be slower, you can perform the same chunking logic to transcribe chunks as they come and obtain strong results.

*Timestamps*

Having timestamps that indicate the start and end time for short audio passages can be useful to align a transcription with the input audio. For example, if you're generating subtitles from a video call, you will want to know to which time segment each transcription belongs. This can easily be enabled using `return_time stamps`. Under the hood, we know each outputted token's context window and the `sampling_rate` for CTC models.

Let's combine all of these with a longer (1-minute) audio:

```
from genaibook.core import generate_long_audio

long_audio = generate_long_audio()

device = get_device()

pipe = pipeline(
    "automatic-speech-recognition", model="openai/whisper-small", device=device
)
pipe(
    long_audio,
    generate_kwargs={"task": "transcribe"},
    chunk_length_s=5,
    batch_size=8,
    return_timestamps=True,
)
```

```
{'chunks': [{'text': ' the second in importance is as follows.',
             'timestamp': (0.0, 3.0)},
            {'text': ' Sovereignty may be defined to be the right of '
                     'making laws.',
             'timestamp': (3.0, 6.33)},
            {'text': ' In France, the king really exercises a '
                     'portion of the sovereign power, since the laws '
                     'have no weight till he has given his assent to '
                     'them.',
             'timestamp': (6.33, 16.89)},
            {'text': ' He is moreover the executor of the laws, but '
                     'he does not really cooperate in their '
                     'formation since the refusal of his asset does '
                     'not annul them. He is therefore merely to be '
                     'considered as the agent of the sovereign '
                     'power.',
             'timestamp': (16.89, 36.61)},
            {'text': ' But not only does the king of France exercise '
                     'a portion of the sovereign power, He also '
                     'contributes to the nomination of the '
                     'legislature, which exercises the other '
                     'portion. He has the privilege of appointing '
                     'the members of one chamber and of dissolving '
                     'the United States has no share in the '
                     'formation of the legislative body',
             'timestamp': (36.61, 59.75)},
            {'text': ' and cannot dissolve any part of it. The king '
                     'has the same right of bringing forward '
                     'measures as the chambers.',
             'timestamp': (59.75, 67.09)},
            {'text': ' A right which the president does not possess.',
             'timestamp': (67.09, 70.43)}],
 'text': ' the second in importance is as follows. Sovereignty may '
         'be defined to be the right of making laws. In France, the '
         'king really exercises a portion of the sovereign power, '
         'since the laws have no weight till he has given his assent '
         'to them. He is moreover the executor of the laws, but he '
         'does not really cooperate in their formation since the '
         'refusal of his asset does not annul them. He is therefore '
         'merely to be considered as the agent of the sovereign '
         'power. But not only does the king of France exercise a '
         'portion of the sovereign power, He also contributes to the '
         'nomination of the legislature, which exercises the other '
         'portion. He has the privilege of appointing the members of '
         'one chamber and of dissolving the United States has no '
         'share in the formation of the legislative body and cannot '
         'dissolve any part of it. The king has the same right of '
         'bringing forward measures as the chambers. A right which '
         'the president does not possess.'}
```

You may notice that the transcript is mostly accurate, but one or two sentences that are present in the audio are missing from the transcript. This is a common issue with the smaller Whisper models. Since these models are generative (i.e., they generate text rather than directly classifying sounds into tokens), they can occasionally miss words or even hallucinate content. Let's discuss some strategies for evaluating these models.

## Evaluation

With so many models that can perform audio tasks, deciding which one to pick can be complex. For pretrained models, we usually look at multiple tasks' downstream performance. Although the most common evaluation downstream task is ASR, we can also evaluate pretrained models fine-tuned in other tasks such as keyword spotting, intent classification, or speaker identification. Apart from performance in downstream tasks, we also need to look into other factors like the model's size, inference speed, languages for which it was trained, and proximity of the training data with the inference data. For example, if you're working with a specific accent, you might want to fine-tune a model with data from that accent. If you need real-time inference, you will want a smaller variant.

In this section, we'll do a high-level evaluation of different models for English speech recognition. Although this won't provide an end-to-end evaluation framework for picking the best model for your use case, it does give some insights into practical ways for analyzing model performance. Let's evaluate two small multilingual models: the 74-million-parameter version of multilingual Whisper and the 94-million-parameter version of Wav2Vec2. We can compare the inference speed and peak amount of GPU used to get started:

```
from genaibook.core import measure_latency_and_memory_use

wav2vec2_pipe = pipeline(
    "automatic-speech-recognition",
    model="facebook/wav2vec2-base-960h",
    device=device,
)
whisper_pipe = pipeline(
    "automatic-speech-recognition", model="openai/whisper-base", device=device
)

with torch.inference_mode():
    measure_latency_and_memory_use(
        wav2vec2_pipe, array, "Wav2Vec2", device, nb_loops=100
    )
    measure_latency_and_memory_use(
        whisper_pipe, array, "Whisper", device=device, nb_loops=100
    )

Wav2Vec2 execution time: 0.009195491333007812 seconds
Wav2Vec2 max memory footprint: 1.7330821120000002 GB
Whisper execution time: 0.092218232421875 seconds
Whisper max memory footprint: 1.6933248 GB
```

Unsurprisingly, the maximum memory footprint (how much VRAM was used) of both models is very similar, which makes sense given both have a similar number of parameters. A 1.7 GB footprint is relatively small, as it can run on laptops and even on some powerful phones. Wav2Vec2 is significantly faster, which is expected given that Whisper's decoder generates text one token at a time.

Let's now look at how good both models are regarding high-quality predictions. The most common metric for evaluating ASR models is the word error rate (WER), which calculates the number of errors by looking at the differences between a prediction and the original label. The error is determined based on how many substitutions, insertions, and deletions are needed to get from the prediction to the label. For example, given the source truth "how can the llama jump" and prediction "can the lama jump up", we have the following:

- One deletion, as "how" is missing
- One substitution, as "llama" was replaced with "lama"
- One insertion, as "up" is in only the prediction

The WER is the sum of the errors divided by the number of words in the label, so we have a WER of 0.6 (three errors divided by five predictions). Note that although there's just one character differing between "llama" and "lama", that's counted as a full error. Many alternative metrics, such as character error rate (CER), evaluate the difference based on each character. Still, the industry widely adopts WER as the go-to metric for ASR evaluation. The *evaluate* library provides a high-level API interface to use these metrics. Using the examples, let's learn how to load and calculate the WER metric:

```
from evaluate import load

wer_metric = load("wer")

label = "how can the llama jump"
pred = "can the lama jump up"
wer = wer_metric.compute(references=[label], predictions=[pred])

print(wer)

0.6
```

A second aspect to consider before doing evaluation is that different ASR models have different output formats based on their training data. For example, Whisper was trained with casing and punctuation, so its transcriptions contain them. To be fair when evaluating models, we can normalize the labels and predictions before computing the WER. This is not perfect, as a model that does learn casing and punctuation would not get a lower error than a model that does not, but it's a solid starting point.

The *transformers* library offers normalizers (`BasicNormalizer`, `EnglishTextNormal` izer, etc.). `BasicTextNormalizer` removes successive whitespaces and basic punctuation and lowercases the text. `EnglishNormalizer` is more advanced, standardizing numbers ("million" to "1000000"), managing contractions, and more. Let's use `Basic Normalizer`, as it will work well; the important part is that we normalize all text and transcriptions consistently:

```
from transformers.models.whisper.english_normalizer import BasicTextNormalizer

normalizer = BasicTextNormalizer()
print(normalizer("I'm having a great day!"))

i m having a great day
```

We'll compare the models using Common Voice, a popular crowd-sourced multilingual dataset. We'll use a part of the English and French test splits of the dataset for demonstration purposes, but we could use other languages (although we would need to be careful with the tokenization). We'll evaluate both WER and CER on 200 samples of each language.

 The Common Voice dataset is public, but you need to accept the terms and conditions and share your name and email with its author, the Mozilla Foundation. You can easily complete this step by visiting the dataset page (*https://oreil.ly/7tMt5*) and clicking the button to signal acceptance. If you don't agree with the terms, feel free to use another dataset or your own data for evaluation.

Let's begin by implementing the evaluation pipeline:

```
# This code example is optimized for explainability
# The inference could be done in batches for speedup, for example.
from datasets import Audio


def normalize(batch):  ❶
    batch["norm_text"] = normalizer(batch["sentence"])
    return batch


def prepare_dataset(language="en", sample_count=200):
    dataset = load_dataset(
        "mozilla-foundation/common_voice_13_0",
        language,
        split="test",
        streaming=True,
    )  ❷
    dataset = dataset.cast_column("audio", Audio(sampling_rate=16000))  ❸
    dataset = dataset.take(sample_count)  ❹
    buffered_dataset = [sample for sample in dataset.map(normalize)]  ❺
```

```
        return buffered_dataset


def evaluate_model(pipe, dataset, lang="en", use_whisper=False):
    predictions, references = [], []

    for sample in dataset:
        if use_whisper:
            extra_kwargs = {
                "task": "transcribe",
                "language": f"<|{lang}|>",
                "max_new_tokens": 100,
            } ❻
            transcription = pipe(
                sample["audio"]["array"],
                return_timestamps=True,
                generate_kwargs=extra_kwargs,
            )
        else:
            transcription = pipe(sample["audio"]["array"])
        predictions.append(normalizer(transcription["text"]))
        references.append(sample["norm_text"])
    return predictions, references
```

❶ Implement function to normalize a batch using Whisper English normalization.

❷ Load the Common Voice dataset in streaming mode.

❸ Resample the audio dataset to 16 kHz.

❹ Sample 200 samples from the dataset.

❺ Normalize the dataset. We also buffer the dataset so it's stored in a list rather than a streaming dataset.

❻ For Whisper, we add additional parameters for its generation (e.g., specifying the language and task).

Now that we have the evaluation pipeline, let's try it with the two models and two languages. We'll first specify the suite:

```
eval_suite = [
    ["Wav2Vec2", wav2vec2_pipe, "en"],
    ["Wav2Vec2", wav2vec2_pipe, "fr"],
    ["Whisper", whisper_pipe, "en"],
    ["Whisper", whisper_pipe, "fr"],
]
```

Now that we have all components in place, let's run the evaluation:

```
cer_metric = load("cer")

# Pre-process the English and French datasets
processed_datasets = {
    "en": prepare_dataset("en"),
    "fr": prepare_dataset("fr"),
}

for config in eval_suite:
    model_name, pipeline, lang = config[0], config[1], config[2]

    dataset = processed_datasets[lang]

    predictions, references = evaluate_model(
        pipeline, dataset, lang, model_name == "Whisper"
    )

    # Compute evaluation metrics
    wer = wer_metric.compute(references=references, predictions=predictions)
    cer = cer_metric.compute(references=references, predictions=predictions)

    print(f"{model_name} metrics for lang: {lang}. WER: {wer}, CER: {cer}")
Reading metadata...: 16372it [00:00, 26197.69it/s]
Reading metadata...: 16114it [00:00, 36235.41it/s]

Wav2Vec2 metrics for lang: en. WER: 0.44012772751463547, CER: 0.22138
Wav2Vec2 metrics for lang: fr. WER: 1.0099113197704748, CER: 0.57450
Whisper metrics for lang: en. WER: 0.2687599787120809, CER: 0.14674
Whisper metrics for lang: fr. WER: 0.5477308294209703, CER: 0.27584
```

Let's discuss the results:

- Whisper clearly outperforms Wav2Vec2 in both English and French (lower error rate is better).

- Although Wav2Vec2 WER for English is high, you can notice that the CER is much lower. As discussed before, Wav2Vec2 is an acoustic model, and it can generate spelling errors. Whisper, on the other hand, has engrained language modeling, so it's more likely to generate the correct words.

- Whisper outperforming Wav2Vec2 in French is not surprising; after all, Whisper was trained with multilingual data, while Wav2Vec2 was trained with English data.

We could experiment with a larger Whisper variant and further reduce the French WER (the largest variant is 20 times larger than the base version). A second interesting aspect is that Whisper performed better than Wav2Vec2 in English. Whisper is multilingual, so we could expect it to perform worse in English than a model tuned entirely with English data. Apart from this, OpenAI also released a Whisper model of the same size but entirely trained on English data. If we wanted to put Whisper in production and knew all our users would speak in English, then it would be better to switch to the English variant.

Remember that Whisper is an autoregressive model. Because of this, it can "hallucinate," and sometimes it can keep generating tokens. This is one of the main issues compared to encoder-only approaches. Given that WER has no upper bound, a single hallucination can significantly drive up the WER. One approach is to limit the maximum number of generated tokens. Since Whisper is designed to transcribe 30-second segments, we could assume 60 words or approximately 100 tokens. Another method is to ground the model to discourage hallucination by forcing it to return the timestamps. In an initial experiment of 100 samples, the WER went from 1.72 to 0.84, just by applying this method.[6] If hallucination is an issue, how come Whisper outperformed Wav2Vec2 in the previous evaluation? The answer is a mix of Whisper's language modeling, the labeled data, and the massive amount of data used for pretraining.

We suggest spending some time experimenting with the following:

- Different model sizes (e.g., Whisper Tiny, of 39 million parameters, versus Large V2, of 1.5 billion parameters, versus the distilled variants)
- Different models (e.g., Wav2Vec2 models fine-tuned in French) or the Whisper variant trained only for English
- Different generation parameters

 If the ASR evaluation topic interests you, we suggest reading the End-to-End Speech Benchmark paper (*https://arxiv.org/abs/2210.13352*). The benchmark proposes comparing multiple end-to-end systems with a unified evaluation using many datasets. There is also a public open source leaderboard (*https://oreil.ly/MKes3*) for speech recognition models, updated regularly with the latest models.

That was a fun dive into ASR technologies. Let's now explore how to do the inverse: convert text to speech, and then generalize to audio generation.

---

6 Empirically, people have found that setting `return_timestamps=True` helps reduce hallucinations in long-form evaluation. There's a high-level explanation about it in the Hugging Face forum (*https://oreil.ly/HzHrI*).

# From Text to Speech to Generative Audio

So far, you've learned how to do high-quality transcriptions with transformer-based models. In this third part of the audio chapter, we'll dive into audio-generation techniques, their evaluations, and challenges. You'll learn about two popular TTS models: SpeechT5 and Bark. Then we'll briefly discuss models that can go beyond speech and generalize to other forms of audio (e.g., music), such as MusicGen, AudioLDM, and AudioGen. Finally, we'll explore how to use diffusion models to generate audio with Riffusion and Dance Diffusion.[7]

Training and evaluating text-to-audio (TTA) models from scratch can be significantly expensive and challenging. Unlike ASR, TTA models can have multiple correct predictions. Think of a TTS model:[8] the generation can have different pronunciations, accents, and speaking styles, and all can be correct. On top of that, popular ASR datasets, such as Common Voice, tend to contain noise, as we want to build robust systems for different conditions. Unfortunately, noise in datasets is an undesired trait for TTA as the models would also learn to generate it. Imagine your generated speech has a dog barking or a car honking in the background. For this reason, training datasets for TTA need to be of high quality.

## Generating Audio with Sequence-to-Sequence Models

SpeechT5 is a pretrained open model by Microsoft that can perform speech-to-text tasks such as ASR and speaker conversion, speech-to-speech tasks such as enhancement and voice conversion, and TTS. SpeechT5, whose architecture is depicted in Figure 9-9, uses an encoder-decoder setup where the inputs and outputs can be either speech or text. To manage inputs from different modalities, speech and text pre-nets convert the input into a hidden representation that the encoder receives afterward. More specifically, the encoder pre-nets convert the input waveforms and texts to a common hidden representation used by the encoder. Similarly, the decoder inputs and outputs are preprocessed and postprocessed with speech and text decoder pre-nets and post-nets. This yields six additional nets, which provide flexibility to accomplish multiple tasks with the same model:

*Text encoder pre-net*
    A text-embedding layer that maps to the hidden representations the encoder expects.

---

7 The selection of models in this section was based on a few factors, including their popularity, size, and quality. SpeechT5 is versatile for handling multiple tasks. Bark is one of the best open models for generating expressive speech. Diffusion-based techniques, although not used as much, have periods of great popularity.

8 Recall that TTS is a type of text-to-audio task.

*Speech encoder pre-net*
> Same idea as the feature extractor from Wav2Vec2: a CNN that preprocesses the input waveform.

*Text decoder pre-net*
> During pretraining, this is the same as the text encoder pre-net. In fine-tuning, this is modified.

*Speech decoder pre-net*
> Takes a log-mel spectrogram and compresses it into a hidden representation.

*Text decoder post-net*
> Single linear layer that projects into probabilities over vocabulary.

*Speech decoder post-net*
> Predicts the output spectrogram and refines it using additional convolutional layers.

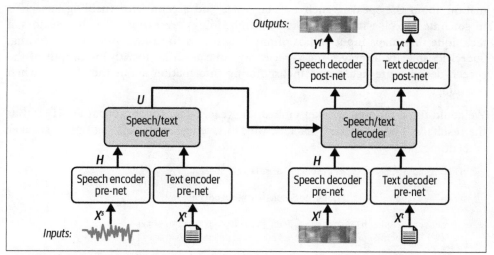

*Figure 9-9. Architecture of the SpeechT5 model (adapted from an image in the original paper (https://arxiv.org/abs/2110.07205))*

For example, if we want to perform ASR, our input will be audio and the output will be text. In that case, we'll want to use the speech encoder pre-net and the text decoder nets (both pre- and post-nets). The *transformers* library comes with a processor class (SpeechT5Processor) that offers the functionalities to process audio and text inputs and outputs. The structure is very similar to that in "Encoder-Based Techniques" on page 308:

```
from transformers import SpeechT5ForSpeechToText, SpeechT5Processor
```

```
processor = SpeechT5Processor.from_pretrained("microsoft/speecht5_asr")
model = SpeechT5ForSpeechToText.from_pretrained("microsoft/speecht5_asr")

inputs = processor(
    audio=array, sampling_rate=sampling_rate, return_tensors="pt"
)
with torch.inference_mode():
    predicted_ids = model.generate(**inputs, max_new_tokens=70)

transcription = processor.batch_decode(predicted_ids, skip_special_tokens=True)
print(transcription)
```

```
['chapter sixteen i might have told you of the beginning i might '
 'have told you of the beginning of the beginning of the beginning '
 'of the beginning of the beginning chapter sixteen']
```

Now, we want to perform TTS. We expect text input and speech output, so we use the text encoder pre-net and the speech decoder nets. To support multispeaker TTS, SpeechT5 expects to receive *speaker embeddings*. These embeddings represent information about the speaker, such as their voice and accent, later enabling SpeechT5 to generate speech with such style. The embeddings are extracted with x-vectors, a technique that maps input audios of any length to a fixed-dimensional embedding. SpeechT5 smartly leverages the x-vector by concatenating it with the output of the speech-decoder pre-net, hence incorporating information about the speaker when decoding.

We could use a random speaker embedding (e.g., using `torch.zeros(1, 512)`), but the results will be very noisy. Luckily, we can leverage some existing online speaker embeddings:

```
from transformers import SpeechT5ForTextToSpeech

from genaibook.core import get_speaker_embeddings

processor = SpeechT5Processor.from_pretrained("microsoft/speecht5_tts")
model = SpeechT5ForTextToSpeech.from_pretrained("microsoft/speecht5_tts")

inputs = processor(text="There are llamas all around.", return_tensors="pt")
speaker_embeddings = torch.tensor(get_speaker_embeddings()).unsqueeze(0)

with torch.inference_mode():
    spectrogram = model.generate_speech(inputs["input_ids"], speaker_embeddings)

plt.figure()
plt.imshow(np.rot90(np.array(spectrogram)))
plt.show()
```

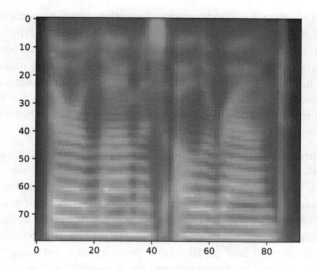

As you can observe, the model output is a log-mel spectrogram rather than a waveform. Spectrograms are powerful tools, but they also have their limitations. While converting waveforms to spectrograms using Short-Time Fourier Transforms is straightforward, the reverse process of converting spectrograms to waveforms is not. Unfortunately, spectrograms don't contain all the information required to reconstruct the original sound. To understand this limitation, let's look at the general formula for a sine wave:

$$F(t) = A \sin (2\pi f t + \Phi)$$

$A$ tells us the amplitude, $f$ is the frequency, and $t$ is the input time. All this information is present in the spectrogram. One element is missing, $\Phi$ (Phi). $\Phi$ represents the phase, which provides additional information about the signal. While magnitude and pitch are the more relevant properties, phase information is essential for accurate audio reconstruction. As a result, we need techniques to reconstruct the original waveform (including the phase information) from a spectrogram. This is an excellent opportunity to learn about vocoders.

A classical reconstruction approach is the Griffin–Lim algorithm, an iterative algorithm that reconstructs a waveform from the predicted spectrogram. This algorithm is popular as it's simple and fast, but it can lead to low-quality audio. The Griffin–Lim algorithm is good enough for some spectrogram generations, but, unfortunately, if you look at the spectrogram generated in the previous example, you might notice that the image quality could improve. Using classical techniques to convert it to waveforms will produce lots of noise and artifacts, so we must dive into fancier techniques that involve neural networks.

Obtaining training data for spectrogram-to-waveform reconstruction is extremely easy, which has led to a rise in recent years of research on trainable models, called *neural vocoders*, that receive some feature representations or spectrograms and convert them to waveforms. WaveNet was one of the first—a famous model from Deep-Mind that got high-quality reconstructions. WaveNet, while being of high quality, is an autoregressive model with slow results, making it unusable for real-world use. There has been work on top of WaveNet to make it much faster, but unfortunately, it required lots of optimization and powerful GPUs.

GAN-based approaches have become popular, high-quality, real-time alternatives for spectrogram-to-waveform reconstruction. At a high level, they use an adversarial training approach in which a model (called generator) receives mel spectrograms and outputs waveforms, and a discriminator model determines if the quality of the audio is close enough to the ground truth, hence leading to both the generator and discriminator to improve. MelGAN and HiFiGANs are popular GAN-based approaches. They are fast and parallelizable, have quality matching WaveNet's, and have good open source implementations. We'll use HiFiGAN as a vocoder for SpeechT5. HiFiGAN's generator is a CNN with two discriminators that help evaluate different aspects of the audio, pushing the CNN to generate high-quality audio. We can use `SpeechT5HifiGan` with *transformers* by passing the spectrogram directly (alternatively, we can specify the `vocoder` parameter when generating speech):

```
from transformers import SpeechT5HifiGan

vocoder = SpeechT5HifiGan.from_pretrained("microsoft/speecht5_hifigan")
with torch.inference_mode():
    # Alternatively
    # model.generate_speech(
    #    inputs["input_ids"],
    #    speaker_embeddings,
    #    vocoder=vocoder)
    speech = vocoder(spectrogram)
```

Remember that you can play the audio via `Audio(array, rate=sampling_rate)` in a notebook or explore some generations we've compiled (*https://oreil.ly/a5Yn_*).

We can generate a spectrogram with SpeechT5 and convert the spectrogram into a waveform with HiFiGAN. SpeechT5 was trained in English, so it will perform poorly in other languages. It's possible to fine-tune it for other languages, but it will have some limitations, such as not supporting characters outside the English language. Fine-tuning for other languages also requires obtaining speaker embeddings for non-English speakers, so the model is expected to perform worse. If you played with different speaker embeddings, the quality of the results highly depends on the speaker embeddings. Maybe we can do better?

An ideal TTS setup is to have a single model (rather than a spectrogram generator plus a vocoder), train it end-to-end, be flexible to use it for multiple speakers, generate long audios, and have fast inference. This leads us to a new model called *VITS*, a parallel end-to-end method. At a high level, VITS can be seen as a conditional VAE. VITS combines multiple tricks, some of which are familiar to us. VITS uses a transformer encoder as the main encoder and the HiFiGAN generator as the decoder. Other components help improve quality and flexibility to tackle the one-to-many challenge of TTS. During training, another trick was to compare the mel spectrogram rather than the final raw waveform when computing the reconstruction loss. This helps the training focus on improving the perceptual quality; if you remember, mel spectrograms approximate how we perceive sound. The model is pushed to generate better perceivable speech by incorporating it in the reconstruction loss.

VITS was released in 2021 by Kakao Enterprise and was among the SOTA models. In 2023, Meta released Massively Multilingual Speech (MMS), a massive multilingual dataset. This dataset led to many exciting results. First, it contains data to identify among 4,000 spoken languages (audio-classification task). Meta also released TTS and ASR data for more than 1,100 languages. The authors built a new pretrained Wav2Vec2 model and released a multilingual ASR fine-tune for the 1,100 languages. What does all this have to do with TTS? The MMS authors also trained separate VITS models for each language, leading to high-quality TTS models for many languages such as Vietnamese and Dutch, obtaining better results than the original VITS models.[9] This is an excellent example of how improving training data can lead to better results. Let's use this model to generate some speech:

```
from transformers import VitsModel, VitsTokenizer, set_seed

tokenizer = VitsTokenizer.from_pretrained("facebook/mms-tts-eng")
model = VitsModel.from_pretrained("facebook/mms-tts-eng")

inputs = tokenizer(text="Hello - my dog is cute", return_tensors="pt")

set_seed(555)  # make deterministic
with torch.inference_mode():
    outputs = model(inputs["input_ids"])

outputs.waveform[0]
```

# Going Beyond Speech with Bark

You just learned how to generate speech with SpeechT5 and VITS. This can be applied to many use cases, but other generative audio applications go beyond speech. For example, you might want a model that can generate sounds like laughing or crying. You could also want to have a model that can generate songs.

---

9  You can find all MMS-based models on Hugging Face (*https://oreil.ly/pzh5u*).

The third generative model we'll visit is Bark (Figure 9-10), by Suno AI (*https://suno.com*), another transformer-based model. Bark is one of the most popular open generative audio models out there. It can generate sounds apart from speech. For example, you can have laugh or sigh in the prompt, and corresponding sounds will be integrated into the speech. We can even make it a bit musical by using ♪ in the prompts. Bark is multilingual and includes a library of voice presets (similar to the speaker embeddings), which allows us to generate speech with different voices.

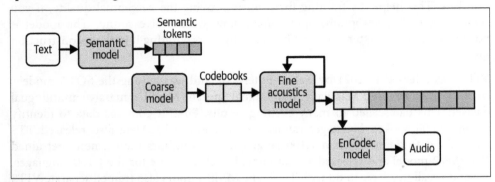

*Figure 9-10. The Bark pipeline uses three components: text-to-semantic tokens, semantic-to-coarse tokens, and coarse-to-fine tokens*

Before we explore the details of Bark, there's one more concept to cover: audio *codecs*. When compressing audio, the goal is to reduce the file size (or bitrate) while keeping the sound quality as high as possible. Researchers have been trying to use neural networks for this purpose for years, leading to advanced tools like SoundStream and EnCodec. EnCodec, developed by Meta, is a popular open source neural codec that can compress audio in real time with high quality.

EnCodec uses a three-step process. First, the encoder compresses the audio into a latent representation. Next, a quantization layer turns this into a compact, more efficient format (a compressed representation).[10] Finally, the decoder reconstructs the audio from the compressed data. The quantized latent space is represented by codebooks, each containing multiple possible vectors. For example, an input audio might be represented using 32 codebook vectors (each with 1,024 entries) in the quantized latent space.

With codecs in our toolkit, let's go back to Bark. The goal of Bark is to receive text and map it into codebooks. Then, Bark uses the decoder component of a neural codec to convert the codebooks to audio. Four components make this possible:

---

10 How to quantize the encoder's output is a design decision. The EnCodec authors used a technique called *residual vector quantization*.

### Text model

An autoregressive decoder transformer with a language-modeling head on top that maps text prompts into high-level semantic tokens. Thanks to this, Bark can generalize to sounds beyond the training data, such as sound effects and lyrics.

### Coarse acoustics model

Same architecture as the text model, but it maps the semantic tokens from the text model into the first two audio codebooks.

### Fine acoustics model

A noncausal AutoEncoder transformer that iteratively predicts the following codebooks based on the sum of the initial ones. It outputs in total two coarse codebooks plus six generated ones.

### Codec

Once all eight codebook channels are predicted, the decoder part of the EnCodec model decodes the output audio array.

There are multiple configurable parameters. For example, we can modify the number of codebooks generated by the coarse and fine acoustics models. We can also play with the size of each codebook, which is 1,024 in the official implementation. This architecture allows the model to generate new sounds, speech in multiple languages, and more. Let's try it out:

```python
from transformers import AutoModel, AutoProcessor

processor = AutoProcessor.from_pretrained("suno/bark-small")
model = AutoModel.from_pretrained("suno/bark-small").to(device)

inputs = processor(
    text=[
        """Hello, my name is Suno. And, uh — and I like pizza. [laughs]
        But I also have other interests such as playing tic tac toe."""
    ],
    return_tensors="pt",
).to(device)


speech_values = model.generate(**inputs, do_sample=True)
```

Those are some nice results. Suppose we wanted to condition the output to sound according to a predefined speaker. In that case, we can also use speaker embeddings from an official library (*https://oreil.ly/ozUYr*) shared by the authors. It's also possible to train these speaker embeddings on your own voice, hence being able to generate synthetic audio following your prosody. Let's use one of the predefined voices:

```python
voice_preset = "v2/en_speaker_6"

inputs = processor("Hello, my dog is cute", voice_preset=voice_preset)
```

```
audio_array = model.generate(**inputs.to(device))
audio_array = audio_array.cpu().numpy().squeeze()
```

## AudioLM and MusicLM

Controlling speech generation with additional sounds is neat, but could we generate entire melodies? The answer is yes. Let's begin the journey with AudioLM and MusicLM, two exciting models from Google from 2023 that can perform audio and music generation. This can be used for all kinds of applications, such as generating noise effects in videos, adding background music to a podcast, or designing sounds for games.

AudioLM receives an audio recording that is a few seconds long and then generates high-quality continuations that preserve the speakers' identity and way of speaking. The model is trained without transcripts and annotations, making it quite impressive. How does AudioLM achieve this? Conceptually, AudioLM is similar to Bark but with a different task: sound continuation rather than TTA.

AudioLM (Figure 9-11) first uses w2v-BERT, a pretrained model that maps the waveform to rich semantic tokens (similarly to how we used an LM to generate semantic tokens from text in Bark). Then, a semantic model predicts the future tokens, modeling the high-level structure of the audio sequence. A second model, the coarse acoustic model, uses the generated semantic tokens and the past acoustic tokens to generate new ones. How are the past acoustic tokens generated? We can pass the input waveform to a codec and retrieve the codebooks (the quantized latent representation). This helps conserve the speaker's characteristics and generates more coherent audio. A fourth model, the fine acoustic model, adds more detail to the audio, refining it, improving the quality, and removing lossy compression artifacts from previous stages. Finally, the tokens are fed into a neural codec to reconstruct the waveform.

AudioLM can also be trained in music, such as piano recordings, to generate coherent continuations that conserve the rhythm and melody. Although the underlying models are different, you might notice that the stages are similar to Bark: we train a series of models that lead to generating high-quality codebooks and then use a neural codec (EnCodec in Bark and SoundStream in AudioLM) to generate the final waveform.

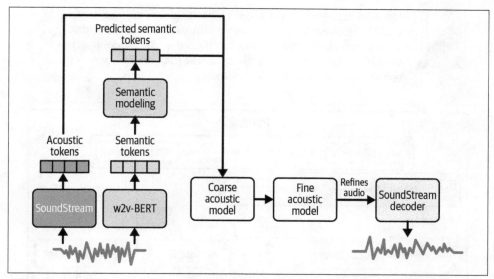

*Figure 9-11. In the AudioLM model pipeline, AudioLM converts the input audio to a sequence of tokens and performs audio generation using language-modeling techniques (adapted from an image in the original paper (https://arxiv.org/abs/2209.03143))*

MusicLM (Figure 9-12) takes things further by focusing on high-quality music generation that accurately matches text descriptions.[11] For example, you can have a text description such as "an intense rock concert with violins" as a prompt. MusicLM uses AudioLM's multistage setup and incorporates text conditioning.

If obtaining high-quality labeled TTS data is complex, labeled TTA can be much more complicated. TTA systems might involve a much broader range of audio types, including environmental sounds and music. Annotating a diverse range of sounds with high accuracy can be more challenging and intensive. To approach this, MusicLM uses an additional model, MuLan, which, similarly to CLIP for image-text pairs, can map texts and their corresponding audio to the same embedding space. Thanks to this, MuLan removed the need for captions during training and enabled training on vast amounts of audio data. To be more concrete, during training, MusicLM uses the embeddings computed from the audio to condition the models, and during inference, MusicLM uses text embeddings.

---

11 MusicCaps, the evaluation dataset used for MusicLM, is open source and can be found online (*https://oreil.ly/cRh9X*).

None of these models are open source at the time of writing. LAION released an alternative to MuLan called CLAP (*https://arxiv.org/abs/2211.06687*). Although trained with 20 times less data than MuLan, it can generate diverse music samples. EnCodec is the open source alternative to SoundStream.

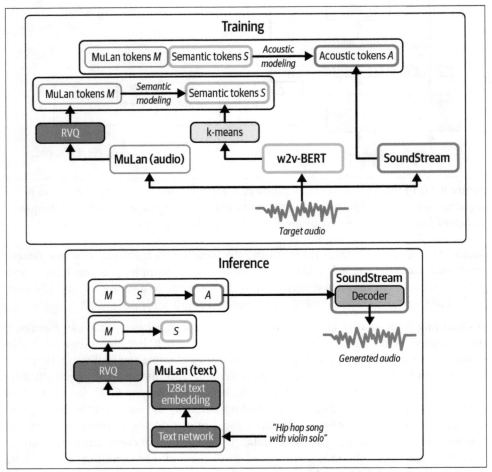

*Figure 9-12. MusicLM incorporates text conditioning to the AudioLM architecture, to generate audio based on a prompt (adapted from an image in the original paper (https://arxiv.org/abs/2301.11325))*

## AudioGen and MusicGen

In parallel, in 2022 and 2023, Meta released multiple open models for audio generation guided by text. AudioGen can generate sound and environmental effects (e.g., a dog barking or a door knock). AudioGen follows a flow similar to Bark and AudioLM. It uses the text encoder from T5 to generate text embeddings and condition the generation with them. The decoder autoregressively generates audio tokens conditioned on the text and audio tokens from the previous steps. The final audio tokens can finally be decoded with a neural codec.

The open source version of AudioGen is a variation of the original architecture; for the neural codec, they retrained an EnCodec on environmental sound data. If you feel this is familiar, it's because it is—we're once again doing a similar process to Bark and AudioLM. So, what can we do with AudioGen? Three tasks with a single model:

- With the full architecture, we can create text-conditioned audio, e.g., "a dog barks while somebody plays the trumpet".
- If we remove the text encoder, we can unconditionally generate sounds.
- We can do audio continuation by using input audio tokens from an existing audio.

Building upon AudioGen, Meta released MusicGen, which was trained to generate music conditioned on text and achieved better results across various metrics than MusicLM. MusicGen passes the text descriptions through a text encoder (such as the ones from T5 or Flan T5) to obtain embeddings. Then, it uses an LM to generate audio codebooks conditioned on the embeddings. Finally, the audio tokens are decoded using EnCodec to get the waveform. Multiple MusicGen models were released.

 AudioGen was trained with public datasets (AudioSet, AudioCaps, etc.). MusicGen, on the other hand, was trained with 20K hours of Meta-owned and specifically licensed music, combining an internal dataset, Shutterstock, and Pond5 music data.

Let's try the smallest MusicGen variant of 300 million parameters and load each component:

```python
from transformers import AutoProcessor, MusicgenForConditionalGeneration

model = MusicgenForConditionalGeneration.from_pretrained(
    "facebook/musicgen-small"
).to(device)
processor = AutoProcessor.from_pretrained("facebook/musicgen-small")
inputs = processor(
    text=["an intense rock guitar solo"],
    padding=True,
```

```
        return_tensors="pt",
    ).to(device)

    audio_values = model.generate(
        **inputs, do_sample=True, guidance_scale=3, max_new_tokens=256
    )
```

You've learned to use multiple audio generation models: Bark, SpeechT5, and Music-Gen. Depending on the API abstractions you expect, rather than loading the model and processor independently and doing all the inference code ourselves, we can use the `text-to-audio` and `text-to-speech` pipelines available in *transformers*. They abstract the logic away and are great for running inference:

```
from transformers import pipeline

pipe = pipeline("text-to-audio", model="facebook/musicgen-small", device=device)
data = pipe("electric rock solo, very intense")
```

## Audio Diffusion and Riffusion

Let's explore diffusion approaches for audio generation. With spectrograms, we have an informative visual representation of audio that can serve as a blueprint to be converted back into sound. If only we knew of a model that could generate images, we could do exciting things…. Wait, we know diffusion models. As discussed in Chapter 4, we can use diffusion pipelines to create images (both conditioned and unconditioned).

*Audio Diffusion* extrapolates this straightforward idea to audio: we can pick thousands of mel spectrograms from a database of songs and then train an unconditional diffusion model to generate mel spectrogram images, which can be converted to audio afterward. Although it sounds surprisingly simple, this yields decent results. For example, *teticio/audio-diffusion-ddim-256* (*https://oreil.ly/cbXde*) is a model trained with 20,000 images from the author's liked songs. Let's generate a song with this model:

```
from diffusers import AudioDiffusionPipeline

pipe = AudioDiffusionPipeline.from_pretrained(
    "teticio/audio-diffusion-ddim-256"
).to(device)

output = pipe()
```

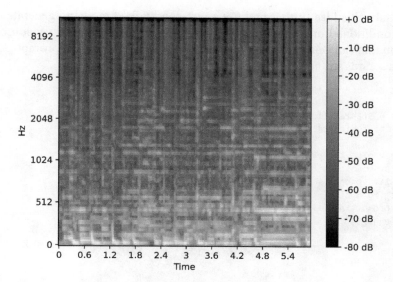

We can access the spectrogram by inspecting the result from `AudioDiffusionPipeline` (`output.images`). Fortunately, `AudioDiffusionPipeline` handles the conversion of the spectrogram to audio for us (by using Griffin–Lim under the hood, which works given the spectrogram's quality) and returns the corresponding audio (`output.audios`). Note that this model is denoising the spectrograms directly. Alternatively, we could use an AutoEncoder to encode the images and work in the latent space (as done in Chapter 5), significantly speeding up model training and inference. This could be an excellent exercise if you'd like to dive deeper.

When you plot the spectrogram from `output.images[0]`, you'll observe differences compared to the preceding spectrogram, which was obtained from the audio output. The model is trained to generate grayscale images, whereas the mel spectrogram is in color. Additionally, the generated spectrogram is horizontally flipped because of the structure of the training data. The displayed spectrogram has been flipped to maintain consistency with others shown in the chapter.

We can take this idea further and use a text-conditioned model to generate spectrograms conditioned on text. Riffusion, for example, is a fine-tuned version of Stable Diffusion that can generate images of spectrograms based on a text prompt. Although this idea sounds strange, it works surprisingly well:

```
from diffusers import StableDiffusionPipeline

pipe = StableDiffusionPipeline.from_pretrained(
    "riffusion/riffusion-model-v1", torch_dtype=torch.float16
)
pipe = pipe.to(device)
prompt = "slow piano piece, classical"
negative_prompt = "drums"
spec_img = pipe(
    prompt, negative_prompt=negative_prompt, height=512, width=512
).images[0]
```

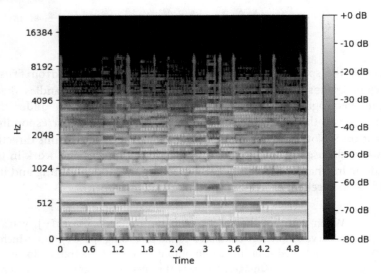

The simplicity of using Stable Diffusion brings lots of advantages. Common tools such as image to image, inpainting, negative prompts, and interpolation work out of the box. For example, you can convert an acoustic solo into an electric guitar solo or smoothly transition between genres, like going from ambient typing sounds to jazz, to create unique sound effects. Let's take the previously generated spectrogram and use an image-to-image pipeline with a new prompt to convert the piano to a guitar song:

```
from diffusers import StableDiffusionImg2ImgPipeline

pipe = StableDiffusionImg2ImgPipeline.from_pretrained(
    "riffusion/riffusion-model-v1", torch_dtype=torch.float16
)
```

```
pipe = pipe.to(device)

prompt = "guitar, acoustic, calmed"
generator = torch.Generator(device=device).manual_seed(1024)
image = pipe(
    prompt=prompt,
    image=spec_img,
    strength=0.7,
    guidance_scale=8,
    generator=generator,
).images[0]
```

# Dance Diffusion

Although generating spectrograms and converting them to audio clips works decently, using images to train an audio model is only somewhat intuitive. Rather than using a spectrogram, we can explore training a model that can directly work with raw audio data (the array of numbers) rather than images. As done in Chapter 4, the UNet is a CNN with a series of downsampling layers followed by a series of upsampling layers. Although so far we've been using a UNet that works for 2D data (by using `UNet2DModel`), we can also use a UNet that works with the raw audio instead, that is, have the UNet work with an array of float numbers (`UNet1DModel`).[12]

Dance Diffusion is an open source family of models for unconditional audio generation that generates audio waveforms directly. There are different models trained with different datasets. For example, `harmonai/maestro-150k` is a model trained with 200 hours of piano clips, so it can unconditionally generate piano sounds:

```
from diffusers import DanceDiffusionPipeline

pipe = DanceDiffusionPipeline.from_pretrained(
    "harmonai/maestro-150k", torch_dtype=torch.float16
)
pipe = pipe.to(device)
audio = pipe(audio_length_in_s=5, num_inference_steps=50).audios[0]
```

The setup for Dance Diffusion is similar to the one we saw in Chapter 4. By changing the `UNet2DModel` and data, you can get decent results out of the box. Setting a minimal training loop for Dance Diffusion with your data can be relatively simple and requires little setup. The quality of these models is OK but could clearly be better.

---

12 If you peek into the generated audio data, you will notice two arrays. This is because Dance Diffusion was trained with stereo sound.

## More on Diffusion Models for Generative Audio

One of the significant issues of diffusion models is that their inference speed is very slow. Inspired by Stable Diffusion, the DiffSound and AudioLDM models were designed to operate on a latent space. This latent space is the CLAP latent embedding space. Just like MuLan in MusicLM and CLIP in the image domain, CLAP is a model that maps texts and audio into a shared latent space. This makes the diffusion process much faster and removes the need for labeled data.

This is similar to Stable Diffusion but in a different modality: we use CLAP rather than CLIP; we still use UNet backbones (actually, the same specifications as Stable Diffusion); and we use a VAE to decode the latent space and generate mel spectrograms. As done in our early TTS adventures, we use a vocoder, HiFiGAN, to synthesize the audio waveform from the spectrogram. This architecture design gives AudioLLM a framework for doing multiple text-guided audio manipulations. For example, it can do inpainting, super-resolution, and style transfer.

MusicLDM modifies AudioLDM to focus entirely on music. CLAP would not work out of the box as it's pretrained on datasets dominated by sound effects and other sounds, but not that much music. The authors retrained CLAP on text-music pair datasets, improving understanding of music data. The authors also retrained the HiFiGAN vocoder on music data to ensure the reconstructed waveforms correspond to the music.

One of the risks with text-to-music generation is that, given the scarcity of permissive data, the diffusion process is more likely to reconstruct examples from the original training data. To avoid this, MusicLDM uses data-augmentation techniques to encourage the model to explore more space in the music data. For example, they use mixup, a technique that combines two audio samples by interpolating them to create a new one. This helps prevent overfitting and improve generalization.

# Evaluating Audio-Generation Systems

TTS and TTA, just like image generation, are tricky to evaluate as there's no single correct generation. On top of that, the audio quality depends a lot on human perception: imagine that you use different models to generate a song based on a prompt; different persons will have different preferences, making it challenging and expensive to compare models.

There have been approaches to defining objective metrics. The Frechet Audio Distance (FAD) can be used to evaluate the quality of audio models when there isn't any reference audio. This metric is correlated with human perception and allows identifying plausible audio but might not necessarily evaluate that the generated audios adhere to the prompts. Another approach, if there are reference audios, is to use a classifier to compute class predictions for both the prediction and the reference audio and then measure the KL divergence between both probability distributions. In case of a lack of reference data, CLAP can map the input prompt and output audio to the same embedding space and compute the similarity between the embeddings. This approach would be strongly biased toward the pretraining data used for CLAP.

Ultimately, human evaluation is always needed for TTS and TTA systems. As mentioned before, the generations' quality is subjective, so multiple humans from diverse backgrounds should ideally evaluate the system's quality. A way to do this is to compute the mean opinion score (MOS), which requires humans to evaluate generations on a certain scale. Another approach is to show humans the input prompt and two different generations from different models. Humans are then required to say which of the two generations is preferred.

# What's Next?

The world of generative audio is experiencing a moment of unprecedented innovation and growth. Recent advancements in audio and speech have been substantial, yet the field remains constantly evolving, continuously offering new frontiers for exploration.

For example, developing real-time, high-quality audio generation is an exciting emerging area. The prospect of generating high-quality audio in real time opens up many possibilities for applications across domains, from accessibility tools to game development. Recent releases such as Coqui's released XTTS (*https://oreil.ly/0OUgv*), ElevenLabs TTS tools (*https://oreil.ly/k0hd2*), and Moshi by Kyutai (*https://kyutai.org*) are great examples of this.

Another emerging topic is unified modeling, which creates models that can be flexible among different tasks. Models such as SeamlessM4T (*https://oreil.ly/WTVBw*) that introduce a scalable unified speech-translation system are a great example of this area. This single model can support various audio tasks, such as TTS, speech-to-speech translation, text-to-speech translation (generating synthetic speech in another language), and more. This chapter explored popular high-quality speech-, audio-, and music-generation models. The differences between these three data domains pose challenges for training a unified model to generate audio in the three forms. However, recent model techniques like AudioLDM 2 are exploring this direction. These models propose a unified language of audio that enables it to create all of them and obtain decent results comparable to or better than the other task-specific models.

Audio challenges and discussions extend beyond modeling. Key ethical concerns include data provenance, copyright laws, memorization, and ownership. While cloning one's voice is technically impressive, it raises serious ethical questions when applied to other people's voices without consent. Training a music model can be an exciting intellectual and creative experiment, but determining fair dataset usage remains an open question. For instance, creating a synthetic version of a celebrity's voice for advertisements without their consent could be seen as a violation of their personal rights.

Additionally, most recent ML research for audio has primarily focused on the English language, leaving significant progress to be made in multilingualism. If speech-recognition models are developed predominantly for a few languages, others may receive subpar or inaccessible services and tools. These ethical considerations underscore the importance of responsible development and application of ML technologies. Addressing these issues proactively can help foster trust and ensure that the benefits of these technologies are equitably distributed.

## Project Time: End-to-End Conversational System

Across the chapters, you've learned to use transformer models for generating text (Chapters 2 and 6), diffusion models for image generation (Chapters 4 and 5), and models to transcribe and generate speech (this chapter), as well as building Gradio demos (Chapter 5). In this challenge, the goal is to build an end-to-end Gradio app in which:

- The user can either write or speak a prompt.
- The prompt can either be conversational or ask to generate an image.
- Based on the prompt, the model generates a response that could be an image or text.
- The model will output the image and text, as well as the corresponding generated speech in case of text.

This project requires many design decisions. Which model would you pick? How do you balance quality and speed? How can you determine if a prompt is asking to generate an image?[13] This open-ended project will require you to use the skills you've learned across the chapters. We suggest starting with a simple version and then iterating on it. You shouldn't need to train any models for this project, but you can fine-tune models if you want to. The goal is to build a fun and interactive conversational system that can generate images, text, and audio based on user prompts.

## Summary

What an adventure! The generative audio space is living in an inspiring moment, with new models popping up every few weeks, higher-quality datasets being released, and new labs entering the generative audio landscape. It's normal to feel overwhelmed

---

13 Hint: You can try heuristics, zero-shot classification, or sentence similarity, for example.

by the number of models being used in the audio domain; after all, the field is progressing extremely fast. Insights from other modalities, such as language or diffusion models in the latent space, have inspired many of the tools we've employed. Audio's inherent complexity has led us to uncover new components like vocoders for spectrogram-to-waveform reconstruction and neural codecs for audio compression and decompression. While this chapter has introduced just the audio domain, it has equipped us with the foundational knowledge to delve deeper into recent research.

If you wish to explore the field further, we suggest researching the following topics:

*CTC*

To learn about the CTC algorithm used by Wav2Vec2, we recommend reading the interactive blog post "Sequence Modeling with CTC" (*https://oreil.ly/7v4tV*).

*ParlerTTS*

ParlerTTS is a training and inference library (as well as a family of models) for TTS. The library is lightweight and can generate high-quality and customizable speech. We recommend exploring the ParlerTTS GitHub repository (*https://oreil.ly/UWhq0*) and trying its inference and training examples.

*Vocoders*

In this chapter, we briefly introduced vocoders, such as HiFiGANs, which do mel spectrogram to speech. We suggest reading about the WaveNet, MelGAN, and HiFiGAN vocoders for a more substantial overview. What are their differences? How are they evaluated?

*Model optimization*

Different model optimization techniques can lead to much faster audio generation with minimal quality degradation. We recommend reading the blog posts "AudioLDM 2, but Faster ⚡" (*https://oreil.ly/Hs1BQ*) and "Speculative Decoding for 2x Faster Whisper Inference" (*https://oreil.ly/0HoGz*).

*Other popular models*

We covered many models in this chapter. Apart from diving into them, we suggest exploring other popular models, such as Tacotron 2, FastSpeech, FastSpeech 2, TorToiSe TTS, and VALL-E. A high-level understanding of these models will provide a complete picture of the ecosystem.

As we've encountered a multitude of datasets and models, Tables 9-1 and 9-2 succinctly summarize the key resources for further exploration.

*Table 9-1. Summary of datasets*

| Dataset | Description | Training hours | Recommended use |
|---------|-------------|----------------|-----------------|
| LibriSpeech | Narrated audiobooks | English: 960 | Benchmarking and pretraining models |
| Multilingual LibriSpeech | Multilingual equivalent of LibriSpeech | English: 44,659 Total: 65,000 | Benchmarking and pretraining models |
| Common Voice 13 | Crowd-sourced multilingual with varying quality | English: 2,400 Total: 17,600 | Multilingual systems |
| VoxPopuli | European Parliament recording | English: 543 Total: 1,800 | Multilingual systems, domain-specific uses, nonnative speakers |
| GigaSpeech | Multidomain English from audiobooks, podcasts, and YouTube | English: 10,000 | Robustness over multiple domains |
| FLEURS | Parallel multilingual corpus | 10 hours for each of 102 languages | Evaluation in multilingual settings (including "low digital resource" setting) |
| MMS-labeled | New Testament read out loud | 37,000 hours for a total of 1,100 languages | Multilingual systems |
| MMS-unlabeled | Recordings of stories and songs | 7,700 hours for 3,800 languages | Multilingual systems |

*Table 9-2. Summary of models*

| Model | Task | Model type | Notes |
|-------|------|------------|-------|
| Wav2Vec2 | English ASR | Encoder transformer with CTC | Trained on unlabeled English data. Can easily be fine-tuned. |
| HuBERT | English ASR | Encoder transformer with CTC | Trained on unlabeled English data. Can easily be fine-tuned. |
| XLS-R | Multilingual ASR | Encoder transformer with CTC | Trained on unlabeled data for 128 languages. |
| Whisper | Multilingual ASR | Encoder-decoder transformer | Trained on a massive amount of multilingual labeled data. |
| SpeechT5 | ASR, TTS, and S2S | Encoder-decoder transformer | Adds pre- and post-nets to map speech and text to the same space. |
| HiFiGAN | Spectrogram to speech | GAN with multiple discriminators | It's one type of vocoder. |
| EnCodec and SoundStream | Audio compression | Encoder-decoder | Uses quantized latent space. |
| Bark | Multilingual TTA | Multistage autoregressive | Predicts codebooks and uses EnCodec to reconstruct. |
| MuLan and CLAP | Map text and audio to the same space | Transformer encoder for text and CNN for audio | CLAP is the open source replication of MuLan. |
| AudioLM | Audio continuation | Multistage autoregressive | Similar conceptually to Bark but uses audio input. |
| MusicLM | Text to music (TTM) | Combines MuLan and AudioLM | Incorporates MuLan to remove need for labeled data. |

| Model | Task | Model type | Notes |
|-------|------|-----------|-------|
| AudioGen | TTA | Multistage autoregressive | EnCodec is retrained on environmental sound data. |
| MusicGen | TTM | Same as AudioGen | Multiple variants are open source. |
| AudioLDM | TTA | Latent space diffusion (same as Stable Diffusion) | Uses CLAP for latent space. |
| MusicLDM | TTM | Same as AudioLDM | Retrains CLAP and HiFiGAN on music domain. |

# Exercises

1. What are the pros and cons of using waveforms versus spectrograms?

2. What's a spectrogram, and what's a mel spectrogram? Which one is used in models?

3. Explain how CTC works. Why is it needed for encoder-based ASR models?

4. What would happen if the inference data had a sampling rate of 8 kHz, while the model was trained with one of 16 kHz?

5. How does adding an n-gram model to an encoder-based model work?

6. What are the pros and cons of encoder-based versus encoder-decoder–based models for ASR?

7. In which case would you prefer to use CER over WER to evaluate ASR?

8. What are the six nets used by SpeechT5? Which setup would be needed to perform voice conversion?

9. What's a vocoder? In which cases would you use one?

10. What's the purpose of the EnCodec model?

11. How do TTA models leverage MuLan/CLAP to relax the need for labeled data?

You can find the solutions to these exercises and the following challenges in the book's GitHub repository (*https://oreil.ly/handsonGenAIcode*).

# Challenges

1. *Whisper exploration.* The following code snippet creates a random array and a Whisper feature extractor from scratch:

```python
import numpy as np
from transformers import WhisperFeatureExtractor

array = np.zeros((16000, ))
feature_extractor = WhisperFeatureExtractor(feature_size=100)
features = feature_extractor(
```

```
    array, sampling_rate=16000, return_tensors="pt"
)
```

Explore the impact of changing `feature_size`, `hop_length`, and `chunk_length` in the shape of the input features. Then, look at the default values of the `Whisper FeatureExtractor` in its documentation (*https://oreil.ly/zhipN*) and what each of them means, and try calculating how many features would be generated for an audio chunk.

2. *Voice conversion*. Implement voice conversion with SpeechT5 so that an input audio is spoken by a different speaker.

3. *Training Dance Diffusion*. Implement a small training pipeline for Dance Diffusion. You can use the code from Chapter 4 as a starting point.

# References

Agostinelli, Andrea, et al. "MusicLM: Generating Music From Text." arXiv, January 26, 2023. *http://arxiv.org/abs/2301.11325*.

Ao, Junyi, et al. "SpeechT5: Unified-Modal Encoder-Decoder Pre-Training for Spoken Language Processing." arXiv, May 24, 2022. *http://arxiv.org/abs/2110.07205*.

Ardila, Rosana, et al. "Common Voice: A Massively-Multilingual Speech Corpus." arXiv, March 5, 2020. *http://arxiv.org/abs/1912.06670*.

Babu, Arun, et al. "XLS-R: Self-Supervised Cross-Lingual Speech Representation Learning at Scale." arXiv, December 16, 2021. *http://arxiv.org/abs/2111.09296*.

Baevski, Alexei, et al. "Wav2vec 2.0: A Framework for Self-Supervised Learning of Speech Representations." arXiv, October 22, 2020. *http://arxiv.org/abs/2006.11477*.

Barrault et al. SeamlessM4T web page. August 22, 2022. *https://oreil.ly/WTVBw*.

Borsos, Zalán, et al. "AudioLM: A Language Modeling Approach to Audio Generation." arXiv, July 25, 2023. *http://arxiv.org/abs/2209.03143*.

Chen, Ke, et al. "MusicLDM: Enhancing Novelty in Text-to-Music Generation Using Beat-Synchronous Mixup Strategies." arXiv, August 3, 2023. *http://arxiv.org/abs/2308.01546*.

Conneau, Alexis, et al. "FLEURS: Few-Shot Learning Evaluation of Universal Representations of Speech." arXiv, May 24, 2022. *http://arxiv.org/abs/2205.12446*.

Conneau, Alexis, et al. "Unsupervised Cross-lingual Representation Learning for Speech Recognition." arXiv, December 15, 2020. *http://arxiv.org/abs/2006.13979*.

Copet, Jade, et al. "Simple and Controllable Music Generation." arXiv, June 8, 2023. *http://arxiv.org/abs/2306.05284*.

Défossez, Alexandre, et al. "High Fidelity Neural Audio Compression." arXiv, October 24, 2022. *http://arxiv.org/abs/2210.13438*.

Gandhi, Sanchit. "A Complete Guide to Audio Datasets." Hugging Face blog, December 15, 2022. *https://oreil.ly/CXGff.*

Gandhi, Sanchit, et al. "ESB: A Benchmark for Multi-domain End-to-End Speech Recognition." arXiv, October 24, 2022. *http://arxiv.org/abs/2210.13352.*

Gandhi, Sanchit, et al. Hugging Face audio course. Hugging Face, June 14, 2023. *https://oreil.ly/Z-IZ0.*

Hollemans, Matthijs. "Speech Synthesis, Recognition, and More With SpeechT5." Hugging Face blog, February 8, 2023. *https://oreil.ly/xar9H.*

Hsu, Wei-Ning, et al. "HuBERT: Self-Supervised Speech Representation Learning by Masked Prediction of Hidden Units." arXiv, June 14, 2021. *http://arxiv.org/abs/2106.07447.*

Huang, Qingqing, et al. "MuLan: A Joint Embedding of Music Audio and Natural Language." arXiv, August 25, 2022. *http://arxiv.org/abs/2208.12415.*

Kim, Jaehyeon, et al. "Conditional Variational Autoencoder with Adversarial Learning for End-to-End Text-to-Speech." arXiv, June 10, 2021. *http://arxiv.org/abs/2106.06103.*

Kong, Jungil, et al. "HiFi-GAN: Generative Adversarial Networks for Efficient and High Fidelity Speech Synthesis." arXiv, October 23, 2020. *http://arxiv.org/abs/2010.05646.*

Kreuk, Felix, et al. "AudioGen: Textually Guided Audio Generation." arXiv, March 5, 2023. *http://arxiv.org/abs/2209.15352.*

Kucsko, Georg. 2023. Bark GitHub repository. September 17, 2023. *https://oreil.ly/Pq2K5.*

Liu, Haohe, et al. "AudioLDM: Text-to-Audio Generation with Latent Diffusion Models." arXiv, September 9, 2023. *http://arxiv.org/abs/2301.12503.*

Panayotov, Vassil, et al. "Librispeech: An ASR Corpus Based on Public Domain Audio Books." In *2015 IEEE International Conference on Acoustics, Speech and Signal Processing*, pp. 5206–10. IEEE, 2015. *https://oreil.ly/MOIUF.*

Patry, Nicolas. "Making Automatic Speech Recognition Work on Large Files with Wav2Vec2 in 🤗 Transformers." Hugging Face blog, February 1, 2022. *https://oreil.ly/gh8O1.*

Pratap, Vineel, et al. "Scaling Speech Technology to 1,000+ Languages." arXiv, May 22, 2023. *http://arxiv.org/abs/2305.13516.*

Radford, Alec, et al. "Robust Speech Recognition via Large-Scale Weak Supervision." arXiv, December 6, 2022. *http://arxiv.org/abs/2212.04356.*

Von Platen, Patrick. "Boosting Wav2Vec2 with N-Grams in 🤗 Transformers." Hugging Face blog, January 12, 2022. *https://oreil.ly/o0HLV.*

Wu, Yusong, et al. "Large-Scale Contrastive Language-Audio Pretraining with Feature Fusion and Keyword-to-Caption Augmentation." arXiv, April 7, 2023. *http://arxiv.org/abs/2211.06687*.

Yang, Dongchao, et al. "Diffsound: Discrete Diffusion Model for Text-to-Sound Generation." arXiv, April 28, 2023. *http://arxiv.org/abs/2207.09983*.

Zeghidour, Neil, et al. "SoundStream: An End-to-End Neural Audio Codec." arXiv, July 7, 2021. *http://arxiv.org/abs/2107.03312*.

# CHAPTER 10

# Rapidly Advancing Areas in Generative AI

The generative AI landscape is moving very fast. Since we began working on this book, we've witnessed the release of new models like GPT-4, Llama 3, Gemini, and Sora. In addition to these, numerous new base LLMs, audio models, and diffusion techniques have emerged. As mentioned in the Preface, this book focuses on general principles and fundamentals that provide generalizable skills and understanding that will allow you to follow the field as it keeps evolving.

Before wrapping up the book, we want to provide a glimpse into some of the most exciting and rapidly advancing areas within generative AI. This chapter offers a high-level overview of these topics and resources to allow you to dive further if you find them interesting. Rather than aiming to make you proficient in the topics, think of this chapter as a guide to continue your learning as you go forward.

## Preference Optimization

In Chapter 6, we trained a chat model based on the Open Assistant dataset of conversations in a supervised fashion. We used traditional fine-tuning, but there's been a strong wave of models that integrate preferences. These models are trained to generate responses that are *aligned* with certain expectations. For example, some people might want to train very helpful models that will always try to help, regardless of the request. Other companies might want to train models that are more neutral and avoid generating toxic outputs.

When a model says that it can't help, this happens because of its preference optimization. Preference optimization is used to steer an LLM toward a desired behavior, which could be anything from generating less buggy code and generating text in a conversational style to refusing to generate content about certain topics.

Reinforcement Learning with Human Feedback (RLHF), one of the methods used for preference-tuning, switches the traditional fine-tuning process a bit. Just as we did in Chapter 6, the first step is to fine-tune the model via supervised fine-tuning. With RLHF, the fine-tuned model is then used to train a *reward model*. For each prompt, the model will generate multiple potential options. Then, a judge ranks the options, and the reward model is trained to predict the judged score. The judges are usually humans, but there has been a tendency to use other, large models as judges (for example, the RLAIF paper (*https://arxiv.org/abs/2309.00267*) uses LLMs for ranking). The final stage is to use the reward model to further fine-tune the original supervised fine-tuned model so that the model learns to generate outputs that resemble the high-scoring (according to judges) examples. RLHF was a critical component for the Llama 2 chat model as well as for ChatGPT.

While the concept of introducing a reward model in the fine-tuning process is intriguing, it also adds a layer of complexity, as shown in Figure 10-1. This has spurred a significant amount of research aimed at replacing the reward model with a new loss function. Recent studies, such as Direct Preference Optimization (DPO) (*https://arxiv.org/abs/2305.18290*), Identity Preference Optimization (IPO) (*https://arxiv.org/abs/2310.12036*), and Kahneman–Tversky Optimization (KTO) (*https://arxiv.org/abs/2402.01306*), are notable examples of this ongoing exploration. These methods entirely remove the RL component, which is known to be unstable and challenging to train.

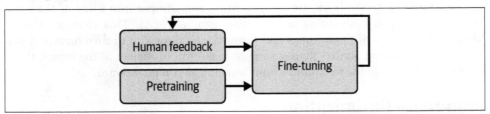

*Figure 10-1. RLHF has three core components: pretraining, fine-tuning, and human feedback*

RLHF can also be applied to diffusion models. Denoising diffusion policy optimization (DDPO) (*https://arxiv.org/abs/2305.13301*) is a way to augment diffusion models using Reinforcement Learning to fine-tune the model and improve the quality of the generated images. RLHF can also be applied to diffusion models, as shown in Figure 10-2.

Figure 10-2. *RLHF applied for diffusion models*

These are some additional reads on the topic:

- The Hugging Face RLHF introductory blog post (*https://oreil.ly/RjZ8c*) is a great step-by-step overview of RLHF.

- Sebastian Rashka's RLHF blog post (*https://oreil.ly/SlmvA*) provides a good overview of RLHF and its alternatives.

- To learn about RLHF in the context of diffusion models, we recommend reading the DDPO blog post (*https://oreil.ly/zoWD2*) or Tanishq Abraham's blog (*https://oreil.ly/um6Vq*).

- To learn more about DPO, IPO, and KTO, we recommend reading the HF blog post (*https://oreil.ly/bEdGk*).

- Constitutional AI is another approach for aligning an LLM to a set of values. The HF blog post (*https://oreil.ly/EBOjt*) is a good resource to dive into it.

# Long Contexts

Most LLMs discussed in the book can handle a context of up to a few thousand tokens, with Llama 3.1 shining at 128,000 and some going up to a few hundred thousand tokens. Proprietary models have achieved much longer contexts, such as Gemini handling up to 2 million tokens and Anthropic Claude supporting 200,000 tokens. Handling extremely long contexts can be very useful for RAG systems (such as the one implemented in the project of Chapter 6) or for systems that do code generation or understanding, where an entire codebase could be used as context.

As the input grows too long, multiple issues arise:

- LLMs require more VRAM to be able to process long contexts.

- The quality of the generations tends to degrade as the context grows. As models were not trained on such long contexts, they may not be able to capture the dependencies between tokens.

- Generation becomes slow. The traditional attention mechanism is a bottleneck as it requires quadratic complexity.

One solution is to use window attention, which limits the number of tokens fed to the LLM. You can think of window attention as a sliding window through the input text. This keeps the GPU usage capped, but the quality still degrades as there may be tokens that carry essential information before the beginning of the window. Window attention can be adapted to take into account the initial tokens using methods such as Attention Sinks, which is great for multiround dialogues. A different approach is to make the attention mechanism more efficient. There are many proposals for sub-quadratic scaling, such as Longformer (*https://arxiv.org/abs/2004.05150*) (which combines window techniques with global attention features) and Flash Attention (*https://arxiv.org/abs/2205.14135*) (which optimizes memory transfers by fusing operations). Flash Attention has become a popular solution as it makes space requirements linear during inference.

While the mentioned approaches focus on making the attention algorithm faster or more computationally efficient, there has also been research on extending pre-trained LLMs with rotary position embeddings (RoPE) scaling (*https://arxiv.org/abs/2104.09864*). Can we pick Llama and make it handle more tokens than what it was pretrained for? RoPE changes how positional information is incorporated into transformers, which allows them to capture long-range dependencies. By doing minimal fine-tuning, we can extend the context window. For example, Meta was able to extend the context window from the original LLaMA model from 2,048 tokens to 32,768 tokens.

Another wave of research is also exploring arbitrarily long contexts. Ring Attention (*https://arxiv.org/abs/2310.01889*) and Infini-Attention (*https://arxiv.org/abs/2404.07143*) are two examples of research in the direction of being able to handle infinite context. The research on evaluation of long context models is still in early stages. Needle in a Haystack (*https://oreil.ly/xqxL9*), shown in Figure 10-3, is an example method for long context retrieval.

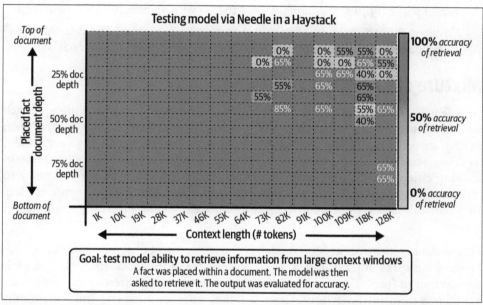

*Figure 10-3. Needle in a Haystack evaluates in-context retrieval on long contexts*

There are parallel ongoing efforts in the ecosystem to use alternative architectures altogether. One of them is using RNNs: RWKV (*https://oreil.ly/Crkoi*) is a family of open source models that achieve efficient inference thanks to linear attention while preserving very efficient and parallelizable training. Another alternative is using State Space Models (SSMs). Mamba (*https://oreil.ly/vQx4R*) uses SSMs to achieve linear memory scaling with respect to the number of tokens and has very fast inference.

Some recommended reads on this topic include the following:

- The Attention Sinks blog post (*https://oreil.ly/pThW2*) explains how Attention Sinks work and the results of different experiments.
- The Flash Attention (*https://arxiv.org/abs/2205.14135*) and Flash Attention 2 (*https://arxiv.org/abs/2307.08691*) papers.
- There have been many concurrent efforts to extend context using RoPE, from a practitioner jumping into ML (*https://oreil.ly/nfVf7*) to research from Meta (*https://arxiv.org/abs/2306.15595*).
- To learn more about RWKV, we recommend reading its announcement blog post (*https://oreil.ly/224i0*), its paper (*https://arxiv.org/abs/2305.13048*), or a more recent paper (*https://arxiv.org/abs/2404.05892*) with architectural improvements.
- To learn about SSMs and Mamba, we recommend reading "The Annotated S4" (*https://oreil.ly/W5rQ7*) and "Mamba: The Hard Way" (*https://oreil.ly/IV35L*).

## Mixture of Experts

In recent years, Mixture of Experts (MoE) has emerged as a compelling approach for LLMs, with the most notable release being Mixtral 8x7B by the Mistral team in December 2023.[1] In the context of transformer models, MoEs are very similar to dense (traditional) transformers (see Figure 10-4), but they offer advantages in training efficiency and production scalability. Given a fixed amount of compute to train a model, MoEs will get you further along the training curve than dense models. In large-scale usage, MoEs can be more efficient in handling many requests per second.

One of the key elements of MoE models is the replacement of some or all of the feed-forward networks in transformer blocks with sparse MoE blocks. Each MoE block is a collection of "expert" networks, with each expert being a different model (usually another feed-forward network). Given a token, only some experts will dynamically activate,[2] and the rest will be idle. To learn which experts to activate, MoEs use a gate network (or router) that dynamically assigns tokens to different experts during training and inference. This gate network acts as a traffic controller, ensuring tokens are distributed effectively among the experts. This makes the gate a critical component of MoEs, and much research is aimed at training better gate networks.

---

1 It is rumored that GPT-4 is also using an MoE architecture.

2 The number of activated experts is a configuration parameter that can be modified.

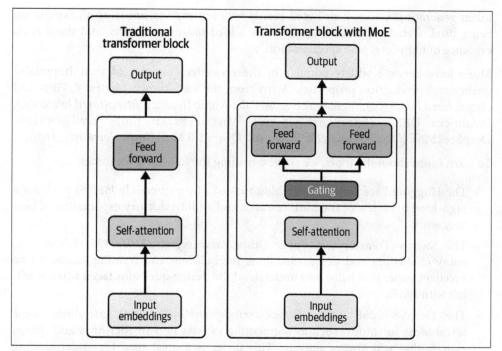

*Figure 10-4. A simplified traditional transformer block and its MoE equivalent having two experts*

It's essential to clarify that the number of experts in MoEs does not directly lead to a linear parameter increase. For instance, in the case of Mixtral 8x7B, the model's name might suggest eight experts of 7 billion parameters each, and hence 56 billion parameters, but in reality, it comprises 47 billion parameters because of shared components, and the eight refers to the number of experts for each MoE block! Remember that only the feed-forward networks are replaced with MoE blocks. The rest of the network, such as the attention blocks, is still shared.

This means that to load the model, you will need a GPU to hold 47 billion parameters. On the other hand, for a given token, only some experts will activate (2 for Mixtral). Therefore, the number of *activated parameters* is much lower (12 billion for Mixtral). This makes MoEs less interesting for local inference (because you need a lot of GPU memory) but compelling for production setups, where you may receive many requests at the same time. Given that fewer parameters per token will be activated for each request being handled in parallel, an MoE should be able to handle more requests than a dense model.

A second misconception about MoEs is that the experts become specialized in different tasks or subsets of data. Experts are trained with a loss function that ensures the token generation load is distributed evenly between experts, ensuring all experts are being used. Gated experts work more like a load balancer of sorts, and there is no evidence of high-level task specialization.

MoEs have become widely popular in the ecosystem because of their impressive quality and production properties. Apart from the well-known Mixtral 8x7B model (*https://oreil.ly/N5d0z*), there is also Snowflake Arctic Instruct (*https://oreil.ly/eSSVK*), Databricks DBRX (*https://oreil.ly/k-Yr6*), Mixtral 8x22B (*https://oreil.ly/A04z8*), DeepSeekMoE (*https://oreil.ly/DDBOa*), and Qwen 1.5 MoE (*https://oreil.ly/c_Hg0*).

To learn more about the topic, we suggest reading the following resources:

- The Hugging Face Introductory blog to MoEs (*https://oreil.ly/J6EN6*) provides a high-level overview of the MoE research and an introductory explanation of how they work.
- The Switch Transformers paper (*https://arxiv.org/abs/2101.03961*) dives into many challenges and design decisions for building and training MoEs. It's an excellent paper that helps you understand the design questions faced when working with MoEs.
- The DeepSeekMoE paper (*https://arxiv.org/abs/2401.06066*) introduces some novel ideas for MoEs, such as segmenting experts into smaller ones and shared experts that will always activate. This paper is a great read for understanding some of the cutting-edge research in the field.
- The Mixtral paper (*https://arxiv.org/abs/2401.04088*) is a nice read on how Mixtral 8x7B was trained. It does not introduce new architecture or training ideas, but it's a good read for understanding how MoEs are trained in practice. This is particularly interesting given that Mixtral was the first high-quality openly available MoE model.

## Optimizations and Quantizations

Optimization techniques were traditionally sought after for two reasons:

- To maximize model performance in high-load scenarios, such as chat UIs or generative APIs used by thousands of users. Serving more users per server and time unit minimizes costs and allows more users to enjoy the service.
- To reduce training time or training resources. For large models, a moderate reduction in the amount of memory used or in the time it takes to complete a training step can result in dramatic speedups and the use of a lot less hardware. Even for small labs or individual practitioners training smaller models, faster training allows faster iteration cycles and more experiments to be completed.

In addition, the past few years have shown the community's overwhelming interest in running all kinds of models, including LLMs, on consumer hardware. There are many reasons for this: to experiment with models without an API clock ticking over your head, to understand how models work by looking at internal activations, to run tasks privately on your computer and even without an internet connection, to fine-tune with your data without spending a lot of money and effort on cloud services, etc.

As a consequence, the community is coming up with many optimization techniques and clever tricks. We've already briefly explored quantization, a collection of techniques that aim to reduce the precision of the model parameters (with minimal impact on quality) to reduce memory and fit models on consumer hardware. Another widespread technique we just mentioned in this chapter is Flash Attention, which not only allows longer context windows but also reduces memory consumption of all types of transformer-based models (including LMs and many other generative models, as we saw in Chapter 4).

Another interesting speedup technique is *speculative decoding*, also called *assisted generation*, which applies to regressive models such as LLMs. This method uses two models with the same architecture for the same task. One of the models is small and fast, while the other is large and has much better quality. The small model generates several tokens as usual, and after a few of them are collected, they are passed together to the large model for confirmation. The large model verifies them in a single pass instead of going through the generation loop. Only the tokens confirmed by the large model are used (the rest are discarded), but as long as the small and large models agree frequently, this is faster than using the large model alone. This is especially useful for structured text such as code. Memory consumption will be larger because we will use two models instead of one, but throughput will be higher.

A somewhat similar method is *Medusa decoding*. This is a fine-tuning specialization that adds new *heads* to an existing model so that a sequence of several tokens can be generated at once. As in the previous case, several candidates are examined so that the generated text is the same as if Medusa was not used.

Here are some resources to learn more about this active topic:

- This post by Merve Noyan (*https://oreil.ly/79V4L*) is a gentle introduction to quantization, and in turn, it provides additional references to dive into the topic.
- The llama.cpp codebase (*https://oreil.ly/DprKF*) contains multiple quantization and optimization techniques, including custom kernels, to accelerate inference on consumer hardware, including Windows and Apple Silicon.
- Quantized, ready-to-use versions of multiple LLMs are prepared and shared by community members such as TheBloke (Tom Jobbins) (*https://oreil.ly/BHVH_*).

The models this solo community member prepared have been downloaded millions of times.

- The Hugging Face documentation about speculative methods (*https://oreil.ly/hJ-CS*) discusses speculative decoding and how to use it.

- This blog post by Joao Gante (*https://oreil.ly/AUJp8*) is a great introduction to assisted generation/speculative decoding.

- Lossy variants of speculative decoding are also possible. In this post (*https://oreil.ly/6q80C*), Vivien Tran-Thien does a fantastic job of exploring this direction.

# Data

While much of this book has focused on models and their applications, the data used to train these models is a crucial aspect of ML. Most pretrained models are trained on vast amounts of web data. Still, by filtering this data or generating synthetic data with other LLMs, smaller models can achieve performance comparable to much larger ones. High-quality data can significantly enhance the performance of even small models, such as Microsoft Phi-3 (*https://oreil.ly/naQMt*). FineWeb (*https://oreil.ly/_Ge0a*) is a high-quality filtered dataset of open web data released as a fully open source dataset and has a technical report (*https://oreil.ly/ddh7Q*) that shows how the tokens were filtered for high quality.

Although synthetic data is not new, Phi opened the doors to exploring large-scale datasets (billions of tokens) created entirely with LLMs. The first iteration of Phi, a 1.3 billion parameter model, was trained with 6 billion tokens of high-quality web data and 1 billion tokens of textbooks and exercises generated with GPT-3.5. Cosmopedia (*https://oreil.ly/StEIR*) is an initial effort that released a dataset of 25 billion tokens of synthetic data covering multiple topics and was created with Mixtral 8x7B.

Tools like Argilla's *distilabel* (*https://oreil.ly/3PhBd*) make it easy to create synthetic data and AI feedback, which can be used for both pretraining and RLHF. While Phi and Cosmopedia focus on large amounts of synthetic data for pretraining, ML models are increasingly used to create preference datasets and scale up model evaluation.

Apart from the Cosmopedia release blog, we recommend reading Eugene Yan's blog post on generating and using synthetic data (*https://oreil.ly/sKgmn*), the TinyStories paper (*https://arxiv.org/abs/2305.07759*), and Phi's original paper, "Textbooks Are All You Need" (*https://arxiv.org/abs/2306.11644*), as well as the follow-up reports for Phi-1.5 (*https://arxiv.org/abs/2309.05463*) and Phi-3 (*https://arxiv.org/abs/2404.14219*).

For other modalities, such as image or audio, we need not only the image and audio datasets but also text datasets that either caption or transcribe the data. Web-scale datasets with text-image pairs have been released such as LAION-2B (used to train the early models of Stable Diffusion), COYO 700M, and DataComp 1B. However, scraping billions of unfiltered images from the open internet may include inappropriate or illegal content, so models trained on this unfiltered data can pose open questions regarding copyright and fair use, as well as safety challenges. Alternative datasets with openly licensed Creative Commons image-text pairs, such as CommonCanvas (*https://oreil.ly/Qzq0k*), have been released to mitigate such challenges. For audio, open datasets for speech, such as Mozilla's Common Voice (*https://oreil.ly/ngE2F*), and for sound effects those such as FreeSound (*https://freesound.org*) and Free Music Archive (*https://oreil.ly/zFWQB*) are well adopted. Internet-scraped and licensed datasets also exist for audio, but there's no centralized dataset index equivalent to COYO or DataComp in the image domain.

# One Model to Rule Them All

There are three main approaches to using LLMs and other generative models for your specific use case, listed here in decreasing order of complexity:

1. Train a new model from scratch.
2. Fine-tune a pretrained model for your use case.
3. Use an existing model with prompt engineering or RAG.

The choice among these approaches depends on your resources and priorities. Training a model from scratch is now prohibitively expensive for most companies because of the high costs involved. Fortunately, the rise of high-quality open source models has made it easier to obtain high-quality results with fine-tuning. Models like BloombergGPT (*https://arxiv.org/abs/2303.17564*) (for finance), AstroLLaMA (*https://arxiv.org/abs/2309.06126*) (for Astronomy), and BioMistral (*https://oreil.ly/amvEB*) (for medical domains) have demonstrated that fine-tuning a strong pretrained model with domain-specific data can sometimes yield better results than using a model out of the box.

That said, as models' zero-shot capabilities improve, their performance might be good enough for many use cases without any fine-tuning. Depending on the project requirement, the time invested in data quality and iterating on the model could be better invested in the end product. As an example, when Meta released Llama 3 and its very high-quality instruct version, the community struggled to achieve better results with fine-tuning, as the model was already very strong out of the box.

Another important consideration is how you deploy and consume the model. Options include self-hosting, using a cloud provider's out-of-the-box solutions, or leveraging the API provided by the model trainer (e.g., OpenAI or Cohere). The best choice depends on your specific needs. The community is increasingly adopting tools (like *langchain* and *llamaindex*) that facilitate easy switching between solutions, preventing dependency on a single model provider. We recommend building your system in a way that allows easy evaluation and swapping of models as needed.

# Computer Vision

Computer Vision is a vast field with a rich history that predates ML techniques. It tries to derive meaningful information from images and apply it to make decisions or actions, such as guiding an autonomous vehicle, detecting defects in a factory line, counting objects, or monitoring traffic. ML methods revolutionized the Computer Vision field, and, in turn, continued improvement on Computer Vision tasks sparked research on increasingly powerful representation learning methods that gave rise to the generative image explosion.

Traditionally, Computer Vision is approached as a set of distinct tasks because it's easier to break those tasks into smaller problems than attempting to *solve* vision understanding in one go. Computer Vision tasks include the following:

*Image classification*
> The problem of deciding which one among a set of categories best describes the content of a given image. Progress on this task has increased dramatically since 2009, when the open ImageNet dataset (*https://oreil.ly/8fMPA*) was published alongside the ImageNet Large Scale Visual Recognition Challenge (ILSVRC). In 2012, a deep neural network (*https://oreil.ly/fwc_I*) created by Alex Krizhevsky, Ilya Sutskever, and Geoffrey E. Hinton won that year's challenge, showing an unbelievable performance 41% better than the second-best solution, after years of crawling marginal progress. This event is traditionally regarded as the beginning of the deep learning revolution, and it shook the way ML and Computer Vision tasks were approached.

*Object detection*
> The task of finding specific types of objects or subjects inside an image (Figure 10-5). Given an input image, an object-detection model generates rectangles (bounding boxes) around the objects belonging to classes the model recognizes and provides a confidence score about the probability that the object inside each box belongs to the predicted class.

*Figure 10-5. Some objects detected by the YOLOv10 model, from the set of object classes it recognizes*

*Segmentation*

Goes one step beyond detection. This task attempts to solve the problem of classifying each individual pixel inside an image according to a set of predefined classes. A segmentation model trained on urban photographs, for example, would predict the pixels in an image corresponding to a road, a tree, people walking down the street, or cars. This is called *semantic segmentation* when there's no distinction between multiple objects of the same class (all pixels belonging to persons would be assigned the same label identifier) or *panoptic segmentation* when the model is capable of discerning different instances of distinct objects that belong to the same class.

*Depth estimation*

Estimates how far objects are in an image, given just a single image with no additional information (Figure 10-6). This is called *monocular* depth estimation to distinguish from other systems that use stereo inputs (two images) or other types of additional data. Monocular depth estimation is useful for computer graphics, 3D, gaming, photography, and artistic tasks.

*Figure 10-6. Apple's Depth Pro model used to estimate a depth map from a photo*

Image classification, detection, and segmentation models were traditionally trained on a specific set of known classes. For example, the ImageNet challenge was conducted on 1,000 categories (even though the original dataset contains about 22,000 classes). This poses a scale problem: to train models that understand the world, we'd need to use sufficient training data to cover all possible classes and nuanced distinctions between them. *Zero-shot tasks* refer to the ability of a model to perform these tasks without having been trained for a specific set of classes. For example, the CLIP model is trained from image-text pairs downloaded from the internet, so it gets a good understanding of image and text features that usually go together. As we saw in Chapter 3, a trained CLIP model can be used to classify an image among a set of arbitrary classes the user provides, without having ever been trained on images classified in those categories.

As larger models are trained on increasingly larger amounts of data, they can solve tasks in a zero-shot fashion without being explicitly trained for them. In addition, these large models learn to use rich and descriptive representations, making it easy to fine-tune for specific tasks. Furthermore, multimodal models that combine text and visual representation (also known as *vision LM*) can answer natural-language questions about image data so that they can be used in various workflows instead of task-specific specialized models. This begs the question, are we on the verge of another Computer Vision revolution, where it may be more fruitful to train on vast datasets rather than focusing on specific tasks? Or will smaller fine-tuned models keep an edge over generalist ones?

# 3D Computer Vision

While traditional Computer Vision primarily focuses on 2D data, such as images and videos, there is a growing interest in understanding, interpreting, and generating 3D data. 3D Computer Vision is widely applied in robotics, augmented reality, healthcare, video production, gaming, and autonomous driving. Traditionally, 3D data has been represented using meshes—a collection of vertices, edges, and faces that define the shape of an object (see Figure 10-7). However, ML techniques often struggle with meshes, prompting the exploration of alternative representations such as neural radiance fields (NeRFs) and Gaussian splatting.

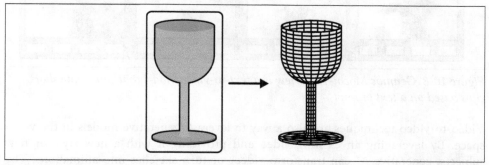

*Figure 10-7. A mesh can be generated even from a single image*

Unlike NLP, the 3D ML ecosystem is small and highly research oriented. As a result, many open tools are experimental and in the early stages of development. The field is rapidly evolving; for example, the first NeRF paper was published in 2020, and Gaussian splatting emerged in 2023. For those interested in exploring this field further, here are some resources:

- Frank Dellaert has published blog posts (*https://oreil.ly/VrvrH*) in 2020, 2021, and 2022 with a recap of what has happened in the NeRF ecosystem. We suggest reading them chronologically.

- Hugging Face has a free course on Machine Learning for 3D (*https://oreil.ly/pdFMo*). The course is a high-level, practical overview of generative ML techniques that can be applied at different steps of the 3D rendering pipeline.

# Video Generation

As image-generation models have established themselves as viable use cases in generative ML, a natural inquiry and research frontier is video. Video is, after all, a sequence of images moving fast enough to create the illusion to the human brain that they are in motion. As such, one approach for video generation is to leverage pretrained image-generation models to generate temporally and visually coherent sequences of pictures (see Figure 10-8). Frameworks such as AnimateDiff (*https://oreil.ly/u0MKW*) derive a motion prior to steer models like Stable Diffusion to produce temporally coherent videos. Pipelines such as Deforum (*https://oreil.ly/U4ytr*) create animations with camera control while embracing frame variations as part of the aesthetic.

*Figure 10-8. Genmo's Mochi-1 Preview is a text-to-video model that can create short clips based on a text prompt*

Video-to-video techniques are also a way to leverage generative models in the video space. By leveraging an existing video and providing it with a new style or new subjects, generative AI can transform videos or turn sketches into animations. The Gen-1 paper (*https://arxiv.org/abs/2302.03011*) by RunwayML showcases an efficient and performant method for video-to-video transformations. This model is currently part of the company's commercial offerings.

However, native techniques for generating novel videos more efficiently are a research frontier with fast-paced developments. One challenge in training native video-generation models is the difficulty of producing video-text pairs that can be semantically meaningful and efficient to train.

To overcome this challenge, models such as CogVideo (*https://oreil.ly/bYCY3*) by Tsinghua University (the first open access text-to-video model) and Make-A-Video (*https://oreil.ly/S1yhT*), released by Meta AI in 2022, employ techniques to pair uncaptioned videos with text-to-image datasets and methods. Make-A-Video, in particular, overcomes the video-text pair data limitation by learning visual-text understanding from image-text pairs and combining that knowledge with motion understanding learned from unsupervised and non-captioned videos. Therefore, the model can learn what things look like and how they move without explicit video-text pairing, enabling text-to-video and image-to-video tasks.

This technique applied on Stable Diffusion enabled further iterations on more efficient text-to-video open models such as ModelScope text-to-video (*https://oreil.ly/aGMGS*) by Alibaba. Scaling up the size of video datasets to train such models has also been achieved with the Stable Video Diffusion model (*https://arxiv.org/abs/2311.15127*), which trains a video Latent Diffusion model and pairs it with a Stable Diffusion text-to-image model. The image-to-video variant of Stable Video Diffusion was released with open weights (*https://oreil.ly/YQS6y*) and increased model quality compared to Make-A-Video and ModelScope samples.

Additional scaled-up approaches for video generation have also been announced, starting with Sora (*https://oreil.ly/zXwRf*), the super-high-quality, realistic, and temporally coherent text-to-video model by OpenAI. While the model is impressive, few technical details have been revealed in its technical report. In this same space, Google DeepMind unveiled Veo (*https://oreil.ly/g1z_i*)—its Sora competitor. Kuai released Kling (*https://oreil.ly/nzT9U*), the first Sora-level model with public access, and RunwayML released Gen-3 (*https://oreil.ly/YK9C4*) a few weeks after.

On the open source and open-weights side, THUDM group at Tsinghua University released CogVideoX 2B (*https://oreil.ly/KR41E*) and CogVideoX 5B (*https://oreil.ly/Ctxka*), a family of open-weight models that can generate realistic and temporally coherent text to video on par with the closed source alternatives previously referenced. There is also an active project on providing an open source replication of Sora with Open-Sora (*https://oreil.ly/o2Rp4*), which displays fast-paced progress.

# Multimodality

In the previous chapters, we explored using generative models for several modalities, such as text, image, and audio. Some models we examined, like Stable Diffusion, have input conditions in one modality (text) and generate outputs in another modality (images). However, models that take in a single modality as input and produce their outputs in a single modality (here, we can also include text-to-speech and speech-to-text models) are not typically what the community refers to regarding multimodality and multimodal models. Multimodality usually means that a single model can either process inputs or yield outputs in more than one modality at once. Let's go through some of the most recent advancements in multimodality.

CLIP is a model architecture introduced by OpenAI in 2021 trained on millions of images and descriptive captions of those images. Once trained, the model can take in both image and text as inputs, and these inputs are encoded to live on the same semantically relevant vector space. This characteristic allows the model to perform a wide range of zero-shot tasks, such as image classification, and semantically compare image to image or text to text. An introduction to CLIP was presented in Chapter 3. Chapter 5 showed how the CLIP text encoder is a component of the Stable Diffusion model.

Bootstrapping Language-Image Pre-training for Unified Vision-Language Understanding and Generation (BLIP) (*https://oreil.ly/pm9fY*) is a framework and model architecture introduced by Salesforce in 2022 that, like CLIP, is trained on image-text pairs. However, the model was trained to further decode the output into text. The multimodal input of either text, image, or both allows the model to perform zero-shot tasks such as image captioning and visual question answering (see Figure 10-9). Follow-up works such as BLIP-2 (*https://arxiv.org/abs/2301.12597*) further refined this concept by combining a frozen image encoder and an LLM.

A pizza with pepperoni and cheese on a plate

*Figure 10-9. BLIP captioning*

*Visual language models* (VLMs), sometimes called *visual large language models* (VLLMs), can take in both images and text as inputs and provide text outputs (see Figure 10-10). A seminal work in this space is the Flamingo paper (*https:// arxiv.org/abs/2204.14198*) by DeepMind in 2022, but the model was not released. Open source replications such as IDEFICS (*https://oreil.ly/5lXpU*) do exist. However, training VLMs from scratch has proven costly. Approaches where an already existing pretrained LLM is further fine-tuned to take in image outputs through a frozen (nontrainable) image encoder have proven efficient and performant. Architectures like BLIP-2 pioneered such an approach, but they still had relatively narrow domain applications (captioning, question answering, etc.) and did not retain all the capabilities of the LLMs. LLaVA (*https://oreil.ly/MgsMl*), an architecture introduced by Microsoft Research in 2023, allows this vision encoder and LLM connection while retaining all its reasoning abilities. This approach brought in an explosion of techniques and models in the open source community, from tiny and efficient models to SOTA VLMs competitive with commercial models. To keep up with the space, follow the Open VLM Leaderboard (*https://oreil.ly/owXmF*) or the image-text-to-text trending models (*https://oreil.ly/7EVZg*) on Hugging Face. To get hands-on experience in this area, you can start with VLM inference on *transformers* (*https://oreil.ly/0vMqw*). Commercial models such as OpenAI's GPT-4 or Anthropic's Claude also have a VLM vision component.

*Figure 10-10. VLM interface*

Using the same logic as VLMs, other modalities can be achieved by leveraging a frozen encoder. For example, Gazelle (*https://oreil.ly/NJU2r*) is a joint speech-language model that leverages a pretrained LLM (Mistral 7B) and a frozen audio encoder (Wav2Vec2). The model gets supercharged as it's able to process and reason directly from an audio input.

Multimodal output models are the next frontier. Research and commercial models in this space are advancing, and we expect a new wave of open multimodal output models soon. Some foundational research in this space is the Chameleon architecture (*https://oreil.ly/voppT*), by Meta AI, which can take in text and image inputs and also generate text and image outputs. It has zero-shot capabilities for tasks such as image instruction following, image editing, image captioning, question answering, and others. Architectures for even broader multimodal input/output capabilities such as Unified-IO and Unified-IO 2 (*https://oreil.ly/gxHqt*) by Allen Institute for AI have been presented, but they have yet to be scaled significantly. As for the commercial models, OpenAI released in May 2024 a multimodal GPT-4o model that can take in image, text, and audio and output the same modalities of image, text, and audio.

# Community

As you've probably realized throughout the chapter and the book, the pace of the ML ecosystem is moving very fast. The best way to keep up with the latest research and developments is to be part of the community. There are many ways to do this, such as joining Discord servers or Reddit communities, sharing your work with others, reading papers, and following researchers and practitioners on X (formerly Twitter).

Surprisingly, we've moved from a world where all research was happening in traditional labs to very impactful research in decentralized setups. EleutherAI, Nous Research, BigCode, and LAION are all examples of the latter, and becoming involved with their efforts can be as simple as joining their Discord servers. Many of these communities also hold paper-reading sessions, great async chat discussions, and hackathons.

Some of these communities were started by individual community contributors who began their journey by tinkering with open models to scratch their own itch to solve the problems that mattered to them. Despite the high cost of training big models from scratch, plenty of research and development opportunities exist for anyone interested in the field. There has never been a better time to get started than now.

# Open Source Tools

This book wouldn't have been possible without open source. Most of the subjects we discussed and the majority of ML research rely on open source contributions—not to mention the production toolchain we used, with open source software such as Jupyter Notebook, Quarto, nbdev, and many more.

In this appendix, we will explore a variety of open source tools for the ML practitioner. Some of these we've used in the book, while others are good to know about. By making yourself familiar with these tools, you'll be well equipped to extend the applications and techniques you just learned.

## The Hugging Face Stack

Throughout this book, you've become familiar with the core libraries of the Hugging Face stack. These are the two main libraries we used:

*transformers*
> The main library to train and run inference with transformer-based models across modalities. It provides multiple levels of abstraction, from the high-level `pipeline` and `Trainer` to supporting running your own *PyTorch* training loops.

*diffusers*
> Similarly to *transformers*, the *diffusers* library allows running pretrained diffusion-based models. Although it's mostly known for its image-generation capabilities, the library also supports audio, video, and 3D.

Both libraries have an opinionated design that prioritizes usability, simplicity, and customizability. What does this mean for end users? First, both libraries aim to offer consistent specifications across models. Whether you're using Llama or Gemma, switching between them should ideally be a single-line code change. While both libraries have many features for fast inference, models are always loaded with the highest precision and lowest optimization by default. This ensures usability across platforms and avoids complex installations, but it also means that models will be slower out of the box unless optimizations are configured.

Two additional Hugging Face libraries are commonly used as well:

*accelerate*
> Allows running PyTorch code in distributed settings, both for training and inference. Whether you want to run the model on a GPU, multiple GPUs, a GPU with CPU offloading, or entirely on a CPU, *accelerate* abstracts away all the complexities. It's used under the hood by both *transformers* and *diffusers*, so most users don't need to learn much about the *accelerate* APIs.

*peft*
> This library enables parameter-efficient fine-tuning techniques to fine-tune models with lower computational and storage costs. It's well integrated with *transformers* and *diffusers*. Although the book mostly explores LoRA, there are many other methods such as p-tuning, prefix tuning, IA3, OFT, and DoRA.

# Data

The open source ecosystem for dataset processing, labeling, and generation has grown significantly in recent years. Here is a brief list of some of the tools being built for working with data:

*datasets*
> This book heavily relies on *datasets*, a popular library for accessing, sharing, and processing open datasets for multiple modalities. Just as *transformers* and *diffusers*, *datasets* provides a consistent API, allowing users to easily swap datasets for a given modality.

*argilla*
> Argilla is a tool for building high-quality datasets. It provides a simple UI where humans can rate data, useful for tasks like comparing model generations (important for RLHF), creating datasets for classical NLP tasks (e.g., entity recognition), or creating evaluation datasets.

*distilabel*
> With the rise of synthetic data generation, new tools like *distilabel* have emerged. It allows creating pipelines to generate synthetic data.

# Wrappers

As the ecosystem has grown, various community and research tools have been built around *transformers*:

*axolotl*

This tool streamlines model fine-tuning; you just need to create a simple configuration file to set up your fine-tuning task. It supports common dataset formats and model architectures.

*unsloth*

Unsloth aims to provide extremely fast fine-tuning of LLMs on top of *transformers*, using a `FastLanguageModel` class that incorporates optimized kernels.

*sentence-transformers*

As discussed in Chapter 2, transformer models can also be used to compute embeddings for a whole sentence, paragraph, or document. The *sentence-transformers* library provides simple APIs to compute embeddings with pretrained models or to fine-tune your own models.

*trl*

With the rise of RLHF, *trl* provides a simple API for fine-tuning and aligning transformer and diffusion models. Chapter 6 showed how to do supervised fine-tuning (SFT), but *trl* contains many other methods such as reward modeling and DPO.

# Local Inference

One major advantage of open models is that you can run many of them locally on your own hardware, offering benefits such as privacy, customizability, and local integrations (e.g., using a code model as a local IDE extension). Depending on your use case, various tools can be used:

*llama.cpp*

Allows doing LLM inference on a variety of hardware. It supports multiple quantization techniques (from 1.5 bits to 8 bits) and has massive community adoption. It's usually used to either chat with an LLM locally or to set up a local endpoint for use by another local service.

*Transformers.js*

Allows running models directly in the browser without the need for a server. This can be very useful to easily deploy services with low latency and no inference costs, or for privacy-first use cases such as writing call transcriptions or subtitles in real time.

# Deployment Tools

While running inference for a single query can be simple, deploying an LLM in production is more complex. Many tools are available for this, including these two popular ones:

*vLLM*
> A simple library for LLM serving that is flexible and well integrated with popular models.

*TGI*
> A production-ready toolkit for LLM deployment.

Other options include *lmdeploy* and NVIDIA's TensorRT-LLM. With so many alternatives, you might wonder which one to pick. Our suggestion is to explore them and find out which one best fits your use cases. All of them are in active development, with different levels of model coverage, community adoption, scalability, integration with cloud services and self-hosted environments, etc.

# LLM Memory Requirements

Models come in all sizes! Llama 3.1, for example, was released with 8B, 70B, and 405B variants. To load and use an LLM, you need enough memory to store the model. The number of parameters and their precision, among other factors, influence the memory requirements for an LLM.

What can you do if you do not have enough memory? Try these options:

- Reduce the precision of the model you are using. Rather than using `float16`, you can use `int8`.

- Use a smaller model. There are many high-quality small models.

- Unload parts of the model that you are not using. This can be done with CPU RAM offloading, a common technique to reduce a model's memory requirements at the cost of slower inference speeds. What happens if there is not enough memory? We can then store the remaining model parts on the disk and load them as needed. Fortunately for us, the *accelerate* library takes care of this via `device_map="auto"`, which will automatically offload parts of the model as needed.

## Inference Memory Requirements

You can roughly estimate the memory requirements as follows:

GPU memory needed = Number of parameters × Bytes per parameter

The bytes per parameter depends on the precision used. Without going into too much detail, Table B-1 shows the memory needed to load 2B, 8B, 70B, and 405B models using different levels of precision (float32, float16, int8, int4, and int2).

*Table B-1. Inference memory requirements for models and levels of precision*

| Model | float32 | float16 | int8 | int4 | int2 |
|-------|---------|---------|------|------|------|
| 2B | 8 GB | 4 GB | 2 GB | 1 GB | 512 MB |
| 8B | 32 GB | 16 GB | 8 GB | 4 GB | 2 GB |
| 70B | 280 GB | 140 GB | 70 GB | 35 GB | 17.5 GB |
| 405B | 1.62 TB | 810 GB | 405 GB | 202.5 GB | 101.25 GB |

For reference, an H100 has 80 GB of memory, so loading Llama 3.1 405B would require at least a full node (of 8 H100s) to load the model in 8-bit integers. This is a rough estimate. You also need to consider the memory required for the input and output tensors and the memory needed for the intermediate computations. For example, long sequences require more memory than short sequences, especially as we go to over 100,000 tokens.

At the time of writing, we can quantize models to int8 with minimal loss in performance. Techniques that go lower than 8 bits per parameter come with performance degradation and are an active area of research.

# Training Memory Requirements

Calculating training requirements can become trickier as they depend on the implementation details of the model and training script. The memory requirements can also significantly change depending on the batch size, the number of tokens in the dataset samples, the training technique (e.g., full fine-tuning versus PEFT), and the training parallelism setup.

The details of the memory requirements of training are beyond the scope of this book. However, we can provide rough estimates for the memory requirements of training LLMs. Table B-2 shows rough GPU requirements for fine-tuning Llama.

*Table B-2. Training memory requirements for models and training techniques*

| Model | Full fine-tuning | LoRA | QLoRA |
|-------|------------------|------|-------|
| 8B | 60 GB | 16 GB | 6B GB |
| 70B | 500 GB | 160 GB | 48 GB |
| 405B | 3.25 TB | 950 GB | 250 GB |

# Further Reading

If you're interested in learning more about the memory requirements of LLMs, you can check the following resources:

- "Transformer Math 101" (*https://oreil.ly/ECVgw*) by EleutherAI, which explains in detail the memory requirements for training a model in different setups.
- "Breaking Down GPU VRAM Consumption" (*https://oreil.ly/FX3zH*) is a short blog post that explains the components that consume GPU memory.

# End-to-End Retrieval-Augmented Generation

A popular application of LLMs is using them for content generation based on both input prompts and externally retrieved information. In this appendix, we will demonstrate how to build a pipeline that leverages a pretrained LLM and a pretrained sentence transformer to generate content based on user input and a set of documents. We've explored the building blocks for this throughout the book. Chapter 2 discussed text generation with LLMs and how to use sentence transformers for encoding text. Chapter 6 also contained a project where we built a minimal RAG pipeline.

Let's discuss the components of a RAG system (shown schematically in Figure C-1):

1. The user inputs a question.
2. The pipeline retrieves the most similar documents to the question.
3. The pipeline passes both the question and the retrieved documents to the LLM.
4. The pipeline generates a response.

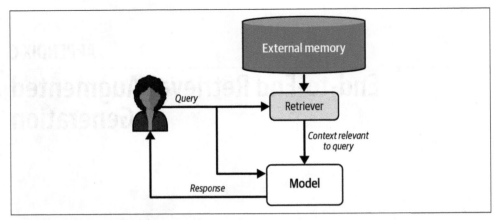

*Figure C-1. A simplified RAG pipeline*

# Processing the Data

As with any ML project, the first step is loading and processing the data. We'll keep it simple by focusing on a single topic. Imagine we want our model to generate content related to the European Union AI Act, which is unlikely to be part of the LLM's training data because the model we'll use was trained before work on the AI Act started. First, we'll load the document:

```
import urllib.request

# Define the file name and URL
file_name = "The-AI-Act.pdf"
url = "https://artificialintelligenceact.eu/wp-content/uploads/2021/08/The-AI-
Act.pdf"

# Download the file
urllib.request.urlretrieve(url, file_name)
print(f"{file_name} downloaded successfully.")
```

```
The-AI-Act.pdf downloaded successfully.
```

The document is likely too long to be processed in one go, so we'll split it into smaller chunks and embed each chunk separately. Each chunk will be a separate *document* we'll compare against the user input. For simplicity, we'll use some preprocessing tools from *langchain*, a library that provides utility functions to create RAG systems. For example, it has a handy `PyPDFLoader` class (*https://oreil.ly/m-1Wj*) that extracts text from PDFs and handles chunking.

First, install the necessary dependencies:

```
!pip install langchain_community pypdf langchain-text-splitters
```

Now, let's load and preprocess the document by using `PyPDFLoader`:

```
from langchain_community.document_loaders import PyPDFLoader

loader = PyPDFLoader(file_name)
docs = loader.load()
print(len(docs))
```

108

PyPDFLoader splits the PDF into one document per page, which leads to 108 documents in this case. We'll split them into even smaller chunks. The *langchain* library provides classes that help with different types of text splitting. We'll use RecursiveCharacterTextSplitter, which has two key parameters:

chunk_size

The number of characters in each chunk. In general, it's a good idea to connect this with the maximum number of tokens the embedding model can handle, which is low for most sentence transformers. Otherwise, you risk having part of the document truncated.

chunk_overlap

The number of characters each chunk overlaps with the previous one. This is useful to avoid splitting sentences in the middle. We'll arbitrarily set it to 100 characters (a fifth of the chunk size we chose).

```
from langchain_text_splitters import RecursiveCharacterTextSplitter

text_splitter = RecursiveCharacterTextSplitter(
    chunk_size=500, chunk_overlap=100
)
chunks = text_splitter.split_documents(docs)
print(len(chunks))
```

854

Let's save the text chunks to an array:

```
chunked_text = [chunk.page_content for chunk in chunks]
```

This is what one of the chunks looks like:

```
chunked_text[404]
```

```
('user or for own use on the Union market for its intended '
 'purpose; \n'
 '(12) 'intended purpose' means the use for which an AI system is '
 'intended by the provider, \n'
 'including the specific context and conditions of use,  as '
 'specified in the information \n'
 'supplied by the provider in the instructions for use, promotional '
 'or sales materials \n'
 'and statements, as well as in the technical documentation;  \n'
 '(13) 'reasonably foreseeable misuse' means the use of an AI system '
 'in a way tha t is not in')
```

# Embedding the Documents

Now that we have the documents (our chunks), we need to create their embeddings. We'll be using a sentence transformer model as a *retriever*, which acts like a search engine to find the most relevant snippets to a given question. This process relies on computing the similarity between the embeddings of the user query and the embeddings of the documents in our collection. To precompute all the document embeddings, we'll use a pretrained sentence transformer model, using the example from "Exercises" on page 52. The following snippet loads a pretrained sentence transformer model, BAAI/bge-small-en-v1.5, and uses it to encode two sentences:

```
from sentence_transformers import SentenceTransformer, util

sentences = ["I'm happy", "I'm full of happiness"]
model = SentenceTransformer("BAAI/bge-small-en-v1.5")

# Compute embedding for both sentences
embedding_1 = model.encode(sentences[0], convert_to_tensor=True)
embedding_2 = model.encode(sentences[1], convert_to_tensor=True)
```

Sentence transformers return a single embedding for the whole sentence. Although transformer models usually output one embedding per token, sentence transformers are trained to pool the token embeddings into a single sentence embedding that captures the semantic meaning of the text:

```
embedding_1.shape
```

```
torch.Size([384])
```

You can then compare the documents based on the cosine similarity:

```
util.pytorch_cos_sim(embedding_1, embedding_2)
```

```
tensor([[0.8367]], device='cuda:0')
```

The cosine similarity, as we saw in Chapter 3, is just the dot product of the two embedding vectors:

```
embedding_1 @ embedding_2
```

```
tensor(0.8367, device='cuda:0')
```

Or, alternatively:

```
import torch
```

```
torch.dot(embedding_1, embedding_2)
```

```
tensor(0.8367, device='cuda:0')
```

Now that we know how to embed a sentence, let's embed all the documents:

```
chunk_embeddings = model.encode(chunked_text, convert_to_tensor=True)
```

This returns a 384-dimensional embedding vector for each chunk:

```
chunk_embeddings.shape
```

```
torch.Size([854, 384])
```

# Retrieval

With the embedded documents, we can retrieve the most relevant ones to a given question. We'll use the same approach as before to calculate the cosine similarity between the question and each document.[1] Fortunately, the similarity computation does not require iteration: it can be efficiently performed by using the built-in PyTorch matrix multiplication primitives:

```python
def search_documents(query, top_k=5):
    # Encode the query into a vector
    query_embedding = model.encode(query, convert_to_tensor=True)

    # Calculate cosine similarity between the query and all document chunks
    similarities = util.pytorch_cos_sim(query_embedding, chunk_embeddings)

    # Get the top k most similar chunks
    top_k_indices = similarities[0].topk(top_k).indices

    # Retrieve the corresponding document chunks
    results = [chunked_text[i] for i in top_k_indices]

    return results
```

Let's try an example. We'll truncate the output in the book to keep it short, but you can run the code in your local environment to see the full output:

```python
search_documents("What are prohibited ai practices?", top_k=2)
```

```
('TITLE  II \n'
 'PROHIBITED  ARTIFICIAL  INTELLIGENCE  PRACTICES \n'
 'Article 5  \n'
 '1. The following artificial intelligence practices shall be '
 'prohibited:  \n'
 '(a) the placing on the market, putting into service o')
('low or minimal risk. The list of prohibited practices in Title II '
 'comprises all those AI systems \n'
 'whose use is considered unacceptable as contravening Unio n '
 'values, for instance by violating \n'
 'fundame')
```

The model correctly retrieves relevant information from the input question.

---

1 You can also use *sentence_transformers'* convenient semantic_search method for this use case.

# Generation

The next step is to generate a response based on the question and the retrieved documents. Let's use our good old friend, the instruct version of SmolLM.[2] Feel free to experiment with other models:

```python
from transformers import pipeline

from genaibook.core import get_device

device = get_device()
generator = pipeline(
    "text-generation", model="HuggingFaceTB/SmolLM-135M-Instruct", device=device
)
```

We'll use an instruct model with a chat template. As discussed in Chapter 6, *transformers* has utilities that format the prompt to meet the model expectations. We'll want to add the retrieved documents to the prompt in the RAG case:

```python
def generate_answer(query):
    # Retrieve relevant chunks
    context_chunks = search_documents(query, top_k=2)

    # Combine the chunks into a single context string
    context = "\n".join(context_chunks)

    # Generate a response using the context
    prompt = f"Context:\n{context}\n\nQuestion: {query}\nAnswer:"

    # Define the context to be passed to the model
    system_prompt = (
        "You are a friendly assistant that answers questions about the AI Act. "
        "If the user is not making a question, you can ask for clarification"
    )
    messages = [
        {"role": "system", "content": system_prompt},
        {"role": "user", "content": prompt},
    ]

    response = generator(messages, max_new_tokens=300)
    return response[0]["generated_text"][2]["content"]
```

Let's try one example:

```python
answer = generate_answer("What are prohibited ai practices in the EU act?")

print(answer)

('The EU Act prohibits the use of artificial intelligence practices '
 'that are harmful to individuals, such as:\n'
```

---

2 You can learn more about how this model was trained on the Hugging Face blog (*https://oreil.ly/GkxE5*).

```
'\n'
'* The placing on the market, putting into service or use of an A I '
'system that is subliminal, that is, it is not intended to be used '
'for any purpose other than to deceive or manipulate individuals.\n'
'* The use of A I systems that are designed to deceive or '
'manipulate individuals, such as those used in advertising, '
'marketing, or customer service.\n')
```

The model generates a response based on the input question and correctly retrieves information. We're using a tiny generative model, so scaling to a larger model can help us obtain higher-quality generations and grow the context length, increasing the number of retrieved documents we can pass to the context.

# Production-Level RAG

The code we've shown is a simple example of a RAG system. In a production-level system, you'd need to consider several additional factors:

*Chunking*
> One of the challenges with real data is that the documents can be very long. Finding the right chunk size is a design decision that depends on the data and the model: snippets that are too small will truncate ideas, and those that are too large will dilute them. You can learn more about splitting in "5 Levels Of Text Splitting" (*https://oreil.ly/WV5A4*).

*Smaller embeddings*
> Large embeddings can be memory intensive. Active research is being conducted to make embeddings smaller while maintaining their quality. If you are interested in these topics, we recommend reading about Matryoshhka Embedding Models (*https://oreil.ly/ZCsWv*) and Embeddings Quantization (*https://oreil.ly/t1yFL*).

*Re-ranking*
> The retrieval step is crucial in RAG systems. Our retrieval models are fast and essential for comparing thousands or millions of documents, but they are not necessarily the most accurate. Once we retrieve the top_k documents, we can re-rank them using a slower but higher-quality model. You can learn more about re-ranking in *sentence_transformers* documentation (*https://oreil.ly/Eu-Ub*) or in "Deep Dive into Cross-encoders and Re-ranking" (*https://oreil.ly/-ogvA*).

*Embedding model evaluation*
> There are dozens of sentence transformer models. To choose the best one for your use case, we suggest checking out the Massive Text Embedding Benchmark (*https://oreil.ly/8m_wr*), which has information such as model size, embedding dimensions, and quality across dozens of tasks. Note that we usually want very small and fast models for retrieval tasks, so that should be a key factor in your decision.

*Production components*

In real-world usage, you might want to integrate other components such as query rewriting, personally identifiable information (PII) redaction, caching, and input guardrails to prevent your model from being used inappropriately. Chip Huyen has an excellent post, "Building a Generative AI Platform" (*https://oreil.ly/l4R4h*), to learn more about this.

Finally, there are many open source tools for building RAG systems. Here are some recommendations to check out:

*ColBERT (https://oreil.ly/JEfYG)*

A fast and accurate BERT-based retrieval model

*RAGatouille (https://oreil.ly/fPMGq)*

A system to use and train retrieval models

Open vector databases such as Milvus (*https://oreil.ly/vX05S*), Weaviate (*https://oreil.ly/BWy95*), and Qdrant (*https://oreil.ly/pARYU*) may prove useful when you have to work with massive datasets. Diving into vector databases is outside the scope of this book, but they are also a quickly growing field. You can see a comparison from 2023 in the "Picking a Vector Database" blog post (*https://oreil.ly/875vL*).

# Index

model() method, 20
average pooling, 137
axolotl, 371

# B

BAAI/bge-small-en-v1.5 sentence transformer, 380
bad_words_ids parameter, 23
Bark, 329-331
BART (Bidirectional and Auto-Regressive Transformers), 37
base models, 32
  (see also diffusion models; LMs)
  evaluation, 230-233
  fine-tuning, 212, 219
  freezing, 195, 213
  selecting, 190, 204-208
batch normalization, 61, 141
BBH dataset, 206
beam search, 21, 23
BeautifulSoup, 241
BERT (Bidirectional Encoder Representations from Transformers), 38, 42, 190, 195
bfloat16 (BF16; brain floating-point) type, 221-222
bias
  datasets, 9
  transformer models, 46
Bidirectional and Auto-Regressive Transformers (BART), 37
Bidirectional Encoder Representations from Transformers (BERT), 38, 42, 190, 195
BigCode, 368
BigCode Models Leaderboard, 208
BioMistral, 359
BLEU, 231
BLIP (Bootstrapping Language-Image Pre-training for Unified Vision-Language Understanding and Generation), 104, 242, 365
Bloom, 39
BloombergGPT, 359
brain floating-point (bfloat16; BF16) type, 221-222
"Building a Generative AI Platform" (Huyen), 384

# C

CapPa, 104

catastrophic forgetting, 247
causal language models (see autoregressive models)
CelebA-HQ dataset, 112
CelebFaces Attributes dataset, 93, 108
CER (character error rate), 319-322
CFG (classifier-free guidance), 172-173
Chameleon, 367
character-level tokenization, 15
chat templates, 228-230
ChatGLM2, 216
ChatGPT, 37
chunking, 383
CLAP (Contrastive Language-Audio Pretraining), 95, 333, 340
classifier-free guidance (CFG), 172-173
Claude, 37, 39
CLIP (Contrastive Language-Image Pretraining), 93-105
  alternatives to, 104
  contrastive loss, 94-95
  image variations, 283
  multimodality, 365
  overview, 107
  steps for, 95-102
  use cases, 103
  zero-shot classification, 101-103
    pipeline, 102
    using, 101-102
  zero-shot tasks, 362
CLIP Guidance method, 104
CNNs (Convolutional Neural Networks), 119
  (see also UNets)
  overview, 9
  speech to text, 308
  transfer learning and, 41
  ViTs and, 47
CoCa, 104
codecs, 330
CogVideo, 364
CogVideoX, 171, 365
Cohere Command R+, 208
ColBERT, 384
"Cold Diffusion" (Bansal et al.), 127
collators, 209
"Common Diffusion Noise Schedules and Sample Steps Are Flawed" (Lin et al.), 134
Common Voice dataset, 293, 320, 359
CommonCanvas dataset, 178, 359

# About the Authors

**Omar Sanseviero** was the chief llama officer and head of platform and community at Hugging Face, leading the developer advocacy engineering, on-device, and moonshot teams. Omar has extensive engineering experience working at Google in Google Assistant and TensorFlow Graphics. Omar's work at Hugging Face was at the intersection of open source, product, research, and technical communities.

**Pedro Cuenca** is a machine learning engineer at Hugging Face, working on diffusion software, models, and applications. He has 20+ years of software development experience in fields like internet applications and iOS. As a cofounder and CTO of LateNiteSoft, he worked on the technology behind Camera+, a successful iPhone app that used custom ML models for photography enhancement. He created deep-learning models for tasks such as photography enhancement and super-resolution. He was also involved in the development of and operations behind DALL·E mini. He brings a practical vision of integrating AI research into real-world services and the challenges and optimizations involved.

**Apolinário Passos** is a machine learning art engineer at Hugging Face, working across teams on multiple machine learning use cases for art and creativity. Apolinário has 10+ years of professional and artistic experience, alternating between holding art exhibitions, coding, and product management, having been a head of product at World Data Lab. Apolinário aims to ensure that the ML ecosystem supports and makes sense for artistic use cases.

**Jonathan Whitaker** is a data scientist and deep learning researcher focused on generative modeling. He has previously worked on several courses related to the topics covered in this book, including the Hugging Face diffusion models class and Fast.AI's *From Deep Learning Foundations to Stable Diffusion*, which he cocreated with Jeremy Howard in 2022. He has also applied these techniques in industry during his time as a consultant and now works full-time on AI research and development at Answer.AI.

## Colophon

The animal on the cover of *Hands-On Generative AI with Transformers and Diffusion Models* is the giant African swallowtail butterfly (*Papilio antimachus*).

The giant African swallowtail is one of the largest species of butterfly, with a wingspan of up to 9–10 inches (around the size of, say, a dinner plate or vinyl record). Yet, for all of their impressive size, relatively little is known about these colossal insects.

First discovered in 1782, swallowtails live in the tropical rainforests of west and central Africa, where they spend most of their time in the forest canopy; males have occasionally been observed mud-puddling at the forest floor, a behavior in which butterflies aggregate on wet organic matter such as soil or dung in a quest for nutrients.

Because of their diet, giant African swallowtails are highly toxic, and they have no known predators. Though there have been some reports of a population decline resulting from habitat destruction and poaching (specimens are highly prized and can fetch prices of over $1,000), the IUCN has listed the giant African swallowtail as Data Deficient: more information is needed in order for a conservation assessment to be made. Many of the animals on O'Reilly covers are endangered; all of them are important to the world.

The cover illustration is by Karen Montgomery. The series design is by Edie Freedman, Ellie Volckhausen, and Karen Montgomery. The cover fonts are Gilroy Semibold and Guardian Sans. The text font is Adobe Minion Pro; the heading font is Adobe Myriad Condensed; and the code font is Dalton Maag's Ubuntu Mono.

O'REILLY®

# Learn from experts.
# Become one yourself.

60,000+ titles | Live events with experts | Role-based courses
Interactive learning | Certification preparation

**Try the O'Reilly learning platform free for 10 days.**